COGNITIVE AGING

COGNITIVE AGING:
A Primer

Edited by

Denise C. Park
Norbert Schwarz

Psychology Press
Taylor & Francis Group

First published by Routledge
This edition published 2012 by Psychology Press
27 Church Road, Hove, East Sussex BN3 2FA
711 Third Avenue, New York, NY 10017, USA
Routledge is an imprint of the Taylor & Francis Group, an informa business

International Standard Book Number-10: 0-86377-692-2 (Softcover)
International Standard Book Number-13: 978-0-86377-692-2 (Softcover)
Library of Congress Card Number 99-043572

Library of Congress Cataloging-in-Publication Data

Aging and cognition : a primer / edited by Denise Park and Norbert Schwarz.
    p. cm.
Includes bibliographical references and index.
ISBN 0-86377-692-2
1. Cognition in old age. 2. Cognition—Age factors. I. Park, Denise C.
II. Schwarz, Norbert, Dr. Phil.
BF724.85.C64 A35 1999
155.67'13—dc21   99-043572

Taylor & Francis Group
is the Academic Division of Informa plc.

Visit the Taylor & Francis Web site at
http://www.taylorandfrancis.com

and the Psychology Press Web site at
http://www.psypress.com

Contents

List of contributors

Denise C. Park is Professor of Psychology at the University of Michigan and Senior Research Scientist at the University of Michigan Institute for Social Research. She studies both basic and applied cognitive processes associated with normal aging with a particular interest in memory. She directs the Center for Applied Cognitive Research on Aging sponsored by the National Institute on Aging, is Past President of the Division of Adult Development and Aging of the American Psychological Association and presently serves as Chair of the Board of Scientific affairs of the APA.

Norbert Schwarz is Professor of Psychology at the University of Michigan and Senior Research Scientist at the Research Center for Group Dynamics and the Survey Research Center of Michigan's Institute for Social Research. His research focuses on human judgment, including the interplay cognition and communication, the role of feelings and subjective experiences in cognition, and changes in these processes across the adult lifespan.

John C. Cavanaugh, Provost and Vice Chancellor for Academic Affairs, University of North Carolina, Wilmington, North Carolina, USA

Fergus I. M. Craik, Department of Psychology, University of Toronto, Toronto, Ontario, Canada

Roger Dixon, Department of Psychology, University of Victoria, Victoria, British Columbia, Canada

Angela Hall Gutchess, Department of Psychology, University of Michigan, Ann Arbor, MI, USA

Lynn Hasher, Department of Psychology, Duke University, Durham, NC, USA

Reid Hastie, Department of Psychology, University of Colorado, Boulder, CO, USA

Susan Kemper, Department of Psychology, University of Kansas, Lawrence, KS, USA

Karen Kemtes, Volen National Center for Complex Systems, Brandeis University, Waltham, MA, USA

Bärbell Knäuper, Assistant Professor of Psychology, Free University of Berlin, Germany

Cynthia May, Department of Psychology, College of Charleston, Charleston, SC, USA

Patricia Reuter-Lorenz, Department of Psychology, University of Michigan, Ann Arbor, MI, USA

Wendy A. Rogers, School of Psychology, Georgia Institute of Technology, Atlanta, GA, USA

David C. Rubin, Department of Experimental Psychology, Duke University, Durham, NC, USA

Timothy Salthouse, School of Psychology, Georgia Institute of Technology, Atlanga, GA, USA

Alan G. Sanfey, Department of Psychology, University of Colorado, Boulder, CO, USA

Arthur Wingfield, Department of Psychology and Volen National Center for Complex Systems, Brandeis University, Waltham, MA, USA

Carolyn Yoon, University of Michigan Business School, Ann Arbor, MI, USA

Preface

As our society ages, there is increasing interest in understanding the effects of aging on cognitive function. Moreover, we are shifting to a society where acquiring, managing, and disseminating information, often via new technologies, not only are integral aspects of work life, but are also surprisingly important aspects of everyday life in the home and community. These two aspects of contemporary life—the increased age of our population and the importance of managing information and technology in daily life—have resulted in the topic of cognitive aging becoming increasingly crucial. *Aging and Cognition: A Student Primer* is a comprehensive overview of what is known about normal cognitive function in older adults. Although there are several books that treat this topic with considerable breadth, these other volumes largely have been written for advanced graduate students and researchers in the field. The present volume is designed to fulfill a need for courses at the advanced undergraduate and beginning graduate level, as well as to provide thoughtful, comprehensive, and highly readable overviews of various aspects of cognitive aging to individuals from all disciplines. Each chapter is written by a distinguished researcher with expert knowledge and considerable hands-on research expertise in his or her topic.

The book is divided into four sections. In the first section, Basic Mechanisms, broad overviews of basic issues are presented by three researchers. In chapter 1, Denise Park discusses the basic mechanisms of speed, working memory, and inhibition that have been hypothesized to be fundamental to all aspects of age-related decline in cognitive function. As a counterpart to the Park chapter about decline, Roger Dixon discusses in chapter 2 the notion that there are gains in some aspects of cognitive function with age and what is meant by the idea of cognitive gains across the life span. Finally, in chapter 3, Timothy Salthouse discusses what he views as pressing issues in the study of cognitive aging, and the interaction of cognitive processes with cognitive products. The second section of the book focuses on attention and memory. Wendy Rogers provides a thorough overview of the important topic of attention in chapter 4, followed by Fergus Craik's review of age changes in basic memory processes and structures in chapter 5. Chapter 6 is devoted to an illuminating discussion of the cognitive neuropsychology of the aging brain by Patricia Reuter-Lorenz. This is a highly accessible, readable treatment integrating what is known about basic cognitive processes and structures discussed in earlier chapters with state-of-the-art work in neuroimaging and neuroanatomy. Chapter 7 is a discussion of metamemory (what an individual believes to be true about his or her memory function), and presents a social-cognitive framework written by John Cavanaugh. In chapter 8, the topic of memory for one's past and how it changes with age is addressed by David Rubin. Finally, chapter 9, written by Carolyn Yoon, Cynthia May, and Lynn Hasher, explores the fascinating view that cognitive function is governed by circadian arousal patterns and that these patterns differ for older and younger adults. They argue that cognitive differences between younger and older adults are relatively small when older adults are tested at their optimal time of day. In the third section, the focus is on language and speech. In chapter 10, Arthur Wingfield reviews the extensive literature on how older adults perceive speech and comprehend spoken language. This is followed by Susan Kemper and Karen Kemtes's discussion in chapter 11 of how older adults produce speech and comprehend both written and spoken language.

Finally, this book is somewhat unusual in that it includes a significant Applications section, focused on the implications of age-related changes in cognitive function for everyday life. We believe strongly that, as knowledge about cognitive aging develops, it is important to understand the implications of this knowledge for function in the real world. Denise Park and Angela Hall Gutchess present in chapter 12 an overview of how age-related changes in cognitive function, combined with increased knowledge across the life span, impact on medical behaviors, driving, and work behaviors—all important everyday behaviors. In chapter 13, Norbert Schwarz and Bärbel Knäuper discuss how age-related decline might affect the manner in which older adults answer questions and how these effects may distort survey results of life span samples. Finally, Chapter 14, written by Alan Sanfey and Reid Hastie, is a review of judgment and decision making across the adult life span, a rarely explored topic of enormous importance for everyday function.

This book is an adaptation of a volume published in 1998 by Psychology Press entitled *Cognition, Aging, and Self-Report.* This earlier book, edited by Norbert Schwarz, Denise Park, Bärbel Knäuper, and Seymour Sudman, contained earlier versions of some of the chapters in the present book written as tutorials for survey researchers, along with a number of chapters of specific interest to only survey researchers. The tutorials were sufficiently broad and comprehensive, so we recognized that we had the makings of an excellent book on cognitive aging that would serve a more general audience well. Thus, after some discussion with Alison Mudditt of Psychology Press, we decided to invite some additional chapters and requested revisions of the original tutorials, resulting in this new volume.

A number of people deserve particular thanks for the fact that this book ever happened. First, we thank Denise Taylor-Moon for her outstanding editorial support in putting this volume together at the University of

Michigan. Second, Alison Mudditt of Psychology Press has been a wonderful editor and good friend throughout this process—motivating, enthusiastic, knowledgeable, and infinitely patient about deadlines. Finally, we thank the authors for their excellent and prompt work, and the Behavioral and Social Research Program of the National Institute on Aging for generous and consistent support of our research efforts in cognitive aging.

Denise Park
Norbert Schwarz

Basic mechanisms

The basic mechanisms accounting for age-related decline in cognitive function

1

Denise C. Park

What happens to the cognitive system as we get older? There are some common age-related stereotypes which suggest that older adults are slower at performing many tasks and have poorer memories than when they were younger. Other stereotypes have suggested that with age come increased knowledge and wisdom, which can be important in solving many dilemmas of contemporary life (Hummert, Garstka, Shaner, & Strahm, 1994). It is often the case that there is considerable truth in folk wisdom, and this is no exception. There actually is a great deal of scientific evidence indicating that, as we age, our mental processes do become somewhat less efficient, and that is the focus of the present chapter. Similarly, there also is evidence that with age come growth and experience, which can be useful in solving complex moral and social problems (Baltes & Staudinger, 1993). Although perhaps more is understood about the losses associated with cognitive aging, there also is considerable impetus to understand how knowledge and experience, which increase with age might translate into gains for older individuals, and that is the focus of the second chapter in this volume by Dixon. This overview of losses and gains that occur with cognitive aging, which is addressed in the first two chapters, will set the stage for the additional topics covered in this book.

The work described in this chapter was supported by the National Institute on Aging through several grants. Grant R01AG14111, entitled *Aging, Cognition, and Self-Report*, was awarded to Norbert Schwarz and Denise Park. The Center for Applied Cognitive Research on Aging also supported this research (grant P50AG11715), as did grant R01AGO6265l, entitled *Effects of Context on the Aging Memory*. The author gratefully acknowledges this assistance. A Website with more information about related research is located at http://www.isr.umich.edu/rcgd/parklab/

Over the past 25 years, cognitive aging psychologists not only have documented many of the declines that occur in cognitive function with age, but they have attempted to discover whether there is a single, fundamental cognitive mechanism that may control all of the age-related declines that are observed on numerous tasks. This chapter provides an overview of major cognitive mechanisms that are sensitive to age-related decline and that have been hypothesized to be the fundamental bases for age differences in cognitive function, which have been demonstrated in thousands of research studies. All of these mechanisms have been considered to be indices of cognitive resources, that is, the quantity of mental processing power or mental energy that a given individual has available to use when performing a cognitive task. These fundamental mechanisms or processing resources not only account for decreased performance in the laboratory, but the concept of processing resources also has substantial implications for performance of many everyday activities. Many theorists believe that the amount of cognitive processing resource that an individual has available to bring to bear in a situation, governs how effective that individual will be in many everyday situations, such as learning how to use new technology, driving in unfamiliar environments, managing finances, managing medications, and making medical decisions (Park, 1997, 1999).

What is meant by cognitive resources is empirically well defined in the cognitive aging literature. Before discussing empirical measures of the construct, it is worthwhile to point out what a pervasive and intuitive construct it is. The concept of resource permeates every day discourse about our cognitive processes. Statements from older adults to the effect that "I'm not as sharp as I used to be," "I'm much fresher in the morning and don't think as well at night," "I just don't have it today," and "I didn't feel well and couldn't remember what you told me" are all reflections of a socially shared cognitive metaphor about the need for cognitive resources to perform mental tasks. Implicit in the metaphor is that there is a pool of mental energy that can be brought to bear in situations to help solve problems or manipulate information, and that this resource somehow declines as one gets older, becomes tired, or is ill. Although notions of fatigue, illness, and low energy all have been applied in the past to views of what cognitive aging might be like (Craik & Byrd, 1982), resource models of aging actually are considerably more precise than this. Generally, resource views of cognitive aging have as a common element that, as one gets older, one has diminished mental resources to draw on quickly, and this limits one's ability to perform mental tasks. At issue among different conceptualizations is the nature of this mental energy, that is, the mechanism that accounts for this apparent limitation on processing capacity or resource. This is an extraordinarily important issue in cognitive aging because many cognitive aging scientists believe that it is a decline in a single mechanism that drives all subsequent cognitive function (e.g., Salthouse, 1996).

This chapter might be viewed as the "bad news" of cognitive aging, given that there is compelling evidence these fundamental processing mechanisms decline with age. Despite the present focus on bad news, there also is some "good news." It is naive to think of the older adults' cognitive system in terms of only processing mechanisms and capabilities. As mentioned earlier, it also is important to recognize that older adults bring vast stores of knowledge and experiences to situations. There is considerable evidence that access to much of this information is maintained across the life span and even grows as one continues to have experiences and learn new information. Perhaps a useful analogy is to conceptualize the aging cognitive system as a computer with a large hard drive that has an enormous amount of information stored on it, but the hard drive is part of a computer with limited random access memory. In this situation, we all know that the computer will behave in a slow and somewhat labored manner, despite its vast informational resources, because the processing capacity of the computer is not sufficient to use all of the information stored on it in an efficient manner. The computer works, but perhaps a little less efficiently than one would like.

One of the major challenges of cognitive aging research that has not necessarily been met by researchers to date is to understand the meaning simultaneously of growth of knowledge and decline of processing efficiency, particularly in every day life. This would seem to be a very important issue for understanding how older adults function in complex, real-world situations outside of the laboratory. It is relatively easy to demonstrate cognitive losses in the laboratory, when older adults must perform unfamiliar tasks where their past experiences and existing stores of knowledge are not very useful. However, when these same adults perform complex tasks in the real world that are familiar, they may function at a very high level due to the support provided by their knowledge and experience. The declines in processing capacity will not be at all apparent in such a familiar environment. It needs to be recognized that the impact of cognitive decline or loss with age is moderated when the older adult is functioning in a familiar environment and will be most apparent in unfamiliar situations where acquired knowledge and past experiences will not be so important.

Before presenting four different cognitive mechanisms that have been hypothesized to be indices of processing resources, I will characterize cognitive function across the life span by providing an overview of performance on a range of cognitive tasks. Then, I will present four different but related views of mechanisms hypothesized to account for these cognitive aging effects, and discuss how the constructs associated with each view are interrelated to one another. I will conclude with challenges that the construct of processing resources present for researchers interested in the basic mechanisms of cognitive aging present. A detailed discussion of the implications of limited processing resources for everyday life occurs in chapter 12 by Park and Hall Gutchess.

Overview of findings from the cognitive aging literature

In a recent study, we collected multiple measures of cognitive function from a life span sample of 301 adults, age 20 to 90 (Park, 1996). We measured performance on a broad range of cognitive tasks, including speed of processing, working memory, free recall, cued recall, and vocabulary knowledge. The results from this study provide a representative snapshot of cognitive functions on many tasks across the life span. Speed of processing is a measure of how rapidly individuals can process information. To measure it, individuals make simple same-different judgments about pairs of comparisons of symbols, patterns, or letters as rapidly as possible. Speed of processing is assessed by how many of these judgments can be made in a short interval. Working memory measures subjects' ability to both simultaneously manipulate and store information in an on-line fashion by asking subjects to both answer a question about a sentence or an equation, while, at the same time, remembering an element of the sentence or equation. The number of elements to be remembered systematically increases until a subject reaches his/her limit. A working memory score is an estimate of overall cognitive resource capacity. In free-recall tasks, subjects are presented with words to study and asked to remember as many as they can in any order, whereas in cued recall, they are presented with word pairs for study and must recall the target word in the pair when later presented with the cue item. Both free recall and cued recall are good estimates of long-term memory function. Figure 1.1 provides a summary of the results from this large study. The figure demonstrates that there is evidence for systematic declines in performance across the life span on speed of processing, working memory, and free- and cued recall tasks. The declines are regular, generally linear, and of considerable magnitude. Notice, however, that the measure of world knowledge presented in Figure 1.1 (vocabulary) does not show age-related decline. It appears that measures of knowledge or crystallized intelligence are somewhat more stable across the life span.

Although Figure 1.1 spans many types of cognitive function, it is important to note that age-related decline is not universal to all types of memory. Generally, age differences are not found on memory tasks that do not require a substantial expenditure of cognitive resource. Figure 1.2, for example, shows that when younger and older subjects are asked to recognize pictures that they studied earlier, there are no age differences in their ability to recognize these meaningful pictures (Park, Puglisi, & Smith, 1986). This age invariance in recognition occurs both when the pictures are relatively simple drawings of objects and when they are drawings of rich complex scenes. Picture recognition is a relatively passive process that may be based on feelings of familiarity or automatic processes rather than on active, effortful, resource-intensive retrieval. Jacoby (1991) has demonstrated convincingly that the familiarity component of memory is age invariant. In

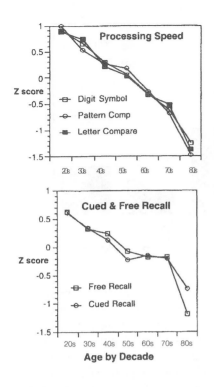

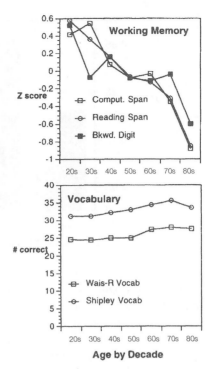

FIG. 1.1.
Performance on multiple measures of processing speed, working memory, cued and free recall, and vocabulary across the life span from a sample of 301 community-dwelling adults. Adapted with permission from Park et al. (1996).

a similar vein, Park and Shaw (1992) have demonstrated that there are large differences in explicit memory for words, but not in implicit memory, as depicted in Figure 1.3. In the explicit recall task, subjects studied words and were later shown word stems that included the first three or four letters of the studied words. Subjects were told to recall words that they had studied. Under these conditions of deliberate, effortful retrieval, large age differences emerged in recall. However, when subjects were told to com-

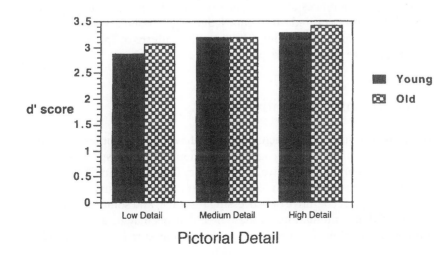

FIG. 1.2.
The effects of three levels of pictorial detail on picture recognition as measured by d'scores. Adapted with permission from Park, Puglisi, and Smith (1986).

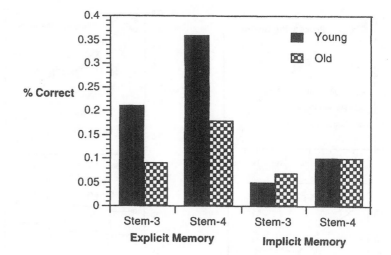

% Correct

FIG.1.3.
Age differences in an
explicit and implicit
stem completion task
as a function of stem
length. Adapted with
permission from Park
and Shaw (1992).

plete the word stems with any words that came to mind, an implicit retrieval task that does not require a resource intensive search of memory,
many subjects reported words that they had studied earlier, even though
they were not necessarily aware that they were reporting words for which
they recently been "primed." Of particular interest is that young and old
adults showed equivalent amounts of word-stem completion from the studied lists in this indirect or implicit retrieval task. The indirect retrieval task
is a situation that does not require a directed, effortful memory search, and
so there are minimal or nonexistent age differences.

The data presented in Figures 1.1 through 1.3 are typical of the laboratory findings in cognitive aging. Generally, studies have indicated that there
are declines in memory tasks that require a great deal of self-initiated processing (Craik & Jennings, 1992), but age invariance on memory tasks that
require less effortful retrieval (see Light, 1991, for more discussion of these
issues). Age differences also are small or nonexistent on cognitive tasks
that rely more on acquired world knowledge (e.g., vocabulary scores) rather
than active cognitive processing. These are the patterns of data which theories of cognitive aging must explain.

Mechanisms of cognitive aging

There are four important mechanisms that have been hypothesized to account for age differences in cognitive functioning: (a) the speed at which
information is processed, (b) working memory function, (c) inhibitory function, and (d) sensory function. Each of these mechanisms can be conceptualized as a type of cognitive or processing resource, and some authors have
suggested that combinations of these mechanisms may be an even better
estimate of cognitive resource than any single measure (Salthouse, 1991).

In any discussion of cognitive aging, it is important to recognize that an important goal is to explain the cause of the age-related variance that occurs on any given cognitive task. If a group of individuals from age 20 to 75 is tested on a cognitive task, there will be variability in performance on that task across individuals. The causes of this variability can be partitioned into many categories. Some of the variability will be caused by how much education the different individuals have had. Some of the variability will be caused by how experienced individuals are on the particular task—those with more experience might perform somewhat better. Another source of differences in performance would be age; that is, younger individuals would perform better than older individuals. Theories of cognitive aging are interested in explaining only the variability in performance that is due to age.

Thus, it is important to note at the outset that we are not necessarily interested in explaining all of the variance on a cognitive task with these mechanisms that we believe underlie cognitive aging. Rather, we are interested in understanding whether the portion of the variance on a cognitive task that is related to age can be explained or is mediated by one of these four mechanisms. It is, of course, logically possible that age-related variance has multiple causes and that more than one of these mechanisms will account for age-related differences in performance on a cognitive task. Therefore, it is important to recognize that evidence in favor of one mechanism being an important underlying influence accounting for aging effects is not necessarily evidence against another mechanism also playing an important role.

The processing speed theory

Salthouse (1991, 1996) has proposed a well-developed theory building on earlier work by Birren (1965) and others, which suggests that the fundamental mechanism that accounts for age-related variance in performance is a generalized, decreased speed of performing mental operations. Salthouse (1996) marshalled an impressive amount of evidence indicating that nearly all age-related variance on almost any kind of cognitive task, ranging from memory to reasoning, can be explained by knowledge of the rate at which the individual makes speeded comparisons on perceptual speed tasks. Perceptual speed tasks are simple paper-and-pencil measures that require the individual to make rapid perceptual same-different judgments about pairs of digit or letter strings or two similar symbols. Speed of processing is measured by the number of comparisons correctly made in a fixed period of time, typically somewhere between 1 and 3 minutes.

Salthouse (1996) hypothesized that there are two important mechanisms responsible for the relationship between speed of processing and cognition. The "limited time mechanism" suggests that "the time to perform later operations is greatly restricted when a large proportion of the available time is occupied by the execution of earlier operations" (p. 404), and the simultaneity mechanisms suggests that "the products of earlier processing may be lost by the time that later processing is completed" (p. 405). Thus, performance deteriorates on cognitive tasks with age because older adults are slow to perform early steps or stages in a complex cognitive tasks, and this slowing also can result in older adults never reaching the later stages because the products of earlier operations are not available to them. The speed-of-processing construct has proven itself to be very powerful when used as an individual difference measure to explain age-related variance on a cognitive task.

An important point about the slowing hypothesis which must be emphasized is that the effects of the slowed processing speed are hypothesized to be global and to have an impact on all aspects of cognition, even tasks that may not appear to have an obvious speed component. When performing a complex cognitive task, older adults may not have the products of earlier mental operations available to them that are necessary to perform later steps on the tasks, due to cognitive slowing. Thus, older adults may not complete some mental operations necessary for accurate final performance on the task. Thus, older adults' performance will differ substantially from younger adults on tasks such as working memory, recall, and reasoning due to slowing even though these tasks do not necessarily appear to have a speed component. The more complex the mental operations required to perform a cognitive task are, the more likely it will be that the processes older adults engage in to perform the task will be quite different from the processes younger adults engage in, due to constraints imposed by age-related slowing. Thus, the largest differences in performances between older and younger adults will be observed when the tasks are very difficult.

Working memory

Craik and Byrd (1982) developed an important framework to explain cognitive aging effects that relates to the construct of working memory. They suggested that older adults were deficient in the ability to engage in what they called "self-initiated processing." What Craik and Byrd referred to as "processing resource" is best measured by working memory tasks. Working memory can be conceptualized as the amount of on-line cognitive resources available at any given moment to process information, and can involve storage, retrieval, and transformation of information. It is the total amount of mental energy available to perform on-line mental operations (Baddeley, 1986). We typically measure working memory by asking subjects to both store and process information simultaneously. For example, in a computational span task (a task represented in Figure 1.1), subjects are asked to solve a series of simple addition problems, but also to remember the second number in each equation. Working memory is measured by how many equations subjects can solve while remembering the relevant number in the equations without error.

Despite this age-related deficiency in processing resource operationalized as working memory, Craik and Byrd (1982) made the important suggestion that this can be repaired by the provision of "environmental supports" for older adults. Environmental supports are elements of a cognitive task that decrease the processing requirements of the memory task. In other words, although older adults may have a more limited working memory capacity, cognitive tasks can be structured so that they require somewhat less capacity to perform. For example, there is evidence that older adults answer survey questions differently based on whether the questions are presented in a written format so that the respondent can see all of the alternatives, or whether the questions are presented auditorily followed by response alternatives presented one at a time. The differences in performance on these types of questions can be explained by environmental support. A survey question that is presented auditorily with alternatives likewise presented auditorily would be quite low in environmental support and have high processing demands, as the respondent would have to hold the questions and response alternatives in working memory as well as simultaneously perform the judgments and comparisons required to answer the question. In contrast, a written question with all answers simultaneously visible and available to the respondent would be very high in environmental support, because the respondent would not have to hold any information in working memory to answer the questions, and merely would have to perform judgments and comparisons. Using the Craik and Byrd model, one would expect larger differences in the kinds of responses older and younger adults might endorse when the questions were presented auditorily compared to visually.

A research group at the University of Michigan consisting of Norbert Schwarz, Bärbel Knäuper, Natalie Davidson, Pam Smith, and me has collected preliminary data on this topic, and we have found that patterns of responses between older and younger adults differ substantially more for auditorily presented questions than for visually presented questions. That is, older adults appear more likely to endorse the latest or most recent alternatives presented to them in multiple choice format questions (as Schwarz and Knäuper report later in chapter 13 in this volume) when the questions are presented auditorily. We also have found that the pattern of differences between young and old is smaller or nonexistent when the same questions are presented visually. It is of considerable interest to us whether these differences are controlled by processing resources, and we are conducting individual differences analyses based on measures of working memory to address this question. The hypothesis is that the quantity of processing resources that an individual has as measured by working memory function will predict response patterns on auditorily presented questions, where working memory is highly relevant, but not on visually presented questions, where subjects can refer back to the material presented as much as they desire.

The importance of environmental support in mitigating age differences is illustrated by a number of studies in the literature. Park, Smith, Morrell, Puglisi, and Dudley (1990) presented younger and older adults with pictures of concrete objects in the presence of either an unrelated cue (e.g., "cherry-spider") or a related cue (e.g., "ant-spider"). The subjects' task was to recall the word "spider" when presented with one of these two cues. Park et al. (1990) reported that older adults profited more from the conceptually related cue compared to the unrelated cue than did younger adults. The related cue provided a memory support that was automatically activated (i.e., word meaning), and this support was more beneficial in improving recall for older adults because the use of it did not draw heavily upon working memory. In contrast, the presentation of a target picture with an unrelated cue required active integration of target with cue, a process that requires active engagement of working memory, so that older adults were more disadvantaged in using the cue to support recall than were younger adults.

In another study, Cherry, Park, Frieske, and Smith (1996) presented subjects with a task where they were to learn a critical adjective that was imbedded in a sentence. Subjects studied (a) the adjective "grimacing" in a simple base sentence (e.g., "The grimacing man held the cheese"); (b) the adjective presented in a base sentence, but with a complex picture present that elaborated the relationship of the adjective to the sentence (e.g., the grimacing man was depicted with his hand in a mousetrap); or (c) a sentence and a picture which were complex and which matched one another (e.g., the elaborated picture was presented along with the sentence, "The grimacing man held the cheese while the mousetrap sprang on his finger"). Figure 1.4 shows that age differences were large in the condition where subjects studied only the base sentence, but that the inclusion of an elaborative picture acted as an environmental support, improving the recall of both groups, but with a greater facilitation effect for older adults compared to younger adults. When the elaborated picture was presented along with a complex sentence so that sentence and picture were redun-

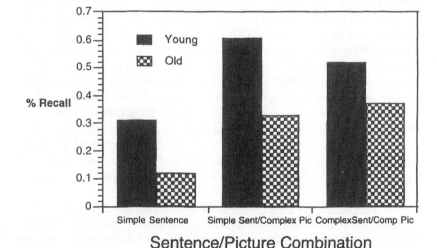

FIG. 1.4. Proportion of recall for a target adjective embedded in a sentence that was sometimes accompanied by an eleborative picture at encoding. Adapted with permission from Cherry, Park, Frieske, and Smith (1992).

dant, age differences became smaller and older adults' recall was more than three times greater than in the control base picture condition. The addition of the picture elaborated the relationships described by the sentences, limiting the working memory requirements of the task.

These studies suggest that when designing everyday information for older adults to remember, it is critically important to keep in mind the working memory load associated with material. It always is best to design instructions and other information for older adults so that the memory load is as low as possible. Memory cues at encoding, prompts at retrieval, and teaching older adults to write down information that they might be likely to forget (Park, Smith, & Cavanaugh, 1990) are important forms of environmental support that can result in good memory.

Relationship between speed of processing and working memory

One question that has not received much attention in the literature until recently is the nature of the relationship between speed and working memory. How can both of them be explanatory mechanisms for age-related declines in cognitive function? The use of structural equation modeling and path analysis permits us to determine the interrelationships between these constructs. In a recent study, we investigated this relationship (Park et al., 1996). We also were interested in verifying the ideas advanced earlier in this chapter that some types of memory do indeed require more cognitive resources than others, and that age differences would be largest on the memory tasks that proved to be the most resource intensive. We studied a sample of 301 adults, age 20 to 90, with roughly equivalent numbers at each decade. Subjects were given a complete cognitive battery, which included measures of speed of processing (pattern comparison, letter comparison, and digit-symbol tasks), working memory (reading span, computational span, and backward digits), and verbal ability, as well as a number of other tasks. These resource constructs were used to explain the age-related variance in three different types of memory: free recall, cued recall, and spatial memory. Typically, free recall is hypothesized to be the most effortful type of memory, as there is little environmental support at encoding or retrieval in a free recall task (Craik & Jennings, 1992), and spatial recall could be viewed as the least effortful task (Hasher & Zacks, 1979), with cued recall hypothesized to be intermediate in its resource demands. We hypothesized that (a) age-related variance would be mediated by speed of processing and working memory, (b) speed would be a more fundamental mechanism than working memory and would be related to all types of memory, and (c) working memory would have a stronger relationship to free recall than to spatial recall.

All of these hypotheses were verified in the model presented in Figure 1.5. This figure shows that all significant age-related variance is mediated by speed. Additionally, speed operates through working memory, but working memory has a direct path only to the two more effortful types of memory: free recall and cued recall. The model demonstrates the fundamental importance of the constructs of speed and working memory to long-term memory function, because there is no significant amount of age-related variance remaining to be explained in the model when the speed construct is included. Moreover, because the working memory construct is related to only the two more effortful measures of recall—free and cued recall—but not to the less effortful measure of spatial recall, the model provides independent verification of the importance of speed of processing and working memory constructs in explaining the age-related variance that occurs on a memory tasks. Due to the differential relationship of speed and working memory to the different memory measures, the model illustrates that some constructs might be more important for one type of memory than for another. The model supports the theorizing of both Salthouse (1996) and Craik and Jennings (1992), demonstrating that both speed and working memory are important for understanding age differences in memory and that age differences are largest on memory tasks that we have independently verified require more mental effort.

Inhibition

A third important construct in the cognitive aging literature is inhibition. Hasher and Zacks (1988) have proposed that, with age, we have more trouble

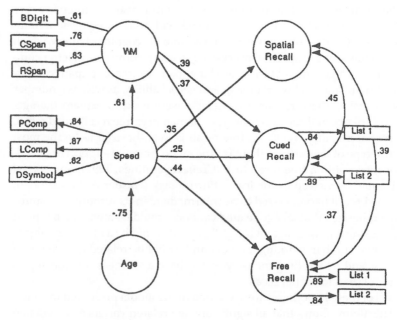

FIG. 1.5. A structural equation model of free recall, cued recall, and spatial recall, portraying the relationships of age, speed, and working memory to these constructs. For each path, the standardized path coefficient is presented. All paths shown are statistically significant. N = 301. BDig't = Backward Digit Span; CSpan - Computational Span; RSpan = Reading Span; PComp = Pattern Comparison; LComp = Letter Comparison; DSymbol = Digit Symbol; List 1 = Recall List 1; List 2 = Recall List 2. Reprinted with permission from Park et al. (1996).

focusing on target information and inhibiting attention to irrelevant material. According to this view, much of what we view as age-related decline in cognition occurs due to the inability of older adults to stay focused on primary information, as they frequently diffuse their attention across both relevant and irrelevant information. Hasher and Zacks suggested that inefficient inhibitory processes permit "the initial entrance into working memory of information that is off the goal path. It will also result in the prolonged maintenance of such information in working memory" (p. 213). Thus, according to this model, although the contents of working memory appear to decrease or shrink with age, the mechanisms underlying this apparent loss are due to the maintenance of a considerable amount of irrelevant information in working memory at the expense of target information due to inefficient inhibitory function. Hasher and Zacks's model is particularly apt for the processing of discourse. They presented compelling data suggesting that older adults are more likely to maintain disconfirmed antecedent information that they heard earlier in memory than are younger adults, and that this irrelevant information affects subsequent cognitive peformance.

In a later study, Hasher, Stoltzfus, Zacks, and Rypma (1991) demonstrated that older adults responded more quickly when a response that should have been inhibited on Trial 1 became the basis for a correct response on Trial 2 (negative priming paradigm), providing evidence for less inhibitory function in older adults at early attentional stages. Unfortunately, the finding of more negative priming in older adults (evidenced by an inability to suppress the effects of the stimulus from the previous trial) reported by Hasher et al. (1991) has not proven to be easily replicable, as there have been a number of studies where negative priming has proven to be age invariant across the life span (McDowd, 1997). The importance of the inhibition construct for understanding cognitive aging phenomena is not clear at this time.

Some theorists have argued that the overall phenomenon of inhibition is not reliable and that other mechanisms and constructs provide a better account of the extant data on language and discourse processing (Burke, 1997) and attention (McDowd, 1997). In response to these criticisms, Zacks and Hasher (1997) have argued that the inhibition mechanism is important and fundamental to understanding cognitive aging. They marshalled considerable support to suggest that inhibition operates in language production situations and other on-line production tasks. They pointed out that inhibition effects are most pronounced when the individual has to inhibit a strong response, and that it is in these situations where older adults are most likely to show evidence for poor inhibitory function. Although they agreed that alternative explanations are possible for individual studies where the inhibition construct has been invoked as the explanatory mechanism, they argued that inhibition is the most parsimonious explanation for the corpus of data that exists, and that it thus is the preferred explanation. More discussion of the inhibition construct occurs in this volume in chapter 9, by Yoon, May, and Hasher.

The notion of poor inhibitory function may be of great importance for understanding the behavior of older adults in many everyday situations. Older adults may be more susceptible to distraction when they are presented with multiple sources of information and must pay attention to only one, such as when multiple conversations are occurring at a party. Additionally, the difficulty older adults have with the inhibition process may result in their having poorer mental control in social situations. The stereotype that older adults are more likely to speak their minds could be related to less effective inhibitory processes operating in social situations rather than to a lack of concern about social mores.

We recently conducted a study where we measured subjects' tendency to say "uh" and insert other filler sounds while they were telling simple stories (Hunter, Park, & Schwarz, 1998). Later, when we asked subjects to inhibit these filler sounds when they told the stories, we found that older adults had more difficulty inhibiting the sounds effectively than younger adults, particularly when they had a high concurrent working memory load. Thus, telling older adults not to do something or to inhibit some type of social response may not have the same effect on their behavior as it does on younger adults. We argue that some aging stereotypes ("crotchety," "blunt," "low tolerance for others") could be a result of the inability of older adults to inhibit strongly activated, but inappropriate, responses in social situations. We know considerably less about inhibitory function and aging than we do about speed and working memory. There have been some methodological limitations to developing this construct, as it has proven difficult to develop a reliable individual difference measure of inhibitory function. We had hoped to examine the relative contributions of inhibition to memory function in the model presented in Figure 1.5, but could not develop a reliable measure of the construct.

Thus, at this point, the attenuation of age-related variance through inhibitory function on cognitive tasks has yet to be demonstrated. Nevertheless, the rich theorizing that surrounds this construct, the existence of inhibitory neural circuits, and the considerable amount of data supporting the Hasher and Zacks (1988) argument suggest inhibition to be a construct that will continue to be invoked as an explanation for cognitive aging and one to be a construct meritorious of continued investigation.

Sensory function

Startling data on mechanisms underlying cognitive function in older adults recently have emerged from the Berlin Aging Study. Lindenberger and Baltes (1994) collected extensive medical, sensory, cognitive, and social measures from a large sample of older adults in Berlin age 70 to 103, with equal representation of subjects at each decade, even for the very old. Lindenberger and Baltes reported compelling evidence indicating that nearly all of the age-related variance in 14 tests of cognitive ability (including measures of speed of processing, reasoning, memory, world knowledge, and verbal fluency) was mediated by sensory functioning as measured by simple tests of visual and auditory acuity. The sensory measures appeared to be a more fundamental index of cognitive resource even than speed of processing. The sensory measures mediated all of the variance in speed of processing, but the reverse was not true, adding credence to the notion that sensory function may be a fundamental index of cognitive aging. Lindenberger and Baltes argued that sensory function is a crude measure of brain integrity. They proposed the "common cause" hypothesis: that sensory function, as a general index of neurobiological architecture, is fundamental to cognitive function and thus is a powerful mediator of all cognitive abilities.

In a later study, Baltes and Lindenberger (1997) conducted analyses similar to those just described, but with a life span sample that included subjects ranging in age from 25 to 103 years. As shown in Figure 1.6, they demonstrated systematic decline across the life span in all aspects of cognitive function, including, somewhat surprisingly, measures of world knowledge and verbal fluency, domains that typically have been considered to be more resistant to age-related decline (e.g., see Figure 1.1). The decline functions did not change when older adults in early stages of dementia were excluded from the sample. In addition, there was strong evidence for mediation of cognitive decline by sensory function, both with demented subjects included and excluded. Finally, Lindenberger and Baltes (1997) demonstrated that the slope of the decline gradient did not vary as a function of education, occupation, social class, and income. This suggests that the declines are indeed based on biology rather than social history, adding some confidence to the notion that the sensory measures provide an index of neuronal integrity which, in turn, mediates cognitive function.

It also should be noted that it is plausible that Figure 1.6 underestimates age-related decline in these functions, due to selective survival or mortality (Baltes & Smith, 1997). It is likely that individuals who survive into very late adulthood may be healthier and cognitively more elite than those who do not survive. Extensive analyses by Baltes and Smith (1997) of individuals for whom they had cognitive data but who died or declined to continue to participate indicated that the Berlin Aging sample was positively selected on all 25 variables that it examined, including the measures of cognition.

The findings from the Berlin Aging Study are profoundly important for understanding cognitive aging. Many different types of cognition were studied, and a sample that was representative of all aspects of the population was included, unlike other cognitive aging studies where only more select individuals have been studied. Additionally, this is a rare study that includes large numbers of individuals in their eighties, nineties, and even over age 100, so it provides a complete view of cognitive aging in very late adulthood, something that we know relatively little about. One important message from the Berlin Aging Study is that being highly educated, affluent, or of high cognitive ability does not protect an individual from age-related decline. The finding that sociobiographical variables such as social

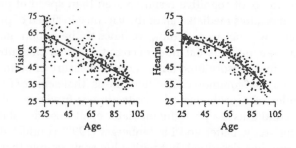

Intellectual Functioning

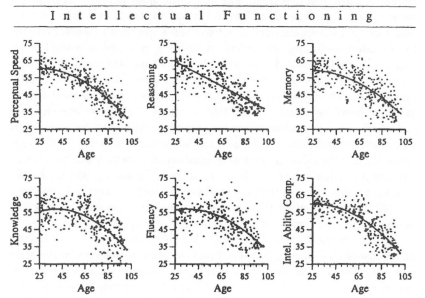

FIG. 1.6.
Declines in sensory and intellectual functioning across the life span (*N* = 315). Reprinted with permission from Baltes and Lindenberger (1997).

class and education did not mitigate age effects suggests that individuals age at the same rate and show age-related decline regardless of initial level of ability. Nevertheless, these data should not be interpreted to suggest that individuals of diverse initial abilities will show the same effects of cognitive aging in their everyday environment.

Data from Baltes and Lindenberger (1997) as well as from Cherry and Park (1993) clearly indicate that more educated individuals have higher levels of cognitive resource. Thus, despite the uniform decline in cognitive ability for all socioeconomic groups, sociobiographical variables are almost certain to be important in understanding situations where cognitive aging puts individuals at risk. As Park (1997) noted, an individual who starts out with a high amount of cognitive resource and experiences significant age-related decline will continue to possess an adequate amount of cognitive resource to perform the tasks of daily living, such as handling routine financial affairs, managing a medication regimen, and dealing with shopping and cooking. In contrast, an individual who is relatively low in cognitive resource initially but is able to manage these tasks as a younger adult might fall below some critical threshold of needed resources to perform these tasks as he or she ages, necessitating institutionalization of the individual. The importance of cognitive resources for everyday life is considered more completely in chapter 12, which focuses on the applied aspects of cognitive aging research.

Summary

There is good evidence that age-related changes in mechanisms of cognitive aging are the basis for age-related decline observed in a broad range of cogntive tasks that span many types of cognitive behavior, including attention, memory, reasoning, and problem solving. The constructs of speed, working memory, inhibition, and sensory function will come up again and again in the subsequent chapters in this book. Evidence to date suggests that sensory function and speed may be crude indicators of the overall neuronal integrity of the individual's central nervous system, but it remains a challenge to directly link these behavioral measures of cognitive aging to neurobiological function within the individual. Working memory function appears to be directly related to speed of processing, but nevertheless it is an important construct in its own right and it does appear to control independent variance from speed on effortful cognitive tasks. Finally, the role of inhibition in age-related decline on cognitive tasks is less well understood compared to the three other fundamental mechanisms. Future research is needed to establish the relationship of inhibition to the other fundamental mechanisms of cognitive aging: sensory function, speed, and working memory capacity.

References

Baddeley, A. (1986). *Working memory*. Oxford, England: Clarendon Press.

Baltes, P. B., & Lindenberger, U. (1997). Emergence of powerful connection between sensory and cognitive functions across the adult life span: A new window to the study of cognitive aging? *Psychology and Aging, 12*, 12–21.

Baltes, P. B., & Smith, J. (1997). A systemic-wholistic view of psychological functioning in very old age: Introduction to a collection of articles from the Berlin Aging Study. *Psychology and Aging, 12*, 395–409.

Baltes, P. B., & Staudinger, U. (1993). The search for a psychology of wisdom. *Current Directions in Psychological Science, 2*, 75–80.

Birren, J. E. (1965). Age changes in speed of behavior: Its central nature and physiological correlates. In A. T. Welford & J. E. Birren (Eds.), *Behavior, aging, and the nervous system*, (pp. 191–216). Springfield, IL: Charles C Thomas.

Burke, D. M. (1997). Language, aging, and inhibitory deficits: Evaluation of a theory. *Journal of Gerontology: Psychological Science, 6*, 52B, 254–264.

Cherry, K. E., & Park, D. C. (1993). Individual difference and contextual variables influence spatial memory in younger and older adults. *Psychology and Aging, 8*, 517–526.

Cherry, K. E., Park, D. C., Frieske, D. A., & Smith, A. D. (1996). Verbal and pictorial elaborations enhance memory in young and older adults. *Aging, Neuropsychology, and Cognition, 3*, 15–29.

Craik, F. I. M., & Byrd, M. (1982). Aging and cognitive deficits: The role of attentional resources. In F. I. M. Craik & S. Trehub (Eds.), *Aging and cognitive processes*, (pp. 191–211). New York: Plenum Press.

Craik, F. I. M., & Jennings, J. M. (1992). Human memory. In F. I. M. Craik & T. A. Salthouse, (Eds.), *The handbook of aging and cognition*, (pp. 51–110). Hillsdale, NJ: Erlbaum.

Earles, J. L., Connor, L. T., Frieske, D. A., Park, D. C., Smith, A. D., & Zwahr, M. (1997). Age differences in inhibition: Possible causes and consequences. *Aging, Neuropsychology, and Cognition, 4*, 45–57.

Hasher, L., Stoltzfus, E. R., Zacks, R. T., & Rypma, B. (1991). Age and inhibition. *Journal of Experimental Psychology: Learning, Memory, and Cognition, 17*, 163–169.

Hasher, L., & Zacks, R. T. (1979). Automatic and effortful processes in memory. *Journal of Experimental Psychology: General, 108*, 356–388.

Hasher, L., & Zacks, R. T. (1988). Working memory, comprehension, and aging: A review and a new view. In G. H. Bower (Ed.), *The psychology of learning and motivation*, (Vol. 22, pp. 193–225). San Diego, CA: Academic Press.

Hummert, M. L., Garstka, T. A., Shaner, J. L., & Strahm, S. (1994). Stereotypes of the elderly held by young, middle-aged, and elderly adults. *Journal of Gerontology: Psychologial Sciences, 49*, P240–P249.

Hunter, S., Park, D. C., & Schwarz, N. (1998). *Mental control and aging: Don't, uh, say uh.* Paper presented at the Cognitive Aging Meeting, Atlanta, GA.

Jacoby, L. L. (1991). A process dissociation framework: Separating automatic from intentional uses of memory. *Journal of Memory and Language, 30*, 513–541.

Light, L. L. (1991). Memory and aging: Four hypothesis in search of data. *Annual Review of Psychology, 42*, 333–376.

Lindenberger, U., & Baltes, P. B. (1994). Sensory functioning and intelligence in old age: A strong connection. *Psychology and Aging, 9*, 339–355

Lindenberger, U., & Baltes, P. (1997). Intellectual functioning in old and very old age: Cross-sectional results from the Berlin Aging Study. *Psychology and Aging, 12*, 410–432.

McDowd, J. M. (1997). Inhibition in attention and aging. *Journal of Gerontology: Psychological Sciences, 52B*, 265–273.

Park, D. C. (1997). Psychological issues related to competence: Cognitive aging and instrumental activities of daily living. In W. Schaie & S. Willis (Eds.), *Social structures and aging*, (pp. 66–82). Mahwah, New Jersey: Erlbaum.

Park, D. C. (1999). Aging and the controlled and automatic processing of medical information and medical intentions. In D. C. Park, R. W. Morrell, & K. Shifren (Eds.), *Processing of medical information in aging patients: Cognitive and human factors perspectives.* Mahwah, NJ: Erlbaum.

Park, D. C., Puglisi, J. T., & Smith, A. D. (1986). Memory for pictures: Does an age-related decline exist? *Psychology and Aging, 1*, 11–17.

Park, D. C., & Shaw, R. J. (1992). Effect of environmental support on implicit and explicit memory in younger and older adults. *Psychology and Aging, 7*, 632–642.

Park, D. C., Smith, A. D., & Cavanaugh, J. C. (1990). The metamemories of memory researchers. *Memory and Cognition, 18*, 321–327.

Park, D. C., Smith, A. D., Lautenschlager, G., Earles, J., Frieske, D., Zwahr, M., & Gaines, C. (1996). Mediators of long-term memory performance across the life span. *Psychology and Aging, 11*, 621–637.

Park, D. C., Smith, A. D., Morrell, R. W., Puglisi, J. T., & Dudley, W. N. (1990). Effects of contextual integration on recall of pictures by older adults. *Journal of Gerontology: Psychological Sciences, 45*, 52–57.

Salthouse, T. A. (1991). *Theoretical perspectives on cognitive aging*. Hillsdale, NJ: Erlbaum.

Salthouse, T. A. (1996). The processing-speed theory of adult age differences in cognition. *Psychological Review, 103*, 403–428.

Zacks, R., & Hasher, L. (1997). Cognitive gerontology and attentional inhibition: A reply to Burke and McDowd. *Journal of Gerontology: Psychological Sciences, 52*, 274–283.

Dell, R.K. in and Stranks, D.R. (1980) The Preparation of the Pure
magnesium. Internal ICI Publication, Pp4.

Bell, O.L., Smith, D.D. and Jones, A.C. (1983) F.T.I.R. Analysis of
C_x O_y Adsorption of Metal Surfaces. Int Chem. Adv. xxx, Pp
xxx.

Baker, C.J., Davies, G.A. and R.W.L. John, J.K. Prentice, V.C. Walton
(1984) Practical Information. A short comment on data which per-
vades of Page. J.Int Sym. xxx. 325.

Holliday, A.J. (1981) Graphics reporting C_x results. Int Tribase. P 230.

Fairbrother, A. (1980) Physical methods of surface Area determination.
Int Journal of xxx. 9th Conf. Pp 760 425.

Abersham, J.D. (1983) Polymer processing and Rheological behaviour.
4th ICI Internal Publication. Company Central xxx. 2579 xxx.

Concepts and mechanisms of gains in cognitive aging

2

Roger A. Dixon

The term "gains" has been used with increasing frequency in the study of psychological aspects of human development, especially lifespan human development. Clearly, developmental "gains" are to be distinguished from developmental "losses." Nevertheless, the meaning and use of the former term, and its relationship to the latter term, have not been fully examined. In this chapter, I focus on the concept of "gains" as it applies to development throughout life, and especially in late life.

The idea of gains

In a traditional dictionary-based sense, a gain is something desired that is won or acquired. A gain constitutes an improvement, an advance, progress, or perhaps even movement toward a valued goal. Gains are not necessarily the product of effort, but often they are, as when one seeks to improve a condition or skill. A loss, on the other hand, reflects a failure to win or acquire, or a failure to preserve or maintain what one has. A loss could be a state of being deprived of something that one previously had possessed or otherwise sought, whether in number (fewer than before) or quality (lower than before). Losses are not typically the product of deliberate effort (i.e., one rarely seeks to lose something both that one has and desires to have), but losses could be the product of failing effort, accident, disease, or progressive decline.

Change is a premise of both gains and losses. Change in quantity or quality may be evaluated as (a) a gain if it involves movement from a lower

---

The author acknowledges grant support from the National Institute on Aging (grant AG08235) and the Natural Sciences and Engineering Research Council of Canada. He appreciates the assistance of Anna-Lisa Cohen and the helpful comments of David Hultsch and Denise Park on earlier versions of this chapter.

(worse) to a higher (better) state, or (b) a loss if it involves movement from a higher (better) to a lower (worse) state. If there is no change or alteration in the state of a system or process, it is said (colloquially) to be in steady state, in a period of maintenance or stability.

A fundamental characteristic of development across the lifespan—at multiple levels of analysis, and from birth to death—is that the human organism changes. It becomes different in form, nature, characteristics, and many other respects. The transformations that occur across the lifespan are changes that involve periods and varieties of gains, losses, and maintenance. This may be true both in the latter three quarters of the life course (i.e., adulthood) and in the first quarter of life (i.e., childhood). Although the stereotypes of development in childhood and adulthood may be differentially populated by gains and losses, both directions of change may occur in all phases (Baltes, 1987). A simplistic illustration of how gains and losses may be intrinsically related in adulthood may be seen in the observation that as one "gains" in years of age (i.e., becomes older), one "loses" in time left to live (i.e., becomes closer to death).

As adults get older, however, there are losses in more than just time left to live. In fact, with aging, biological (e.g., Medina, 1996), sensory (e.g., Schieber & Baldwin, 1996), and cognitive (e.g., Salthouse, 1991) changes are reasonably and predominantly evaluated as losses. Are there fundamental and meaningful gains that occur with movement through adulthood? Are there changes with aging that arguably can be evaluated as gains? Or, does the concept of "gains" require some modification to accommodate the phenomena of aging? A specific purpose of this chapter is to review the concept of "gains" as it has been used in scholarship on cognitive changes in adulthood, otherwise known as the field of cognitive aging. An additional purpose is to note new empirical and theoretical directions in the study of gains and losses.

Conceptualizing gains and losses

That cognitive development in adulthood may not be characterized entirely as losses—and, in fact, could include some manner of gains—occasionally has been noted by psychologists for most of the twentieth century. To be sure, the gains of cognitive aging typically are placed in the context of losses. For example, observing age differences in intellectual performance in favor of younger (as compared to older) adults, some early scholars also noted apparent exceptions (e.g., Jones & Conrad, 1933; Pressey, 1919; Sanford, 1902; see Dixon, Kramer, & Baltes, 1985, for review). The exceptions to the "rule" of aging losses have included processes that appeared to be at least generally delayed in the onset of decline, processes that developed with broader bands of individual differences, and processes linked to possible supportive mechanisms. Several recent observers have focused on possible mechanisms for maintenance of cognitive competence and skills and on dynamics between gains and losses (e.g., Baltes, 1987; Baltes & Baltes, 1990; Perlmutter, 1990; Salthouse, 1987, 1990; Uttal & Perlmutter, 1989). Other recent observers have identified processes that are thought to be relatively decoupled from aging decline and, in fact, fundamentally growth oriented. Such gains are viewed not as exceptions to the rule of losses, but rather as independent of decline, produced as a function of an unfolding (or growing) organism or environment. Overall, intriguing ideas have been issued regarding whether, how, and why gains can appear in cognitive aging.

Complementary perspectives

This chapter is a companion to chapter 1 in this volume by Park, which focuses on basic mechanisms of cognitive aging, and thus more on losses than gains. I emphasize companion rather than contrast, because, although the two chapters have different foci, the theoretical perspectives represented in these chapters are not incommensurable. Indeed, despite some divergence in proximal theoretical and empirical goals, the perspectives represented in the two chapters may be complementary in the study of cognitive aging. Not only do they both attend to issues of gains and losses in cognitive aging—at both a descriptive and an explanatory level—but they have relatively shared many constraints and global purposes. In addition, both perspectives address the essential tension of cognitive aging; namely, the changing balance between losses and gains across the lifespan.

As argued elsewhere (e.g., Dixon & Hertzog, 1996), divergent theoretical perspectives in cognitive aging differ in numerous matters of focus, assumptions, balance, and methods, but they may not yet so much clash, as competing paradigms might, as complement one another through their differences. Nevertheless, in the field of cognitive aging, alternative perspectives are not often fighting over the same territory, as indeed informal examinations of the citation patterns of the respective proponents have confirmed. The circle of cognitive aging phenomena may be quite large, encompassing a wide variety of: (a) issues, concepts, methods, and theories; (b) skills, performances, behaviors, abilities, responses, and beliefs; and (c) observations, directions, interpretations, reasons, and perhaps even causes. It is useful that different sectors of this circle of cognitive aging are, in fact, being explored. Among these different sectors are phenomena thought to represent aging-related gains and losses.

Treatments of gains and losses issue

There are four principal treatments of the gains-losses issue in cognitive aging. Whereas I address the first three issues briefly, the fourth is covered in somewhat more detail. These four treatments, posed as questions, follow.

1. What do scholars say (theoretically, speculatively) about gains and losses in cognitive aging?
2. What do textbook authors teach students about gains and losses in cognitive aging?
3. What do researchers find when they survey the beliefs of individuals about gains and losses in cognitive aging?
4. How are gains represented conceptually and empirically in the context of losses?

Scholars' perspectives

As noted above, several scholars have constructed theoretical positions that include the concept of gains in cognitive aging. Baltes (1987, 1997) has been a central proponent of the notion that there may be gains in cognitive aging. To be sure, his perspective is a comprehensive one, for he never failed to note that there also are considerable losses. Overall, lifespan development is portrayed as a complex process reflecting simultaneous transformations of gains, losses, and maintenance. Baltes emphasized that the gains-losses issue is a lifespan issue and, more specifically, that the ratio of gains to losses changes throughout life. Put simply, whereas there are more gains than losses in early life, there are more losses than gains in late life. Perhaps most notable about this portrayal is the idea that there indeed are losses occurring in child development and gains occurring during aging. This constitutes a provocative reformulation of the traditional gains-oriented concept of development. The broader concept of development does not rest, however, on a precise value of the gains:losses ratio at any particular point in the life course or on a precise representation of the shape of the function. Other scholars have produced complementary treatments of the gains-losses issue in cognitive aging (e.g., Perlmutter, 1990; Uttal & Perlmutter, 1989). Similarly, the problem of expanding the concept of development to include both gains and losses has been discussed elsewhere (e.g., Dixon, Lerner, & Hultsch, 1991; Harris, 1957; Lerner, 1984; Wohlwill, 1973).

Textbook portrayals

How do prominent textbooks on adult development and aging portray the concepts of gains and losses? I informally selected and examined four recently published textbooks in the area. My two principal criteria in selecting these texts were that (a) they be written by one or more active contributors to scholarship in the psychology of adult development, and (b) they be published within the past several years. My perusal was guided by four major concerns:

1. whether and to what extent the gains-losses issue was prominent,
2. the extent to which gains were represented as a feature of cognitive aging,

3. whether the gains as described were related to cognitive losses, and

4. the extent to which prominent theories about aging-related cognitive loss were represented.

Overall, the four textbooks I examined included substantial coverage of aging-related decrements in sensory, health, social role, and cognitive abilities. Specifically, age differences in favor of younger adults were reported for a variety of memory and other cognitive processes. Accompanying the substantial empirical literature on such cognitive losses, however, are well-established and well-tested theories regarding the range, ramifications, and causes of these losses (see, e.g., Cerella, 1990; Craik & Jennings, 1992; Light, 1991; Park, chapter 1 in this volume; Salthouse, 1991; Zacks & Hasher, 1994). To what extent did the textbooks present this relatively large and influential theoretical literature, as compared to published ideas, empirical results, and theories pertaining to cognitive gains?

In terms of both number of text pages and number of figures or tables, these four textbooks presented far more information pertaining to cognitive gains than to theories of cognitive losses. Indeed, three of the textbooks contained virtually no mention of such prominent theories of cognitive aging as Salthouse's (1991) influential and cogent views on generalized slowing. In contrast, at the theoretical level, the textbooks appeared to focus more on the possible gains of cognitive aging, including postformal operations, dialectical-relativistic thinking, wisdom, creativity, and expertise. Some textbooks in the psychology of adult development and aging identify and highlight ideas about gains with aging, but place such discussion only marginally in the context of theoretical developments regarding cognitive losses. This observation may be more meaningful if one recognizes that the relative size and influence of the literature pertaining to cognitive gains and losses is decidedly in favor of the latter. Quite possibly, an optimistic perspective regarding cognitive aging was adopted deliberately by the authors and publishers.

Research on beliefs about gains and losses

What do lay adults believe about gains and losses with aging? Heckhausen and colleagues (e.g., Heckhausen, Dixon, & Baltes, 1989; Heckhausen & Krueger, 1993) have conducted research on beliefs about gains and losses associated with aging, and some of their results pertain to cognitive aging. In a typical procedure, Heckhausen et al. (1989) presented younger and older adults with a series of over 350 adjectives describing a wide range of personality (e.g., skeptical), social (e.g., friendly), and cognitive (e.g., intelligent) characteristics. They used adjectives referring to desirable, undesirable, and neutral characteristics. The participants were asked to rate each adjective for sensitivity to developmental change (i.e., does it increase, become stronger, become more common; 1 = *not at all,* 9 = *very*) and desirability (the desirability of the change; 1 = *very undesirable, 9 = very desirable*). It is not too much of a speculative leap to view very desirable increases in attributes as gains and very undesirable increases in attributes as losses. Following this, the participants rated the expected *onset age* (age at which the increase starts) and *closing age* (age at which the increase ends) on a scale of adult ages from 20 to 90 years. The overall proportional relationship between gains and losses in adulthood is quite similar to that presented hypothetically by Baltes (1987). That is, the proportion of gains to losses is greater in childhood and much lower in adulthood.

For the purposes of the present chapter, I reexamined the original tables from the Heckhausen et al. (1989) article. In so doing, I conducted a secondary selection of items from the original data. The selection involved the following criteria. The attributes selected were arguably cognitive ones:

- believed to be increasing across adulthood ($M > 6$);
- believed to be gains (M desirability ≥ 6.6) or losses (M desirability ≤ 3.8);
- considered *aging gains* if they were believed to be gains and had onset ages later than 30 and closing ages no earlier than 70;
- considered *aging gains-to-losses* if they were believed to be gains but had closing ages earlier than 70;
- considered *aging losses* if they were believed to be losses and had onset ages greater than 30 and closing ages no earlier than 70.

It is possible that a category termed *aging losses-to-gains* might have emerged, but it did not.

The results of this informal selection—how these categories are populated—can be easily summarized. The German adults participating in the Heckhausen et al. (1989) study rated as virtually unqualified cognitive gains with aging the following attributes: human knowledge, open-minded, smart, experienced, well-read, reasonable, levelheaded, wise, and educated. Cognitive attributes that fit the characteristics of gains-to-losses were: logical, productive, methodical, ready-witted, adaptive, industrious, and planful. In contrast, cognitive attributes that were believed by the participants to be losses with aging were: moralistic, overcautious, complicated, obstinate, forgetful, headstrong, stubborn, and absentminded.

In sum, when asked to characterize adult development in terms of a wide range of attributes, the participants produced a pattern of life course change in the gains:losses ratio that fits the figurative patterns generated by scholars (e.g., Baltes, 1987). Moreover, they identified a set of cognitive attributes that they believed to be desired and to follow trajectories of sustained improvement with aging. These data overlap with recent studies on conceptions of intelligence (e.g., Berg & Sternberg, 1992) and stereotypes of aging (e.g., Hummert, Gartska, Shaner, & Strahm, 1994). For example, in both the Heckhausen et al. (1989) and Hummert et al. (1994) studies, attributes seen as cognitive gains, such as witty, wise, intelligent, well-informed, knowledgeable, and productive (gains-to-losses) emerged under some conditions as stereotypic attributes of older adults. Both studies found that lay persons believed cognitive losses included attributes such as inflexible, slow-thinking, and forgetful.

Summary

According to these brief reviews, the first three treatments of the concept of gains have revealed that many observers—theoretical authors, textbook authors, and laypersons—believe there are reasons to consider the possibility of at least selected gains in cognitive aging. Theoretical scholars have established a conceptual basis for the idea of cognitive gains, textbook authors have instructed university students in optimistic tones about the possibilities of cognitive gains with aging, and adult research participants, with apparently no special stake in the case, have identified several processes that might undergo improvement with aging.

It would be unfair to say that the scholars have not yet taken up the challenge of linking aspects of gains and losses in human development (Baltes, 1997). It might be fair, however, to say that thus far the predominant tendency has been to discuss gains and losses separately or in parallel. For example, some authors may comment on the gains and then the losses in the abstract, but may not necessarily link the two ideas in theoretical or empirical work. Perhaps there is a disconnection in explanations of cognitive competence and adaptivity (gains or losses) in late adulthood. Whereas there is considerable empirical and theoretical work pertaining to the description and explanation of decline in cognitive abilities with aging, there is very little parallel descriptive and explanatory work pertaining to those cognitive processes that allegedly are maintained or improved with aging. More thorough examination of these linkages should be pursued.

In the next section, I turn to the fourth major category of scholarship on the treatment of gains and losses. This category includes research on how gains may be conceptualized in the context of losses.

Conceptualizing gains in the context of losses

The fourth major category of treatments is the largest and most complex. This category pertains to both empirical and theoretical work concerning cognitive gains and losses with aging. After examining extensive literature, I divided it into three main approaches to the issue of cognitive aging gains.

1. *Gains qua gains*, or the idea that gains emerge and continue despite or independent of the constraints provided by losses. It includes the "never the twain shall meet" principle, which reflects my informal observation that researchers who focus on gains qua gains rarely

mention the observations or theories of colleagues who focus on cognitive losses, and vice versa.

2. *Gains as losses of a lesser magnitude,* or the idea that some consolation may be taken in cognitive losses that occur (a) later than expected, (b) not universally, (c) at a level less than feared or predicted, (d) at a level that is not debilitating to everyday skills, and so forth.

3. *Gains as a function of losses,* or apparent gains that are linked to specific or general losses, that are occasioned by losses, or that compensate for losses.

Each of these subcategories is summarized in turn.

Gains qua gains

This alternative is perhaps the boldest and most optimistic of the three, in that it represents some aspects of cognitive aging as undergoing continued or renewed growth throughout adulthood. In some instances, it may derive from a perspective on human development that incorporates the neo-organismic (e.g., neo-Piagetian) idea that there is continued growth in thinking or reasoning with advancing age. The growth may even be "structural" or qualitative in nature (see, e.g., Commons, Sinnott, Richards, & Armon, 1989). Examples include research on (a) fifth or postformal "stages" of cognitive development (beyond Piaget's fourth formal operations stage (Sinnott, 1996); (b) dialectical, transactional, relativistic thinking or reasoning (Kramer & Woodruff, 1986); and perhaps (c) wisdom in late life (Baltes & Staudinger, 1993; Sternberg, 1990). Some observers refer to this approach as the "developmental" approach, presumably because a traditional concept of development is employed in which processes that grow are developmental and processes that decline are not developmental. As noted above, however, a broader concept of development includes both growth and decline. If the term "development" is not tantamount to growth, then developmental approaches include all manner of foci of lifespan change. Elsewhere, other terms are used to refer to this approach, including organismic, structural, and neo-Piagetian (e.g., Dixon & Hertzog, 1996).

Postformal operations.   A basic research question in postformal operations concerns whether there is a type of rationality that is qualitatively higher than (Piaget's) formal operations (Sinnott, 1996). The stage of formal operations represents a major cognitive advance for those adolescents and young adults who achieve it. Logical, abstract thinking offers many useful problem-solving tools. Some researchers have argued, however, that it is important for mature adults to consider the relativistic, contradictory, and inherently ambiguous nature of some cognitive problems (e.g., Perry, 1968). The use of formal logic and the pursuit of absolute solutions may not be the most adaptive strategy. Abilities or styles of problem solving that are not constrained by formal reasoning (but probably are preceded by it) are referred to as "postformal" operations. Sinnott (1996, p. 362) wrote that the "essence of postformal operations" is "knowing the general-operation rule and letting it filter your reality, consciously choosing the formal operations logical system you'll impose and living it out as 'true'." From this description, postformal operations appear to involve some metacognitive characteristics, including some evaluation and monitoring of when and where to deploy a given analysis or logic.

As Sinnott (1996) acknowledged, however, an important gap in the research base has not yet been closed. Perhaps further specificity regarding the cognitive skills representative of postformal operations will help. For example, Sinnott provided examples of postformal operations that reflect numerous everyday cognitive and social-cognitive skills: "Ability to 'speak' in 'others' languages' or belief systems; better communication; the ability to argue within others' logics; a flexible view of what is possible for a family; . . . awareness of one's own biases and filtered world-views; . . . more creative problem solving; more flexible interpersonal relations" (p. 370) and so forth. A challenge for proponents of this perspective will be to differentiate their view on how these valued skills might develop and be maintained from the views of researchers from other approaches. Theoretically, it may be a challenge for scholars in this area to address the question of whether and how gains in postformal operations can or do develop independently of cognitive, sensory, and neurological losses. Are the mechanisms of cognitive growth in adulthood the same as those promoting cognitive growth in early life? Empirically, it will be important for scholars sharing this perspective to generate more studies testing their provocative and optimistic views of cognitive aging (Sinnott, 1996).

Wisdom. Equally provocative has been the multifaceted research conducted in the past several decades on the development of wisdom with aging. That wisdom may be an aging-related gain can be established by reference to studies on beliefs about aging (e.g., Heckhausen et al., 1989) and common sense definitions of wisdom (e.g., Berg & Sternberg, 1992; Sternberg, 1990). That is, wisdom is a positively valued feature of cognition and often is viewed as increasing with age. That it is a gain qua gain can be inferred from a review of the literature, which does not typically place it in the context of cognitive losses. Wisdom is dissimilar to postformal operations in two important ways. First, it has an enduring common sense quality that invokes similar meanings across a broad range of adults. Second, the development of wisdom in adulthood has been a topic of considerable empirical research.

One of the largest research programs devoted to wisdom is that emanating from Baltes and colleagues (see reviews by Baltes & Smith, 1990; Baltes & Staudinger, 1993). Whereas the definition of wisdom in terms of a growing and expert knowledge system pertaining to fundamental issues of life and living is not entirely unlike that for postformal operations (Sinnott,

1996), casting it explicitly in an expertise framework provides a crucial benefit. Knowledge development and the acquisition of expertise in general are well-understood processes (e.g., Ericsson & Charness, 1994). The facts and pertinent mechanisms of the development of expertise are actively researched in a variety of domains. A well-known principle of expertise is that practice and experience in the domain are fundamental premises and mechanisms for further development. Thus, theoretically, given certain assumptions, wisdom as an expertise is established on firm and promising ground.

In the past decade, a growing body of research regarding wisdom and aging has emerged. It is beyond the purposes of this commentary to review that research, but several features deserve to be highlighted. First, the domain of "life pragmatics" has been operationalized in terms of three main exemplars: life planning, life management, and life review. Notably, these domains bear some resemblance to the description of cognitive activities provided by a postformal operation researcher, Sinnott (1996). Baltes and colleagues, however, have taken this operational definition further in that they have empirically examined each of these areas separately and in a variety of ways (e.g., Baltes & Smith, 1990; Baltes & Staudinger, 1993). Thus, the data base from which conclusions are drawn about wisdom as a gain with aging is substantial. As yet, no firm conclusions are available about whether wisdom is a process that shows gains across adulthood—whether as a rule or an exception—and what the constraints and supportive conditions are on its development.

Summary.   Cognitive aging researchers have not yet established firmly that there are demonstrable gains qua gains through late adulthood. Two examples of research in this area have been mentioned. Research methods have included experiments, interviews, and questionnaire studies. Further efforts are encouraged.

Gains as losses of a lesser magnitude

Perhaps only a few observers would assert blithely that losing is in any way tantamount to winning, even if one only just falls short or does better than expected. But, this category is populated by numerous everyday examples. For example, competitors in sports often testify that performing a personal best in a losing effort is nevertheless a victory of sorts. Giving the competition the "old college try," but losing with dignity, can be a consolation to many performers. It can be heartening to find a new way, through innovative strategy or upgraded technology, of performing a leisure or professional skill and thereby managing to meet your own expectations or maintain your own level of performance.

In cognitive aging, this idea is that some consolation may be taken in selected features of certain cognitive losses, such as those that occur later than expected, less universally than expected, and at a level less than feared or predicted, and that seem to be independent of (unrelated to) other abilities or everyday skills and competencies. I have identified numerous examples of this category from the cognitive aging literature, but summarize only selected illustrations here.

Gains as losses occurring later, less uniformly, or less universally than expected. This exemplar is a pivotal one. Given stereotypes of declining cognitive abilities and a vast reservoir of evidence to support these views, it is possible that some consolation may be taken in the evidence that there are some exceptions to the rule. The exceptions need not be of enormous proportions; in fact, evidence pertaining to more modest than expected losses may be theoretically more promising. An excellent example is that provided by Schaie (e.g., 1990, 1994, 1996). In several recent reviews of his prodigious Seattle Longitudinal Study, Schaie has presented a figure with data pertaining to maintenance of intellectual abilities across a 7-year interval by four cohorts; namely, those age 53 to 60, 60 to 67, 67 to 74, and 74 to 81. His analyses suggest that very high proportions of different age samples maintain one or more intellectual abilities across the 7-year interval. For example, 90% or more of people in the all four age groups (including those up to age 81) maintained at least two intellectual abilities. Critics may quibble with Schaie's definition of maintenance and other issues, but the importance of his analysis in the present context is that it illustrates the implicit notion that losses occur in intellectual abilities, but they may not be as great, as uniform, or as universal as some observers would expect. This fact may be viewed, with some optimism, as a gain.

Gains as losses that can be accommodated. The second illustration also is a prominent one. An excellent example of this phenomenon may be found in the work of Brandtstädter (e.g., Brandtstädter & Greve, 1994; Brandtstädter & Wentura, 1995). The overall effect of losses may be mitigated by processes that serve to compensate through redefinition and redirection. Accommodation and its connection to compensation have been discussed elsewhere (e.g., Bäckman & Dixon, 1992; Dixon & Bäckman, 1995; Salthouse, 1995). Examples of accommodation include:

1. Reducing one's criterion of success, such that one may proclaim success in areas of diminished potentiality simply by lowering the standard by which one evaluates performance. Such "bar lowering" occurs regularly in competitive sports, in which there are competitions and records for junior, senior, or master performers. In any activity in which the effects of aging reduce the potential performance, adjusting downward the standard of successful performance may be a form of accommodating to losses.
2. Adjusting one's goals, which could include devaluing and disengaging from blocked goals, as well as selecting new and more feasible goals. As Brandtstädter and Wentura (1995) noted, with de-

clining productive resources in late life, it may not be possible to maintain the highest standards in multiple domains. The task is to manage one's resources efficiently, such that some novel weighted set of goals can be pursued as resources change with age. For example, the accommodating individual may boost or maintain performance in one valued task only if another task requiring a similar constellation of resources is dropped from the set of goals. Rearranging priorities may be an effective means of adjusting to some aspects of aging-related losses.

3. Constructing palliative meanings is a form of accommodation by which an individual experiencing losses can find and focus on selected positive interpretations. Brandtstädter and Wentura (1995) carefully noted that it is possible to construct palliative meanings while still being rational, and that even some serious losses may be accommodated in this way. As such, it is perhaps most effective in the relief it provides to the experience of losses. Unless linked with another compensatory process, however, it does not directly address, overcome, or cure the deficit.

Gains from constructing forgiving environments.   The role that the environment can play in preventing, managing, or compensating for aging-related losses has been reviewed extensively by Charness and Bosman (1995). An early view of how gains can be forged from aging-related losses through efforts at managing the environment was provided by Skinner (1983). Indeed, Skinner referred to his method of intellectual self-management in older age as providing a "prosthetic environment." Based on his own experience, Skinner emphasized that biological decline (which he characterized colorfully as "decay and rot") is inevitable with aging. Nevertheless, despite inevitable reduction in biological capacities, it is possible to provide prosthetic environments in which older adults' productive behaviors could be reinforced. He noted several examples of managing the environment of older people, such as arranging the environment to contain cues, using collaborators to improve memory performance, influencing the criteria with which others will evaluate one's performance, and avoiding formidable on-line memory tasks through the use of assistive devices and techniques.

Summary.   This category, gains as losses of a lesser magnitude, has been a fertile one in recent cognitive aging research. Three examples of subcategories have been briefly summarized. The theme of each is that although biologically based cognitive losses inevitably occur with aging, some of these losses are not as uniform or universal as expected, or are of a magnitude that can be prevented, postponed, overcome, overlooked, devalued, modified, or otherwise accommodated. As such, losses of this (minor) magnitude can be viewed as "gains," in that individuals can continue to perform at an acceptable, successful, if not optimal, level despite decline.

Gain as a function of losses

I now turn to the third approach to the issue of how gains can be conceptualized in the context of losses in cognitive aging. This approach is referred to as gains as a function of losses. The basic principle is that cognitive losses or deficits are a fundamental and inevitable fact of adult development and aging. Describing and explaining aging-related decrements are major empirical and theoretical goals. Formidable progress in meeting these challenges has been made (e.g., Salthouse, 1991). Nevertheless, some observers have noted an attendant conundrum; namely, that, despite the ineluctable and substantial aging-related cognitive losses, there are conditions under which older adults perform in surprisingly effective ways and at notably efficient levels of achievement (e.g., Dixon, 1995; Salthouse, 1990). Therefore, some attention has been directed at questions pertaining to the linkage of losses and gains. Most basic among these questions is whether and how some specific gains could be a function of specific losses.

Research pertaining to this approach exists at several levels of analysis, including those of the brain, psychological skills, and interaction-communication. Although this research naturally exists under different preferences regarding terminology, I will ignore this for my present purpose in favor of focusing on the similarities of the approach and issues. A key term and perspective in this regard is *compensation.* In addition to the forms of compensation described above, one that functionally links losses to gains is evident in research in the current perspective. Compensation refers to processes through which a gap between current accessible skills and environmental demands is reduced or closed (Bäckman & Dixon, 1992; Dixon & Bäckman, 1995). The deficit could be due to aging-related decline, injuries to neurological or sensory systems, organic progressive neurological diseases, or congenital deficits. In the present context, relevant compensatory mechanisms include the recruitment and substitution of either new or existing (i.e., latent) skills, resources, or pathways. Thus, in this context, the term gain refers to the development of new or supplemental means of performing a cognitive task. The gain, however, is a function of a loss because it presumably would not have developed if the deficit had not come into existence, whether through decline or injury. Several examples of research in which gains are assumed to be inextricably linked to losses can be summarized.

Gains as a function of losses in the brain.   At the level of the brain, several recent and different examples may be noted. This issue has been summarized in more detail elsewhere (e.g., Dixon & Bäckman, 1999). Buckner, Corbetta, Schatz, Raichle, and Petersen (1996) studied the mechanisms through which speech abilities could be maintained following prefrontal damage, such as that occurring as a result of stroke. Predictably, lesions to the left frontal cortex produce speech impairments, such as nonfluent aphasia. After a period of recovery, there are individual differences in the extent of impairment. Buckner et al. (1996) found direct evidence from Positron Emission Tomography (PET) assessment that, at least for one 72-year-old stroke patient, preserved speech and language apparently was due to activation of an area of the brain outside the left prefrontal cortex. That is, the brain apparently developed and activated a new pathway that served a compensatory function. Presumably, this pathway was not available to non-injured individuals. Therefore, in this sense, this gain (new pathway for performing a cognitive function) was a function of the loss (lesion to a specific area of the brain). There is a growing body of research showing such gains (e.g., recruitment of alternative sites and pathways in the brain) as a function of losses (e.g., injury, disease).

Behavioral gains as a function of organic impairment. Cognitive deficits resulting from severe head injuries, organic diseases (e.g., dementia), or aging-related declines in the brain also can be linked with behavioral compensation (Bäckman & Dixon, 1992; Dixon & Bäckman, 1999). The losses associated with a brain-related deficit can be counteracted to some extent by a variety of mnemonic strategies, external memory aids, and environmental adaptations (e.g., Wilson, 1995). Wilson and Watson (1996) have proposed a framework for understanding how specific organic memory deficits can be compensated by particular trainable strategies. The focus is on losses associated with brain injury that can be counteracted and managed by behavioral compensation. New techniques for performing old tasks can be generated by the cognitive neurorehabilitation specialist and learned by the injured person. Specific behavioral gains are linked to identifiable neurological losses. The extent of recovery of function—or the extent of gains—is, however, also dependent on several organic characteristics of the injury. For example, more gains may be possible when the injury occurs earlier in life (e.g., before age 30) and when the injury is of lesser (rather than greater) severity. In addition, Wilson and Watson (1996) contend that the extent and duration of gains following organic memory impairment may be associated with the type of rehabilitation program followed.

Gains in substitutable skills. The speed with which information is processed declines at a regular rate with human aging (Salthouse, 1991). One implication is that with aging, skills requiring speeded performance may be executed at slower rates. For skills in which speed of performance is an important criterion of success, such aging-related slowing may have far-reaching detrimental repercussions. For example, transcription typing is a skill in which both speed and accuracy of performance are valued. Task analyses have revealed that among the multiple determinants of this skill are speed-related components such as finger-tapping speed and choice reaction time. If performance on these components declines with aging (as it does), then speed of transcription typing also should decline with aging. Interestingly, the molar skill does not necessarily decline with aging. Active, older professional typists who perform accurate transcription typing at a speed comparable to that of younger typists can be identified (e.g., Salthouse, 1984). Moreover, they perform this complex skill at high levels despite losses in speed-related components. Maintenance, despite decline, may be accomplished through gains in substitutable mechanisms, a principal form of compensation (Bäckman & Dixon, 1992; Dixon & Bäckman, 1995; Salthouse, 1987, 1995). As researchers have shown, transcription typists may be using a compensatory mechanism of increased eye–hand span (Bosman, 1993; Salthouse, 1984). That is, the older typist may be processing the text to be typed further ahead of the current keystroke than do other skilled typists. One possible inference is that this gain in eye–hand span is a function of the loss of finger speed and reaction time.

Gains in or via collaborative contexts. Recent research in communicative and collaborative mechanisms has focused on their relevance to cognitive deficits, whether as a function of organic injury or aging-related loss. One brief example of each of these is presented.

First, Ahlsén (1991) studied a 47-year-old individual who became aphasic after a sudden illness. The recovery phase was quite long, but after several years, the individual began developing "body communication" with semantic loading. That is, the patient, who could not communicate semantic information orally, developed complex gestures to communicate this information visually. Moreover, as verbal expression and communicative patterns returned, the use of body communication declined. The gain was a function of a loss and, as recovery of normal functioning occurred, the new skill declined.

Second, some researchers recently have examined the extent to which older individuals may effectively use collaborators as living external cognitive aids in performing demanding cognitive tasks (e.g., Dixon & Gould, 1998; Gould, Kurzman, & Dixon, 1994; Gould, Trevithick, & Dixon, 1991). That is, can individual cognitive deficits be compensated by recruiting alternative pathways not within the individual's brain, but by accessing other brains? Researchers have examined normal older adults (with typical aging-related cognitive declines) as well as adults with organic impairments, such as those associated with Parkinson's disease. Testing has occurred in both individual and collaborative settings; that is, performance has been measured at both the standard individual level of analysis as well as at the group level of performance. Measurements have included multiple aspects of cognitive products as well as multiple indicators of collaborative processes (e.g., strategic negotiations). Participants have included unacquainted groups as well as married couples (experienced collaborators). Early results of these studies have shown that experienced older dyads may indeed compensate for individual-level aging-related decline through unique interactive processes (e.g., Dixon, 1996; Gould et al., 1994). In addition, the patterns of collaborative performance are indicative of some degree of benefit as a function of interactive experience (Dixon & Gould, 1998). In this example, the losses are typical aging-related cognitive ones. The compensatory gains are not, however, at the individual level of analysis. They instead are at the level of the (human) environment: some older adults may work selectively and strategically with a partner such that the overall level of performance is greater than either partner could achieve and greater than that achieved by numerous comparison groups, including younger and healthier ones (Dixon, 1996). In this sense then, the gains in recruiting and using other brains may be linked to individual-level losses, or possibly even a function of them.

Summary.   This third approach to the issue of cognitive aging gains focuses on how gains may be a function of losses. Several examples of research pertaining to this approach have been presented briefly. In all cases, the crucial question of determining precisely that a given gain was, in fact, a function of a given loss has not been settled. For the present purposes, this is not viewed as a major omission or flaw, because (a) it is extremely difficult to obtain such definitive empirical data, (b) arguments pertaining to the issue usually are based on patterns of results rather than single relationships, and (c) the present goal is to show brief examples of the direction of this research and theory. Nevertheless, it is important to differentiate gains as a function of losses from gains qua gains and gains as losses of a lesser magnitude. The former approach is unique in that cognitive losses are taken as targets of analysis, whether at the theoretical or the empirical level. Given a cognitive loss, the question becomes how maintenance of overall performance can be maintained. Typically, such maintenance involves the mechanism of compensatory substitution. Alternative, if not novel, mechanisms are used adaptively to overcome a specific loss.

Conclusion

In this initial analysis of the concept of gains in cognitive aging, I have developed a modest taxonomy representing how this term is used (whether explicitly or implicitly) in the cognitive aging literature. The pertinent literature includes publications in the field, beliefs about aging, and empirical research representing various perspectives. The taxonomy has three major categories: (a) gains qua gains, (b) gains as losses of a lesser magnitude, and (c) gains as a function of losses. These categories may be updated by a variety of research projects, including those for which differential, experimental, clinical, self-report, and survey research procedures are employed. The concept of gains in cognitive aging is a complex one, perhaps more complex than often is realized. The phenomena of cognitive aging actually are characterized by multiple determinants, multiple directions, and multiple aspects. This multiplicity is reflected in the variety of cogent and legitimate perspectives and theories on cognitive aging, whether they focus on gains, losses, or both.

References

Ahlsén, E. (1991). Body communication as compensation for speech in a Wernicke's aphasic: A longitudinal study. *Journal of Communication Disorders, 24,* 1–12.

Bäckman, L., & Dixon, R. A. (1992). Psychological compensation: A theoretical framework. *Psychological Bulletin, 112,* 259–283.

Baltes, P. B. (1987). Theoretical propositions of life-span developmental psychology: On the dynamics between growth and decline. *Developmental Psychology, 23,* 611–626.

Baltes, P. B. (1997). On the incomplete architecture of human ontogeny: Selection, optimization, and compensation as foundation of developmental theory. *American Psychologist, 52,* 366–380.

Baltes, P. B., & Baltes, M. M. (Eds.). (1990). *Successful aging: Perspectives from the behavioral sciences.* New York: Cambridge University Press.

Baltes, P. B., & Smith, J. (1990). Toward a psychology of wisdom and its ontogenesis. In R. J. Sternberg (Ed.), *Wisdom: Its nature, origins and development* (pp. 87–120). Cambridge, England: Cambridge University Press.

Baltes, P. B., & Staudinger, U. M. (1993). The search for a psychology of wisdom. *Current Directions in Psychological Science, 2,* 75–80.

Berg, C. A., & Sternberg, R. J. (1992). Adults' conceptions of intelligence across the adult lifespan. *Psychology and Aging, 7,* 221–231.

Bosman, E. A. (1993). Age-related differences in the motoric aspects of transcription typing skill. *Psychology and Aging, 8,* 87–102.

Brandtstädter, J., & Greve, W. (1994). The aging self: Stabilizing and protective processes. *Developmental Review, 14,* 52–80.

Brandtstädter, J., & Wentura, D. (1995). Adjustment to shifting possibility frontiers in later life: Complementary adaptive modes. In R. A. Dixon & L. Bäckman (Eds.), *Compensating for psychological deficits and declines: Managing losses and promoting gains* (pp. 83–106). Mahwah, NJ: Erlbaum.

Buckner, R. L., Corbetta, M., Schatz, J., Raichle, M. E., & Petersen, S. E. (1996). Preserved speech abilities and compensation following prefrontal damage. *Proceedings of the National Academy of Sciences, 93,* 1249–1253.

Cerella, J. (1990). Aging and information processing rate. In J. E. Birren & K. W. Schaie (Eds.), *Handbook of the psychology of aging* (pp. 201–221). San Diego, CA: Academic Press.

Charness, N., & Bosman, E. A. (1995). Compensation through environmental modification. In R. A. Dixon, & L. Bäckman (Eds.), *Compensating for psychological deficits and declines: Managing losses and promoting gains* (pp. 147–168). Mahwah, NJ: Erlbaum.

Commons, M. L., Sinnott, J. D., Richards, F. A., & Armon, C. (Eds.). (1989). *Adult development: Comparisons and applications of developmental models.* New York: Praeger.

Craik, F. I. M., & Jennings, J. M. (1992). Human memory. In F. I. M. Craik & T. A. Salthouse (Eds.), *The handbook of aging and cognition* (pp. 51–110). Hillsdale, NJ: Erlbaum.

Dixon, R. A. (1995). Promoting competence through compensation. In L. Bond, S. Cutler, & A. Grams (Eds.), *Promoting successful and productive aging* (pp. 220–238). Newbury, CA: Sage.

Dixon, R. A. (1996). Collaborative memory and aging. In D. J. Herrmann, C.

McEvoy, C. Hertzog, P. Hertel, & M. K. Johnson (Eds.), *Basic and applied memory: Theory in context* (pp. 359–383). Mahwah, NJ: Erlbaum.

Dixon, R. A., & Bäckman, L. (1995). Concepts of compensation: Integrated, differentiated and Janus-faced. In R. A. Dixon & L. Bäckman (Eds.), *Compensating for psychological deficits and declines: Managing losses and promoting gains* (pp. 3–19). Mahwah, NJ: Erlbaum.

Dixon, R. A., & Bäckman, L. (1999). Principles of compensation in cognitive neurorehabilitation. In D. T. Stuss, G. Winocur, & I. H. Robertson (Eds.), *Cognitive neurorehabilitation: A comprehensive approach* (pp. 59–72). Cambridge, England: Cambridge University Press.

Dixon, R. A., & Gould, O. N. (1998). Younger and older adults collaborating on retelling everyday stories. *Applied Developmental Science, 2,* 160–171.

Dixon, R. A., & Hertzog, C. (1996). Theoretical issues in cognition and aging. In F. Blanchard Fields & T. M. Hess (Eds.), *Perspectives on cognitive change in adulthood and aging* (pp. 25–65). New York: McGraw-Hill.

Dixon, R. A., Kramer, D. A., & Baltes, P. B. (1985). Intelligence: A life-span developmental perspective. In B. B. Wolman (Ed.), *Handbook of intelligence: Theories, measurements, and applications* (pp. 301–350). New York: Wiley.

Dixon, R. A., Lerner, R. M., & Hultsch, D. F. (1991). The concept of development in the study of individual and social change. In P. van Geert & L. P. Mos (Eds.), *Annals of theoretical psychology* (pp. 279–323). New York: Plenum.

Ericsson, K. A., & Charness, N. (1994). Expert performance: Its structure and acquisition. *American Psychologist, 49,* 725–747.

Gould, O. N., Kurzman, D., & Dixon, R. A. (1994). Communication during prose recall conversations by young and old dyads. *Discourse Processes, 17,* 149–165.

Gould, O. N., Trevithick, L., & Dixon, R. A. (1991). Adult age differences in elaborations produced during prose recall. *Psychology and Aging, 6,* 93–99.

Harris, D. B. (Ed.). (1957). *The concept of development*. Minneapolis: University of Minnesota Press.

Heckhausen, J., Dixon, R. A., & Baltes, P. B. (1989). Gains and losses in development throughout adulthood as perceived by different adult age groups. *Developmental Psychology, 25,* 109–121.

Heckhausen, J., & Krueger, J. (1993). Developmental expectations for the self and most other people: Age grading in three functions of social comparison. *Developmental Psychology, 29,* 539–548.

Hummert, M. L., Garstka, T. A., Shaner, J. L., & Strahm, S. (1994). Stereotypes of the elderly held by young, middle-aged, and elderly adults. *Journal of Gerontology: Psychological Sciences, 49,* 240–249.

Jones, H. E., & Conrad, H. S. (1933). The growth and decline of intelligence: A study of a homogeneous group between the ages of ten and sixty. *Genetic Psychology Monographs, 13,* 223–298.

Kramer, D. A., & Woodruff, D. S. (1986). Relativistic and dialectical thought in three adult age-groups. *Human Development, 29,* 280–290.

Lerner, R. M. (1984). *On the nature of human plasticity*. New York: Cambridge University Press.

Light, L. L. (1991). Memory and aging: Four hypotheses in search of data. *Annual Review of Psychology, 42,* 333–376.

Medina, J. J. (1996). *The clock of ages: Why we age, how we age, winding back the clock*. Cambridge, England: Cambridge University Press.

Perlmutter, M. (Ed.). (1990). *Late life potential*. Washington, DC: Gerontological

Society of America.

Perry, W. I. (1968). *Forms of intellectual and ethical development in the college years.* New York: Holt, Rinehart, & Winston.

Pressey, S. L. (1919). Are the present psychological scales reliable for adults? *Journal of Abnormal Psychology, 14,* 314–324.

Salthouse, T. A. (1984). Effects of age and skill in typing. *Journal of Experimental Psychology: General, 113,* 345–371.

Salthouse, T. A. (1987). Age, experience, and compensation. In C. Schooler & K. W. Schaie (Eds.), *Cognitive functioning and social structure over the life course* (pp. 142–157). Norwood, NJ: Ablex.

Salthouse, T. A. (1990). Cognitive competence and expertise in aging. In J. E. Birren & K. W. Schaie (Eds.), *Handbook of the psychology of aging* (pp. 310–319). San Diego, CA: Academic Press.

Salthouse, T. A. (1991). *Theoretical perspectives on cognitive aging.* Hillsdale, NJ: Erlbaum.

Salthouse, T. A. (1995). Refining the concept of psychological compensation. In R. A. Dixon & L. Bäckman (Eds.), *Compensating for psychological deficits and declines: Managing losses and promoting gains* (pp. 21–34). Mahway, NJ: Erlbaum.

Sanford, E. C. (1902). Mental growth and decay. *American Journal of Psychology, 13,* 426–449.

Schaie, K. W. (1990). Intellectual development in adulthood. In J. E. Birren & K. W. Schaie (Eds.), *Handbook of the psychology of aging* (pp. 291–309). San Diego, CA: Academic Press.

Schaie, K. W. (1994). The course of adult intellectual development. *American Psychologist, 49,* 304–313.

Schaie, K. W. (1996). *Intellectual development in adulthood: The Seattle Longitudinal Study.* New York: Cambridge University Press.

Schieber, F., & Baldwin, C. L. (1996). Vision, audition, and aging research. In F. Blanchard-Fields & T. M. Hess (Eds.), *Perspectives on cognitive change in adulthood and aging* (pp. 122–162). New York: McGraw-Hill.

Sinnott, J. (1996). The developmental approach: Postformal thought as adaptive intelligence. In F. Blanchard-Fields & T. M. Hess (Eds.), *Perspectives on cognitive change in adulthood and aging* (pp. 358–383). New York: McGraw-Hill.

Skinner, B. F. (1983). Intellectual self-management in old age. *American Psychologist, 38,* 239–244.

Sternberg, R. J. (Ed.). (1990). *Wisdom: Its nature, origin and development.* Cambridge, England: Cambridge University Press.

Uttal, D. H., & Perlmutter, M. (1989). Toward a broader conceptualization of development: The role of gains and losses across the lifespan. *Developmental Review, 9,* 101–132.

Wilson, B. A. (1995). Memory rehabilitation: Compensating for memor problems. In R. A. Dixon & L. Bäckman (Eds.), *Compensating for psychological deficits and declines: Managing losses and promoting gains* (pp. 171–190). Mahwah, NJ: Erlbaum.

Wilson, B. A., & Watson, P. C. (1996). A practical framework for understanding compensatory behaviour in people with organic memory impairment. *Memory, 4,* 465–486.

Wohlwill J. F. (1973). *The study of behavioral development.* New York: Academic Press.

Zacks, R. T., & Hasher, L. (1994). Directed ignoring: Inhibitory regulation of working memory. In D. Dagenbach, & T. H. Carr (Eds.), *Inhibitory processes in attention, memory, and language* (pp. 241–264). San Diego, CA: Academic Press.

Pressing issues in cognitive aging 3

Timothy A. Salthouse

A distinction between two types of cognition has been recognized since at least the 1920s. For example, Foster and Taylor (1920) found that younger adults were superior in the construction of sentences containing three specific words and in memory for drawings, whereas older adults had a relative advantage in comprehension of questions, detection of absurdities, and definitions of abstract words. The authors interpreted this pattern in terms of young adults being more adaptable, whereas older adults were postulated to have an advantage when they could benefit from accumulated experience. A comparable classification was made several years later by Jones and Conrad (1933). These researchers found the largest age-related declines on tests that they claimed assessed "native capacity" or "sheer modifiability," and the least age-related declines on tests that they felt were influenced by the "accumulative effects of experience."

Similar distinctions between stable and declining cognitive abilities have subsequently been mentioned by Cattell (1972), Hebb (1942), Welford (1958), Baltes (1987), and many others. A variety of labels have been used to characterize the distinction, such as type A versus type B cognition, fluid versus crystallized intelligence, and cognitive mechanics versus cognitive pragmatics. The fluid-crystallized terminology is probably the most familiar, but I believe the terms *process* and *product* are more descriptive of the intended distinction. That is, by *process*, I refer to the efficiency or effectiveness of processing at the time of assessment. This type of cognition reflects the ability to solve novel problems or to transform and manipulate familiar materials. The term *cognitive product* refers to the accumulated products of processing carried out in the past, and, consequently, this type of cognition largely consists of various forms of acquired knowledge.

The two aspects of cognition are not necessarily independent, because all products must be acquired through the operation of processes, and it is also possible that the current level of products influences the efficiency or effectiveness of some processes. It also is important to recognize that these are only two of many possible types of cognition, and that many forms of cognition, such as wisdom, judgment, practical intelligence, and social intelligence, are not represented in this classification. Nevertheless, process and product aspects should be distinguished if for no other reason than the suspected differential developmental patterns across adulthood.

This distinction between two types of cognition provides the foundation for what I will propose are the six major issues in the field of cognitive aging. The issues are represented in the matrix in Figure 3.1 and can be characterized as the what and why of adult age relations on variables reflecting cognitive processes, cognitive products, and the interaction of processes and products. In my opinion, these are pressing issues because if they were to be resolved, enormous progress would have been made toward understanding aging and cognition. I believe we are closer to the answer for some cells in the matrix than for others, but considerable research remains to be done before we can have confidence in any of the conclusions. In the remainder of this chapter, I will elaborate on these issues and report relevant research findings where available.

Process

I will begin with process aspects of cognition because that has been the focus of the bulk of the research concerned with aging and cognition. Process cognition has been evaluated with many types of experimental and psychometric tests of memory, reasoning, and spatial ability. The assessments often have been designed to have minimal influence of prior knowledge, either by the use of highly familiar material, such as digits or common words, or by the use of abstract nonmeaningful material, such as patterns of geometric symbols. Typical tasks used to evaluate efficiency or effectiveness of cognitive processing have involved deliberate recall, abstraction of relations, and transformation of spatial patterns. Other chapters in this volume (chapter 5 by Craik, chapter 9 by Yoon, May, and Hasher; chapter 11 by Kemper and Kemtes; chapter 1 by Park; chapter 10 by Wingfield) refer to research on the relations of age on specific types of cognitive process measures.

Age-process relations are well documented in the research literature. Perhaps the best way to illustrate them is with results from large samples that include a wide range of ages. Furthermore, because several data sets include measures of both cognitive processes and cognitive products, the age trends for the two types of cognition can be directly compared. We will first consider the relations of age to cognitive process measures.

	Process	Product	Process X Product
What age relation?	??	??	??
Why this age relation?	??	??	??

FIG. 3.1. Classification scheme to illustrate the six pressing issues in cognitive aging.

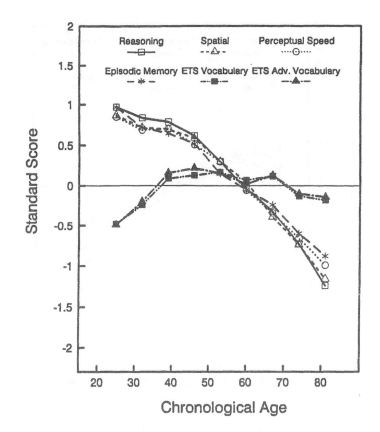

FIG. 3.2.
Age relations on composite measures of different cognitive abilities in the cross-sectional data from the 1984 and 1991 waves of the Seattle Longitudinal Study.

Figure 3.2 illustrates data from the 1,322 participants in the 1984 and 1991 cross-sectional samples in Schaie's Seattle Longitudinal Study (Schaie, 1996). Notice that very similar age relations are evident in the composite measures representing inductive reasoning, spatial, perceptual speed, and episodic memory abilities.

Figure 3.3 illustrates data from over 1,600 adults in the standardization sample for the Woodcock-Johnson Cognitive Abilities Test (Woodcock & Johnson, 1990) for the average of two perceptual speed, reasoning, associative learning, and short-term memory measures in that test battery. Once again, there is a nearly monotonic age-related decline in these process measures, with a total magnitude from the youngest to the oldest of at least one total sample standard deviation.

The consistency of the age relations in process measures of cognition across different samples and specific types of tests suggests that we can have considerable confidence in the *what* of age-process relations. That is, at least in cross-sectional samples, it appears that there is an age-related decline of between one and two standard deviations across a range in age from about 18 to 80.

Unfortunately, relatively little is yet known about the *why* of these

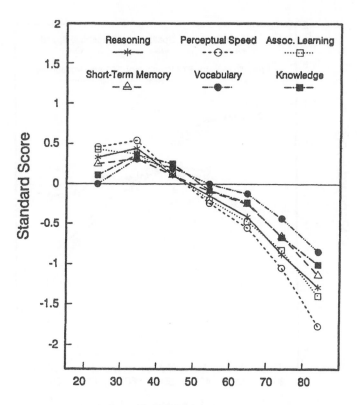

FIG. 3.3.
Age relations on
composite measures of
different cognitive
abilities from the
standardization sample
of the Woodcock-
Johnson
Psychoeducational Test
Battery.

negative age-process relations. Many speculations have been proposed, ranging from generation-specific experiences to changes in working memory, various aspects of attention, or speed of processing, to decreases in the supply of particular types of neurotransmitters, but there has not yet been much agreement about the causes of age-related declines in measures of processing efficiency or effectiveness.

However, I do not mean to imply that nothing is known about the relations between age and process measures of cognition, because some conclusions about age-process relations are clearly possible. For example, because there is now considerable evidence that age-related differences on various cognitive variables are not independent, I believe we can conclude it is unlikely that multiple specific deficits are responsible for a very large proportion of the age-related effects on process aspects of cognition. Evidence relevant to this conclusion has been provided by two different types of analytical methods.

One analytical procedure is based on the notion of mediation, and is often represented in the form of models expressed as path diagrams. For example, a number of studies have investigated the plausibility of structural models in which the age-related effects on various measures of cognitive functioning are mediated by age-related reductions in working memory or speed of processing. Figure 3.4 contains very simple versions of two alternative models of the relations on two variables: one with completely independent age-related effects on the two variables, and the other with shared age-related effects on the variables. Notice that if the age-related effects were independent, as in the top panel of the figure, then there would be no possibility of mediation of age-related effects on one variable through other variables. Over the last 10 years, a great deal of research has been conducted with this type of analytical procedure, and almost without exception it has revealed little support for the idea of completely independent age-related influences. In fact, estimates of the amount of shared age-related variance for many combinations of cognitive variables are moderate to large, often exceeding 50% or more of the total age-related variance (e.g., Salthouse, 1994).

A second analytical procedure for investigating the independence of age-related influences in cognition consists of examining the age-related effects in one variable in the context of age effects in other variables. This procedure is sometimes referred to as single common factor analysis, and is schematically illustrated in Figure 3.5. The single common factor analysis procedure is useful for determining the magnitude of the age-related effects on a given variable after controlling for the effects of age on what all variables have in common. It differs from the mediational approach in that there is no commitment to a particular type of variable as being more fundamental or primitive than others, and there is no attempt to specify linkages among variables except in terms of the age-related influences on the variables. Although this analytical procedure seems rather simplistic, there

Independent Influences

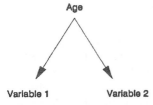

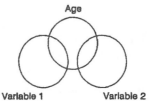

Shared Influences

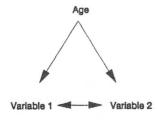

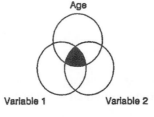

FIG. 3.4. Schematic illustration of two possible outcomes with path analyses of age relations on two different cognitive variables.

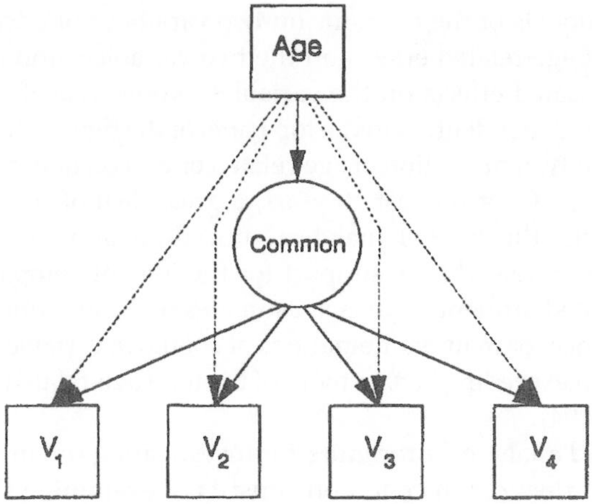

FIG. 3.5.
Schematic illustration of
the single common
factor analytical
method. Dashed lines
represent relations of
age to the cognitive
variables that are
independent of those
through the common
factor. V = variables.

are at least two theoretically interesting ways in which differential age relations could occur within this framework. One way in which a variable could
have little or no relation to age is if it has a weak or non-existent loading on
the common factor, and a second way is if it has unique relations of age
that are independent of the age-related effects through the common factor.
The single common factor analytical procedure is just beginning to be explored, but both of the patterns just described have been reported for different variables. Of greatest interest in the present context is that a consistent finding across numerous single common factor analyses is that the
independent or unique age-related influences on different cognitive variables, represented in the figure by dotted lines, are almost always few in
number and small in magnitude (e.g., Salthouse, 1996; Salthouse, Hancock,
Meinz, & Hambrick, 1996; Verhaeghen & Salthouse, 1997). This implies
that a large proportion of the age-related influences on different cognitive
variables are shared and are not independent.

Therefore, while there is still no consensus regarding the reasons for
age-related declines in process aspects of cognition, some progress has been
achieved because we can now be confident that the number of explanations will be much fewer than the number of variables exhibiting age-related declines. It thus seems reasonable to conclude that task-specific interpretations such as inefficient strategies or defective components that
are used in a limited set of tasks are unlikely to play a major role in accounting for age-process relations found in many different cognitive variables.

Product

Product aspects of cognition have typically been evaluated with variables
reflecting acquired knowledge or other benefits of accumulated experience.

For example, tests of vocabulary or knowledge of other types of information have frequently been used to assess product cognition.

Age-product relations are not as consistent as age-process relations. The lack of consistency can be illustrated with data from the same two data sets described above. Figure 3.2 also contains data from two vocabulary tests administered by Schaie to participants in the 1984 and 1991 cross-sectional samples in his study, and it can be seen that the age trend on these measures is largely one of stability. Figure 3.3 contains the results from a test of vocabulary and a composite measure of knowledge about science, social studies, and humanities from the Woodcock-Johnson standardization data. Note that performance on the knowledge tests of cognitive products in this large and nationally representative sample declines nearly as much as does performance on the perceptual speed, reasoning, associative learning, and short-term memory measures of cognitive processes.

In light of these inconsistent patterns, it is reasonable to ask what is responsible for the discrepancies in the age-product relations. Although a definitive answer is not yet possible, I suspect that in representative samples such as the Woodcock-Johnson standardization sample, there is frequently a negative relation between age and amount of education, and it seems reasonable to assume that education is typically positively associated with level of knowledge. The relations between age and measures of knowledge may therefore be negative in these representative samples because the average older adults has fewer years of education than the average young adult. In contrast, many cognitive researchers often deliberately try to avoid confounding age and amount of education, and consequently in those types of samples, measures of knowledge may either remain stable across adulthood, or possibly may even increase with age. However, differential amounts of education are not responsible for all of the variation in the age-product relations because while control of education has been found to eliminate the age-related decline in measures of product cognition in some analyses, the reduction in the magnitude of the relations with age was only about 50% in the Woodcock-Johnson knowledge measures.

Other factors may also be contributing to the variation in the pattern of age-product relations but because of the inconsistency across samples, no firm conclusions can be reached about the *what* of the relation between age and product measures of cognition at the current time.

Although one might expect an increase with age in knowledge measures, which are presumably based on experience and, more specifically, on opportunities for the acquisition of information, we have seen that the results have not confirmed this expectation. Therefore, the principal *why* question with respect to cognitive products is, What is responsible for the stability in age-product relations? At least three possible explanations could be postulated to account for the lack of the expected increase with age in measures of knowledge.

One possibility is that there is a decrease in the efficiency of new learning, which together with some losses due to forgetting, might offset or balance the cumulative increases in knowledge such that there is an overall steady state across most of the adult years. This interpretation receives some support from evidence of age-related decreases in the effectiveness of many types of learning, which would presumably reduce the rate of growth of knowledge. A second possible explanation for the absence of age-related increases in measures of knowledge is that there may be limitations in the types of experience one encounters, such that there are early plateaus on the benefits of experience. This interpretation seems plausible because much of the experience in many situations could be redundant, and hence not lead to greater knowledge. In circumstances such as these, only the initial periods of experience may be sufficiently diverse and novel to lead to new knowledge, and therefore much of the experiential advantage of older adults may be "wasted" in the sense that it does not contribute to increments in knowledge.

A third possible interpretation attributes the lack of age-related increases in knowledge measures of product cognition to the manner in which knowledge is typically assessed. That is, in order to have wide applicability, most tests of knowledge are designed to assess relatively general information rather than information specific to particular vocations or avocations. However, it is certainly possible that as people become specialized, their interests narrow. Thus, their total amount of knowledge could continue to expand, but it might not be detected if it were in a limited domain that was not well represented in tests of general information or vocabulary. Although these hypotheses all seem plausible, they may be difficult to investigate because it is not clear how losses in acquisition efficiency might be calibrated against gains in cumulative products, it is uncertain how diversity of experience could be accurately evaluated, and assessments of different types of specialized knowledge may not be directly comparable. This is not to say that these interpretations are not meaningful and important, but rather that at the present time it does not seem possible to reach any definitive conclusion about the *why* of age-product relations.

Process times product

The third major aspect of cognition in my proposed classification scheme concerns the joint effects of process and product. More specifically, the focus here is on the *what* and *why* of the relations between the two types of cognition across the period of adulthood. At least two different facets of these issues can be distinguished. The first is how the levels of process and product affect the age relations on one another. The second is how process and product jointly affect the relations of age on the performance of complex tasks involving both types of cognition.

Two possible outcomes can be specified with respect to the first question, concerned with the relations of the two types of cognition with one another; namely, process and product could have either additive or interactive relations with one another. Additive relations would suggest that there are independent influences of age on cognitive processes and cognitive products, whereas interactions would suggest that the age relations on one aspect of cognition depend on the level of the other aspect of cognition. Perhaps the simplest way in which these possibilities could be examined is in the context of a multiple regression model, in which one tests for the presence of an age times predictor interaction when predicting process scores from age and product variables, and when predicting product scores from age and process variables. In order to be meaningful, these types of analyses should be based on relatively large samples in which measures of both process and product aspects of cognition are available. Fortunately, the Woodcock-Johnson data set possesses these characteristics.

Regression analyses on the data from the over 1,600 adults in the Woodcock-Johnson standardization sample revealed no interactions of age and product in the prediction of a cognitive process measure (i.e., a composite measure of inductive reasoning, which is considered by the authors of the test battery to be the best measure of fluid or process cognition). Figure 3.6 illustrates these results with age relations from the top 25%, the middle 50%, and the bottom 25% of the total sample from the distribution of knowledge measures (i.e., vocabulary and a composite of scores from the science, social studies, and humanities tests). Notice that the relations of age to the composite reasoning measure of process cognition were nearly parallel across the three levels of vocabulary performance, and across the three levels of knowledge performance. This implies that although people with higher levels of product cognition also have higher levels of process cognition, the relations between age and measures of process cognition are independent of the level of cognitive products.

In contrast, the interactions of age and process cognition were statistically significant in the prediction of cognitive product measures. Figure 3.7 illustrates these interactions in the form of the age-product relations for the top 25%, the middle 50%, and the bottom 25% of distribution on the composite inductive reasoning process measure. Notice that with the vocabulary product measure (top panel), there is an age-related decrease only among individuals with low reasoning scores, and with the composite knowledge product measure (bottom panel), there is an age-related increase for adults with high reasoning scores. Although these interactions are potentially quite interesting, they need to be interpreted cautiously because of the small number of individuals in some of the groups. To illustrate, only 22 adults over age 60 were in the high-process group, and thus the interaction pattern may be of greater theoretical, than practical, relevance.

The second aspect related to the joint effects of process and product concerns their combined influence on other tasks or activities. That is, the criterion variables in this context are not based on abstract tasks or tests designed to assess process or product forms of cognition, but instead represent more complex activities involving a mixture of processes and prod-

Age - Process Relations

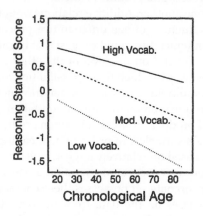

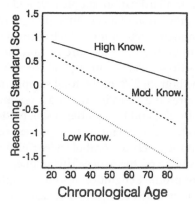

FIG. 3.6. Regression lines relating age to composite inductive reasoning performance for the top 25%, middle 50%, and bottom 25% of the distribution of adults on the vocabulary and composite knowledge product measures.

ucts. When both process and product can affect performance, individual differences in performance might be attributable to variations in the level of the predictors, or in the weighting of the predictors. This can be easily conceptualized in terms of a regression equation in which performance is determined by both process and product, that is, Performance = a(Process) + b(Product). The primary question with respect to aging then becomes, do the weightings of the predictors change with age in addition to their levels, and if so, what is responsible for this change?

This issue is potentially quite interesting because certain patterns within this analytical framework could be interpreted as evidence for the existence of age-related compensation (e.g., Salthouse, 1995). For example, a shift with increased age in the direction of a greater weighting on stable or increasing products and a lesser weighting on declining processes might allow the same, or possibly even increasing, levels of overall performance to be achieved across adulthood despite declines in relevant components.

Some preliminary evidence relevant to this issue is available with very

Age - Product Relations

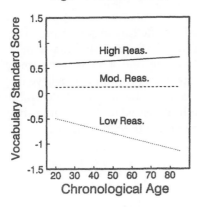

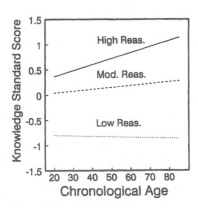

FIG. 3.7.
Regression lines relating age to cognitive product measures for the top 25%, middle 50%, and bottom 25% of the distribution of adults on the composite inductive reasoning measure.

simple criterion tasks such as verbal fluency, with measures of vocabulary serving as the product variable and measures of perceptual speed serving as the process variable (Salthouse, 1993). Two studies in that project revealed that younger and older adults had quite different mean levels of the process and product variables, but that the regression coefficients were very similar in the two groups. These results suggest that there may not be age differences in the relative weighting of process and product, but additional research with more complex tasks is needed before much confidence can be placed in this conclusion.

To summarize, although several intriguing possibilities can be specified, relatively little is currently known about either the nature (i.e., the *what*) or the reasons (i.e., the *why*) of the relations between age and the joint effects of process and product. This is unfortunate because it seems likely that most activities outside of the laboratory involve a combination of the two types of cognition, and yet we know very little about how they function together.

Conclusion

In conclusion, I have identified six major, or pressing, issues in aging and cognition. Furthermore, I have suggested that some consensus about the answers was evident for only one of the issues; namely, the decline of process cognition. Nevertheless, I continue to believe that these issues represent the most important questions in the field and that, once answered, they will lead to greatly increased understanding about how and why cognitive functioning changes with increasing age.

References

Baltes, P. B. (1987). Theorectical propositions of life-span developmental psychology: On the dynamics between growth and decline. *Developmental Psychology, 23,* 611–626.

Cattell, R. B. (1972). *Abilities: Their structure, growth, and action.* Boston: Houghton-Mifflin.

Foster, J. C., & Taylor, G. A. (1920). The applicability of mental tests to persons over fifty years of age. *Journal of Applied Psychology, 4,* 39–58.

Hebb, D. O. (1942). The effect of early and late brain injury upon test scores, and the nature of normal adult intelligence. *Proceedings of the American Philosophical Society, 85,* 275–292.

Jones, H. E., & Conrad, H. S. (1933). The growth and decline of intelligence: A study of a homogeneous group between the ages of ten and sixty. *Genetic Psychology Monographs, 13,* 223–295.

Salthouse, T. A. (1993). Speed and knowledge as determinants of adult age differences in verbal tasks. *Journal of Gerontology: Psychological Sciences, 48,* 29–36.

Salthouse, T. A. (1994). How many causes are there of aging-related decrements in cognitive functioning? *Developmental Review, 14,* 413–437.

Salthouse, T. A. (1995). Refining the concept of psychological compensation. In R. A. Dixon & L. Bäckman (Eds.), *Psychological compensation: Managing losses and promoting gains* (pp. 21–34). Hillsdale, NJ: Erlbaum.

Salthouse, T. A. (1996). Constraints on theories of cognitive aging. *Psychonomic Bulletin & Review, 3,* 287–299.

Salthouse, T. A., Hancock, H. E., Meinz, E. J., & Hambrick, D. Z. (1996). Interrelations of age, visual acuity, and cognitive functioning. *Journal of Gerontology: Psychological Sciences, 51B,* 317–330.

Schaie, K. W. (1996). *Intellectual development in adulthood: The Seattle Longitudinal Study.* New York: Cambridge University Press.

Verhaeghen, P., & Salthouse, T. A. (1997). Meta-analyses of age-cognition relations in adulthood: Estimates of linear and non-linear age effects and structural models. *Psychological Bulletin, 122,* 231–249.

Welford, A. T. (1958). *Ageing and human skill.* London: Oxford University Press.

Woodcock, R. W., & Johnson, M. B. (1990). *Woodcock-Johnson Psycho-Educational Test Battery–Revised.* Allen, TX: DLM. (Original work published 1989.)

Attention and memory ▐▐

Attention and aging 4

Wendy A. Rogers

As far back as 1890, William James claimed that, "Everyone knows what attention is" (James, 1950, p. 403). However, some of us may identify more with what one of my graduate students lamented in a seminar on attention: "No one seems to know what attention is" (Anonymous graduate student, 1996). Part of the confusion may be due to the fact that attention is a multidimensional construct. Thus, even though he claimed we all knew what it was, James (1950) provided a fairly lengthy definition of attention:

> [Attention] is the taking possession by the mind, in clear and vivid form, of one out of what seem several simultaneously possible objects or trains of thought. Focalization, concentration of consciousness are of its essence. It implies withdrawal from some things in order to deal effectively with others, and is a condition which has a real opposite in the confused, dazed, scatterbrained state which in French is called distraction. (pp. 403–404)

Consider the following examples.

> Caroline is preparing Thanksgiving dinner for her family. It is 4:00 PM and everyone is beginning to arrive. She is extremely busy. Everything requires perfect timing. She must remember to stir the gravy every few minutes, check the pies in the oven, and finish mashing the potatoes and seasoning the other vegetables. Amid all of this, Caroline also must monitor the grandchildren who insist on "helping" in the kitchen but are in danger of getting burned or stepped on as they play on the floor.

> Alice is driving to her new doctor's office in the city. As she lives in the country, she is not used to all of the traffic. To make matters worse, she is not familiar with the route. Luckily, Alice has been driving for many years and is familiar with her old sedan. However, Alice must monitor the traffic to ensure safe driving, search the road for the street signs she is looking for, check the written directions periodically to ensure that she is on the right track, and rehearse the questions that she wants to remember to ask the doctor when she arrives.

Caroline and Alice both are engaging in attention-demanding tasks. Caroline is dividing her attention among her many tasks, alternately focusing attention on the various dishes she is cooking, shifting attention among the people in the kitchen, and so forth. Aspects of Alice's task do not require her attention because she is a skilled driver (e.g., steering, shifting gears). However, Alice also is dividing her attention between the task of driving safely and searching for information in the environment. She is also switching attention periodically between the road and her written directions. Her attentional resources may be somewhat limited because she is going to a new doctor and wants to be sure to remember her questions, so she is reviewing them in her mind as she is driving.

These examples illustrate the complexity of the term *attention*. Given the many activities and processes that involve attention, how then should one define attention? Psychologists have come to the conclusion that there are "varieties of attention" (e.g., Parasuraman & Davies, 1984); that is, attention is a construct that is representative of different processes. Thus, we must specify what aspect of attention we are referring to when we discuss the concept. We will discuss selective attention, focused attention, sustained attention, and divided attention. It also is important to realize that some tasks may be attention demanding when we are first learning how to do them but become less demanding (i.e., more automatic) with practice. This transition from attention demanding to the automatic performance of a task or task component also will be discussed.

In addition to specifying the type of attention we are referring to, we also must consider the age of the person involved. Suppose, for example, that Caroline and Alice are both 70 years old. What implications would this have for their ability to select, divide, shift, sustain, and focus attention? Moreover, does the transition from attention demanding to automatic differ for older adults? For each area of attention that we discuss, we will review the impact of age on that process.

Varieties of attention

Selective attention

Attention . . . out of all the sensations yielded, picks out certain ones worthy of its notice and suppresses all the rest. (James, 1950, p. 285)

One major function of attention is to enable us to select certain information for processing. Selective attention involves filtering stimulus information. The classic example of selective attention was termed the "cocktail party problem" by Cherry (1953). Imagine yourself at a cocktail party (or in any other crowded room where a number of conversations are occurring simultaneously). How is it that you are able to selectively attend to the conversation in which you are involved?

Selective attention has been studied in the laboratory using visual search tasks. In a typical visual search task, participants are asked to search for items (e.g., words, letters, pictures) in arrays of distracting objects. For example, individuals might be required to scan lists of letters searching for a particular target letter; thus, they would have to selectively attend to the letter of interest while filtering the other distractor letters. The more similar that the distractor letters are to the target letter, the more difficult the task is (e.g., searching for an *O* in an array of *Q*s is more difficult than in an array of *T*s; see Figure 4.1). Selective attention is affected by the ease with which the target information can be distinguished from the other stimulus information in the environment. Imagine trying to find your sister in a crowd of people. The task would be easier if your sister was 5'6" tall and she was standing amidst a group of 4-year-olds, or if your sister was brunette and she was in a room of blondes. Selective attention also is aided by cues: if I tell you that your sister is in the left side of the room, you will be able to locate her more quickly.

Visual search paradigms have been used extensively to investigate age-related differences in selective attention. Plude and Doussard-Roosevelt (1989) demonstrated that the attention-demanding task of conjunction search reliably yields age-related differences in performance. In a conjunction search, two or more features must be searched. To illustrate, suppose you are searching for a chocolate-covered donut in a bin containing also strawberry-covered donuts. This search does not require a conjunction of features because you have to distinguish only the feature of color (brown vs. pink). However, if you were searching for a chocolate-covered croissant in a bin also containing strawberry-covered croissants and chocolate-covered donuts, your search would require the conjunction of the feature of color (brown vs. pink) and shape (donut vs. croissant).

Plude and Doussard-Roosevelt (1989) demonstrated that in a task requiring conjunction search (i.e., find a red *X* in a field of green *X*s and red *O*s), search rate was faster for the younger adults relative to the older adults. Thus, tasks that require the selection of information on the basis of two or more features will show an age-related deficit.

T T T T T	Q Q Q Q Q
T T T T T	Q Q Q Q Q
T T T T T	Q Q Q Q Q
T T T T T	Q Q Q Q Q
T T T T T	Q Q Q Q Q
T T T T T	Q O Q Q Q
T T T O T	Q Q Q Q Q
T T T T T	Q Q Q Q Q

FIG. 4.1.
Sample visual search task. The task is to find the letter O in each display. Notice that it is much easier to find the letter O among the T's than among the Q's.

Age-related differences in selective attention may be reduced if the older individual has experience with the target and distractor information. Clancy and Hoyer (1994) investigated the ability of middle-aged medical technicians (range: age 40 to 68; mean: age 47.4) to read X-rays. This is a visual search task where the technician must search the X-rays looking for telltale patterns of danger (e.g., tumor). On this familiar search task, the middle-aged medical technicians were able to perform the task as well as younger adults. Interestingly, Clancy and Hoyer also tested their participants on an unfamiliar letter search task and found that the middle-aged participants performed significantly worse. Thus, selective attention ability may be well maintained only for those tasks that are familiar.

Another method of improving the selection of information is to provide cues. For example, Madden (1983) compared cue utilization in a search task for younger and older adults and found that older adults actually showed a greater benefit from cuing than did younger adults. In his task, using a cue to minimize the search requirements of the task substantially reduced age-related differences in performance. Generally speaking, younger and older adults show similar benefits from cuing (Hartley, 1992; Madden & Plude, 1993). However, the details of cuing effects are still being worked out; the time course may differ across age groups, the degree of validity of the cue may have differential effects, and so forth.

In the extreme, cues may turn the selective attention task into a focused attention task, thereby reducing the age-related differences. As we will see in the next section, older adults do not show declines in focused attention.

Focused attention

> One principle object comes then into the focus of consciousness, others are temporarily suppressed (James, 1950, p. 405)

In a focused attention task, the individual knows where the target will appear but distracting information also is present. Think about trying to watch a movie in a crowded theater: the screen location is unchanging but there may be a lot of distractions that must be filtered out. Focused attention involves concentration; that is, intense processing of information from a particular source. To contrast selective with focused attention, suppose that you went to get popcorn and now are searching for your companion. The location of the target is not known and you must search through a complex visual field to find the target. Your attempt to ignore irrelevant information and select only that which is relevant makes this a selective attention task.

Focusing of attention involves blocking out external sources of stimulus information. Sometimes we get so involved in a task that we forget where we are and are oblivious to what is going on around us. Other times it is more difficult to focus attention on the task at hand. Variables such as interest, motivation, and fatigue all can influence our ability to successfully focus attention.

Investigations of focused attention in older adults suggest that this ability remains relatively intact. Older adults are able to focus their attention as well as younger adults, if the target information is clear. For example, Wright and Elias (1979) demonstrated that the effects of irrelevant distracting information were similar for younger and older adults. In their task, the irrelevant information could be ignored because the target information always appeared in the same central location.

Another method to study focused attention is to set up a situation where the target information is categorically distinct from the distractor information. Madden (1982) showed that if targets were letters and distractors were numbers, older adults were able to focus on the relevant information as well as younger adults. For example, in the display K4VCS, both younger and older adults would find it relatively easy to focus on the number 4.

There also is evidence to suggest that focused attention is maintained even for older individuals with Alzheimer's disease. Nebes and Brady (1989) used a color cue in their search task and found that the cue benefits were similar for normal older adults, Alzheimer's patients, and younger adults. They concluded that focused attention ability was intact for their patients who all were diagnosed as probable Alzheimer's.

In a focused attention task, the location of the target is known or the target is easily discriminable from the distractor information. Older adults (even those with Alzheimer's disease) are able to perform these tasks as well as younger adults. However, as discussed above, if the task requires the *selection* of information where the target location is unknown, targets are not easily discriminable from distractors, or the search requires the conjunction of features, older adults are likely to show deficits in performance in comparison with younger adults. However, these deficits may be reduced through experience or through the provision of cuing information.

Sustained attention

> There is no such thing as voluntary attention sustained for more than a few seconds at a time . . . it is a repetition of successive efforts which bring back the topic to the mind. (James, 1950, p. 420)

Sustained attention refers to one's ability to actively process incoming information over a period of time. You can think of it as focusing attention for an extended interval. Sustained attention most often has been measured in vigilance tasks in which an observer must respond to infrequent signals over an extended period of time (see Parasuraman, 1984, for a review). Real-world examples of vigilance tasks include a submarine officer monitoring the radar screen for unfamiliar blips, an assembly line inspector searching for defective products, and a mother listening for her baby's cry.

In the laboratory environment, early studies of vigilance used the clock test (e.g., Mackworth, 1948). In this task, an observer watches a clock hand moving in steps around a blank clock face. The task is to report any time the hand moves a double step. Performance on this task drops significantly after only 30 minutes on task. Presumably, the observer has difficulty sustaining his or her attention for such minimal stimulus activity. Of course, if the consequences of missing a target are dire, the attendant will more successfully be able to sustain attention. During wartime, for example, the radar operator likely will have more success sustaining attention on the radar scope for longer periods of time; however, vigilance decrements in performance still are observed in these situations.

In a recent review of age differences in vigilance tasks, Giambra (1993) reported that the evidence was mixed: some studies reported age differences, whereas others did not. However, vigilance tasks may involve more than just sustained attention, and the other components of the task may account for some of the age differences observed. For example, Giambra suggested that if the exposure time of the stimulus is too short for older individuals to reliably detect it, they might miss the target; however, such a miss would not be indicative of a deficit in sustained attention per se.

Age-related differences also tend to be larger on tasks that require more subtle distinctions between targets and nontargets. For example, Parasuraman and Giambra (1991) required subjects to distinguish between a 17-millimeter square (the target) and 20-millimeter squares (the nontargets). The middle-aged (40 to 55 years) and older (70 to 80 years) subjects in their study showed more of a vigilance decrement than did the younger adults (19 to 27 years).

In sum, the age differences often can be attributed to other aspects of the task (Giambra, 1993). For example, (a) discriminability of stimulus—if the stimulus is easily discriminable from background noise, age differences are minimal; (b) duration of stimulus—if the stimulus is not being "missed" because it is too brief, age differences are reduced; and (c) working memory load—age differences are reduced if the requirement to maintain information active in working memory is low. Thus, the age differences do not appear to be due to sustained attention per se, but to other aspects of the task. The ability to sustain attention may in fact be age invariant. However, it is important to keep in mind that tasks requiring sustained attention often have other components, which may decline with age, and overall performance on such tasks may show age-related decrements.

Attention switching and divided attention

> To how many things can we attend at once? . . . the answer is, not easily more than one, unless the processes are very habitual. (James, 1950, pp. 405, 409)

Divided attention studies assess one's ability to simultaneously perform more than one task. The evidence suggests that for simple tasks, younger and older adults can divide their attention equally well (e.g., Somberg &

Salthouse, 1982). However, for more complex tasks, the older adults' performance declines (e.g., McDowd & Craik, 1988; Salthouse, Rogan, & Prill, 1984). In addition to the complexity of the task, the amount of practice provided also is important. Practice with the simultaneous performance of the tasks may reduce the severity of the age-related decline (e.g., Rogers, Bertus, & Gilbert, 1994).

Dividing attention and switching attention will be considered together because it is difficult to differentiate between the true division of attention and the rapid switching between tasks. For example, consider reading the newspaper and watching television. Do you really simultaneously "divide" your limited attention between the two tasks or do you actually switch back and forth between the two, attending more to the television when something interesting is happening and switching to the newspaper during the commercials. We will use the term *divided attention* to refer to both possibilities because that is what is most often used in the literature, but it is important to remember that attention switching may be involved in what we are calling divided attention.

Are there age-related differences in divided attention? It depends on the complexity of the tasks. The evidence suggests that for relatively simple tasks, younger and older adults can divide their attention equally well. For example, Somberg and Salthouse (1982) used a perceptual identification task where the participants had to look for a small line extending from an X in one display while simultaneously looking for a small line extending from a + (see Figure 4.2). Their results showed no significant difference between the younger and older adults in their ability to divide their attention between these two tasks. Somberg and Salthouse replicated their results in a second experiment that assessed the simultaneous performance of a simple reaction time task (respond when you hear a tone) and a repetitive keying task (entering digit sequences on a keyboard). Again, the older adults were able to divide their attention between the two tasks as well as the younger adults.

For more complex tasks, evidence suggests that the performance of older adults declines. McDowd and Craik (1988) required their subjects to monitor an orally presented list of words to detect words that denoted living things, while simultaneously determining if a visually presented char-

X	+	X̶
✗		+
X	+	X

FIG. 4.2. Sample stimuli used in the Somberg and Salthouse (1982) perceptual identification task. The task is to quickly look for a small line extending from an X while simultaneously looking for a small line extending from a + sign.

acter was a vowel, consonant, odd digit, or even digit. To illustrate, if you were a participant in this study, you might hear "wolf" and see Q. You would have to press a key to respond to the fact that a wolf is a living thing and press the appropriate response key to show that Q is a consonant. Twelve words are presented (one every 2 seconds) and the visual characters are presented continuously for 24 seconds. As you might imagine, performing these two tasks simultaneously is rather difficult. McDowd and Craik showed that this complex dual task revealed significant age-related differences. The older adults had much more difficulty than younger adults in performing both tasks simultaneously, relative to performing them one at a time. These results suggest that age-related differences in divided attention ability may become evident only for difficult or complex tasks.

In addition to the complexity of the task, the amount of practice provided also is important. Practice with the simultaneous performance of the tasks may reduce the severity of the age decline. Studies that have reported an absence of age-related differences have tended to provide substantially more practice. To illustrate, Baron and Mattila (1989) provided subjects with 11,800 trials of memory scanning practice; Somberg and Salthouse (1982, Experiment 1) provided 550 trials of perceptual identification practice; and Wickens, Braune, and Stokes (1987) provided three sessions (3.5 hours) of practice on their tasks (the exact number of trials was difficult to determine). Rogers, Bertus, and Gilbert (1994) provided subjects with over 9,000 trials of practice.

On the contrary, those studies that have reported age differences on dual tasks have provided much less practice. For example, Crossley and Hiscock's (1992) subjects received only 48 experimental trials; Madden's (1986) subjects received between 240 and 280 trials; Ponds, Brouwer, and van Wolffelaar's (1988) subjects spent 26 minutes on the task (the number of trials could not be determined); Salthouse, Rogan, and Prill's (1984) subjects received 100–300 trials; McDowd and Craik's (1988) subjects received approximately 9.5 minutes of time on task in their Experiment 1 and 9 minutes in Experiment 2; and McDowd's (1986) subjects received only 180 total trials of practice. The dual-task data suggest that practice may play a critical role in determining age-related differences in divided attention.

To summarize, the division of attention involves performing two or more tasks at the same time. Investigations of age-related differences suggest that if the tasks are not memory demanding, older adults may successfully be able to divide their attention. However, for more complex tasks, age-related differences emerge. An additional piece of the puzzle is that practice in dividing attention may reduce the age differences.

Automatic processing

Habit diminishes the conscious attention with which our acts are performed. (James, 1950, p. 114)

James may have foreseen some of the changes that occur with age when he said that, "Could the young but realize how soon they will become mere walking bundles of habits, they would give more heed to their conduct while in the plastic state" (James, 1950, p. 127)

For our purposes, we can think of habits as automatic processes. Thus far, we have discussed tasks which require our attention. However, an important component of skill acquisition is the ability to "automatize" task components such that they no longer require attention. Consider a novice driver trying to carry on a conversation. His or her attempts are intermittent because inexperienced drivers must focus most of their attention on the task of driving, especially at critical junctures of switching gears or turning a corner. More experienced drivers, however, are able to perform these activities while talking, changing the radio, or planning their day. The difference between a novice driver and a skilled driver is the amount of attention required for the task components. Consistent components such as changing gears become automatized with extensive practice. However, even for skilled drivers, the overall task of driving is not automatic, as evidenced by the fact that other activities cease when the driver is in heavy traffic or an unfamiliar neighborhood.

There are certain characteristics that define whether something is a controlled or an automatic process (Schneider, Dumais, & Shiffrin, 1984). An automatic process is a process that occurs obligatorily when a specific eliciting stimulus is present; it can occur without intention, and, once initiated, will run to completion; and it does not reveal itself to conscious awareness nor does it consume attentional resources. See Figure 4.3 for a demonstration of an automatic process.

Step 1: Write the following sentence as quickly as you can in your normal handwriting.

I think that this task is a time-consuming and silly exercise.

Result: Writing is an automatic process for you so this task should be trivially easy and you could probably write the sentence very quickly.

Step 2: Write the same sentence again BUT this time do not cross your t's or dot your i's.

I think that this task is a time-consuming and silly exercise.

Result: This demonstration illustrates how, for experienced writers, crossing t's and dotting i's is an automatic process that is difficult to inhibit, even if you try. (Note that you were probably successful at inhibiting the automatic process but much slower than if you had allowed the automatic process to occur naturally.)

FIG. 4.3.
A demonstration of an automatic process.

A controlled process is an intentional process that is focused on achieving a particular goal; it is open to awareness and does require attentional resources. Almost all of our everyday activities involve a combination of automatic and controlled processes. That alone makes the two processes sufficiently important as areas of study in experimental psychology.

Acquisition of new automatic processes.   When children first begin to learn to read, all aspects of the process are effortful and attention demanding. They must learn the features of each letter, what each letter represents, how letters are combined to make sounds and form words, how words are combined to form phrases and sentences, and, of course, what the sentences mean. For experienced readers, many of the lower-level components of the reading task are automatized (LaBerge and Samuels, 1974), thus freeing up more attentional resources for higher-level processes such as comprehension. Such automatization occurs through extensive consistent practice; for example, the features / - \ combine to form the letter *A*, the letters *C A T* combine to form the word *cat*, and so forth.

The acquisition of new automatic processes for older adults has been investigated most frequently in search tasks where the type of practice, the amount of practice, and the individual's prior experience with the task could be closely controlled. Visual search tasks were discussed above in the section, Selective Attention. If the target item is consistent (i.e., always search for words from the category of animals), the search task can become automatized for younger adults (e.g., Fisk & Schneider, 1983; Schneider & Shiffrin, 1977). However, even after extensive consistent practice, visual search tasks remain attention demanding for older adults (e.g., Fisk & Rogers, 1991).

Contrary to visual search tasks, older adults can successfully automatize memory search tasks. Memory search tasks vary from visual search tasks in the following way. In a visual search task, the participant is given a single target item and is asked to find it in an array of multiple items (e.g., find the letter *A* in this list of 50 letters). In a memory search task, on the other hand, the participant is given several potential target items and is then presented with a single probe item for comparison (e.g., the target letters are *A, B, G, O, P* . . . the probe item is *B* . . . is there a match?). Thus, visual search tasks are more perceptually demanding, whereas memory search tasks are more demanding of memory. After extensive consistent practice on a memory search task, performance can become automatic such that individuals can search for all of the memory set items as quickly as any one single item from the memory set. Studies of older adults have revealed that although they may require more extensive practice than younger adults, they are capable of automatizing memory search tasks (e.g., Fisk & Rogers, 1991).

Thus, to answer the question of whether there are age differences in the development of new automatic processes, we must consider the type of task involved. Automatic processes that require perceptual learning (e.g., fast visual processing) do show age differences. However, for memory-dependent automatic processes, as long as older adults are given a sufficient amount of practice, they are able to automatize the task (Fisk & Rogers, 1991).

Previously acquired automatic processes. It is important to make a distinction between the development of new automatic processes and the use of previously acquired automatic processes. There is evidence to suggest that processes which were automatized when individuals were young tend to remain intact into older age. This is particularly important for the maintenance of functioning into older age. Components of many of our daily activities are performed automatically; if we were to lose these automatic abilities as we grew older, all of our activities would become attention demanding and it would be very difficult for us to function.

The retention of the automatized components of reading has been illustrated using the Stroop color-word task. In this task, individuals are presented with a color word in colored ink (e.g., GREEN in red ink). The task is to say the ink color and ignore the word (e.g., say red). However, the word GREEN interferes for experienced readers because they automatically read the word. Inexperienced readers do not show the Stroop effect—the amount of interference increases with the reading experience of the individual (for a review, see MacLeod, 1991). Interference is observed, and in some cases increased, for older adults (e.g., Dulaney & Rogers, 1994), suggesting that the automatic activation of the word remains stable across age. A similar maintenance of a well-learned automatic process was reported by Rogers and Fisk (1991) for arithmetic operations; for example, the automatic retrieval of 5 when presented with 3 + 2 = __.

Another measure of automatic access of information is called lexical access. Lexical means related to words, and access refers to retrieving the information from one's long-term memory. For example, if you are presented with the word "orangutan," you automatically access that word in your memory. Evidence suggests that such lexical access remains fairly stable throughout older age (Light, 1992).

In all of these examples, there is evidence that younger and older adults show similar patterns of automatic activation of well-learned information. These results suggest that automatic processes developed early in life remain reliable well into older age.

To summarize our knowledge about age-related differences in automatic processes, there are two basic questions. First, are automatic processes that were acquired at a younger age maintained into older age? The answer here appears to be yes. This finding is very encouraging because it means that we may rely on automatic processes throughout our lives, provided we first acquire them when we are young. The second question is, How well can older adults acquire new automatic processes? Here the answer is that it depends on the type of task. For memory-based tasks, older adults may take longer, but they can successfully automatize the task. However, for tasks that involve more perceptual learning, such as visual search tasks, older adults continue to devote attention to the task, even after thousands of trials of consistent practice.

A general theory of age-related attention differences

> Always present is the inhibition of irrelevant movements and ideas.
> (James, 1950, p. 445)

Attention often involves the selection of information. In a divided attention task, we must choose how to allocate our attention to the exclusion of some stimulus information. Similarly, in focused and selective attention, we are processing some stimuli more than other stimuli. The selection process can be aided by emphasizing the critical information (e.g., through cuing or consistent practice), or by deemphasizing the noncritical information. Thus, attention has two facets—the selection of some information and the active inhibition of other information. The process of inhibition has been proposed as a potential source of age-related differences in attention tasks (e.g., Hasher & Zacks, 1988).

Hasher and Zacks proposed that, "Central to the efficient operation of . . . selective and intensive [focused] attention . . . are inhibitory mechanisms which, when normally functioning, serve to limit entrance into working memory" (p. 212). They then suggested the possibility that the inhibitory mechanisms of older adults are less efficient.

Such a decrease in inhibitory functioning would affect the selection, focus, and division of attention. The idea is that irrelevant information that is not appropriately inhibited will interfere with the processing of the relevant information. Inhibition is the corollary to selection. As we select some information for further processing, we inhibit other irrelevant or distracting information. If we were completely unable to inhibit distracting information, it would be impossible to function. As you are reading this text, you might be inhibiting extraneous thoughts—the radio in the next room, the fact that your chair is uncomfortable, the sensation of hunger, the wealth of other visual stimulation in the room, and so forth. Imagine if you were unable to inhibit all of this stimulation—you never would be able to complete the chapter! Although this is an extreme example, older adults may have a reduction in their ability to inhibit information, and this "disinhibition" may influence their performance on attention and other types of tasks.

One method for measuring inhibitory processes is called the negative priming effect. Figure 4.4 represents an illustration of this phenomenon. On Trial 1, the participant is supposed to respond to the letter *D* and ignore the *V*s. On Trial 2, the participant is supposed to respond to the letter *V* and ignore the *M*'s. Response time would be slower for Trial 2 because the participant is trying to respond to an item that he or she recently has inhibited. The idea is that by ignoring the stimulus on Trial 1, that stimulus

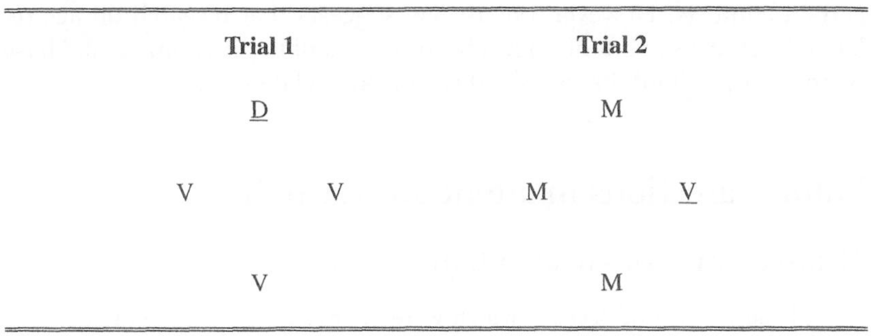

Trial 1		Trial 2	
D̲		M	
V	V	M	V̲
V		M	

FIG. 4.4.
Sample of a negative priming paradigm (adapted from Kramer et al., 1994). The participant must respond to the underlined item on each trial. Having ignored (i.e., inhibited) the letter V on trial 1 would slow the response to the letter V on Trial 2.

has been inhibited and, thus, it is more difficult to attend to it in the near future.

Hasher, Stoltzfus, Zacks, and Rypma (1991) found that older adults showed reduced inhibition on a negative priming task. (Note that the effect is measured relative to a baseline, thus controlling for overall response time differences between younger and older adults.) However, Kramer, Humphrey, Larish, Logan, and Strayer (1994) reported that the magnitude of the negative priming effect did not differ for younger and older adults. The Hasher et al. and Kramer et al. studies used different negative priming tasks. One way to reconcile the discrepant findings is to propose that there are multiple inhibitory systems, only some of which will show age-related declines (Kramer et al., 1994; May, Kane, & Hasher, 1995).

Whether older adults have difficulty inhibiting information remains a controversial issue. Some studies have found evidence of disinhibition for older adults, whereas others have not. Moreover, there is some debate as to whether older adults exhibit a general decline of inhibitory function or whether there may be specific declines in certain inhibitory processes. One thing is clear: the idea of disinhibition for older adults has been an important development in attention research, and it ultimately may provide a unifying theory for age-related differences in attention.

Summary of age-related differences in attention

Clearly, there are varieties of attention and there are varieties of age-related differences in attention. Aspects of attention that remain intact for older adults are: selective, focused, divided, and the transition from attention-demanding to automatic processes. Aspects of attention that decline for older adults are: selective, divided, and the transition from attention demanding to automatic processes. Notice that some attention types appear on both lists. This fact demonstrates the complexity of the question, Does attention decline with age? Some types of attention do show age-related declines, some types do not, and some types show declines only in certain contexts. However, our review suggests that research on age-related differences in attention has been successful in providing a solid base of knowledge about the locus and type of age-related differences.

Future directions in attention research

Neurological bases of attention

> Those brain processes . . . which were connected . . . were kept sub-excited . . . the summation of stimulations will prepare the motor centres. (James, 1950, pp. 433–434)

> Every impression falling on the nervous system must propagate itself somewhither. (James, 1950, p. 457)

Even back in 1890, James understood the importance of mapping behaviors onto neurological and physiological processes. Researchers have shown that different brain regions may control different components of attentional processing. For example, Posner and Petersen (1990) proposed that a posterior brain system mediates attention to spatial locations, whereas an anterior system mediates attention to cognitive operations. Understanding whether age-related changes in brain structure or brain process differ across these systems may help us to understand age-related differences in attention. Researchers have a number of techniques available to investigate these issues. Brain activity can be measured using an electroencephalogram (EEG), positron emission tomography (PET), and magnetic resonance imaging (MRI). This blending of neurological techniques and cognitive measures of attention is called *neuropsychology,* and it holds much promise for broadening our understanding of age-related changes in attention. For example, these methods may enable us to determine whether older adults are less able to inhibit information based on continued activation of information that is no longer relevant to the task at hand.

Practical applications

As we learn more about age-related differences in attention, we can use that information to understand and improve performance outside of the laboratory. For example, researchers have attempted to try to understand the individual differences in attention variables that are predictive of driving success. One such variable is the visual field that can be processed during a brief glance known as the *useful field of view* (UFOV). The UFOV varies as a function of the duration, salience, and eccentricity of a target item. However, the UFOV measure is more than just a measure of vision; it has an attentional component related to the degree of competing attentional demands (Ball & Owsley, 1991). The UFOV varies between individuals, with older adults tending to have a smaller UFOV. Ball and Owsley (1991) reported that a measure of UFOV alone can account for 13% of the variance of all car accidents in a sample of older drivers and 21% of the variance of intersection accidents in the same sample. Thus, individual differences in UFOV appear to be related to individual differences in driving accidents. An encouraging finding is that restricted UFOVs can be improved by as much as 133% after only 5 days of training (Ball, Beard, Roenker, Miller, & Griggs, 1988).

Driving also requires rapid attention switching between sources of information, and there are individual differences in the ability to shift attention, especially for older drivers with various types of dementia (Parasuraman & Nestor, 1991). Such individual differences in attention shifting may be used to measure driving competence (Proctor & Van Zandt, 1994). The UFOV and attention-switching influences on driving ability provide just two examples of how understanding age-related differences in attention may help us to understand age-related differences in practical tasks.

References

Ball, K., Beard, B., Roenker, D., Miller, R., & Griggs, D. (1988). Age and visual search: Expanding the useful field of view. *Journal of the Optical Society of America, 5*, 2210–2219.

Ball, K., & Owsley, C. (1991). Identifying correlates of accident involvement for the older driver. *Human Factors, 33*, 583–595.

Baron, A., & Mattila, W. R. (1989). Response slowing of older adults: Effects of time-limit contingencies on single- and dual-task performances. *Psychology and Aging, 4*, 66–72.

Cherry, C. (1953). Some experiments on the recognition of speech with one and two ears. *Journal of the Acoustical Society of America, 25*, 975–979.

Clancy, S. M., & Hoyer, W. J. (1994). Age and skill in visual search. *Developmental Psychology, 30*, 545–552.

Crossley, M., & Hiscock, M. (1992). Age-related differences in concurrent-task performance of normal adults: Evidence for a decline in processing resources. *Psychology and Aging, 7*, 499–506.

Dulaney, C. L., & Rogers, W. A. (1994). Mechanisms underlying reduction in Stroop interference with practice for young and old adults. *Journal of Experimental Psychology: Learning, Memory, and Cognition, 20*, 470–484.

Fisk, A. D., & Rogers, W. A. (1991). Toward an understanding of age-related memory and visual search effects. *Journal of Experimental Psychology: General, 120*, 131–149.

Fisk, A. D., & Schneider, W. (1983). Category and word search: Generalizing search principles to complex processing. *Journal of Experimental Psychology: Learning, Memory, and Cognition, 9*, 177–195.

Giambra, L. M. (1993). Sustained attention in older adults: Performance and processes. In J. Cerella, J. Rybash, W. Hoyer, & M. L. Commons (Eds.), *Adult information processing: Limits on loss* (pp. 259–272). San Diego, CA: Academic Press.

Hartley, A. A. (1992). Attention. In F. I. M. Craik and T. A. Salthouse (Eds.), *The Handbook of Aging and Cognition* (pp. 3–49). Hillsdale, NJ: Erlbaum.

Hasher, L., Stoltzfus, E. R., Zacks, R. T., & Rypma, B. (1991). Age and inhibition. *Journal of Experimental Psychology: Learning, Memory and Cognition, 17*, 163–169.

Hasher, L., & Zacks, R. T. (1988). Working memory, comprehension, and aging: A review and a new view. In G. H. Bower (Ed.), *The psychology of learning and motivation* (Vol. 22, pp. 193–225), San Diego, CA: Academic Press.

James, W. (1950). *The principles of psychology* (Vol. I). New York: Dover. (Original work published 1890.)

Kramer, A. F., Humphrey, D. G., Larish, J. F., Logan, G. D., & Strayer, D. L. (1994). Aging and inhibition: Beyond a unitary view of inhibitory processing in attention. *Psychology and Aging, 9*, 491–512.

LaBerge, D., & Samuels, S. J. (1974). Toward a theory of automatic information processing in reading. *Cognitive Psychology, 6*, 293–323.

Light, L. L. (1992). The organization of memory in old age. In F. I. M. Craik and T. A. Salthouse (Eds.), *The Handbook of Aging and Cognition* (pp. 111–165). Hillsdale, NJ: Erlbaum.

Mackworth, N. H. (1948). The breakdown of vigilance during prolonged visual search. *Quarterly Journal of Experimental Psychology, 1*, 5–61.

MacLeod, C. M. (1991). Half a century of research on the Stroop effect: An integrative review. *Psychological Bulletin, 109*, 163–203.

Madden, D. J. (1982). Age differences and similarities in the improvement of controlled search. *Experimental Aging Research, 8*, 91–98.

Madden, D. J. (1983). Aging and distraction by highly familiar stimuli during visual search. *Developmental Psychology, 19*, 499–505.

Madden, D. J. (1986). Adult age differences in the attentional capacity demands of visual search. *Cognitive Development, 1*, 335–363.

Madden, D. J., & Plude, D. J. (1993). Selective preservation of selective attention. In J. Cerella, J. Rybash, W. Hoyer, & M. L. Commons (Eds.), *Adult information processing: Limits on loss* (pp. 273–300). San Diego, CA: Academic Press.

May, C. P., Kane, M. J., & Hasher, L. (1995). Determinants of negative priming. *Psychological Bulletin, 118*, 35–54.

McDowd, J. M. (1986). The effects of age and extended practice on divided attention performance. *Journal of Gerontology, 41*, 764–769.

McDowd, J. M., & Craik, F. I. M. (1988). Effects of aging and task difficulty on divided attention performance. *Journal of Experimental Psychology: Human Perception and Performance, 14*, 267–280.

Nebes, R. D., & Brady, C. B. (1989). Focused and divided attention in Alzheimer's disease. *Cortex, 25*, 305–315.

Parasuraman, R. (1984). Sustained attention in detection and discrimination. In R. Parasuraman & D. R. Davies (Eds.), *Varieties of attention* (pp. 243–271). San Diego, CA: Academic Press.

Parasuraman, R., & Davies, D. R. (1984). *Varieties of attention*. San Diego, CA: Academic Press.

Parasuraman, R., & Giambra, L. M. (1991). Skill development in vigilance: Effects of event rate and age. *Psychology and Aging, 6*, 155–159.

Parasuraman, R., & Nestor, P. G. (1991). Attention and driving skills in aging and Alzheimer's disease. *Human Factors, 33*, 539–557.

Plude, D. J., & Doussard-Roosevelt, J. A. (1989). Aging, selective attention, and feature integration. *Psychology and Aging, 4,* 98–105.

Ponds, R. W. H. M., Brouwer, W. H., & van Wolffelaar, P. C. (1988). Age differences in divided attention in a simulated driving task. *Journal of Gerontology, 43,* 151–156.

Posner, M. I., & Petersen, S. E. (1990). The attention system of the human brain. *Annual Review of Neuroscience, 13,* 25–42.

Procter, R. W., & Van Zandt, T. (1994). *Human factors in simple and complex systems.* Boston: Allyn & Bacon.

Rogers, W. A., Bertus, E. L., & Gilbert, D. K. (1994). A dual-task assessment of age differences in automatic process development. *Psychology and Aging, 9,* 398–413.

Rogers, W. A., & Fisk, A. D. (1991). Age-related differences in the maintenance and modification of automatic processes: Arithmetic Stroop interference. *Human Factors, 33,* 45–56.

Salthouse, T. A., Rogan, J. D., & Prill, K. A. (1984). Division of attention: Age differences on a visually presented memory task. *Memory and Cognition, 12,* 613–620.

Schneider, W., Dumais, S. T., & Shiffrin, R. M. (1984). Automatic and control processing and attention. In R. Parasuraman & D. R. Davies (Eds.), *Varieties of attention* (pp. 1–27). San Diego, CA: Academic Press.

Schneider, W., & Shiffrin, R. M. (1977). Controlled and automatic human information processing: I. Detection, search and attention. *Psychological Review, 84,* 1–66.

Somberg, B., & Salthouse, T. A. (1982). Divided attention abilities in young and old adults. *Journal of Experimental Psychology: Human Perception and Performance, 8,* 651–665.

Wickens, C. D., Braune, R., & Stokes, A. (1987). Age differences in the speed and capacity of information processing: 1. A dual-task approach. *Psychology and Aging, 2,* 70–78.

Wright, L. L., & Elias, J. W. (1979). Age differences in the effects of perceptual noise. *Journal of Gerontology, 34,* 704–708.

Duncan, D. J., Ward, R. & Kowalski, J. S. (1990). Active selective attention and feature integration in scanning. *Vision Research*.

Eriksen, R. W. & St. James, J. D. & van Wolffelaar, P. C. (1989). Selective costs in divided attention in a binocular rivalry task. *Journal of Gerontology*.

Fisk, A. D. & Schneider, W. (1981). The attention system of the human brain.

Hoffman, W. C. & Nissen, M. J. (1981). Toward a science. Academic Press.

Pashler, H. E. & LaBerge, D. L. (1990). Stimulus effects in divided attention. *Cognitive Psychology*.

Rogers, W. A. & Fisk, A. D. (1991). Age-related differences in the maintenance and acquisition of automatic processes. *Journal of Gerontology*.

Salthouse, T. A. & Somberg, B. L. (1982). Distributed attention: Age differences in a novel pmnemonics. *Experimental Aging Research*.

Schneider, W. & Detweiler, M. (1987). A connectionist/control architecture for working memory. In The psychology of learning. Academic Press.

Schneider, W. & Shiffrin, R. M. (1977). Controlled and automatic human information processing. *Psychological Review*.

Strayer, D. L. & Kramer, A. F. (1990). Attentional requirements of automatic and controlled processing. *Journal of Experimental Psychology*.

Wickens, C. D. (1980). The structure of attentional resources. In *Attention and performance VIII*. Erlbaum.

Woltz, D. J. (1988). An investigation of the role of working memory in procedural skill acquisition. *Journal of Experimental Psychology*.

Age-related changes in human memory 5

Fergus I. M. Craik

This chapter addresses age-related difficulties and problems to do with various aspects of memory. Age-related changes in memory are well documented (Craik & Jennings, 1992; Light, 1991; Salthouse, 1991; Zacks, Hasher, & Li, 1999). The general consensus is that memory performance does decline in older adults, but also that the amount of loss depends very much on the specific memory task under consideration: performance on some tasks drops considerably in older people, whereas performance on other memory tasks shows little or no decline. It is the memory theorist's job to understand this pattern of differential loss and possible compensation (Dixon & Bäckman, 1995) and the applied researcher's task to show how such age-related changes in memory affect aspects of real-life behavior. The bulk of this chapter is devoted to a review of current theories and data in the field of memory and aging; the practical implications of these findings also are discussed briefly.

Types of memory

Cognitive psychologists typically talk and write about a variety of different memory systems, memory stages, or memory stores. This is a reasonable, and even necessary, response to the results of 100 years of laboratory and clinical research showing that performance on some tasks is unaffected by aging, by brain damage, and by adverse environmental conditions, whereas performance on other memory tasks declines catastrophically in the same individuals. To give some classical examples, the patient H.M., who underwent bilateral surgical excision of his hippocampus and surrounding brain areas for the relief of epilepsy, is unable to recollect any personal events experienced since the operation, yet is essentially unimpaired at learning new motor skills and also in the ability to repeat back a series of words or numbers (Milner, Corkin, & Teuber, 1968). The patient K.C. suffered brain damage in a traffic accident; his access to general knowledge of facts and procedures is normal, yet he has no access to any personal memory from his entire life. Thus he can give a coherent account of the procedures necessary to change a car tire, yet is unable to recollect any occasion on which he changed a tire, and does not even remember that his brother died in an accident many years ago (Tulving, Hayman, & Macdonald, 1991). In the case of normal aging, older adults (typically between the ages of 60 and 85 in the work discussed here) are typically impaired relative to younger control subjects (typically age 20 to 30) in free-recall tasks, in their ability to recall highly specific facts such as names, and in their ability to remember details of where and when events occurred. They are much less impaired, and sometimes superior to their younger counterparts, on other tasks, such as word priming, recognition memory, and knowledge of word meanings (Craik & Jennings, 1992; Salthouse, 1991; Zacks et al., 1999).

Such findings drive the necessary conclusion that "memory" is not some monolithic entity, but cognitive psychologists unfortunately disagree about how the overall concept should be decomposed. One early scheme suggested a tripartite division into the three successive stages of sensory memory, short-term (or primary) memory, and long-term (or secondary) memory (Atkinson & Shiffrin, 1968; Murdock, 1967). This classification provides an explanation of why amnesic patients and, to a much lesser degree, normal older people have difficulties in retrieving personal events from hours or days ago, yet can repeat back strings of digits or words at the same level as their younger counterparts (Baddeley & Warrington, 1970; Craik, 1977). That is, their long-term memory is impaired, but their short-term memory (in the sense of material "still in mind") is unaffected. An extended and modified version of this tripartite scheme has been suggested by Tulving and his colleagues (e.g., Schacter & Tulving, 1994). They suggested that memory can be divided into five major systems that differ fundamentally from one another. Their five candidates are procedural memory, the perceptual representational system (PRS), primary memory, episodic memory, and semantic memory. Of these five, PRS corresponds roughly to sensory memory, primary memory corresponds to short-term memory, and episodic memory and semantic memory together map onto the former long-term memory. The new system, procedural memory, is responsible for learning associative relations, simple conditioning, and motor and cognitive skills.

One of the main categories of evidence for separate memory systems is the existence of "dissociations" among various tasks that presumably tap the systems differentially. Thus, if aging, brain damage, or some other manipulation affects performance on one task, but has no effect on a second task, it is inferred that the tasks are mediated by separate systems. Further convergent evidence from different sources usually is sought before concluding that tasks do indeed tap into different systems (Schacter & Tulving, 1994). This five-system framework provides a good account of such cases as H.M. (impaired episodic memory, intact procedural memory and primary memory) and K.C. (impaired episodic memory, intact semantic and procedural memory), and normal aging (impaired episodic memory and aspects of semantic memory, intact procedural memory). Although the memory systems viewpoint has its critics (McKoon, Ratcliff, & Dell, 1986), it undoubtedly provides a good descriptive framework within which the main age-related changes in memory may be understood. The following sections provide brief reviews of age-related changes in the different memory systems, and a final section draws these findings and conclusions together to point out their implications for the design and interpretation of questionnaire assessments of cognitive changes in older people.

Procedural memory

The term "procedural memory" is used to cover the learning and retention of a rather wide assortment of motor and cognitive skills (e.g., playing the piano, driving a car, solving a jigsaw puzzle or a Tower of Hanoi problem) as well as academic skills such as counting, spelling, and reading. These abilities all have a large automatic component associated with them, and typically do not involve the conscious recollection of the initial learning episode. For this reason, procedural memory often is described as involving *implicit* memory processes, in contrast to the *explicit* recollection that necessarily is involved in episodic recall and recognition. It appears to be this bypassing of conscious recollection and conscious decision making on the one hand, and the heavy involvement of well-learned, automatic mental processes on the other hand, that work together to protect procedural memory skills from the effects of aging and brain damage.

In the cognitive realm, procedural memory often is assessed by means of priming paradigms. For example, reading a word appears to prime the specific perceptual, lexical, and semantic operations involved in the word's analysis, with the result that subsequent analysis of either the same word (e.g., doctor-DOCTOR) or a related word (e.g., doctor-NURSE) is carried out more easily and rapidly. Laver and Burke (1993) carried out a meta-analysis of semantic priming tasks and found that the effect is, if anything, greater in older people. One variant of the priming procedure involves presenting words to study (e.g., market), then later giving participants a word-stem completion task in which the first few letters of a word are provided (e.g., MAR___) and the task is to complete the word. Light and Singh (1987) tested younger and older people on this task under two instructional conditions; in one condition, subjects were asked to complete each word fragment with the first word that came to mind and, in the other condition, they were asked to use the fragments as cues to remember words from the study list. Light and Singh found no age differences in the first (implicit) task; that is, older people were as likely as their younger counterparts to complete MAR___ with market (as opposed to marble, marriage, and so forth), but the investigators found that younger participants outperformed older subjects in the explicit cued recall task.

In a second ingenious variant of the priming paradigm developed by Jacoby and Witherspoon (1982), participants were asked to read sentences biasing the less frequent member of a homophone pair (e.g., reign as opposed to rain, hare as opposed to hair). Subjects therefore read a sentence like, "The wounded hare limped slowly across the field" and, after a series of similar sentences, were given a spelling test in which they were asked to spell auditorily presented words, including the homophones. The finding was that participants are biased to spell the recently encountered variant, and Howard (1988) showed that younger and older subjects did not differ in this respect.

These and other examples have shown that procedural memory processes apparently are unaffected by aging (see reviews by Craik & Jennings, 1992; Light & LaVoie, 1993). Whereas this generally is a positive finding, it also can have negative consequences. In a series of recent articles, Jacoby and his colleagues (e.g., Dywan & Jacoby, 1990; Jacoby, 1991; Jennings & Jacoby, 1997) have pointed out that many cognitive tasks involve a mixture of unconscious, implicit processes, and consciously mediated, explicit processes. If explicit processes are impaired by aging, but implicit processes are not, then an older person's responses will be more governed by these latter mental operations. Thus, Dywan and Jacoby (1990) found that older people were more likely to think that repeated fictitious names were names of real famous people; they misattributed the familiarity associated with repetition to fame in the outside world. Similarly, Jennings and Jacoby (1997) showed that older subjects were more likely than younger subjects to misattribute repetitions of words in a test list to their presentation in a previous study list. These and other examples of false memories experienced more often by older people (see Schacter, Koutstaal, & Norman, 1997, for a review) appear to result from the combination of unimpaired procedural (or implicit) memory processes with impaired explicit memory for the episodic context in which the word or other event originally was experienced.

Such false memories can have serious negative consequences for older people in real-life settings. For example, the confusion of imagined or intended actions with real actions (e.g., taking medications or turning off the stove) could be quite dangerous. In the context of surveys, certain responses could be biased or primed by framing questions in a certain way or by the provision of earlier "examples." Results from the cognitive aging literature suggest that these influences would be stronger in older people.

The perceptual representational system

This "system" clearly is a collection of different subsystems dealing with sensory and perceptual information from the different modalities. Their brain locations typically are those regions associated with the early processing of modality-specific information, and their function is to analyze, integrate, and briefly hold incoming sense data (Tulving & Schacter, 1990). With respect to aging, little direct research has been done on possible age-related changes in PRS functioning (see Craik & Jennings, 1992, for a brief review). Given that procedural memory is essentially intact in older people, it seems reasonable to assume that early processing stages, common to implicit and explicit memory, are comparatively unaffected. On the other hand, it is clear that the sensory mechanisms themselves (e.g., vision, hearing, taste, touch, and smell) show marked changes with age, and it perhaps is a more interesting question in the present context to ask how sensory losses affect higher-order cognitive processes (Schneider & Pichora-Fuller, 1999).

Lindenberger and Baltes (1994) recently have presented some rather dramatic results showing that visual and auditory acuity together accounted for 93% of the age-related variance in intelligence in a large group of older people between age 70 and 103. Intelligence was measured by a battery of 14 cognitive tests, so it seems likely that the result is a valid one. However, it need not be the case that losses in vision and hearing cause losses in intelligence; another possible interpretation is that normal aging is associated with a reduction in a whole variety of physical and mental abilities, and that some "common cause" underlies this generalized reduction in efficient functioning (Lindenberger & Baltes, 1994). That is, to the extent that aging affects a wide range of somatic systems (e.g., the cardiovascular, muscular, respiratory, and central nervous systems), it might be expected that substantial correlations would be found among all functions. Brain function may correlate with muscular strength, for example, although no direct causal mechanism links the two sets of abilities.

Another research line explores the effects of degrading sensory input on cognitive performance in younger adults. Spinks, Gilmore, and Thomas (1996) showed that younger adults performed like 50-year-olds on symbol-digit substitution and on Raven's Advanced Progressive Matrices when visual contrast was degraded to the levels experienced by patients with Alzheimer's disease. Correspondingly, Alzheimer's patients' cognitive performance can be improved differentially if the visual contrast of the display is enhanced (Gilmore, Thomas, Klitz, Persanyi, & Tomsak, 1996). In a similar study carried out by Murphy and colleagues (Murphy, Craik, Li, & Schneider, in press), memory for recently presented paired associates was reduced greatly in younger adults when the auditorily presented stimuli were presented in a background of noise. It is important to note that the younger adult subjects perceived the stimuli correctly; nonetheless, the noisy background impaired the ability to lay down adequate memory traces.

Age-related differences in speech comprehension provide another case in which perceptual and cognitive factors interact. This topic is of prime interest to survey researchers who make extensive use of telephone interviews; difficulties in comprehension may result in a different pattern of responses from those obtained in face-to-face interviews. Such potential difficulties may be lessened by the provision of an adequate context, especially the context preceding important information or a crucial question. Wingfield, Alexander, and Cavigelli (1994) explored age differences in identifying spoken words that were presented either in isolation or with varying amounts of preceding and subsequent context or both. The researchers found that younger participants were better able to identify isolated words and made better use of context following the target words. Older and younger subjects were equally able to benefit from preceding context, however. This point also was investigated by Pichora-Fuller, Schneider, and Daneman (1995). Participants listened to short sentences in a range of noisy babble backgrounds, and attempted to identify the final word in each case. The sentences provided a context that was either highly predictive or nonpredictive of the final word; thus, both the sensory signal-to-noise ratios and the level of cognitive support were varied in the study. Figure 5.1A shows typical results from a younger adult, an older adult, and an older adult with marked hearing problems (presbycusis). Figure 5.1B shows the group results in the form of the benefit conferred by the high-context relative to low-context sentences. The figure shows that older and presbycusis subjects benefited more than their younger counterparts from the predictive context, but that higher levels of signal-to-noise ratios were required to reap these benefits.

Primary memory and working memory

The general notion of a separate short-term memory system has been well accepted in cognitive psychology since the early 1960s but, unfortunately, the terminology has been used in a confusing way. Experimental psychologists use the term to refer to a very small fragment of memory–essentially, just that information that is still "in mind" after several stimuli have been presented. Good recall of items from the end of a list (the recency effect) is attributed to this special short-term store, for example. However, clinicians tend to use "short-term memory" to refer to memory for recent events over several hours or even days; clearly, a very different concept. To clarify mat-

FIG. 5.1. (A) Percentage of high-context and low-context words correctly identified as a function of signal-to-noise ratio for three sample subjects, one younger adult (Y3), one older adult (O1), and one older presbycusic adult (P2). (B) Mean difference between high context and low context in percentage of correctly identified words as a function of signal-to-noise ratio, for younger, older, and presbycusic adults. Adapted with permission from research given in Pichora-Fuller, Schneider, & Daneman, 1995.

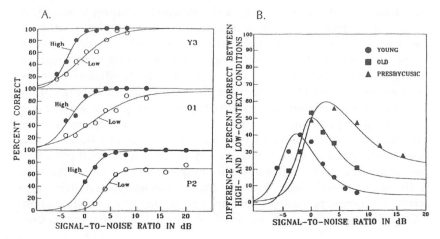

ters, Waugh and Norman (1965) suggested the term *primary memory* (PM) to refer to the fragment still in mind, and *secondary memory* for all other information retrieved from memory. Thus, PM is involved in the recency effect, in span paradigms, in holding telephone numbers in mind, and so forth.

The further important concept of *working memory* (WM) was introduced by Baddeley and Hitch (1974). This notion also refers to information held in mind, but stresses the functions of short-term retention (e.g., the integration of language and other serially presented stimuli, mental calculations, and reasoning in general). Thus, WM is a much more dynamic concept than the passive store suggested by PM. But are PM and WM separate systems? I have suggested not (Craik & Rabinowitz, 1984), proposing instead that short-term memory tasks lie on a passive-active continuum, such that passive tasks (e.g., recall of a list of numbers) are relatively pure PM tasks, whereas active tasks (e.g., the Daneman & Carpenter, 1980, reading span task) requiring manipulation, storage, and transformations of held material are examples of WM tasks.

When age differences are considered, the PM-WM distinction is a useful one in that age-related differences are slight in PM tasks, but substantial in WM tasks. Thus, if the task requires immediate repetition of a small amount of material, adult age differences are quite small. If the task requires active manipulation of stored material, however, or requires rapid alternation between storage and processing of further incoming information, then age-related differences are much greater. Examples of tasks with a high PM component include word and digit span (Parkinson, Lindholm, & Inman, 1982), the Brown-Peterson paradigm (Craik, 1977; Inman & Parkinson, 1983), and recall from the recency portion of free recall lists (Delbecq-Derouesne & Beauvois, 1989). Whereas age-related differences sometimes are statistically reliable in such tasks, the general finding is that the differences are small relative to the much larger differences found in secondary memory tasks (see Craik & Jennings, 1992, for a review).

With regard to practical implications, the comparative absence of an age-related decrement in PM means that older people can copy down telephone numbers accurately or transcribe small amounts of information without error from one part of a form to another. However, other real-life tasks often may tap WM (e.g., telephone surveys that involve long complex sentences, or questions with several alternative responses to bear in mind), and here the research data suggest the existence of large age decrements. A number of studies agree that performance on WM tasks declines systematically from early adulthood on (e.g., Craik, Morris, & Gick, 1990; Dobbs & Rule, 1989; Wingfield, Stine, Lahar, & Aberdeen, 1988). There also is some possibility that the age-related decrements increase with increasing task complexity, although here the picture is less clear (Craik et al., 1990; Salthouse, Mitchell, Skovronek, & Babcock, 1989). There is also debate about the underlying reasons for the age-related decline, with some researchers suggesting a depletion in mental energy or "attentional resources"

(Craik & Byrd, 1982), and others arguing for an age-related decline in processing speed (Salthouse, 1991, 1993) or for a decline in the ability to inhibit unwanted information (Hasher & Zacks, 1988; Zacks & Hasher, 1988). Whatever the underlying cause or causes, it is clear that older adults have particular problems in situations where they must hold, manipulate, and integrate moderate amounts of information over short time spans. These difficulties may be exacerbated when the task involves holding some information while simultaneously dealing with further incoming information (Daneman & Carpenter, 1980; Gick, Craik, & Morris, 1988).

Episodic memory

When older people complain that their memory "isn't what it used to be," they usually are referring to *episodic memory*, the ability to recollect specific autobiographical events that have happened comparatively recently. One laboratory analogue that taps this ability is free recall of words, sentences, stories, or pictures. In this paradigm, subjects are presented with a long list of stimuli and then attempt to recall them, without cues or reminders, at a later time (typically anything from 30 seconds to 24 hours after presentation). There is overwhelming evidence that performance on such tests declines with age from the thirties and forties to the seventies and eighties, and that the age-related decrement in free recall typically is greater than the decrement observed on many other memory tasks, such as PM, procedural memory, and some semantic memory tasks.

Why is episodic memory especially vulnerable to the effects of aging? It seems likely that a number of factors come into play to determine the final outcome. While I would like to believe some optimistic accounts suggesting that such age-related declines are all for the best—that a kindly Mother Nature is protecting older memory systems from being overloaded with trivia, for instance—I find it difficult to believe such adaptive and compensatory theories. First, the inability to remember details of recent events often is a source of embarrassment and frustration to older people; they certainly would like to remember. Second, the notion of "overloaded memory banks" is quite unlikely given all we know about expertise and memory; this work makes it clear that the more we know about a topic, the easier it is to encode and retrieve further episodic events relevant to that topic (Bransford, Franks, Morris, & Stein, 1979). Thus, the metaphor of accrued knowledge as a framework or scaffolding for new events is more apt than the metaphor of a cluttered cupboard. Third, memory is mediated by neural structures in the brain, and the brain is a physical organ like the heart, liver, lungs, and kidneys. These other organs undoubtedly become less efficient with advancing age, and it would be curious indeed if the brain was invulnerable to the effects of aging.

So, what actually changes? Cognitive aging researchers have suggested that "attentional resources" decline from midlife to older age, and that such resources are required to fuel the processes necessary to support cognitive performance. It also is necessary to postulate that episodic memory is particularly resource demanding. Candidates for these "resources" include the availability or utilization of blood glucose, the availability of an adequate blood supply to key areas of the brain, the speed with which mental operations are carried out, and the richness of interconnections among neurons in the central nervous system (Wickens, 1984). The recent enormous upsurge of research in cognitive neuroscience is likely to provide a definitive answer within the next few years. At the behavioral level, one problem associated with episodic memory is that events often are unpredictable and idiosyncratic; we therefore cannot use overlearned schemes and routines to encode and retrieve them. Instead, episodic memory is akin to "fluid intelligence" in that it deals with new information, rather than being able to rely on the accumulated structures of "crystallized intelligence."

One point about age-related differences in episodic memory is that the deficits often are reduced as supportive contextual information is provided, either at encoding (in the form of strategy instructions or the provision of an organized framework into which new events can be placed meaningfully) or at retrieval (in the form of cues, hints, reminders, and reinstatement of the original context). For this effect to appear reliably, it may be necessary to supply cues both at the time of encoding and again at the time of retrieval. For example, Craik, Byrd, and Swanson (1987) gave younger and older subjects lists of unrelated words to learn, either with or without a short descriptive phrase (e.g., a body of water, POND); age differences were smallest when the cues were provided during the learning phase and the retrieval phase. Very much the same result was reported by Shaw and Craik (1989). On the other hand, Park and Shaw (1992) boosted memory performance in an episodic memory task for words by providing the first two, three, or four initial letters of the words at retrieval; these investigators found that younger subjects benefited relatively more from the cues. Finally, Light (1991) concluded from a review of the evidence that the most common finding is both age groups benefit equally from the provision of such "environmental support." The literature thus is clear on the fact that episodic memory performance can be enhanced in older people by providing supportive contextual material at encoding and retrieval, although the conditions under which older people benefit more, less, or equally, relative to younger participants, have still to be worked out in detail.

One finding that is generally accepted concerns the greater difficulties experienced by older adults in remembering where and when they experienced an event or learned a fact. Thus, a face may "seem very familiar," yet an older person (and, indeed, many younger people) may be unable to recollect where and when they saw the face before. In brain-damaged patients, this type of failure is referred to as "source amnesia"; the impairment is much less severe in older people, but it may reflect the same inefficiency of frontal lobe functioning in a subclinical form (Craik, Morris,

Morris, & Loewen, 1990). Moreover, the degree of source amnesia does seem to increase with age in a normal sample. Using a paradigm devised by Schacter, Harbluk, and McLachlan (1984), McIntyre and Craik (1987) presented made-up facts (e.g., "Bob Hope's father was a fireman") to younger and older participants. One week later, the subjects were given "a general knowledge test" in which they were asked questions like, "What was Pablo Picasso's profession?" and "What did Bob Hope's father do for a living?" The participants also were asked to say where and when they had first learned the information, and the researchers found that older people remembered the "new facts" quite well, but forgot that they had learned them during the previous week's session. This age-related forgetting of contextual detail also is seen in the propensity of older people to tell the same anecdote to the same audience a number of times (Koriat, Ben-Zur, & Sheffer, 1988). This failure probably is the result of two age-related inefficiences: first, the greater likelihood that a given context will evoke a certain observation, question, or story; and second, the reduced likelihood that the older person will remember the previous occasion on which the question was asked or the anecdote told.

It seems possible that the age-related difficulty in remembering context is one manifestation of a more general age-related impairment in dealing with associative information. That is, older people may have special problems in forming and using associative connections among mental events. The need to integrate mental events, and the ability to do so is referred to as "binding." Johnson and her collaborators recently have shown that such binding problems increase with age (Chalfonte & Johnson, 1995; Johnson & Chalfonte, 1994).

Semantic memory

As used by cognitive psychologists, the term *semantic memory* refers to our store of factual knowledge, usually dissociated from any episodic recollection of where and when that knowledge was learned. At first, it seems that semantic memory in this sense declines little with age. The general knowledge sections of IQ tests typically are answered as well by older as younger respondents (Salthouse, 1982, 1991), knowledge and use of vocabulary shows very little decline until the late seventies or eighties (Salthouse, 1982), and the age-related declines in the ability to use semantic information are slight or nonexistent (Light, 1992; Light & Burke, 1988). The contrast between the minimal age-related differences in semantic memory performance, on the one hand, and the substantial age-related declines in episodic memory performance, on the other hand, may be taken as a further proof of the existence of at least two separate memory systems (cf., Tulving, 1983). There indeed are substantial age-related decrements in some aspects of semantic memory functioning, however, and such findings detract from any overly simple formulation. For example, word-finding failures increase with age (Burke, MacKay, Worthley, & Wade, 1991), and one of the most noticeable age-related memory failures is the difficulty which almost all older people experience in retrieving names (Cohen & Faulkner, 1986; Maylor, 1990).

It seems possible that it is not the episodic-semantic distinction that determines the presence or absence of age differences in memory, but rather the specificity of the sought-for information. Episodic information typically is quite specific, given that details of the temporal and spatial context are bound up in a satisfactory response, and factual knowledge often is rather general in that it can be expressed in a variety of different ways. When knowledge is specific, and cannot be rephrased or redescribed in alternative ways (e.g., names), then systematic age-related decrements are found; it remains to be seen whether age-related differences in episodic memory are reduced as the episodic context specified by the question becomes more general.

The fuzzy boundary between episodic and semantic memory is further illustrated by a consideration of work on spatial memory and on remote memory for personal events. Whereas it seems at first that memory for where things occurred and memory for long-ago experiences both are clear cases of episodic memory, a closer examination makes this classification less certain. Remembering where I left a book on a specific occasion is unambiguously "episodic," but memory for where I usually place my keys or park my car shades over into the realm of semantic memory. When it comes to memory for the spatial layout of a building or city, the information in question appears to be rather general and "semantic" in nature. Similarly, memory for remote autobiographical events seems to tap episodic memory, but Cermak (1984) made the interesting point that events from childhood and early adulthood may be told and retold so often that they take on the status of personal or family folklore, often drifting substantially away from the facts of the original event as it actually occurred.

Spatial memory

However it is classified, memory for spatial information does seem to decline markedly across the life span, and this result is to be expected in light of the well-established age-related drop in memory for contextual information in general (Spencer & Raz, 1995). Investigations of age differences in spatial memory range from laboratory tasks (e.g., Cherry & Park, 1993; Park, Cherry, Smith, & Lafronza, 1990; Zelinski & Light, 1988) to behavior in real-life settings. In this latter category, Uttl and Graf (1993) tested museum visitors age 15 to 74 on their memory for the spatial layout of museum displays they recently had visited. Participants over age 55 showed clear declines in this form of spatial memory. When the task taps well-learned semantic memory, information deficits are still reported. For example, Evans, Brennan, Skorpovich, and Held (1984) asked subjects to recall the buildings from a familiar part of their city and to place the buildings on a schematic map. Older people were poorer than their younger counterparts on both tasks, despite the fact that the older adults were quite familiar with the areas in question. One note of caution here is that there may be a difference between the abstract ability to recall spatial information, and the ability to use familiar spatial cues in real-life navigation. Older people may well be less impaired (or not impaired at all) on the latter class of tasks. If so, such a contrast would fit with the well-established finding of greater age-related declines in explicit than implicit memory (see Craik & Jennings, 1992, for a review).

Remote memory

The assessment of memories from the remote past presents some interesting methodological challenges. Older adults often contrast their "vivid recollection" of things that happened to them as children or as young adults with their "hazy" memory for things that happened only hours or days before. But, the vivid memory from 50 years ago is likely to be of some salient event; it also is likely that the memory has been retrieved and relived many times, rather than being retrieved for the first time after 50 years. These factors of selection and repeated retrieval make it difficult to compare such remote memories with memories of more banal events from recent times. One solution is to use the diary method, in which people record daily events (without review) and then are tested on their memory for these personal events at a later time. The forgetting functions for these real-life events is an exponential multiplied by a power function (Rubin, 1982), but good data from older adults on this paradigm still are needed. In a second method, participants are presented with a single word and are asked to describe a personal memory that is evoked by the word. The evoked memories are then dated as accurately as possible. Rubin, Wetzler, and Nebes (1986) found that the frequency per hour of such generated memories declines steadily from the present to 20 years ago, and that the forgetting functions were similar for subjects in their twenties and those in their seventies. In addition, there is an overrepresented "bump" of memories from the period of 10 to 30 years of age, suggesting either that this period is particularly rich in salient life events, or perhaps that many events around this time have emotional connotations and therefore are particularly well encoded.

An alternative approach to the study of remote memories is to deal with verifiable public events rather than with personal autobiographical memories. This technique obviously is more objective, but it may fail to capture some aspects of personal memories: the involvement of self, and the emotional interactions of self with others, for example. Nonetheless, studies by Warrington and Sanders (1971) and by Squire (1989) both showed the same general pattern as that reported by Rubin et al. (1986); namely, remembering declined with the remoteness of the event, and the decline was equivalent for younger and older adults.

Truth effect

A final topic with some practical implications is the tendency for people to rate repeated statements as being more valid and believable than statements presented only once (Zajonc, 1968). In the literature on marketing, this tendency is known as the *truth effect*, the perceived validity of an advertisement or a marketing claim increases with repetition (Hasher, Goldstein, & Toppino, 1977). Although little work has been done on this topic with respect to possible age differences, one study by Law, Hawkins, and Craik (1998) showed that the effect is exaggerated in older adults. This could mean that older people may be more susceptible to agreeing with political or marketing statements that are repeated during the course of a broadcast or marketing survey.

In general, the literature on age-related differences in semantic memory suggests that, when questionnaires deal with the recollection of public events, younger and older adults show the same tendency to forget incidents or people as the time interval increases. Older adults typically perform somewhat less well in absolute terms, especially when the sought-for information is very specific as with names of people and places. Remote personal memories (however sincerely believed) are liable to distortion after repeated reproductions (Bartlett, 1932). Factual information can be primed and made more accessible by recent use, so another caveat for researchers concerns the differential likelihood that people of different ages may have dealt recently with the information in question. Finally, contextual details appear to be particularly vulnerable to the effects of aging.

Conclusion

This brief survey of the literature on aging and memory makes it clear that researchers and professionals dealing with older people should be aware of a number of results in this area when designing or administrating questionnaires. Some effects are predictable and obvious, others less so. In the former category, it should be expected that older people might be less accurate in recalling recent events, especially those involving specific details of time and place. Similarly, common sense should guard against giving long and complex instructions or questions in a telephone interview. In the category of less obvious pitfalls, priming effects may have a greater biasing effect on older respondents; as mentioned above, the provision of "helpful" examples may bias older respondents in their choice of answers. Reduced perceptual clarity (either reduced visual contrast or a noisy telephone line) may reduce immediate memory for initial alternatives in a multiple choice format. Both this factor and the decline in WM capacity are likely to bias answers toward the most recent alternative presented. Finally, repetition of information may result in that information being viewed more favorably (the "mere exposure" effect reported by Zajonc, 1968) or being misattributed to some external source (the "false fame" effect reported by Dywan & Jacoby, 1990).

Safeguards against these sources of bias include such obvious measures as counterbalancing the order of questions or alternative answers, confirming answers by checking with relatives, providing supportive context whenever possible, and reducing the involvement of WM and episodic recall. These measures may not always be practicable, of course, but by being aware of possible sources of bias stemming from age-related memory impairments, researchers at least will be able to interpret the responses of older participants with appropriate caution.

References

Atkinson, R. C., & Shiffrin, R. M. (1968). Human memory: A proposed system and its control processes. In K. W. Spence & J. T. Spence (Eds.), *The psychology of learning and motivation* (Vol. 2, pp. 89–195). New York: Academic Press.

Baddeley, A. D., & Hitch, G. J. (1974). Working memory. In G. H. Bower (Ed.), *The psychology of learning and motivation* (Vol. 8, pp. 47–90). New York: Academic Press.

Baddeley, A. D., & Warrington, E. K. (1970). Amnesia and the distinction between long- and short-term memory. *Journal of Verbal Learning and Verbal Behavior, 9,* 176–189.

Bartlett, F. C. (1932). *Remembering: A study in experimental and social psychology.* Cambridge, England: Cambridge University Press.

Bransford, J. D., Franks, J. J., Morris, C. D., & Stein, B. S. (1979). Some general constraints on learning and memory research. In L. S. Cermak & F. I. M. Craik (Eds.), *Levels of processing in human memory* (pp. 331–354). Hillsdale, NJ: Erlbaum.

Burke, D. M., MacKay, D. G., Worthley, J. S., & Wade, E. (1991). On the tip of the tongue: What causes word finding failures in young and older adults? *Journal of Memory and Language, 30,* 542–579.

Cermak, L. A. (1984). The episodic/semantic distinction in amnesia. In N. Butters & L. R. Squire (Eds.), *The neuropsychology of memory* (pp. 55–62). New York: Guilford Press.

Chalfonte, B. L., & Johnson, M. K. (1995). Feature memory and binding in young and older adults. *Memory and Cognition, 24,* 403–416.

Cherry, K. E., & Park, D. C. (1993). Individual difference and contextual variables influence spatial memory in younger and older adults. *Psychology and Aging, 8,* 517–526.

Cohen, G., & Faulkner, D. (1986). Memory for proper names: Age differences in retrieval. *British Journal of Developmental Psychology, 4,* 187–197.

Craik, F. I. M. (1977). Age differences in human memory. In J. E. Birren & K. W. Schaie (Eds.), *Handbook of the psychology of aging* (pp. 384–420). New York: Van Nostrand Reinhold.

Craik, F. I. M., & Byrd, M. (1982). Aging and cognitive deficits: The role of attentional resources. In F. I. M. Craik & S. Trehub (Eds.), *Aging and cognitive processes* (pp. 191–211). New York: Plenum Press.

Craik, F. I. M., Byrd, M., & Swanson, J. M. (1987). Patterns of memory loss in three elderly samples. *Psychology and Aging, 2,* 79–86.

Craik, F. I. M., & Jennings, J. M. (1992). Human memory. In F. I. M. Craik & T. A. Salthouse (Eds.), *The handbook of aging and cognition* (pp. 51–110). Hillsdale, NJ: Erlbaum.

Craik, F. I. M., Morris, L. W., Morris, R. G., & Loewen, E. R. (1990). Relations between source amnesia and frontal lobe functioning in older adults. *Psychology and Aging, 5,* 148–151.

Craik, F. I. M., Morris, R. G., & Gick, M. L. (1990). Adult age differences in working memory. In G. Vallar & T. Shallice (Eds.), *Neuropsychological impairments of short-term memory* (pp. 247–267). Cambridge, England: Cambridge University Press.

Craik, F. I. M., & Rabinowitz, J. C. (1984). Age differences in the acquisition and use of verbal information: A tutorial review. In H. Bouma & D. E. Bouwhuis (Eds.), *Attention and performance* (Vol. 10, pp. 471–499). Hillsdale, NJ: Erlbaum.

Daneman, M., & Carpenter, P. A. (1980). Individual differences in working memory and reading. *Journal of Verbal Learning and Verbal Behavior, 19,* 450–466.

Delbecq-Derouesne, J., & Beauvois, M. F. (1989). Memory processes and aging: A defect of automatic rather than controlled processes? *Archives of Gerontology and Geriatrics, 1*(Suppl. 1), 121–150.

Dixon, R. A., & Bäckman, L. (1995). *Compensating for psychological deficits and declines: Managing losses and promoting gains.* Mahwah, NJ: Erlbaum.

Dobbs, A. R., & Rule, B. G. (1989). Adult age differences in working memory. *Psychology and Aging, 4,* 500–503.

Dywan, J., & Jacoby, L. L. (1990). Effects of aging on source monitoring: Differences in susceptibility to false fame. *Psychology and Aging, 5,* 379–387.

Evans, G. W., Brennan, P. L., Skorpovich, M. A., & Held, D. (1984). Cognitive mapping and elderly adults: Verbal and location memory for urban landmarks. *Journal of Gerontology, 39,* 452–457.

Gick, M. L., Craik, F. I. M., & Morris, R. G. (1988). Task complexity and age differences in working memory. *Memory and Cognition, 16,* 353–361.

Gilmore, G. C., Thomas, C. W., Klitz, T., Persanyi, M. W., & Tomsak, R. (1996). Contrast enhancement eliminates letter identification speed deficits in Alzheimer's disease. *Journals of Clinical Geropsychology, 2,* 307–320.

Hasher, L., Goldstein, D., & Toppino, T. (1977). Frequency and the conference of referential validity. *Journal of Verbal Learning and Verbal Behavior, 16,* 107–112.

Hasher, L., & Zacks, R. T. (1988). Working memory, comprehension, and aging: A review and a new view. In G. H. Bower (Ed.), *The psychology of learning and motivation* (Vol. 2, pp. 193–225). San Diego, CA: Academic Press.

Howard, D. V. (1988). The priming of semantic and episodic memories. In L. L. Light & D. M. Burke (Eds.), *Language, memory, and aging* (pp. 77–100). New York: Cambridge University Press.

Inman, V. W., & Parkinson, S. R. (1983). Differences in Brown-Peterson recall as a function of age and retention interval. *Journal of Gerontology, 38,* 58–64.

Jacoby, L. L. (1991). A process dissociation framework: Separating automatic from intentional uses of memory. *Journal of Memory and Language, 30,* 513–541.

Jacoby, L. L., & Witherspoon, D. (1982). Remembering without awareness. *Canadian Journal of Psychology, 36,* 300–324.

Jennings, J. M., & Jacoby, L. L. (1997). An opposition procedure for detecting age-related deficits in recollection: Telling effects of repetition. *Psychology and Aging, 12,* 352–361.

Johnson, M. K., & Chalfonte, B. L. (1994). Binding complex memories: The role of reactivation and the hippocampus. In D. L. Schacter & E. Tulving (Eds.), *Memory systems 1994* (pp. 311–350). Cambridge, MA: MIT Press.

Koriat, A., Ben-Zur, H., & Sheffer, D. (1988). Telling the same story twice: Output monitoring and age. *Journal of Memory and Language, 27,* 23–39.

Laver, G. D., & Burke, D. M. (1993). Why do semantic priming effects increase in old age? A meta-analysis. *Psychology and Aging, 8,* 34–43.

Law, S., Hawkins, S. A., & Craik, F. I. M. (1998). Repetition-induced belief in the elderly: Rehabilitating age-related memory deficits. *Journal of Consumer Research, 25,* 91–107 .

Light, L. L. (1991). Memory and aging: Four hypotheses in search of data. *Annual Review of Psychology, 42,* 333–376.

Light, L. L. (1992). The organization of memory in old age. In F. I. M. Craik & T. A. Salthouse (Eds.), *The handbook of aging and cognition* (pp. 111–165). Hillsdale, NJ: Erlbaum.

Light, L. L., & Burke, D. M. (1988). Patterns of language and memory in old age. In L. L. Light & D. M. Burke (Eds.), *Language, memory, and aging* (pp. 244–271). New York: Cambridge University Press.

Light, L. L., & LaVoie, D. (1993). Direct and indirect measures of memory in old age. In P. Graf & M. E. J. Masson (Eds.), *Implicit memory: New directions in cognition, development, and neuropsychology* (pp. 207–230). Hillsdale, NJ: Erlbaum.

Light, L. L., & Singh, A. (1987). Implicit and explicit memory in young and older adults. *Journal of Experimental Psychology: Learning, Memory, and Cognition, 13,* 531–541.

Lindenberger, U., & Baltes, P. B. (1994). Sensory functioning and intelligence in old age: A strong connection. *Psychology and Aging, 9,* 339–355.

Maylor, E. A. (1990). Age and prospective memory. *Quarterly Journal of Experimental Psychology, 42A,* 471–493.

McIntyre, J. S., & Craik, F. I. M. (1987). Age differences in memory for item and source information. *Canadian Journal of Psychology, 41,* 175–192.

McKoon, G., Ratcliff, R., & Dell, G. S. (1986). A critical evaluation of the semantic-episodic distinction. *Journal of Experimental Psychology: Learning, Memory, and Cognition, 12,* 295–306.

Milner, B., Corkin, S., & Teuber, H. L. (1968). Further analysis of the hippocampal amnesic syndrome: 14 year follow-up study of H.M. *Neuropsychologia, 6,* 215–234.

Murdock, B. B. (1967). Recent developments in short-term memory. *British Journal of Psychology, 58,* 421–433.

Murphy, D. R., Craik, F. I. M., Li, K. Z. N., & Schneider, B. A. (in press). Comparing the effects of aging and background noise on short-term memory performances. *Psychology and Aging.*

Park, D. C., Cherry, K. E., Smith, A. D., & Lafronza, V. N. (1990). Effects of distinctive context on memory for objects and their locations in young and elderly adults. *Psychology and Aging, 5,* 250–255.

Park, D. C., & Shaw, R. J. (1992). Effect of environmental support on implicit and explicit memory in younger and older adults. *Psychology and Aging, 7,* 632–642.

Parkinson, S. R., Lindholm, J. M., & Inman, V. W. (1982). An analysis of age differences in immediate recall. *Journal of Gerontology, 37,* 425–431.

Pichora-Fuller, K., Schneider, B., & Daneman, M. (1995). How young and old adults listen to and remember speech in noise. *Journal of Acoustical Society of America, 97,* 593–608.

Rubin, D. C. (1982). On the retention function for autobiographical memory. *Journal of Verbal Learning and Verbal Behavior, 21,* 21–38.

Rubin, D. C., Wetzler, S. E., & Nebes, R. D. (1986). Autobiographical memory across the lifespan. In D. C. Rubin (Ed.), *Autobiographical memory* (pp. 202–221). Cambridge, England: Cambridge University Press.

Salthouse, T. A. (1982). *Adult cognition: An experimental psychology of human aging.* New York: Springer-Verlag.

Salthouse, T. A. (1991). *Theoretical perspectives on cognitive aging.* Hillsdale, NJ: Erlbaum.

Salthouse, T. A. (1993). Speed mediation of adult age differences in cognition. *Developmental Psychology, 29,* 722–738.

Salthouse, T. A., Mitchell, D. R., Skovronek, E., & Babcock, R. L. (1989). Effects of adult age and working memory on reasoning and spatial abilities. *Journal of Experimental Psychology: Learning, Memory, and Cognition, 15,* 507–516.

Schacter, D. L., Harbluk, J. L., & McLachlan, D. (1984). Retrieval without recollection: An experimental analysis of source amnesia. *Journal of Verbal Learning and Verbal Behavior, 23,* 593–611.

Schacter, D. L., Koutstaal, W. E., & Norman, K. A. (1997). False memories and aging. *Trends in Cognitive Sciences, 1,* 229–236.

Schacter, D. L., & Tulving, E. (1994). What are the memory systems of 1994? In D. L. Schacter & E. Tulving (Eds.), *Memory systems 1994* (pp. 1–38). Cambridge, MA: MIT Press.

Schneider, B. A., & Pichora-Fuller, M.K. (1999). Implications of perceptual deterioration for cognitive aging research. In F. I. M. Craik & T. A. Salthouse (Eds.), *The handbook of aging and cognition* (2nd Ed.). Mahwah, NJ: Erlbaum.

Shaw, R. J., & Craik, F. I. M. (1989). Age differences in predictions and performance on a cued recall task. *Psychology and Aging, 4,* 131–135.

Spencer, W. D., & Raz, N. (1995). Differential effects of aging on memory for content and context: A meta-analysis. *Psychology and Aging, 10,* 527–539.

Spinks, R., Gilmore, G., & Thomas, C. (1996, April). *Age simulation of a sensory deficit does impair cognitive test performance.* Poster session presented at the Cognitive Aging Conference, Atlanta, GA.

Squire, L. R. (1989). On the course of forgetting in very long-term memory. *Journal of Experimental Psychology: Learning, Memory, and Cognition, 15,* 241–245.

Tulving, E. (1983). *Elements of episodic memory.* New York: Oxford University Press.

Tulving, E., Hayman, C. A. G., & Macdonald, C. A. (1991). Long-lasting perceptual priming and semantic learning in amnesia: A case experiment. *Journal of Experimental Psychology: Learning, Memory, and Cognition, 17,* 595–617.

Tulving, E., & Schacter, D. L. (1990). Priming and human memory systems. *Science, 247,* 301–306.

Uttl, B., & Graf, P. (1993). Episodic spatial memory in adulthood. *Psychology and Aging, 8,* 257–273.

Warrington, E. K., & Sanders, H. I. (1971). The fate of old memories. *Journal of Experimental Psychology, 23,* 432–442.

Waugh, N. C., & Norman, D. A. (1965). Primary memory. *Psychological Review, 72,* 89–104.

Wickens, C. D. (1984). Processing resources in attention. In R. Parasuraman & D. R. Davies (Eds.), *Varieties of Attention* (pp. 63–102). Orlando, FL: Academic Press.

Wingfield, A., Alexander, A. H., & Cavigelli, S. (1994). Does memory constrain utilization of top-down information in spoken word recognition? Evidence from normal aging. *Language and Speech, 37,* 221–235.

Wingfield, A., Stine, E. A., Lahar, C. J., & Aberdeen, J. S. (1988). Does the capacity of working memory change with age? *Experimental Aging Research, 14,* 103–107.

Zacks, R. T., & Hasher, L. (1988). Capacity theory and the processing of inferences. In L. L. Light & D. M. Burke (Eds.), *Language, memory, and aging* (pp. 154–170). New York: Cambridge University Press.

Zacks, R. T., Hasher, L., & Li, K. Z. H. (1999). Human memory. In F. I. M. Craik & T. A. Salthouse (Eds.), *The handbook of aging and cognition* (2nd Ed.). Mahwah, NJ: Erlbaum.

Zajonc, R. B. (1968). Attitudinal effects of mere exposure. *Journal of Personality and Social Psychology, 9,* 1–27.

Zelinski, E. M., & Light, L. L. (1988). Young and older adults' use of context in spatial memory. *Psychology and Aging, 3,* 99–101.

Cognitive neuropsychology of the aging brain 6

Patricia A. Reuter-Lorenz

Aging brings widespread changes in cognitive function. Some cognitive changes may stem from global alterations in brain function; others may result from localized decline of specific neural structures. The neuropsychology of aging must distinguish between these sources of age-related decline and specify the neural mechanisms that underlie cognitive change. With the availability of high-resolution neuroimaging methods, cognitive modeling techniques, and comparisons with focal brain damage, neuropsychologists are well positioned to meet this challenge. The evidence that is beginning to emerge from these combined approaches has the potential to transform our understanding of the aging process.

This chapter summarizes major theories and bodies of evidence linking cognitive changes in aging to their underlying neural substrates. Because the coverage is broad in scope, the scientific review is selective. Numerous references are made to additional works offering further analyses of the major issues discussed in each section. We begin with an overview of cortical organization, introducing relevant terminology, the prominent features of gross cortical anatomy, and some general challenges entailed in relating brain structure to cognitive function. Once the goals of a cognitive neuropsychological approach to aging are summarized, we turn to the empirical review of the field.

Brain structure and the effects of age

The two cortical hemispheres each contain four major lobes that contribute specific processes to the overall repertoire of human thought and be-

The preparation of this chapter was supported by grant AG13027 from the National Institute on Aging. The assistance of Joseph Mikels, Marti Smith, and Richard Bryk is gratefully acknowledged.

havior (see Figure 6.1). The occipital lobes at the very back (posterior) of the brain contain the first or primary cortical regions for vision, along with secondary visual and association areas that process the output from primary visual cortex. The basic hierarchy of primary, secondary, and association cortices exists in the temporal lobes for auditory processing and in the parietal lobes, where somatosensory input is processed from the body surface. Regions at the junction of occipital, parietal, and temporal cortices integrate input from multiple sensory modalities and can be influenced by goals, emotional-attentional state, and body position in the environment. In the front (anterior) of the brain are the frontal lobes. At their most posterior boundary, adjacent to parietal cortex, is the motor strip, which contains the neural machinery for sending motor commands to the body. In right-handers, Broca's area is in the left frontal cortex just anterior to the motor strip. This region is known to play a vital role in the planning and programming of language. Other frontal subregions have reciprocal connections to secondary and association cortices of all modalities and to subcortical centers, such as the thalamus, hippocampus, and amygdala, that are involved in emotion and memory. The frontal lobes are therefore thought to reside at the top of the information-processing hierarchy where they can modulate (i.e., inhibit or promote) neural operations in other brain regions in accord with current intentions, goals, and plans.

Under a microscope, the six layers of cortex can be seen to vary in thickness and cell density depending on the function of each cortical region. A neuroanatomist named Brodmann, working at the turn of the previous century, classified 52 different subregions of cortex based on cytoarchitecture (see Figure 6.1). His numerical classifications are the most widely used reference system in human cognitive neuroscience. Brain areas also can be referred to by the sulci or gyri on which they reside or by their relative location within a particular lobe: toward the side (lateral), middle (medial), top (dorsal), or bottom (ventral).

Older (age 60 and up) and younger (age 18 to 35) brains differ physically. Sulci become more prominent as we age, due to cell loss in some regions and to the widespread shrinkage of brain tissue itself (Haug & Eggers, 1991). Reduced dendritic branching contributes to age-related atrophy and presumably affects the quality and efficiency of neuronal communication. Aging leads to reduced concentrations of neurotransmitters, especially dopamine, which contributes to frontal lobe functions and acetylcholine, which plays an important role in learning and memory (see, e.g., Woodruff-Pak, 1997). Intracellular changes and reduced cerebral blood flow compromise the brain's metabolic efficiency. Change in cerebral blood flow (i.e., hemodynamic changes) with age may complicate the interpretation of results from neuroimaging methods, such as positron emission tomography (PET) and functional magnetic resonance imaging (fMRI), which rely on blood flow to localize neural activity. In PET, a radioactive form of water is injected into the blood and the radioactive emissions from the decaying isotope signal blood flow changes that result from localized

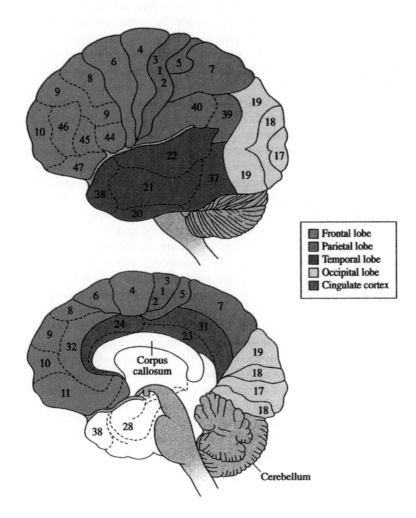

FIG. 6.1.
A lateral view of the left hemisphere and a medial view of the right hemisphere with the cytoarchitectonic fields of Brodmann delimited. The four major lobes are color coded in both views, and cingulate cortex and the corpus callosum are visible from the medial view. Reprinted with permission from Damasio (1995).

changes in neural activity. The fMRI technique detects changes in the magnetic properties of blood that result from localized neural activity. An active area of neuroimaging research aims to distinguish between age differences that are due to hemodynamic factors from those that reflect neurocognitive changes (e.g., D'Esposito, Zarahn, Aguirre, & Rympa, 1999; Ross et al., 1997).

Given the brain's structural diversity, it is not surprising that some regions age more than others. Postmortem studies and in vivo structural imaging studies reveal the greatest atrophy in the hippocampus, dorsolateral prefrontal cortex, and portions of the cerebellum (Raz, in press). But, as the past century of behavioral brain science tells us, the correspondence between structure and function is not perfect. Physical signs of regional dysfunction need not cause measurable deficits due, for example, to reorganization, compensatory processes, and strategy changes. Likewise, the neural substrates underlying behavioral or cognitive changes are not easy to identify. Mapping particular cognitive operations onto neural circuitry is difficult because our cognitive theories are imprecise, our behavioral measurements often are highly variable, and our neural measurements can be course and indirect. Nevertheless, converging evidence from multiple cognitive neuroscience approaches has led to significant advances toward understanding the neural bases of cognition.

What can we hope to learn from a neuropsychological approach to aging? There are several valuable and exciting goals. The first is to gain a deeper understanding of the cognitive abilities and mental operations that are most affected by aging. Drawing largely from purely behavioral studies, cognitive theories of aging offer competing views about whether processing speed, attentional resources, working memory, and other such cognitive constructs are at the root of cognitive aging effects. Studies that combine cognitive and neural methods (i.e., neurocognitive approaches) have the potential to adjudicate among competing accounts of age effects and to specify how and when particular mechanisms limit the performance of older adults. The second goal is to advance our understanding of the neural bases of cognitive function more generally. Neurocognitive studies of aging can inform cognitive theories just as studies of patients with focal brain lesions have advanced cognitive psychology, by testing theoretical assumptions and uncovering new phenomena for the theories to explain. Finally, and perhaps most optimistically, neurocognitive studies of aging may provide key insights into ways to combat aging's affect on cognition. There are new indications that the aging brain may engage compensatory processes that reduce performance decline. By identifying what is optimal in older brains, we stand a better chance of promoting the secrets of successful aging.

Right hemisphere aging

Differential decline of verbal and nonverbal abilities

The hypothesis that the right hemisphere ages more rapidly than the left was one of the original neuropsychological accounts of aging. This theory emerged during the 1970s when left brain–right brain research was at its peak, and it is still being tested today. A rich convergence of clinical evidence and studies of neurologically intact young adults revealed fundamental differences between the two hemispheres: the left hemisphere is dominant in most language tasks but is inferior to the right hemisphere on spatial tasks, such as drawing, copying complex configurations, making size, distance, and orientation judgments, and performing visual-motor tasks that require the construction and manipulation of forms (see Reuter-Lorenz & Miller, 1998, for a review).

These neuropsychological dichotomies gave new meaning to the widely recognized finding that age had a greater effect on nonverbal than on verbal intelligence. For example, when measured by a standardized test instrument like the Wechsler Adult Intelligence Scale ([WAIS]; e.g., Wechsler, 1981), verbal IQ begins to decline around age 60, whereas nonverbal (i.e., performance IQ) decline is evident as early as age 50 (e.g., Albert & Kaplan, 1979; Schaie & Schaie, 1977). Higher verbal than performance subscale scores also are found in patients with right hemisphere damage (Albert & Kaplan, 1979; Botwinick, 1977). Should we infer that the hemispheres age asymmetrically because nonverbal measures show greater decline with age? There are several reasons to refrain from this conclusion. First, when administered with standard procedures, the WAIS is not a suitable neuropsychological instrument for localizing neurological deficit (Kaplan, Fein, Morris, & Delis, 1991). Because there are many ways to do poorly on the performance IQ measures, right hemisphere patients and older adults could have similar scores but for very different reasons. Second, the verbal and performance subtests differ in a way that is critical to aging: the performance subtests are timed and the verbal tests are not. Because perceptual-motor slowing is a basic factor in cognitive aging (Salthouse, 1992), the performance subtests may be more sensitive to general aging effects than the verbal subtests.

So, what if verbal and nonverbal abilities were assessed with speeded response measures? If the verbal and nonverbal tasks were matched for overall difficulty, any age differences between them potentially could be linked to underlying brain mechanisms. Using this approach, Lawrence, Myerson, and Hale (1998) evaluated verbal and nonverbal decline in a large group of adults between age 18 and 90. The verbal tests included speeded lexical decisions, category decisions, and synonym-antonym decisions. The speeded visuospatial tasks included line length discrimination, shape classification, visual search, and design matching. They found that, across the life span, verbal processing times increased by approximately 50%, whereas visuospatial processing times increased by 500%! The authors attributed their results to basic differences between verbal and nonverbal processing rather than to hemispheric asymmetries in aging. However, theirs is precisely the outcome that the right hemisphere aging hypothesis would predict. Yet, one crucial difference between these verbal and nonverbal tasks suggests an alternative explanation. The nonverbal tasks required filtering out (i.e., ignoring) irrelevant properties in the stimulus display, whereas selective attention demands in the verbal tasks were minimal. Selective attention and inhibitory processing depend in part on the prefrontal cortex, which may be disproportionately affected by age (see below). Thus, we cannot determine the locus of dysfunction based only on the striking difference between verbal and nonverbal performance.

The inherent ambiguity of a purely behavioral approach stems from uncertainty about which processes the tasks are measuring. Even if the right hemisphere aging hypothesis is correct, verbal and nonverbal decline could appear to be equivalent if the respective tasks call on similar processes or, at least, processes that depend on the same hemisphere. For example, some nonverbal memory tasks may emphasize analytic or local processing when judgments are based on a component of a larger configuration (e.g., Salthouse, 1995). Such "local" level processing has been linked to the left hemisphere (see Ivry & Robertson, 1998; for a review), even with nonverbal materials. Likewise, mathematical processing may require either or both hemispheres, depending on a subject's strategy.

Differential age effects for verbal and nonverbal tasks also have been attributed to differential novelty of the materials, or of the tasks themselves. For example, defining words is more familiar than constructing block designs, and nonnameable shapes and configurations simply are less familiar than words and sentences. The longer one lives, the greater the familiarity difference becomes. Thus, when Tubi and Calev (1989) found poorer recall of geometric designs than words in older adults, and the opposite in the younger group, they suggested that a lifetime of familiarity with verbal materials makes them more resilient to age effects. Interpretive difficulties such as these motivated the use of more direct measures of hemispheric decline.

Laterality studies of right hemisphere aging

Hemispheric differences can be assessed using the technique of lateralized stimulus presentations, which exploit the neuroanatomical segregation of sensory input pathways from the ears and the eyes to the left and right sides of the brain. The left ear has more numerous connections to right primary auditory cortex, and the right ear has stronger projections to left auditory cortex. The visual modality is more complex because each eye projects to both hemispheres. When gazing straight ahead, everything positioned to the left of fixation falls in the left visual field and projects to right primary visual cortex. Likewise, everything to the right of fixation falls in the right visual field and projects to the left primary visual cortex (see Figure 6.2). The corpus callosum mediates the extensive integration of information from the left and right sides that takes place after primary sensory cortex. Nonetheless, the direct input from the sensory receptors to the contralateral hemisphere produces a measurable processing advantage relative to information conveyed indirectly via the callosum. In visual laterality studies, right-handers typically are faster and more accurate at identifying verbal items presented to the right visual field than to the left visual field. The right visual field advantage is thought to occur because information is presented directly to the hemisphere specialized for processing it, in this case, the left hemisphere for language processing. Similarly, a left visual field advantage for nonverbal materials can result from direct access to the right hemisphere where specialized processing occurs.

Two straightforward predictions of the right hemisphere-aging hypothesis can be tested with these techniques. First, verbal tasks yielding a right

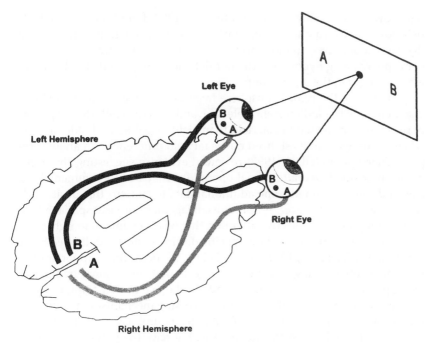

FIG. 6.2.
A schematic diagram of the projection of the left and right visual fields onto the opposite (contralateral) visual cortices. Reprinted with permission from Ivry and Robertson (1998).

ear or right visual field advantage in younger adults should produce a greater advantage in older adults if aging leads to greater right hemisphere decline. Second, on nonverbal tasks, right hemisphere aging should reduce the left ear or left visual field advantage found in the younger adult. Support for the right hemisphere aging hypothesis thus would entail an enhanced left hemisphere advantage on language tasks and a weaker right hemisphere advantage on spatial-nonverbal tasks in older adults relative to their younger counterparts. Alternatively, an absence of age differences in the magnitude of the hemisphere advantage for verbal and nonverbal tasks would challenge the validity of the right hemisphere aging hypothesis.

These predictions have not received strong support, and the right hemisphere aging hypothesis has fared poorly (see Nebes, 1990). For example, Nebes, Madden, and Berg (1983) tested verbal asymmetries by in a word-reading task with items presented to either the left or right visual field. In the nonverbal task designed to elicit a left field advantage, observers named the position of the hour hand on a clock face presented to one visual field or the other. Younger adults showed the expected pattern of visual field differences. The older group showed the same pattern, with field advantages that were approximately of the same magnitude. More recently, Cherry, Hellige, and McDowd (1995) used a visually presented consonant-vowel-consonant task requiring the participants to name aloud the syllable presented on each trial. Older participants performed slightly worse overall, but there was no age difference in the magnitude of the right visual field advantage. Finally, Hoyer and Rybash (1992) found the expected left field advantage on a visual-spatial task that required coordinate judgments (Kosslyn et al., 1989) in older and younger groups. Contrary to the right hemisphere aging hypothesis, the left field advantage tended to be somewhat stronger in the older group.

In favor of the right hemisphere hypothesis, a recent study of object discrimination by Gerhardstein, Peterson, and Rapcsak (1998) found poorer performance in the left visual field than right visual field of older adults, whereas younger adults showed no visual field differences. In another report, Cherry and Hellige (1999) reviewed evidence suggesting that right hemisphere–mediated attentional operations may be more vulnerable to age, and they presented some additional data to support this position. It should be noted, however, that the disengagement of visuospatial attention, a component of selective attention that has been linked to right parietal mechanisms, does not show specific decline in older adults (see Faust & Balota, 1997; Hartley, 1992). Nevertheless, the occasional support for the right hemisphere aging hypothesis suggests that the original framing of the hypothesis was certainly too broad. To the extent that aging is asymmetrical, it is more likely that specific processing mechanisms are affected rather than an entire hemisphere. Functional neuroimaging methods have not yet been used to test this hypothesis, but have the potential to reveal selective aging of right hemisphere mechanisms if it exists. Resolution of these questions awaits future research.

Aging and the neuropsychology of long-term memory

Medial temporal lobe dysfunction in aging

Elderly adults frequently complain of poor memory, and cognitive studies show that they are right: memory declines with age. Yet, twentieth century psychology has taught us that memory is not a single, unitary entity. There are several dissociable types of memory that are mediated by different neural structures and subsystems. Does aging have an equivalent effect on all of them? Or, are aging effects selective, impairing some memory subsystems more than others? These questions have been addressed by comparing the performance of older adults the patterns of deficit and sparing in amnesia due to known focal damage of memory areas in medial temporal lobe regions or the frontal lobes.

Medial temporal lobe amnesia, characterized by patient H.M. (Scoville & Milner, 1957), is the paragon of memory dysfunction. After bilateral surgical removal of the medial temporal lobe structures (hippocampus, entorhinal cortex, parahippocampal gyrus, and portions of temporal cortex), H.M. was left with normal intelligence and normal immediate memory while being virtually unable to learn anything new. His anterograde amnesia affected all types of information, including facts and events (semantic memories) and personal experiences (episodic memories), and was evident on tests of recognition and recall. These memory measures require the conscious recollection of prior learning experiences and have been described as tapping declarative or explicit memory. H.M.'s performance was relatively intact on some implicit memory tests that did not require the explicit recollection of items acquired during a particular learning episode. He could acquire some new skills, such as mirror drawing and backward reading, and he could be classically conditioned. He retained his childhood or remote memories, although his ability to remember the 10 years or so prior to the surgery was compromised.

This basic profile of an inability to retain new episodic and semantic memories over a long delay, together with relatively spared immediate memory, implicit and procedural knowledge, and remote memory, also is evident in patients with damage to the diencephalon. Does it also characterize the memory performance of normal older adults? Bear in mind that our comparisons are qualitative. H.M and other neurological cases have had frank damage to the memory circuitry. The physical effects of normal aging are less dramatic, and so the functional consequences should be quantitatively less than in neurological patients. But, is the pattern the same? The similarities and differences both are informative about the neural basis of memory decline with age (see Prull, Gabrieli, & Bunge [in press] for a review).

Consistent with medial temporal lobe dysfunction, age-related memory decline is evident when explicit measures of delayed recall and recognition are used to probe new verbal and nonverbal learning (Craik & Jennings, 1992). As in medial temporal lobe amnesia, immediate memory and implicit memory evident on certain priming tasks (e.g., perceptual word identification, fragment completion) are far less affected by aging (see Light & Lavoie, 1993; Moscovitch & Winocur, 1995, for reviews). Some implicit tests, such as word-stem completion and classical conditioning, do show aging effects, however, and suggest that age-related decline in memory cannot be fully accounted for by medial temporal lobe dysfunction. According to Moscovitch and Winocur (1995), stem completion engages strategic processing that recruits frontal lobe mechanisms which decline with age. Age-related impairment in classical conditioning has been linked to altered cerebellar functioning in the older brain (Woodruff-Pak, 1997).

One way to characterize the comparison between aging and medial temporal lobe amnesia, then, is that the latter is more severe but also more specific. That is, aging affects new declarative episodic and semantic memories, but its effects also go beyond these types of memory. How, then, do we know that declarative memory loss in aging arises from medial temporal dysfunction rather than generalized neural decline with age? The structural evidence for circumscribed cell loss in the hippocampal formation has implicated a specific role for this structure in age-related memory loss (Simic, Kostovic, Winbald, & Bagdanovitch, 1997; see Morrison & Hof, 1997, for a review). Moreover, greater hippocampal atrophy has been found in individuals with poorer delayed recall, even when the effects of general cortical atrophy were statistically controlled (Golomb et al., 1994; Raz, Gunning-Dixon, Head, Dupuis, & Acker, 1998).

Furthermore, electrophysiological and neuroimaging evidence has revealed age-related changes in medial temporal lobe activity during memory tasks. Electrophysiological recordings from scalp electrodes have revealed an age difference in the event-related potential component known as the N4 (Nielsen-Bohlman & Knight, 1995). This potential is thought to be generated by medial temporal structures, and it was significantly reduced in older adults attempting to recognize an item after a long delay. Older adults also performed more poorly than younger adults, but only in the long delay condition. In a neuroimaging study using PET, Grady and her colleagues (1995) measured brain activity while older and younger adults studied faces and then retrieved them from long-term memory. Compared to younger adults, the older group showed less right hippocampal activity during the study phase (encoding). Age differences in frontal activation also were evident and these are discussed below. Thus, some aspects of age-related memory loss can be linked to alterations in medial temporal lobe activity; however, other brain regions, including the frontal lobes, also have been implicated.

Frontal lobe contributions to content memory and aging

Comprising approximately one third of the cortical mantle, the human frontal lobes are heterogeneous structures containing more than 10 different cytoarchitectonic regions with unique patterns of cortical and subcortical connectivity. As the likely seat of those capacities that set humans apart from other species, the frontal lobes are an important frontier for cognitive neuroscience. The hallmarks of frontal dysfunction include deficits in planning, initiating, and carrying out new goal-directed behaviors and inhibiting inappropriate behaviors (Fuster, 1989; Luria, 1966). Recent work also has shown an important role of the frontal lobes in memory processes, and suggests that a decline in these functions contribute to age-related changes in declarative memory. Understanding these contributions requires that we distinguish between memory for content (what has occurred) and memory for context (where and when it occurred). Studies of patients with focal frontal lobe lesions have indicated that prefrontal cortex makes separable contributions to both content and context memory (e.g., Moscovitch & Winocur, 1995; Prull et al., in press). Neuroimaging studies have corroborated this result and demonstrated that prefrontal correlates of these aspects of memory are affected by age. We first consider prefrontal contributions to the encoding and retrieval of content memory.

In 1994, Tulving and his colleagues reported prominent left frontal activation in PET measurements taken when young participants were studying items in a long-term memory task (Kapur et al., 1994; Tulving, Kapur,

Craik, Moscovitch, & Houle, 1994). Moreover, the magnitude of left frontal activation (Brodmann's Area [BAs] 45/46, 47/10) was greater when study instructions emphasized forming semantic associations, which improved memory performance. Frontal activation also was prominent during memory retrieval, but here it was right lateralized (BAs 10, 46, 44, 6). This pattern of frontal asymmetry characterizes verbal and nonverbal long-term memory and is referred to as hemispheric encoding-retrieval asymmetry ([HERA]; Tulving et al., 1994).

Several studies now indicate a pronounced departure from the HERA pattern in older adults. Grady (1995) were the first to report that older adults did not activate left inferior prefrontal cortex while studying faces. As noted above, this experiment also found less right hippocampal activation in older adults. It is unlikely, however, that these age differences were due to generalized hemodynamic decline or atrophy (see Raz, in press), because some brain regions were equally active in younger and older adults. In particular, Grady et al. found significant right frontal activation in both groups during the recognition phase. Grady et al. attributed the poorer face recognition performance in the older group to the failure to activate left prefrontal sites during the study phase. This may reflect inadequate encoding strategies, which, in turn, may lead to poor memory in older adults (see Schacter, Savage, Alpert, Rauch, & Albert, 1996).

Age-related decreases in prefrontal activation during encoding have been replicated in subsequent studies that also have found age differences in retrieval activations (Cabeza et al., 1997a; see also Schacter et al., 1996). Cabeza (1997a, in press) reported less right frontal activation during retrieval in older than younger adults. However, unlike young adults, older adults also showed left frontal activation during retrieval. Other studies have corroborated this tendency toward bilateral activation in older adults (Cabeza et al., in press; Madden et al., 1999), raising some interesting hypotheses about age effects on the brain. One possibility is that older adults attempt the right frontal retrieval operations used by younger adults, but older adults also must recruit left hemisphere sites to compensate for right frontal deficiencies. Alternatively, older adults could be using different retrieval strategies than younger adults, and the left hemisphere activation may reflect this difference. A further possibility is that impaired interactions between brain regions in older adults lead to the inappropriate activation of left hemisphere sites, which consequently disrupts performance.

To summarize, aging is associated with altered patterns of activation in the prefrontal regions that have been linked in younger adults to the semantic encoding and explicit retrieval of information from long-term memory. While our understanding of the particular memory contributions of these areas is incomplete, organizational and strategic aspects of encoding and retrieval seem to depend on the frontal lobes (e.g., Moscovitch & Winocur, 1995). Age-related changes in prefrontal activity are likely to alter the interactions across a network of brain regions involved in these aspects of memory encoding and retrieval (see Cabeza, McIntosh, Tulving,

Nyberg, & Grady, 1997b), including the hippocampus and related structures, as well as modality-specific or material-specific processing areas located more posteriorly in the brain.

Frontal lobe contributions to context memory and aging

Patients with damage to prefrontal cortex have difficulty remembering context information—where and when they have learned new things. In laboratory tests, for example, frontal lobe patients were poor at remembering whether a word they studied was read by a male or female voice, or presented in the auditory or visual modality, even when their recognition and recall memory for the items themselves was relatively spared (Janowsky, Shimamura, & Squire, 1989; Schacter, Kaszniak, Kihlstrom, & Valdiserri, 1991). Frontal damage also disrupts memory for temporal context such that patients have difficulty judging which item they learned more recently (McAndrews & Milner, 1991; Shimamura, Janowsky, & Squire, 1990).

Some older adults also are impaired at remembering the source or recency of information that they successfully recognize (Craik, Morris, Morris, & Loewen, 1990; Fabiani & Friedman, 1997; Schacter et al., 1991; Spencer & Raz, 1994, 1995), and several lines of evidence have suggested that frontal dysfunction underlies this pattern. First, contextual memory deficits have been found to correlate with impairment on certain psychometric tests of frontal lobe dysfunction (Craik et al., 1990; Parkin, Walter, & Hunkin, 1995; c.f., Degl' Innocenti & Backman, 1996). Comparing recognition and recency memory for pictures, Fabiani and Friedman (1997) observed that older adults were markedly impaired compared to young adults when judging recency, whereas recognition performance did not differ between the two groups. Of importance, recency errors correlated with errors on the Wisconsin Card Sort Test (WCST) of frontal lobe function, whereas recognition errors did not. Similar results also have been found for tests of source memory (Spencer & Raz, 1994).

Second, electrophysiological evidence has linked age-related changes in frontal function to impaired contextual memory. Trott, Friedman, Ritter, and Fabiani (1997) found greater decrements in source memory than item memory in older adults. Electrophysiological measures showed that frontal activity associated with source memory in younger adults was absent in the older group. Finally, a recent PET study found greater right prefrontal activation (BA 10) for temporal order retrieval than for item retrieval, but only in younger adults (Cabeza et al., in press). Cabeza and colleagues pointed out that this result could reveal the role of frontal cortex in temporal order memory per se, or it could reflect greater working memory, attention, or inhibitory demands of recency judgments. Future research can distinguish these possibilities. Frontal regions do indeed contribute to these other capacities, which also show age-related declines.

Frontal contributions to working memory, executive functions, and aging

Beyond its role in explicit memory for content and context, prefrontal cortex has been implicated in a variety of other cognitive abilities, which are commonly referred to as executive functions. These include planning a sequence of processes to complete a goal, the inhibition of distracting events and prepotent responses, and the management of multiple tasks or the subprocesses that make up complex tasks (see Smith & Jonides, 1999, for a review). Regions of frontal cortex also contribute to the short-term (i.e., less than 30 seconds) storage of information that can be used in problem solving and in such tasks as anagrams or mental arithmetic. These entail "working memory," which is thought to have storage (short-term memory) and executive processing components, all of which rely in part on various mechanisms within frontal cortex.

A wealth of behavioral evidence has indicated that working memory and inhibitory processes decline with age (see Park, chapter 1 in this volume, for a review). However, the tasks used to measure these constructs vary greatly from one study to the next, and often are sufficiently complex to rely on numerous other processes that are not specifically "frontal" but also could be affected by aging. Converging evidence from cognitive neuroscience is essential to determine whether the age differences in working memory and executive processes that are measured behaviorally result from frontal dysfunction. Recent reviews by Moscovitch and Winocur (1995) and by R. L. West (1996) detailed the parallels between the performance of patients with frontal damage and the effects of aging on tests such as self-ordered pointing, the Stroop color-word task, and measures of verbal fluency. Here, we review several lines of work on short-term memory and inhibition that offer further evidence for changes in frontal lobe functioning with age.

In the primate literature, the delayed matching-to-sample task has been used widely to measure frontal function. Typically, the animal views two food wells, one of which is baited. The wells are then covered, hidden from view for a few seconds, after which the animal must select the correct well to obtain the reward. Lesions to dorsolateral prefrontal cortex impair performance on this task. Single-unit recordings and lesion studies led Goldman-Rakic (1992) to propose that prefrontal regions are essential to retaining information over a delay. This conclusion is supported by neuroimaging work with humans using verbal and nonverbal materials (e.g., letters and spatial locations). Prefrontal sites (BAs 9, 46, 44, 45, 6), along with parietal sites (BAs 7 and 40), are active during short-term memory, with a predominance of left hemisphere activation for verbal tasks and right hemisphere activation for nonverbal tasks (Smith, Jonides, & Koeppe, 1996).

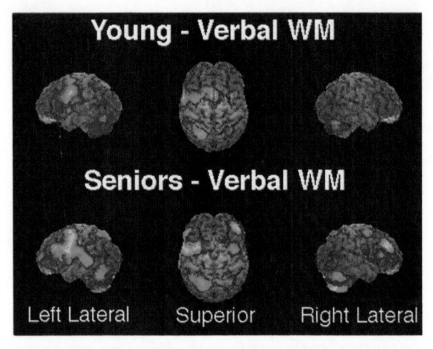

and parietal cortex (BA 7, 40). The activations in the older group appear more robust, but this is due to the greater number of participants in this group. Nevertheless, the different patterns of activation are evident, with greater anterior right hemisphere activation in the older group, and predominantly left lateralized activity in the younger group. The age differences are centered in the activity of frontal regions.

In general, short-term memory is less affected by age than either long-term memory or working memory tasks that require information manipulation and processing (Craik & Jennings, 1992). Nonetheless, the small but reliable age differences on short-term memory tasks suggests that storage operations may be compromised by age—a possibility supported by recent electrophysiological and neuroimaging studies. For example, in an experiment by Chao and Knight (1997a), three identifiable sounds (e.g., dog bark, bell, siren) were followed by a 2.5-second interval and then a probe. Participants indicated whether the probe matched one of the previous three sounds. Stimulus volume was adjusted for each subject individually, using audiometric techniques to compensate for hearing loss in the older group. Nevertheless, older adults erred more on this task than younger adults. Moreover, the most prominent electrophysiological age difference was the reduced amplitude in older adults of a frontally generated electrical signal known as sustained frontal negativity (SFN). Because the SFN has been linked to auditory attention, these results suggest an age-related dysfunction in the attentional requirements of short-term memory.

Neuroimaging studies of short-term memory also have revealed prominent age differences in frontal sites (Grady et al., 1998; Jonides et al., in press; Reuter-Lorenz, Jonides, et al., in press). Reuter-Lorenz, Jonides, et al. (in press) found the expected predominance of left-hemisphere activation for verbal and right hemisphere activation for spatial short-term memory in younger adults (see Figure 6.3). However, older adults performing these tasks showed a markedly different pattern. In frontal sites that are thought to mediate rehearsal (Broca's area [left BA 44] for letters, and supplementary motor area [right BA 6] for locations), older adults showed bilateral activity. In dorsolateral prefrontal sites (BAs 46, 9), thought to mediate encoding and retrieval from short-term memory, older adults as a group showed activation that was opposite to the patterns of left-right asymmetry observed in the younger group. A clue from the verbal study sheds light on this paradoxical laterality pattern. When the older group was divided into good and poor performers, the good performers showed bilateral activation of dorsolateral prefrontal sites, whereas the poorer ones showed the paradoxical pattern (i.e., greater right than left dorsolateral prefrontal activation during verbal short-term memory). Thus, bilateral activation could be indicative of recruitment of additional brain regions that compensate for aging effects. Because the paradoxical laterality was particular to the poor performing older adults, it may signal an alteration in frontal function that has adverse behavioral consequences. Future research is needed to clarify the functional consequences of these and other age differences in laterality.

Often in daily life, we must hold things in mind while avoiding distraction from ongoing events. Our ability to do so also declines with age. A classic laboratory test used to study interference effects in short-term memory is the Brown-Peterson task. Research participants listen to and retain a string of items, and then count backwards continuously during the retention interval. Then, they are asked to recall the items. The counting task is disrupting, and memory is compromised. Parkin and Walter (1991) found that older adults performed more poorly on this task than younger adults, and that the greatest deficits occurred in older adults who also were impaired on the WCST and on verbal fluency (another test sensitive to frontal dysfunction).

The electrophysiological results of Chao and Knight (1997b) also implicated the frontal lobes in age-related increases distractibility. Participants were required to remember the pitch of a single tone during a blank interval or during an interval filled with distracting tones. The older group performed more poorly than the younger one, and failed to show attention-related frontal activity as in the study reported above (Chao & Knight, 1997a). Moreover, the auditor-evoked responses to the distractors were greater in the older group, suggesting that frontal operations did not sufficiently inhibit these signals (see McDowd & Filion, 1992, for a related result). This interpretation is reinforced by the finding that errors on the WCST correlated with the amplitude of responses to the distractors.

A recent study by Jonides et al. (in press) offered additional evidence that frontal inhibitory processes are compromised with age. A short-term letter memory task was modified to increase the inhibitory demands. On some trials, the probe letter did not match the current memory set; however, it did match the memory set on the immediately preceding trial. These probes thus presented participants with a conflict between the high familiarity of the probe (which suggested a positive response) and its lack of membership in the memory set of the current trial (which demanded a negative response). Consequently, participants were slower to respond "no" compared to when the probe was not a member of a recent set. The slowing was even greater for the older group. Moreover, younger adults showed increased activation at a site in left dorsolateral prefrontal cortex (BA 45) that was not active in the older group. Thus, older adults seemed to lack the contribution of a frontally mediated process that would help them to resolve the response conflict created in this condition.

From this brief overview, we see converging indications that age-related changes in frontal function may affect short-term memory and the inhibition of competing sensory events and response tendencies. These are only a subset of the processes associated with the central executive, and future work will be needed to establish whether other executive functions mediated by frontal lobe mechanisms contribute to age-related changes in cognition. The electrophysiological evidence of Chao and Knight (1997b) highlighted the importance of frontal influences on other brain areas, reminding us that localized aging effects may have secondary consequences on the functioning of other parts of the network in which a region operates. The final section explicitly addresses the possible effects of age on interactions between brain regions by considering age-related changes in interhemispheric interactions that are mediated by the corpus callosum.

Age-related changes in interhemispheric interactions

The evidence for greater bilateral activation or paradoxical patterns of activation in older adults found in some neuroimaging studies suggests that interhemispheric dynamics are among those altered with age. The adult corpus callosum is approximately 6 centimeters in length and contains between 200 million and 350 million axons (myelinated and unmyelinated) that interconnect regions in the left and right hemispheres (see Figure 6.1). The corpus callosum is organized topographically, but roughly speaking the frontal lobes are interconnected through the anterior third, the parietal somatosensory regions and auditory areas in the temporal lobes are connected through the midbody, and the visual areas of parietal and occipital cortex are connected through the posterior region known as the splenium. Several structural imaging studies have indicated that callosal atrophy is somewhat greater than in other brain regions, suggesting that this structure may be selectively vulnerable to aging effects (see Dreisen & Raz, 1995; Reuter-Lorenz & Stanczak, in press). Callosal atrophy could be a consequence of cell loss in cortical regions that project through it, but such relationships have yet to be documented in normal aging (see Thompson, Narr, Blanton, & Toga, in press, for a review).

A handful of behavioral studies have suggested that sensorimotor functions of the corpus callosum decline with age (see Jeeves & Moes, 1996; Reuter-Lorenz & Stanczak, in press, for reviews). For example, callosally mediated transfer is required when the left hand responds to a signal in the right visual field, whereas a left hand response to a left visual field signal does not require transfer (see Figure 6.2). The differences in response speed between younger and older adults is greatest when transfer is required, suggesting some decline in the efficiency of the corpus callosum (Jeeves & Moes, 1996; Reuter-Lorenz & Stanczak, in press). Electrophysiological evidence also has indicated that callosally transmitted visual signals used in this task may be reduced in older adults (Hoptman, Davidson, Gudmundsson, Schreiber, & Ershler, 1996).

Yet, age does not appear to depress callosal functions uniformly (e.g., Cherry et al., 1995; Reuter-Lorenz & Stanczak, in press). For example, bilateral activation found in several neuroimaging studies (see above) may reflect compensatory recruitment of left and right hemisphere regions (i.e., bihemispheric processing) and an increased reliance on callosal-mediated interactions. A recent visual laterality study is consistent with this interpretation. Reuter-Lorenz, Stanczak, and Miller (in press) used letter-matching tasks of varying complexity that were performed under two conditions: (a) the matching letters projected to the same visual field-hemisphere; (b) the matching letters projected to opposite visual fields-hemispheres. Older adults generally performed better in the bilateral than unilateral condition, whereas younger adults showed this pattern only for the most complex task. These results show that older adults can benefit from conditions that require interhemispheric interactions. Banich (1998) proposed that these tasks reflect callosal contributions to attentional resource allocation. The results of Reuter-Lorenz et al. suggest, then, that aging does not disrupt callosal processes uniformly. Interhemispheric interactions for sensorimotor control may be more vulnerable to the effects of age than callosally mediated attentional processes. The latter may improve the brain's ability to meet processing demands and thereby compensate for some effects of normal aging.

Understanding how age alters the functions of the corpus callosum may shed light on age-related changes in network interactions more generally. Callosally mediated interactions thus could also serve as a model system to study the effect of age on intrahemispheric dynamics. Future research using combined structural, functional, and behavioral methods should aim to clarify whether age affects the inhibitory or excitatory functions of the callosum, and to identify any variations in these effects that may exist across the functional subregions of the callosum.

Closing remarks

The evidence reviewed in this chapter suggests that changes in specific brain regions and the networks in which they operate underlie age-related decline of specific cognitive functions, including the encoding and retrieval of explicit memories, contextual memory, aspects of working memory, and some forms of inhibition. In this light, accounts that attribute cognitive aging to such global mechanisms as a generalized slowing or loss of resources are incomplete. But clearly there is a great deal more to accomplish. At present, the evidence for age-related alterations of frontal and medial temporal lobe functions is the most compelling. Does this imply that occipital and parietal processes, as well as nonmnemonic functions of the temporal lobes, are unaffected by aging? And, what about the cerebellum? Cognitive neuroscience has a long way to go toward understanding its role in cognitive development and decline. Moreover, a comprehensive neurocognitive account of aging ultimately must consider the potentially widespread effects of neurochemical changes and specify how such changes interact with focal aging effects. Numerous methodological challenges are posed by the new neuroimaging methods used in aging research. Drawing valid conclusions from age differences in brain activations will hinge on meeting these challenges. Refining our cognitive constructs will facilitate our ability to relate them to specific neural processing mechanisms. Neurocognitive research needs to differentiate further among types of inhibition, types of attention, and memory encoding-retrieval processes because each is likely to have a unique set of neural mechanisms that could be selectively affected by age. Finally, the exciting clues about compensation and plasticity in aging point to new research frontiers that could uncover novel approaches to optimizing neurocognitive functioning across the lifespan.

References

Albert, M. S., & Kaplan, E. (1979). Organic implications of neuropsychological deficits in the elderly. In L. W. Poon, J. L. Fozard, L. S. Cermak, D. Ehrenberg, & L. W. Thompson (Eds.), *New directions in memory and aging: Proceedings of the George Talland Memorial Conference* (pp. 406–432). Hillsdale, NJ: Erlbaum.

Banich, M. T. (1998). The missing link: The role of interhemispheric interaction in attentional processing. *Brain and Cognition, 36,* 128–157.

Botwinick, J. (1977). Intellectual abilities. In J. E. Birren, & K. W. Schaie (Eds.), *Handbook of the psychology of aging* (pp. 580–605). New York: Van Nostrand Reinhold.

Cabeza, R., Anderson, N. D., Mangels, J. A., Nyberg, L., & Houle, S. (in press). Age-related differences in neural activity during item and temporal-order memory retrieval: A positron emission tomography study. *Journal of Cognitive Neuroscience.*

Cabeza, R., Grady, C. L., Nyberg, L., McIntosh, A. R., Tulving, E., Kapur, S., Jennings, J. M., Houle, S., & Craik, F. I. M. (1997a). Age-related differences in neural activity during memory encoding and retrieval: A positron emission tomography study. *Journal of Neuroscience, 17*(1), 391–400.

Cabeza, R., McIntosh, A. R., Tulving, E., Nyberg, L., & Grady, C. L. (1997b). Age-related differences in effective neural connectivity during encoding and recall. *NeuroReport, 8,* 3479–3483.

Chao, L. L., & Knight, R. T. (1997a). Age-related prefrontal alterations during auditory memory. *Neurobiology of Aging, 18,* 87–95.

Chao, L. L., & Knight, R. T. (1997b). Prefrontal deficits in attention and inhibitory control with aging. *Cerebral Cortex, 7,* 63–69.

Cherry, B. J., & Hellige, J. B. (1999). Hemispheric asymmetries in vigilance and cerebral arousal mechanisms in younger and older adults. *Neuropsychology, 13,* 111–120.

Cherry, B. J., Hellige, J. B., & McDowd, J. M. (1995). Age differences and similarities in patterns of cerebral hemispheric asymmetry. *Psychology and Aging, 10,* 191–203.

Craik, F. I. M., & Jennings, J. M. (1992). Human memory. In F. I. M. Craik & T. A. Salthouse (Eds.), *Handbook of Aging and Cognition* (pp. 51–109). Hillsdale, NJ: Erlbaum.

Craik, F. I. M., Morris, L. W., Morris, R. G., & Loewen, E. R. (1990). Relations between source amnesia and frontal lobe functioning in older adults. *Psychology and Aging, 5,* 148–151.

Damasio, H. (1995). *Human brain anatomy in computerized images.* New York: Oxford University Press.

Degl'Innocenti, A., & Backman, L. (1996). Aging and source memory: Influences of intention to remember and associations with frontal lobe tests. *Aging, Neuropsychology, and Cognition, 3,* 307–319.

D'Esposito, M., Zarahn, E., Aguirre, G., & Rypma, B. (1999). The effect of normal aging on the coupling of neural activity to the bold hemodynamic response. *Neuroimage, 10,* 6–14.

Driesen, N. R., & Raz, N. (1995). The influence of sex, age, and handedness on corpus callosum morphology: A meta-analysis. *Psychobiology, 23,* 240–247.

Fabiani, M., & Friedman, D. (1997). Dissociations between memory for temporal order and recognition memory in aging. *Neuropsychologia, 35,* 129–141.

Faust, M. E., & Balota, D. A. (1997). Inhibition of return and visuospatial attention in healthy older adults and individuals with dementia of the Alzheimer's type. *Neuropsychology, 11,* 13–29.

Fuster, J. M. (1989). *The prefrontal cortex* (2nd ed.). New York: Raven Press.

Gerhardstein, P., Peterson, M. A., & Rapcsak, S. Z. (1998). Age-related hemispheric asymmetry in object discrimination. *Journal of Clinical and Experimental Neuropsychology, 30,* 174–185.

Goldman-Rakic, P. S. (1992, September). Working memory and the mind. *Scientific American, 267,* 110–117.

Golomb, J., Kluger, A., de Leon, M. J., Ferrs, S. H., Convit, A., Mittelman, M. S., Cohen, J., Rusinek, H., De Santi, S., & George, A. E. (1994). Hippocampal formation size in normal human aging: A correlate of delayed secondary memory performance. *Learning and Memory, 1,* 45–54.

Grady, C. L., McIntosh, A. R., Bookstein, F., Horwitz, B., Rapoport, S. I., & Haxby, J. V. (1998). Age-related changes in regional cerebral blood flow during working memory for faces. *Neuroimage, 8,* 409–425.

Grady, C. L., McIntosh, A. R., Horwitz, B., Maisog, J. Ma, Ungerleider, L. G., Mentis, M J., Pietrini, P., Schapiro, M. B., & Haxby, J. V. (1995). Age-related reductions in human recognition memory due to impaired encoding. *Science, 269,* 218–221.

Hartley, A. A. (1992). Attention. In F. I. M. Craik & T. A. Salthouse (Eds.), *The Hanbook of Aging and Cognition* (pp. 3–50). Hillsdale, NJ: Lawrence Erlbaum Associates.

Haug, H., & Eggers, R. (1991). Morphometry of the human cortex cerebri and corpus striatum during aging. *Neurobiology of Aging, 12,* 336–338.

Hoptman, M. J., Davidson, R. J., Gudmundsson, A., Schreiber, R. T., & Ershler, W. B. (1996). Age differences in visual evoked potential estimates of interhemispheric transfer. *Neuropsychology, 10,* 263–271.

Hoyer, W. J., & Rybash, J. M. (1992). Age and visual field differences in computing visual-spatial relations. *Psychology and Aging, 7,* 339–342.

Ivry , R. B., & Robertson, L. C. (1998). *The two sides of perception.* Cambridge, MA: MIT Press.

Janowsky, J. S., Shimamura, A. P., & Squire, L. R. (1989). Source memory impairment in patients with frontal lobe lesions. *Neuropsychologia, 27,* 1043–1056.

Jeeves, M. A., & Moes, P. (1996). Interhemispheric transfer time differences related to aging and gender. *Neuropsychologia, 34,* 627–636.

Jonides, J., Marshuetz, C., Smith, E., Koeppe, R., Hartley, A. & Reuter-Lorenz, P. A. (in press). Changes in inhibitory processing with age revealed by brain activation. *Journal of Cognitive Neuroscience.*

Kaplan, E., Fein, D., Morris, R., & Delis, D. (1991). *WAIS-R as a neuropsychological instrument.* San Antonio, TX: The Psychological Corporation.

Kapur, S., Craik, F. I. M., Tulving, E., Wilson, A. A., Houle, S., & Brown, G. M. (1994). Neuroanatomical correlates of encoding in episodic memory: Levels of processing effect. *Proceedings of the National Academy of Sciences, USA, 91,* 2008–2011.

Kosslyn, S. M., Koenig, O., Barrett, A., Cave, C. B., Tang, J., & Gabrieli, J. D. E. (1989). Evidence for two types of spatial representations: Hemispheric specialization for categorical and coordinate relations. *Journal of Experimental Psychology: Human Perception and Performance, 15,* 723–735.

LaVoie, D., & Light, L. L. (1994). Adult age differences in repetition priming: a meta-analysis. *Psychology and Aging, 9,* 539–553.

Lawrence, B., Myerson, J., & Hale, S. (1998). Differential decline of verbal and visuospatial processing speed across the adult life span. *Aging, Neuropsychology, and Cognition, 5,* 129–146.

Light, L. L., & Lavoie, D. (1993). Direct and indirect measures of memory in old age. In P. Graf & F. E. J. Masson (Eds.), *Implicit memory: New directions in cognition, development, and neuropsychology* (pp. 207–230). Hillsdale, NJ: Erlbaum.

Luria, A. R. (1966). *Higher cortical functions in man.* New York: Basic Books.

Madden, D. J., Turkington, T. G., Provenzale, J. M., Denny, L. L., Hawk, T. C., Gottlob, L. R., & Coleman, R. E. (1999). Adult age differences in the functional neuroanatomy of verbal recognition memory. *Human Brain Mapping, 7,* 115–135.

McAndrews, M. P., & Milner, B. (1991). The frontal cortex and memory for temporal order. *Neuropsychologia, 29,* 601–618.

McDowd, J. M., & Filion, D. L. (1992). Aging, selective attention and inhibitory processes: A psychophysiological approach. *Psychology and Aging, 7,* 65–71.

Milner, B., Corsi, P., & Leonard, G. (1991). Frontal-lobe contribution to recency judgments. *Neuropsychologia, 29,* 601–618.

Morrison, J. H., & Hof, P. R. (1997, October 17). Life and death of neurons in the aging brain. *Science, 278,* 412–419.

Moscovitch, M., & Winocur, G. (1995). Frontal lobes, memory, and aging. Structure and functions of the frontal lobes. *Annals of the New York Academy of Sciences, 769*, 115–150.

Nebes, R. D. (1990). Hemispheric specialization in the aged brain. In C. Trevarthen (Ed.), *Brain circuits and function of the mind: Essays in honor of R. W. Sperry* (pp. 364–370). New York: Cambridge University Press.

Nebes, R. D., Madden, D. J., & Berg, W. D. (1983). The effect of age on hemispheric asymmetry in visual and auditory identification. *Experimental Aging Research, 9*, 87–91.

Nielsen-Bohlman, L., & Knight, R. T. (1995). Prefrontal alterations during memory processing in aging. *Cerebral Cortex, 5*, 541–549.

Parkin, A. J., & Walter, B. M. (1991). Aging, short-term memory, and frontal dysfunction. *Psychobiology, 19*, 175–179.

Parkin, A. J., Walter, B. M., & Hunkin, N. M. (1995). Relationships between normal aging, frontal lobe function, and memory for temporal and spatial information. *Neuropsychology, 9*, 304–312.

Prull, M. W., Gabrieli, J. D. E., & Bunge, S. A. (in press). Memory and aging: A cognitive neuroscience perspective. In F. I. M. Craik & T. A. Salthouse (Eds.), *Handbook of aging and cognition* (2nd ed.). Mahwah, NJ: Erlbaum.

Raz, N. (in press). Aging of the brain and its impact on cognitive performance: Integration of structural and functional findings. In F. I. M. Craik & T. A. Salthouse (Eds.), *Handbook of aging and cognition* (2nd ed.). Mahwah, NJ: Erlbaum.

Raz, N., Gunning-Dixon, F. M., Head, D., Dupuis, J. H., & Acker, J. D. (1998). Neuroanatomical correlates of cognition aging: Evidence from structural magnetic resonance imaging. *Neuropsychology, 12*, 95–114.

Reuter-Lorenz, P. A., Jonides, J., Smith, E., Marshuetz, C., Miller, A., Hartley, A., & Koeppe, R. (in press). Age differences in frontal lateralization of working memory. *Journal of Cognitive Neuroscience.*

Reuter-Lorenz, P. A., & Miller, A., (1998). The cognitive neuroscience of human laterality: Lessons from the bisected brain. *Current Directions in Psychological Science, 7*, 15–20.

Reuter-Lorenz, P. A., & Stanczak, L. (in press). Aging and the corpus callosum. *Developmental Neuropsychology.*

Reuter-Lorenz, P. A., Stanczak, L., & Miller, A. (in press). Neural recruitment and cognitive aging: Two hemispheres are better than one, especially as you age. *Psychological Science.*

Ross, M. H., Yurgelun-Todd, D. A., Renshaw, P. F., Maas, L. C., Mendelson, J. H., Mello, N. K., Cohen, B. M., & Levin, J. M. (1997). Age-related reduction in functional MRI response to photic stimulation. *Neurology, 48*, 173–176.

Rybash, J. M. (1996). Implicit memory and aging: A cognitive neuropsychological perspective. *Developmental Neuropsychology, 12*, 127–179.

Salthouse, T. A. (1992). *Mechanisms of age-cognition relations in adulthood.* Hillsdale, NJ: Erlbaum.

Salthouse, T. A. (1995). Differential age-related influences on memory for verbal-symbolic information and visual-spatial information? *Journal of Gerontology, 50B*, 193–201.

Schacter, D. L., Kaszniak, A. W., Kihlstrom, J. F., & Valdiserri, M. (1991). The relation between source memory and aging. *Psychology and Aging, 6*, 559–568.

Schacter, D. L., Savage, C. R., Alpert, N. M., Rauch, S. L., & Albert, M. S. (1996). The role of hippocampus and frontal cortex in age-related changes in memory. A PET study. *NeuroReport, 7*, 1165–1169.

Schaie, K. W., & Schaie, J. P. (1977). Clinical assessment and aging. In J. E. Birren & K. W. Schaie (Eds.), *Handbook of the psychology of aging* (pp.692–723). New York: Van Nostrand Reinhold.

Scoville, W. B., & Milner, B. (1957). Loss of recent memory after bilateral hippocampal lesions. *Journal of Neurology, Neurosurgery, and Psychiatry, 20,* 11–21.

Shimamura, A. P., Janowsky, J. S., & Squire, L. R. (1990). Memory for the temporal order of events in patients with frontal lobe lesions and amnesic patients. *Neuropsychologia, 28,* 803–813.

Simic, G., Kostovic, I., Winbald, B., & Bagdanovitch, N. (1997). Volume and number of neurons of the human hippocampal formation in normal aging and Alzheimer's disease. *Journal of Comparative Neurology, 379,* 482–494.

Smith, E. E., & Jonides, J. (1999, March 12). Storage and executive processes in the frontal lobes, *Science, 283,* 1657–1661.

Smith, E. E., Jonides, J., & Koeppe, R. A. (1996) Dissociating verbal and spatial working memory using PET. *Cerebral Cortex, 6,* 11–20.

Spencer, W. D., & Raz, N. (1994). Memory for facts, source, and context: Can frontal lobe dysfunction explain age-related differences? *Psychology and Aging, 9,* 149–159.

Spencer, W. D., & Raz, N. (1995). Differential effects of aging on memory for content and context: A meta-analysis. *Psychology and Aging, 10,* 527–539.

Thompson, P., Narr, K., Blanton, R., & Toga, A. (in press). Mapping structural alterations of the corpus callosum during brain development and degeneration. In E. Zaidel, M. Iacoboni, & A. Pascual-Leone (Eds.), *The role of the corpus callosum in sensory-motor integration: Anatomy, physiology and behavior.* Cambridge, MA: MIT Press.

Trott, C. T., Friedman, D., Ritter, W., & Fabiani, M. (1997). Item and source memory: Differential age effects revealed by event-related potentials. *NeuroReport, 8,* 3373–3378.

Tubi, N., & Calev, A. (1989). Verbal and visuospatial recall by younger and older subjects: Use of matched tasks [Brief reports]. *Psychology and Aging, 4,* 493–495.

Tulving, E., Kapur, S., Craik, F. I. M., Moscovitch, M., & Houle, S. (1994). Hemispheric encoding/retrieval asymmetry in episodic memory: Positron emission tomography findings. *Proceedings of the National Academy of Sciences, USA, 91,* 2012–2015.

Wechsler, D. (1981). *Manual for the Wechsler Adult Intelligence Scale–Revised.* New York: The Psychological Corporation.

West, R. L. (1996). An application of prefrontal cortex function theory to cognitive aging. *Psychological Bulletin, 120,* 272–292.

Woodruff-Pak, D. S. (1997). *The neuropsychology of aging.* Malden, MA: Blackwell.

Metamemory from a social-cognitive perspective 7

John C. Cavanaugh

Being able to think and reflect on our own cognitions, it can be argued, is what separates humans from other species. Self-reflection, and the personal knowledge that results, form the very foundation of human consciousness (Metcalfe & Shimamura, 1994). We are able to monitor what is perceived, judge what we know or what we need to learn, and predict the consequences of our actions.

Self-reflection about cognition is referred to as *metacognition* in the psychological literature. Although this term has been used for only about a quarter century, the issue of what people know about their cognition, how they use this knowledge, and why this knowledge is important have been at the core of philosophy for millennia. Indeed, one of the most widely known (and paraphrased) statements in philosophy concerns metacognition—Descartes's famous point, *cogito, ergo sum*. Clearly, at least some philosophers believe that metacognition cuts to the very core of the human condition.

The claims involving metacognition in cognitive psychology are much more modest. Indeed, whether people even are capable of meaningful conscious reflection on their thinking is open to debate (e.g., Nisbett & Wilson, 1977). Nevertheless, over the past quarter century increased attention has been focused on metacognition, especially in the domain of memory. This latter area, referred to as *metamemory*, is the oldest and most intensively researched aspect of metacognition.

Although the systematic study of people's knowledge and beliefs about their memory is only a century or so old, awareness of the issue predates recorded history. For example, one can easily imagine that ancient storytellers realized remembering a script that took hours (or even days) to recite was a formidable task, which probably led to the use of music as a memory device as well as the creation of classic mnemonic techniques. Indeed, it makes little intuitive sense to argue that the creation of formal memory strategies, such as the method of loci, would have occurred in the absence of awareness of memory fallibility.

This realization that one's memory is not perfect, and that some sort of behavior is necessary to buttress it, is one example of the more general notion that people have knowledge about and certain beliefs in reference to memory. Given the label "metamemory" in the early 1970s by Flavell (1971), memory knowledge and beliefs have moved from a little researched topic to a significant subject within memory research. Although the definition of metamemory has evolved over the years, in general it refers to knowledge about how we remember, the process of monitoring our memory processing, and the beliefs we hold about memory (Cavanaugh & Perlmutter, 1982; Hertzog & Dixon, 1994).

In this chapter, two major aspects of metamemory research as it pertains to older adults are addressed. First, a brief summary of the major lines of theory and investigation will be presented, focusing mainly on self-report questionnaires assessing memory knowledge and memory self-efficacy as well as their relation to memory performance. Second, key issues from the social cognition literature, along with a framework from viewing metamemory as a type of social cognition, will be presented that focuses on the genesis of individuals' responses to the items. Finally, several specific avenues for future research will be presented.

This chapter is not intended to be a comprehensive review of the metamemory and aging literature. Several excellent articles and chapters fulfilling this function are available (e.g., Cavanaugh, 1996; Hertzog & Dixon, 1994; West & Berry, 1994). Self-ratings of memory ability also have been routinely used in large survey and interview studies. Although not typically included in reviews of the metamemory literature, they nevertheless provide additional evidence regarding what people know and believe about their memory. Thus, the focus here is on identifying key issues in the metamemory literature.

Theory and research on metamemory

Although investigations of children's and adults' metamemory have been conducted for roughly a century, a specific focus on older adults' metamemory dates only from the late 1970s and early 1980s. This relatively recent emphasis is due, in part, to the common stereotype of memory decline and complaint in older adults (Levy & Langer, 1994). At a time when the prevailing worldview was inevitable decline, there was little need for theory or research on what older adults knew or believed to be true about memory. However, as it became clear that memory development in late life depends on the type of memory being examined (e.g., working memory, very-long-term memory) and that differences across individuals in memory development are large, metamemory in late life became a potential explanatory variable. These twin notions of intra- and inter-individual differences in memory would provide an important conceptual basis for metamemory theory and research.

At roughly the same time, researchers began developing memory questionnaires aimed at assessing what adults knew about memory. This early research (e.g., Herrmann & Neisser, 1978) resulted in the first generation of questionnaires (e.g., the Short Inventory of Memory Experiences). This survey research approach has become the major way that systematic developmental research is conducted on age differences in what adults know about their memory and the beliefs they hold about it.

With the joint developments of intra- and inter-individual differences and memory questionnaires, the stage was set for the creation of comprehensive survey instruments. Psychometrically sound questionnaires (e.g., Memory Functioning Questionnaire; Metamemory in Adulthood Instrument) appeared in the 1980s, as did early attempts at developing theoretical models. Nearly all subsequent work has been grounded in these early approaches, which has resulted in the creation of metamemory taxonomies.

A taxonomy of metamemory

Developing a taxonomy of metamemory is a little more difficult than it seems. Part of the complication stems from the inclusion of several different types of processes and information in the definition of metamemory. For example, the inclusion of monitoring aspects implies that metamemory includes feelings of knowing (also known as tip-of-the-tongue phenomena) as well as "facts about memory" (e.g., verbatim recall usually is more difficult than gist recall). Although I will briefly discuss feelings of knowing, for purposes of this chapter, I will focus more on the informational aspects.

Hertzog and Dixon (1994) provided a very useful taxonomy of metamemory using three general categories (see also Cavanaugh & Green, 1990; Cavanaugh & Perlmutter, 1982; Gilewski & Zelinski, 1986; Lovelace, 1990): "(1) declarative knowledge about memory tasks and memory processes—defined as knowledge about both how memory functions and the viability of strategic behaviors for tasks requiring memory processes; (2) memory monitoring—defined as the awareness of the current state of one's memory system; and (3) self-referent beliefs about memory" (p. 229). Memory self-efficacy (Cavanaugh & Green, 1990) is the central construct of memory beliefs, defined as one's sense of mastery or ability to use memory effectively when required.

A multidimensional view of metamemory is critical if one wants to understand the role that metamemory plays in remembering (Hertzog & Dixon, 1994) and in order to reconcile discrepant data (Berry, in press). If the conceptualizations of metamemory differ across researchers, then the operationalizations (and measurement) and the explanatory power of the construct will vary across studies. Such problems have plagued metamemory research (e.g., Berry, 1999; Cavanaugh, Feldman, & Hertzog, 1998).

Theoretical frameworks

To date, the most thoroughly articulated theoretical framework from an adult developmental perspective concerning metamemory in older adults has been offered by Cavanaugh and colleagues (e.g., Cavanaugh, 1989; Cavanaugh & Morton, 1989). Based on an earlier framework (Cavanaugh, Kramer, Sinnott, Camp, & Markley, 1985), Cavanaugh and colleagues proposed a complex set of reciprocal dynamic interrelationships that denote the influence of cognitive developmental level, personality, situational factors, general knowledge, self-efficacy, effort, memory strategies, and various feedback and evaluation processes.

A critical aspect of the model is that metamemorial self-evaluations are not conducted only on the basis of direct input from content knowledge about memory processes and functions. Rather, the influence of stored content knowledge is mediated through memory beliefs. The importance of this mediation cannot be overemphasized. Cavanaugh and colleagues' framework implies that evaluations of memory ability are not made simply by retrieving and applying objective "memory facts." Instead, evaluations of ability in a given context are constructed by using previously stored information in addition to contemporaneous information processing. This means that people's responses to items may be based on the retrieval of previously stored judgments, the construction of responses at the time they are needed, or both (Cavanaugh et al., 1998).

Most of the adult developmental research on metamemory has focused on the memory beliefs and self-efficacy aspects of Cavanaugh and colleagues' framework. Although the entire framework has not yet been subjected to empirical test, there is, as we will see, a growing body of evidence that at least some of its hypothesized relations have support. It is to this research that we now turn.

Empirical research on metamemory

Research on metamemory across adulthood began in part as an outgrowth of research indicating that one reason children do not use efficient memory strategies is that they do not know they should (Cavanaugh & Borkowski, 1980; Flavell, 1971; Schneider & Pressley, 1989). So, for example, some researchers provided older adults with information about the efficacy of various memory strategies. However, this approach was not very successful; for instance, Rabinowitz (1989) demonstrated that additional opportunities and encouragement to use memory strategies is insufficient by itself to produce optimal strategic performance. Specific training to use memory strategies, while somewhat more effective, also does not produce long-term improvement (e.g., Anschutz, Camp, Markley, & Kramer, 1985, 1987).

Early on, though, much metamemory research in gerontology focused on two key questions: What do older people know about their memory? What beliefs about memory do older adults hold?

Memory beliefs. Most questionnaire research in metamemory has examined memory beliefs. In particular, work has focused on the concept of memory self-efficacy, which is a derivative of Bandura's (1986, 1989) general notion of self-efficacy: the extent to which one believes in his or her ability to mobilize the motivation, cognitive resources, and courses of action necessary to exert control over task demands. Memory self-efficacy can be constructively viewed as hierarchically organized beliefs about the self as rememberer ranging from global ("my memory isn't very good") to domain specific ("I can't remember names, but I'm good at faces") to context specific ("I can't remember where I parked in the lot") to local or concurrent ("I can remember this phone number so I don't need to write it down") (Hertzog, Dixon, & Hultsch, 1990). Memory self-efficacy is viewed as a primary, but mediated, influence on performance (Bandura, 1989; Berry & West, 1993; Cavanaugh & Green, 1990) in three ways: (a) on the construction and selection of strategies, (b) on the level of effort or persistence, and (c) on affect-related outcomes of performance. Current adult developmental theories of metamemory have postulated that memory self-efficacy, memory abilities, and performance are mutually influential, and that individual differences in each must be taken into account (Cavanaugh & Green, 1990; Hertzog et al., 1990).

To date, researchers have relied mostly on three questionnaires to investigate age differences in memory self-efficacy (see Cavanaugh, 1996, for a discussion of measurement issues): the Metamemory in Adulthood Instrument (MIA), the Memory Failures Questionnaire ([MFQ]; Gilewski & Zelinski, 1988), and the Memory Self-Efficacy Questionnaire ([MSEQ]; Berry, West, & Dennehey, 1989). Psychometric research has indicated that the MIA subscales of Capacity (measuring perceived ability), Change (measuring perceived change in ability), and Locus (measuring perceived control over memory) converge with the MFQ to identify a factor identified as memory self-efficacy (Hertzog, Hultsch, & Dixon, 1989). Several investigations have found age-related differences in memory self-efficacy (e.g., Berry et al., 1989; Dixon & Hultsch, 1983).

Due to the predicted relationship between self-efficacy and performance, much research also has examined this issue. The data clearly have indicated that memory self-efficacy beliefs often are inaccurate, and that memory self-efficacy judgments and performance typically are only moderately correlated (for reviews, see Cavanaugh & Green, 1990; Hertzog & Dixon, 1994; West & Berry, 1994). However, the relation between the two is mediated (e.g., Berry, 1999; Cavanaugh et al., 1998; Cavanaugh & Green, 1990) and varies across types of memory tasks (Berry, 1999; West, Dennehy-Basile, & Norris, 1996) and instructional conditions (Baldi & Berry, 1996). In the former case, self-efficacy beliefs have been shown to predict better verbal memory performance for men (but not for women), and to have no relation with nonverbal memory (Seeman, McAvay, Merrill, Albert, & Rodin, 1996). In the latter case, for example, respondents who completed memory self-efficacy questionnaires in descending order (i.e., from most to least difficult task demands) showed higher self-efficacy than those completing the questionnaires in ascending order (Baldi & Berry, 1996). Additionally, there is growing evidence that memory beliefs are extremely complex, and not easily parsed into neat categories (e.g., Hertzog, Lineweaver, & McGuire, 1999; Lineweaver & Hertzog, 1998).

These data have suggested to some that memory self-efficacy (and memory beliefs in general) must be examined as types of social cognition (Cavanaugh et al., 1998). For example, memory self-efficacy is likely to be influenced by individuals' implicit theories about cognition (Dweck & Leggett, 1988) and how these implicit theories explain memory aging (Hertzog & Dixon, 1994). Similarly, the affect that results from performance (e.g., anxiety, confidence) may be the result of specific levels of self-efficacy (Bandura, 1986, 1989). It is to this integration of metamemory with social cognition that we now turn.

Interfaces between metamemory and social cognition

Despite the fact that metamemory has been viewed as including beliefs about one's memory and aspects of self-efficacy, and that the typical metamemory assessment approach is to ask people to respond to collections of questions about many different aspects of memory, surprisingly little attention has been paid to a number of basic issues such as how people go about responding to metamemory questions (Cavanaugh et al., 1998). The lack of research is especially surprising given the considerable attention that has been given to this issue and a host of related issues (e.g., the diagnosticity of information, context effects, the role of affect in judgments) in the social cognition literature (Cavanaugh et al., 1998; Schwarz, 1996).

Fortunately, a few authors have begun making explicit theoretical connections between the metamemory and social cognition literatures (Cavanaugh et al., 1998; Schwarz, 1996). These forays have followed relatively parallel paths, drawing on several central constructs from the social cognition judgment literature and applying them to the case of judgments about one's memory. For purposes of this chapter, I will highlight only several of the most important connections; the interested reader is encouraged to read the more extended discussions for a more complete account. Additionally, the reader is reminded that these connections, for the most part, have no empirical data directly addressing the presumptions. Thus, the points of contact, at this point, are purely speculative.

Nevertheless, several aspects of this approach have been applied successfully to other aspects of metamemory, most notably feelings of knowing and memory monitoring. For example, several researchers in cognitive psychology have used the notions of accessibility and availability to help explain how monitoring succeeds and fails (e.g., Koriat, 1994; Nelson &

Narens, 1990, 1994). Such convergence on similar constructs provides support for the dynamic view of metamemory discussed above.

A theoretical framework of metamemory from a social cognition perspective

The social cognition literature has a host of both constructs and data to support it that provides the basis for creating a theoretical framework describing the knowledge and beliefs aspects of metamemory (Cavanaugh et al., 1998). This framework is based on the four core notions of schematicity, accessibility, availability, and diagnosticity, as well as the range of things that influence them (such as context and affect). Cavanaugh et al. (1998) argued that these constructs set the stage for complex, reciprocal interactions among stored self-knowledge about memory, prior judgments about memory, affect, and response constructions triggered by the question being asked. These interactions form the basis for responding to survey items about memory.

To preview a bit, we consider answers to metamemory questions to be based partly on reporting of already stored information and partly as the result of on-the-spot constructions. Individual differences are apparent in the underlying cognitive structures and the degree to which they are flexible and context dependent (Barsalou, 1987; Kelly, 1955). Coupled with environmental (e.g., task) demands, these structures influence the metamemory judgments people make, which in turn influence subsequent behavior and the cognitive structures themselves (e.g., Cavanaugh & Morton, 1989). Such reciprocity merely acknowledges the reciprocal role of affect, which both is inherent in any existing cognitive structure as well as a result of the judgment process itself. Because the specific assumptions underlying the framework are described in detail in Cavanaugh et al. (1998), the focus here will be on highlighting a few of the more central constructs from social cognition research.

Implications of social cognition for metamemory

The most important implication of a social cognition view of metamemory is that representations of the self concerning memory actually are complex and multifaceted cognitive structures. What one believes at any given moment about oneself as a rememberer, for example, depends in complex ways on how and on which stored judgments about oneself are accessed. Indeed, there is no such thing as a permanent cognitive structure about the self (Anderson, 1987; Bargh, 1989; Feldman & Lynch, 1988; Markus & Wurf, 1987). By extension, there is no such thing as a permanent set of self-judgments about memory ability or beliefs. In practical terms, how one views oneself as a rememberer changes over time, an important point to consider (remember?) when trying to interpret the stability of self-judgments.

This implication that the self is a constantly evolving, dynamic process allows for direct connections between metamemory and social cognition research. For example, concepts from the social cognition literature such as schematicity, attributions, self-efficacy, automaticity, and the recall of personal attributes, all of which have been researched extensively, may be brought to bear to understand the nature of metamemory. Of course, such points of contact reveal fundamental (and glaring) gaps in the metamemory literature as well as fruitful avenues for future research.

Schematicity.   Referring to traits and other concepts that are highly elaborated components of self-concept or of theories of persons, Markus (1977) used the term *schematicity* to imply that individuals differ in the concepts they habitually and automatically use to describe themselves and others (Bargh, 1989, 1994), such as "outgoing" or "forgetful." Because these concepts are heavily elaborated and affect-laden (Fiske & Pavelchak, 1986), information processing in their domains is more efficient than is processing in other domains (e.g., responses to these survey items are generated more quickly), and conflicting information is processed more thoroughly (e.g., responses to these survey items take longer to formulate; Kihlstrom & Klein, 1994). In simple terms, people are schematic with respect to a concept (such as "good rememberer") if they rate the concept as highly self-descriptive and highly important; otherwise, they are aschematic. In general, schematic concepts are the ones that people use when asked to describe themselves.

Schematic concepts are chronically accessible, more elaborated, and likely to have affective loading; aschematic concepts are less likely to have these characteristics. Schematic concepts are used more often for evaluating self and others; aschematic concepts can be used, but only after direct questioning, and are subject to higher levels of context dependence. In short, schematic concepts are much more likely to be invoked when responding to items in a survey. Only with great difficulty and careful design will aschematic concepts be used.

Whether schematicity results in stable metamemory judgments (i.e., the degree to which judgments are susceptible to context effects) is open to debate. Cavanaugh et al. (1998) argued that older adults are schematic regarding memory and memory loss (i.e., more likely to refer to memory as "very important" or to describe themselves as "forgetful"), making them much like experts who have long-term or "trait" involvement in a domain (Feldman & Lynch, 1988) or people with well-developed value systems and ideologies (Fischoff, Slovic, & Lichtenstein, 1980). Such memory "experts" would be likely to attend to domain-relevant information automatically, to be capable of accurate analytic and intuitive processing, to organize material in memory around the schematic construct, to process impression-inconsistent information more elaborately, to generate affect automatically, to have context-independent judgment standards and well-developed abstract category representations, and to be less susceptible in general to contextual influences on judgment (Alba & Hutchinson, 1987; Fazio, Sanbonmatsu, Powell, & Kardes, 1986; Feldman & Lindell, 1989; Feldman & Lynch, 1988; Wyer & Srull, 1986). This means that questions dealing with memory-related information, for example, would invoke these characteristics more in older adults than younger adults. Of particular importance for metamemory is that influencing such "expert" judgments (e.g., trying to get people to consider additional factors or another viewpoint) would not be easy, as it would require the suppression of automatic responses, which would require considerable effort on the respondent's part.

Although none of these implications has been tested directly in the metamemory domain, there are several findings that are consistent with the conclusion that older adults are more schematic with respect to memory decline. For example, Cavanaugh, Grady, and Perlmutter (1983) found that older adults reported being more upset at memory failures, even when the personal importance of the to-be-remembered information was rated as low. Cavanaugh (1987) reported high correlations among older adults' self-ratings of memory ability across several domains. Cavanaugh et al. (1983), Cavanaugh and Morton (1988), and Dixon and Hultsch (1983) all reported that older adults claimed that having a good memory is important to them, rated themselves as having an adequate memory, yet reported more instances of memory failures compared to younger adults. Most attempts at training or modifying memory self-efficacy in older adults has met with modest success at best, with no studies showing strong, long-lasting effects (e.g., see Cavanaugh, 1996, for a review).

Despite suggestive findings, no firm conclusions can be drawn. Schwarz (personal communication, February 16, 1996) pointed out that the assumption of the stability of judgments over time may not be warranted in the area of self-judgments, which at least in college students does not follow the patterns described above for older adults. Also, there is some evidence (Schwarz & Knäuper, chapter 12 in this volume) that older adults are more susceptible to response order effects and less affected by item order effects than younger respondents, although this research has not focused on self-ratings of memory ability. It would seem that the only way to find out whether these speculations hold for metamemory would be to conduct the appropriate experiments.

Attributional processes. People ascribe causes to events and behaviors, a point that routinely is incorporated into conceptions of metamemory (e.g., Cavanaugh, 1996). Whether these ascribed causes are logical or not is a function of how the information is framed and how it is processed. Well-known biases in attributional processes exist, caused in part by automatic processing; that is, by the degree to which schematicity holds. In domains in which a person is schematic, information is processed via a chronically accessible causal scenario; in aschematic domains, information is processed via more general structures. For a schematic older adult, this may mean that forgetting an item at the store would be due to "getting old"; having one's attention diverted by other events, a potentially plausible explanation, likely would not even be considered. To the extent that a person experiences self-inconsistent task experience (e.g., high rates of success on memory tasks), the individual eventually may differentiate a specific task performance impression from a general memory ability impression on which he or she is schematic (Brewer, 1988; Cavanaugh & Morton, 1988; Cavanaugh, Morton, & Tilse, 1989). In other words, the person may differentiate remembering at the grocery store (which is associated with good performance) and remembering in other stores (which is associated with poor performance). However, in cases of weak or nonexistent general impressions, specific task experience may serve to create or change such impressions due to the incorporation of specific, noncritical features into category representations. This is especially true for topics the person has never thought about before, which may occur when responding to items in a survey.

Automaticity and awareness. People may not be aware of the many influences on their responses to metamemory questions. This assumption is compatible with Bargh's (1989) concept of conditional automaticity. His framework described a system in which perceptions of memory events, for example, and judgments about these events are flexible, based on past experience and present context, but are experienced phenomenally as states of the world or of the self. People become aware of this process only by consciously attending to variations across situations and, even then, probably only with difficulty. Most important, automatic processes cannot be deconstructed through introspection without a great deal of effort, making them very difficult (at best) to describe in response to items in a survey.

Metamemory is no exception. We may "know" a great deal about memory, but essentially be unable to introspect and explain how we came to this knowledge (e.g., Nisbett & Wilson, 1977). To the extent that a memory event, such as forgetting to get bread at the grocery store, is categorized automatically, a reasonably accurate estimation of the frequency of such events and a self-judgment on some accessible trait or ability category can be made. If a metamemory question taps this same category, an answer could be directly retrieved and provided as a response. But, if the question taps a category not typically used by the person, both specific event memories and existing relevant judgments would be jointly retrieved in order to construct a response, which would be vulnerable to various biasing factors. Understanding how such biasing factors operate is an important avenue for future metamemory research.

Clearly, this aspect of metamemory has major implications for survey construction. Any frequency estimation question is subject to these effects. Without understanding whether the items' and the person's trait categories match, it is nearly impossible to understand the meaning of the responses, especially once they are aggregated across items and respondents.

Recall of personal attributes. Responding to metamemory questions requires one to take prior responses into account in creating the present answer, termed the "recall of personal attributes" in the social cognition literature. Ross (1989) proposed that this entails a two-step process: (a) establishing one's present status on the attribute in question, and (b) invoking an implicit theory of stability or change over time on the attribute in order to make a judgment. According to Ross, people view some attributes as relatively more stable than others, and that some normally stable attributes may change under some circumstances that are neither controllable nor positive. Additionally, implicit theories may bias judgments by resulting in underestimation or overestimation of the true change in an attribute, depending on whether the judgment is biased in favor of normative consistency or normative change.

Some data in the metamemory literature are relevant here. Beliefs about memory ability appear to be quite similar, regardless of whether people are rating unspecified age-graded targets or themselves (Ryan, 1992; Ryan & Kwong See, 1993). Cavanaugh and Morton (1988) reported that some older adults expressed strong opinions in favor of normative changes in memory with age, but simultaneously stated that such changes were outside of their control. Additionally, they reported that implicit theories tended to result in inflated ratings of ability earlier in life, a finding verified by McFarland, Ross, and Giltrow (1992), who found that older adults rated themselves as healthier and as having a better memory at age 38 than a group of 38-year-olds currently rated themselves. McDonald-Miszczak, Hertzog, and Hultsch (1995) found that scales measuring self-reported change in memory ability are influenced more by implicit theories of change than by adults' accurate monitoring of actual changes in memory; indeed, they found that actual longitudinal changes were not related strongly to perceived changes. Together, the findings suggest that implicit theories about change and beliefs about current status drive judgments about change that may or may not be accurate reflections of true changes in memory ability. The age differences so often noted in the metamemory questionnaire literature simply may be artifacts of the influence of implicit theories about how aging affects memory. Thus, to gain insight into people's perceptions of change in their memory ability, it is essential to understand their implicit theories about it. Only then will we be able to design appropriate and effective intervention strategies (see also Cavanaugh, 1996).

Future directions

As can be surmised from the preceding discussion, adult developmental research on the knowledge and beliefs aspects of metamemory is at a key crossroads. At this point, we know that psychometrically sound questionnaires assessing memory knowledge and beliefs can be constructed and that, under certain circumstances, responses to these questionnaires predict memory performance. However, due in part to the focus on creating psychometrically sound questionnaires, and in part to historical biases in adult developmental cognitive research, little effort has been directed toward understanding how people arrive at their responses. In this chapter, several core constructs from social cognition have been discussed that may prove useful in understanding these processes. For additional progress to be made, several issues must be examined systematically. Among the most important of these are the following.

- What standards of judgment do people use to make their responses? How do these standards change with different instructional sets? To what extent do memory self-efficacy and attributions about performance vary with standards of judgment? In this context, standards of judgment refer to two separate things: the reference group against which a respondent makes a judgment (e.g., "other people my age," "people older/younger than me") and the level of performance assumed to be typical for this memory situation. Presumably, each type of standard (reference group and performance) could vary independently.
- How accurately do people remember their prior memory performances? What forces shape accuracy? Under what conditions does this represent an episodic memory task (i.e., recall of a specific number of items remembered) versus one in which the respondent uses an estimation strategy?
- What types of memory situations have the most affect-laden outcomes? Which aspects of memory knowledge and beliefs are most influenced by affect?
- Are there systematic age differences in schematicity of memory? If so, does this vary across different memory situations? Does schematicity vary across memory content domains?
- How do implicit theories of memory shape adults' responses? Are implicit theories linked to standards of judgment, schematicity, self-efficacy, and experience of affect?
- Can meaningful patterns of individual differences be identified in how people respond to items in metamemory questionnaires? If so, can such differences be used to better predict performance, maladaptive beliefs, and the like?
- How do all of these aspects change across adulthood? Are some processes more important at different ages? If so, how and why do they change?

By addressing these issues, we will uncover many interesting details on how people's beliefs about their memory influence their ability to remember. Such understanding will be a significant advance in our knowledge about cognition and aging.

References

Alba, J. W., & Hutchinson, J. W. (1987). Dimensions of consumer expertise. *Journal of Consumer Research, 13*, 411–454.

Anderson, J. R. (1987). Skill acquisition: Compilation of weak-method problem solutions. *Psychological Review, 94*, 192–210.

Anschutz, L., Camp, C. J., Markley, R. P., & Kramer, J. J. (1985). Maintenance and generalization of mnemonics for grocery shopping by older adults. *Experimental Aging Research, 11*, 157–160.

Anschutz, L., Camp, C. J., Markley, R. P., & Kramer, J. J. (1987). Remembering mnemonics: A three-year follow-up on the effects of mnemonic training in elderly adults. *Experimental Aging Research, 13*, 141–143.

Baldi, R. A., & Berry, J. M. (1996). *Memory self-efficacy and memory performance in older adults: Anchoring and choice effects.* Unpublished manuscript, University of Richmond, Richmond, VA.

Bandura, A. (1986). *Social foundations of thought and action: A social cognitive theory.* Englewood Cliffs, NJ: Prentice-Hall.

Bandura, A. (1989). Regulation of cognitive processes through perceived self-efficacy. *Developmental Psychology, 25*, 729–735.

Bargh, J. A. (1989). Conditional automaticity: Varieties of automatic influence in social perception and cognition. In J. S. Uleman & J. A. Bargh (Eds.), *Unintended thought: Causes and consequences for judgment, emotion, and behavior.* New York: Guilford Press.

Bargh, J. A. (1994). The four horsemen of automaticity: Awareness, intention, efficiency, and control in social cognition. In R. S. Wyer, Jr., & T. K. Srull (Eds.), *Handbook of social cognition* (2nd ed., Vol. 1, pp. 1–40). Hillsdale, NJ: Erlbaum.

Barsalou, L. W. (1987). The instability of graded structure: Implication for the nature of concepts. In U. Neisser (Ed.), *Concepts and conceptual development: Ecological and intellectual factors in categorization* (pp. 101–140). Cambridge, England: Cambridge University Press.

Berry, J. M. (1999). Memory self-efficacy in its social cognitive context. In F. Blanchard-Fields & T. M. Hess (Eds.), *Social cognition and aging* (pp. 69–96). San Diego, CA: Academic Press.

Berry, J. M., & West, R. L. (1993). Cognitive self-efficacy in relation to personal mastery and goal setting across the life span. *International Journal of Behavioral Development, 16*, 351–379.

Berry, J. M., West, R. L., & Dennehey, D. M. (1989). Reliability and validity of the Memory Self-Efficacy Questionnaire. *Developmental Psychology, 25*, 701–713.

Brewer, M. B. (1988). A dual process model of impression formation. In T. K. Srull & R. S. Wyer (Eds.), Advances in social cognition (Vol. 1, pp. 1–32). Hillsdale, NJ: Erlbaum.

Cavanaugh, J. C. (1987). Age differences in adults' self reports of memory ability. *International Journal of Aging and Human Development, 24*, 271–277.

Cavanaugh, J. C. (1989). The importance of awareness in memory aging. In L. W. Poon, D. C. Rubin, & B. Wilson (Eds.), *Everyday cognition in adulthood and late life* (pp. 416–436). New York: Cambridge University Press.

Cavanaugh, J. C. (1996). Memory self-efficacy as a key to understanding memory change. In F. Blanchard-Fields & T. M. Hess (Eds.), *Perspectives on cognitive changes in adulthood and aging* (pp. 488–507). New York: McGraw Hill.

Cavanaugh, J. C., & Borkowski, J. G. (1980). Searching for metamemory-memory connections: A developmental study. *Developmental Psychology, 16*, 441–453.

Cavanaugh, J. C., Feldman, J. M., & Hertzog, C. (1998). Memory beliefs as social cognition: A reconceptualization of what memory questionnaires assess. *Review of General Psychology, 2*, 48–65.

Cavanaugh, J. C., Grady, J., & Perlmutter, M. (1983). Forgetting and use of memory aids in 20- and 70-year-olds' everyday life. *International Journal of Aging and Human Development, 17*, 113–122.

Cavanaugh, J. C., & Green, E. E. (1990). I believe, therefore I can: Self-efficacy beliefs in memory aging. In E. A. Lovelace (Ed.), *Aging and cognition: Mental processes, self-awareness, and interventions* (pp. 189–230). Amsterdam: North-Holland.

Cavanaugh, J. C., Kramer, D. A., Sinnott, J. D., Camp, C. J., & Markley, R. J. (1985). On missing links and such: Interfaces between cognitive research and everyday problem solving. *Human Development, 28*, 146–168.

Cavanaugh, J. C., & Morton, K. R. (1988). Older adults' attributions about everyday memory. In M. M. Gruneberg & P. Morris, (Eds.), *Practical aspects of memory: Current research and issues* (Vol. 1, pp. 209–214). Chichester, England: Wiley.

Cavanaugh, J. C., & Morton, K. R. (1989). Contextualism, naturalistic inquiry, and the need for new science: A rethinking of everyday memory aging and childhood sexual abuse. In D. A. Kramer & M. Bopp (Eds.), *Transformation in clinical and developmental psychology* (pp. 89–114). New York: Springer-Verlag.

Cavanaugh, J. C., Morton, K. R., & Tilse, C. S. (1989). A self-evaluation framework for understanding everyday memory aging. In J. D. Sinnott (Ed.), *Everyday problem solving: Theory and application* (pp. 266–284). New York: Praeger.

Cavanaugh, J. C., & Perlmutter, M. (1982). Metamemory: A critical examination. *Child Development, 53*, 11–28.

Dixon, R. A., & Hultsch, D. F. (1983). Structure and development of metamemory in adulthood. *Journal of Gerontology, 38*, 682–688.

Dixon, R. A., Hultsch, D. F., & Hertzog, C. (1988). The Metamemory In Adulthood (MIA) questionnaire. *Psychopharmacology Bulletin, 24*, 671–688.

Dweck, C. S., & Leggett, E. L. (1988). A social-cognitive approach to motivation and personality. *Psychological Review, 95*, 256–273.

Fazio, R. H., Sanbonmatsu, D. M., Powell, M. C., & Kardes, F. R. (1986). On the automatic activation of attitudes. *Journal of Personality and Social Psychology, 50*, 229–238.

Feldman, J. M., & Lindell, M. K. (1989). On rationality. In I. Horowitz (Ed.), *Organization and decision theory* (pp. 83–164). Amsterdam: Kluwer-Nijhoff.

Feldman, J. M., & Lynch, J. G., Jr. (1988). Self-generated validity and other effects of measurement on belief, attitude, intention, and behavior. *Journal of Applied Psychology, 73*, 421–435.

Fischoff, B. Slovic, P., & Lichtenstein, S. (1980). Knowing what you want: Measuring labile values. In T. Wallsten (Ed.), *Cognitive processes in choice and decision behavior* (pp. 117–142). Hillsdale, NJ: Erlbaum.

Fiske, S. T., & Pavelchak, M. (1986). Category-based versus piecemeal-based affective responses: Developments in schema-triggered affect. In R. M. Sorrentino & E. T. Higgins (Eds.), *Handbook of motivation and cognition* (pp. 167–203). New York: Guilford Press.

Flavell, J. H. (1971). First discussant's comments: What is memory development the development of? *Human Development, 14,* 272–278.

Gilewski, M. J., & Zelinski, E. M. (1986). Questionnaire assessment of memory complaints. In L. W. Poon (ed.), *Handbook for clinical memory assessment of older adults* (pp. 93–107). Washington, DC: American Psychological Association.

Gilewski, M. J., & Zelinski, E. M. (1988). Memory Functioning Questionnaire (MFQ). *Psychopharmacology Bulletin, 24,* 665–670.

Herrmann, D. J., & Neisser, U. (1978). An inventory of everyday memory experiences. In M. M. Gruneberg, P. E. Morris, & R. N. Sykes (Eds.), *Practical aspects of memory* (pp. 35–51). New York: Academic Press.

Hertzog, C., & Dixon, R. (1994). Metacognitive development in adulthood and old age. In J. Metcalfe & A. P. Shimamura (Eds.), *Metacognition: Knowing about knowing* (pp. 227–251). Cambridge, MA: MIT Press.

Hertzog, C., Dixon, R. A., & Hultsch, D. F. (1990). Metamemory in adulthood: Differentiating knowledge, belief, and behavior. In T. M. Hess (Ed.), *Aging and cognition: Knowledge organization and utilization* (pp. 161–212). Amsterdam: North-Holland.

Hertzog, C., Hultsch, D. F., & Dixon, R. A. (1989). Evidence for the convergent validity of two self-report metamemory questionnaires. *Developmental Psychology, 25,* 687–700.

Hertzog, C., Lineweaver, T. T., & McGuire, C. L. (1999). Beliefs about memory and aging. In F. Blanchard-Fields & T. M. Hess (Eds.), *Social cognition and aging* (pp.43–68). San Diego, CA: Academic Press.

Kelly, G. A. (1955). *The psychology of personal constructs.* New York: Norton.

Kihlstrom, J. F., & Klein, S. B. (1994). The self as a knowledge structure. In R. S. Wyer, Jr., & T. K. Srull (Eds.), *Handbook of social cognition* (2nd ed., Vol. 1, pp. 153–208). Hillsdale, NJ: Erlbaum.

Koriat, A. (1994). Memory's knowledge of its own knowledge: The accessibility account of the feeling of knowing. In J. Metcalfe & A. P. Shimamura (Eds.), *Metacognition: Knowing about knowing* (pp. 115–135). Cambridge, MA: MIT Press.

Levy, B., & Langer, E. (1994). Aging free from negative stereotypes: Successful memory in China and among the American deaf. *Journal of Personality and Social Psychology, 66,* 989–997.

Lineweaver, T. T., & Hertzog, C. (1998). Adults' efficacy and control beliefs regarding memory and aging: Separating general from personal beliefs. *Aging, Neuropsychology, and Cognition, 5,* 264–296.

Lovelace, E. A. (1990). Aging and metacognitions concerning memory function. In E. A. Lovelace (Ed.), *Aging and cognition: Mental processes, self-awareness, and interventions* (pp. 157–188). Amsterdam: North-Holland.

Markus, H. (1977). Self-schemata and processing information about the self. *Journal of Personality and Social Psychology, 35,* 63–78.

Markus, H., & Wurf, E. (1987). The dynamic self-concept: A social-psychological perspective. *Annual Review of Psychology, 38,* 299–337.

McDonald-Miszczak, L., Hertzog, C., & Hultsch, D. F. (1995). Stability and accuracy of metamemory in adulthood and aging: A longitudinal analysis. *Psychology and Aging, 10,* 553–564.

McFarland, C., Ross, M., & Giltrow, M. (1992). Biased recollections in older adults:

The role of implicit theories of aging. *Journal of Personality and Social Psychology, 62*, 837–850.

Metcalfe, J., & Shimamura, A. P. (Eds.). (1994). *Metacognition: Knowing about knowing*. Cambridge, MA: MIT Press.

Nelson, T. O., & Narens, L. (1990). Metamemory: A theoretical framework and new findings. In G. Bower (Eds.), *The psychology of learning and motivation* (Vol. 26, pp. 125–141). New York: Academic Press.

Nelson, T. O., & Narens, L. (1994). Why investigate metacognition? In J. Metcalfe & A. P. Shimamura (Eds.), *Metacognition: Knowing about knowing* (pp. 1–25). Cambridge, MA: MIT Press.

Nisbett, R. E., & Wilson, T. D. (1977). Telling more than we can know: Verbal reports on mental processes. *Psychological Review, 84*, 231–259.

Rabinowitz, J. C. (1989). Age deficits in recall under optimal study conditions. *Psychology and Aging, 4*, 378–380.

Ross, M. (1989). Relation of implicit theories to the construction of personal histories. *Psychological Review, 96*, 341–357.

Ryan, E. B. (1992). Beliefs about memory changes across the adult lifespan. *Journal of Gerontology: Psychological Sciences, 47*, 41–46.

Ryan, E. B., & Kwong See, S. (1993). Age based beliefs about memory changes for self and others across adulthood. *Journal of Gerontology: Psychological Sciences, 48*, 199–201.

Schneider, W., & Pressley, M. (1989). *Memory development between 2 and 20*. New York: Springer-Verlag.

Schwarz, N. (1996, September). *Metacognition*. Presented at the National Institute on Aging Workshop on Social Cognition and Aging, Washington, DC.

Seeman, T., McAvay, G., Merrill, S., Albert, M., & Rodin, J. (1996). Self-efficacy beliefs and change in cognitive performance: MacArthur studies of successful aging. *Psychology and Aging, 11*, 538–551.

West, R. L., & Berry, J. M. (1994). Age declines in memory self-efficacy: General or limited to particular tasks and measures? In J. D. Sinnott (Ed.), *Handbook of adult lifespan learning* (pp. 426–445). New York: Greenwood.

West, R. L., Dennehy-Basile, D., & Norris, M. (1996). Memory self-evaluation: The effects of age and experience. *Aging and Cognition, 3*, 67–83.

Wyer, R. S., Jr., & Srull, T. K. (1986). Human cognition in its social context. *Psychological Review, 93*, 322–359.

Autobiographical memory and aging 8

David C. Rubin

Autobiographical memory has been a fruitful areas of study over the past few decades (Brewer, 1996; Conway, 1990; Conway & Rubin, 1993; Conway, Rubin, Spinnler, & Wagenaar, 1992; Jobe, Tourangeau, & Smith, 1993; Neisser & Fivush, 1994; Rubin, 1986, 1996, 1998; Schwarz & Sudman, 1994). Because older adults have more life to remember, much of this work has been integrated into the study of cognitive aging. Here, I concentrate on how autobiographical memories are distributed over the lifespan, both because it is one topic for which we have a good quantitative description and because clear differences exist in the availability of autobiographical memories from different parts of the life span.

Two issues need to be mentioned briefly. The first is the accuracy of the memories themselves. The second is the accuracy of the dates. If the autobiographical memories people report from their life are mostly confabulations, or if the dates given bear no direct relation to the actual dates, then the results reported here would be of little use for survey research. Neither condition appears to hold.

The issue of the accuracy of autobiographical memories is one of the most complex and heated in psychology (Brewer, 1996; Robinson, 1996; Schacter, 1996; Winograd & Neisser, 1992). After an extensive review of the philosophical and psychological literature, Brewer (1996, p. 61) came to the following conclusion: "Recent recollective memories tend to be fairly veridical unless they are influenced by strong schema-based processes. Recollective memories give rise to high confidence in the accuracy of their contents and that confidence can frequently predict objective memory accuracy." Most of the time, people are mostly accurate unless there are biasing factors at work. This summary offers little comfort for individual courtroom cases, but is the best we have and is less troubling for survey data that are to be aggregated. Depending on the goals of the survey, some of the biasing may not be a problem. People tend to keep their memories consistent with their current views of themselves (Robinson, 1996) and so may distort in ways that are useful for some, but not all, purposes.

The question of the accuracy of the dating of memories is easier to discuss because the data are better (Friedman, 1993; Huttenlocher, Hedges, & Prohaska, 1988; Larsen, Thompson, & Hansen, 1996; Thompson, Skowronski, Larsen, & Betz, 1996). It is clear that people do not store the exact dates of most events (Brewer, 1996), but rather construct them using a cyclical timescale of years, seasons or months, and weeks. A person may know an event occurred on a Sunday in June, but not know the year. Thus, there are a disproportionate number of events that have dating errors of approximately plus or minus 1 day, 7 days, 30 days, and 365 days. Nonetheless, the dates people give to events when temporal boundaries are not set are unbiased estimates of when the events actually occurred (Rubin, 1982; Rubin & Baddeley, 1989). There are some exceptions to this generalization (Brown, Shevell, & Rips, 1986; Kemp & Burt, 1998), but they are not common.

With these preliminary considerations, we can turn to the distribution of autobiographical memories. The scientific beginnings of the study of autobiographical memory and of their distribution can be traced to Galton (1879; see Crovitz, 1970, and Crovitz & Schiffman, 1974, for an integration into modern cognitive psychology).

Memories from the recent past

Galton (1879) studied his own memories by taking a "leisurely walk along Pall Mall" (p. 151), pausing at approximately 300 objects and using each one to cue a memory. To bring the study into the laboratory, he made a list of words, viewed the words one at a time, recorded the time it took for the word to elicit a memory, recorded a brief response, and noted the age of the memory. His distribution of memories was 39% from "boyhood and youth," 46% from "subsequent manhood," and 15% "quite recent events" (p. 157). This research can be seen as the foundation of two directions in research. The first is the free associations of Freud and Jung. The second is Crovitz and Schiffman's (1974) revival of the technique to study autobiographical memory. Whereas Galton accepted all memories as responses, Crovitz and Schiffman intended that their subjects' responses be episodic memories as defined by Tulving (1972, 1983); that is, memories for events that occurred at one specific time and place.

In order to obtain a temporal distribution, Crovitz and Schiffman (1974) assumed that when a respondent reported a memory occurred n time units ago, the implied precision meant that the memory could be distributed evenly over ± ½ of the time unit. Thus, a memory that was reported as occurring 24 hours ago was assigned to a bin ranging from 23.5 to 24.5 hours ago, whereas a memory reported as occurring 1 day ago was assigned to a bin ranging from 12 to 36 hours ago. They plotted these densities at each time marker of English from 1 hour to 17 years ago using the time units of hours, days, weeks, months, and years. Another technique (Rubin, 1982) asked for exact dates and times, rank ordered these, and formed bins of an odd number of reported memories, using the range of each bin to determine the density and the median date of each bin to determine the time ago. The results were the same. A sample distribution (Rubin, 1982, Experiment 2) from 18-year-old undergraduates using the latter technique is shown in Figure 8.1. Each of the points in the figure is based on the median and range of 85 successively dated memories.

Several points are worthy of note. First, there is a large range of both times and densities—so large that logarithmic scales are used on both axes to allow all the data to be shown. Second, the data closely fit a smooth curve, even though there is no control at learning and little control at recall. Third, the data are close to linear on the log-log paper and thus fit a power function, $\ln(y) = \ln(a) - b \cdot \ln(t)$ or $y = at^{-b}$, with an exponent, b, of about .8. The power function also is a good fit to studies of laboratory learning (Anderson & Schooler, 1991; Rubin, 1982; Rubin & Wenzel, 1996; Wixted & Ebbesen, 1991). In a review of 210 data sets from the literature on human and animal memory, Rubin and Wenzel (1996) found that, overall, the power function fit as well as any of the 125 two-parameter functions they tested. The power function clearly was superior to the logarithmic and other two-parameter functions only for the autobiographical memory data sets. This difference could be due to autobiographical memory being different or to the much larger range of recall values present in the autobiographical memory data sets.

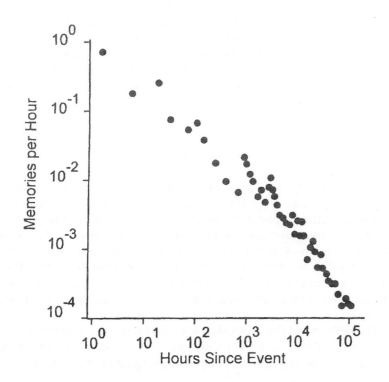

FIG. 8.1.
The relative number of autobiographical memories per hour reported by undergraduates as a function of the age of those memories. Both axes are logarithmic, so a straight line would be a power function. Adapted with permission from Rubin, 1982, Figure 2.

If the most recent 10 to 20 years of life of people ranging in age from 12 to 70 are examined, similar results can be obtained (Rubin & Schulkind, 1997b, 1997c; Rubin, Wetzler, & Nebes, 1986). A power function fits a collection of data sets with r^2s all over .95. The slopes vary between .69 and 1.07 across studies from laboratories using different subject populations, stimuli, and methods of aggregating the data, but the slopes do not differ systematically with the average age of the respondents. Thus, for adults of any age, it appears that recent memories will be most available, with a monotonically decreasing retention function of the form at^{-b}, with b in the range of .7 to 1.1. The lack of a consistent difference in the slope parameter with the age of the respondent is consistent with the literature on other forms of retention (Giambra & Arenberg, 1993; Hulicka & Weiss, 1965; Rubin & Wenzel, 1996; Wickelgren, 1975). There are differences in learning with age but, once the level of learning is equated, there at most are small differences in the rate of retention with age.

The power function description of autobiographical memory has been shown to hold for individual people and individual cue words and for conditions in which people are asked to provide 50 autobiographical memories from their life without any cue words (Rubin, 1982). Different cues have different effects. For instance, concrete, easy-to-image words, such as fire, house, ship, and tree, which usually have objects as referents, produce older memories (i.e., shallower slopes) than hard-to-image words such as contents, context, memory, and time (Rubin, 1982). This may be one reason that odorants tend to produce old memories (Herz & Cupchik, 1992), though not older than words with the same referent (Rubin, Groth, & Goldsmith, 1984). Odors do, however, produce memories that are less often thought about. Nonetheless, the basic power function is maintained. In summary, there is a robust interpretable, quantitative description of the relative availability of autobiographical memories from the most recent decade or two of life.

Memories from early childhood

We now turn briefly to people's early childhood memories. The retention function is expressed as a function of time ago (i.e., time measured from response). Another component is needed that is expressed as a function of age (i.e., time measured from birth). This is because people tend to recall fewer memories from the first few years of life and no memories from before birth. If the distributions of autobiographical memories of people of different ages are to be described, both a function of time ago, the t in at^{-b}, and a function of time since birth (age – t) are needed. Figure 8.2 shows distributions of early memories from several sources.

The left panel of Figure 8.2 shows results from three studies in which undergraduates were asked to provide memories from before age 8. For each study, the percentage of memories at each year is shown. In the first

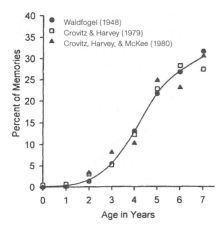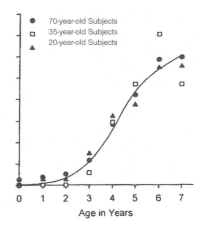

FIG. 8.2.
The distributions of
early childhood mem-
ories from several pub-
lished studies. Percent-
ages of the total num-
ber of memories prior
to age 8 in each distri-
bution are used so that
the plots can be easily
compared. The curve
fit to the data in both
panels is the average
distribution of the
8,610 early childhood
memories from all
studies combined.

study, Waldfogel (1948) had 124 undergraduates each spend two 85-minute
sessions separated by 35 to 40 days recording experiences up to their eighth
birthday. He then tabulated the number of unique, nonrepeated, memories for each person as a function of age. In the second study, Crovitz and
Harvey (1979) collected memories of episodes from before age 8 from 17
undergraduates. Each student was instructed to spend 4 hours a week for
each of 12 weeks. For these subjects, there was a tendency to produce memories from later in the period between 0 and 8 years as the 12 weeks pro-
gressed, but this effect is ignored here. In the third study, Crovitz, Harvey,
and McKee (1980) had 18 undergraduates spend up to 3 minutes trying to
recall an autobiographical memory from before age 8, cued by each of 20
nouns. These nouns were drawn from words that described the memories
produced in the earlier Crovitz and Harvey study. As can be seen in the left
panel, the data are remarkably similar given the differences in procedures,
so one curve is drawn for all three data sets.

The right panel of Figure 8.2 shows data from Rubin and Schulkind
(1997c) for subjects of three different ages: 40 undergraduates who were
20 years old, 20 adults who were 35 years old, and 60 adults who were 70
or 73 years old. The task for these subjects was to produce an autobiographical memory for each of 124 cue words. In contrast to the left panel
just discussed, in the right panel memories were requested from anywhere
in the life span, not just from the first 8 years; however, only the data from
the first 8 years are analyzed here. For each group, the number of memories dated as occurring before the eighth birthday was set equal to 100% in
the figure. As will be discussed later, some subjects were biased toward
earlier memories and, although they did produce more early memories,
the shape of their distributions did not differ. Similarly the 20-, 35-, and 70-
year-old subjects varied widely in the percentage of the 124 cue words
memories that were from before age 8 (6.0%, 1.4%, and 4.2%, respectively),
but the relative distributions from the three age groups are remarkably
similar, with the obvious exception that data from groups with more sub-

jects are more regular. The curve fit to the data is the same as that in the left panel. Thus, it appears that, independent of the age of the adult and independent of whether all episodic memories or only those from early childhood are to be retrieved, the same distribution is obtained.

Averaging overall the data shown in Figure 8.2, by summing the total number of memories produced in each year independent of the study in which the memory was collected and then dividing by the total number of memories, yields the following percentages for ages 0 through 7: 0.13%, 0.38%, 1.68%, 5.54%, 12.96%, 21.80%, 27.05%, and 30.45%. This set of values, to which the curves in Figure 8.2 are fit, provides my best estimate of the relative frequency of childhood memories by age. It is based on a total of 8,610 memories from before age 8.

Memories from the remainder of the life span

The discussion so far is sufficient to describe the distribution of autobiographical memories of 20-year-old respondents. However, most of the lives of older adults has not been considered. When the total distribution of older adults is considered, a third component is needed: a *bump*, or increase in memories, from the period after the childhood decline to about age 30. Figure 8.3 shows a distribution for 70-year-old respondents from several laboratories.

The third component could be termed reminiscence, but the term bump is used to stress the empirical nature of the finding because all that is implied is that more autobiographical memories are recalled from when a person is between 10 and 30 years old than would be expected from the

FIG. 8.3.
The distribution of autobiographical memories over the life span for older adults from several published studies. The data are normalized so that the area under each curve is approximately the same.

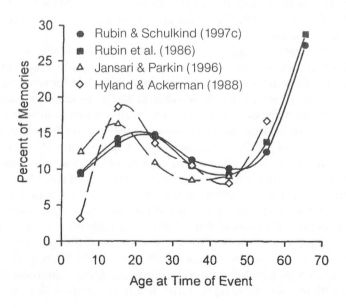

other two components. The term bump also serves to highlight the lack of a suitable theoretical framework. Reminiscence, while usually lacking the kind of explicit quantitative definition provided here for the bump, has been a topic of great interest in the aging literature (e.g., Butler, 1964; Costa & Kastenbaum, 1967; Havighurst & Glasser, 1972; Romaniuk, 1981). For integrations of studies of the distribution of autobiographical memory with studies of the theoretically richer term reminiscence, see Fitzgerald (1996) and Webster and Cappeliez (1993). Additionally, people with many forms of amnesia often have better memory for older than for more recent events (Butters & Cermak, 1986; Ribot, 1882; Squire, Chace, & Slater, 1975), and the description of the bump provides a comparison measure of the extent to which such a pattern occurs in nonclinical populations.

The definition of the bump used here was derived from empirical studies of autobiographical memory that used the cue word technique. The oldest plot in Figure 8.3 was taken from Rubin et al. (1986) and is a summary of 1,373 memories of 70 adults sorted into the decades in which the individuals reported that the remembered event had occurred. The subjects, who were about 70 years old, were tested in three different laboratories under slightly different conditions (Fitzgerald & Lawrence, 1984; Franklin & Holding, 1977; Rubin et al., 1986). At the time of data collection, none of the laboratories were expecting a bump, which appeared only on reanalysis of the data in Rubin et al. (1986). In all cases, the subjects were asked to provide an autobiographical memory for each cue word. There were between 20 and 50 cue words per subject. On completing this task, the subjects were asked to date each memory. Roughly half the memories produced by these subjects are not in Figure 8.3. Memories that occurred within the most recent year of life were not included because doing so would have required extending the vertical axis, making the rest of the curve less visible. Data from 50- and 60-year-olds from the same three and one additional laboratory (Zola-Morgan, Cohen, & Squire, 1983) yielded similar curves. Data from 40-year-olds did not show a clear bump.

The second plot in Figure 8.3 is a combination of the twenty 70- and twenty 73-year-old subjects from Rubin and Schulkind (1997c) who each provided autobiographical memories to 124 cue words. Again, all memories from the most recent year were eliminated and the area under the curve set to 100%.

The third plot is from Hyland and Ackerman (1988). Subjects were cued with object nouns, activity verbs, and feeling terms from Robinson (1976). Older volunteers showed a clear increase in memories, which peaked in their teens and early twenties. In Figure 8.3, we plot the data from 12 volunteers with a mean age of 70. Hyland and Ackerman did not exclude recent memories, but reported that 47% of the 70-year-old subjects' memories occurred within the subject's most recent decade. In order to make their data comparable with the first two studies, the area under the first six decades of the Hyland and Ackerman data and the Rubin et al. (1986) plot were set equal to each other. Adults in their sixties also showed a clear reminiscence effect. Adults in their fifties showed a possible reminiscence effect, whereas those in their forties had a nearly equal number of memories from their teens, twenties, and thirties, with 80% of their reports falling in the most recent decade of life. For these adults, as well as the 40-year-old subjects analyzed by Rubin et al. (1986), it is likely that any reminiscence effect was overshadowed by memories for recent events.

Jansari and Parkin (1996) also asked adults to provide autobiographical memories to each of Robinson's (1976) cue words. Half of the subjects were under normal instructions and half received the added requirement that all memories had to be older than 2.5 years. Independent of these instructions, for reasons that are not clear, the data differ slightly from the other data sets in that they have fewer recent memories and more memories from childhood. Nonetheless, if the area under the curves from both of Jansari and Parkin's conditions are equated, the two conditions show patterns similar to each other and to the other data sets. The data for the average of their two conditions for their oldest group, whose members were between 56 and 60 years old, are plotted in Figure 8.3, with the area under the curve up to age 50 set equal to that of the Rubin et al. (1986) data set up to age 50.

In the studies reviewed so far, the bump occurs at one period in the life span. A standard developmental question to ask is whether this is due to maturation or environment. As usual, the answer appears to be both. Schrauf and Rubin (1998) tested a dozen older adults who lived in a Spanish speaking culture for at least 20 years and then lived in an English speaking culture for at least 30 years. Although their sample was small, they found that the bump was evident and followed the age of emigration, though the bump was largest for those whose emigration occurred earlier.

Thus, the bump is a robust and substantial effect. When older adults are asked to provide autobiographical memories from their lives without restrictions to the content or time period, they show a marked increase in memories for events that occurred in adolescence and early adulthood. The only way not to get this result seems to be to ask adults to recall events from individual thirds, quarters, or fifths of their life span for 5 or 10 minutes and to then see if some periods have more memories than others (Howes & Katz, 1992; Rabbitt & Winthorpe, 1988).

One question that remains with a method that lets people select whatever memory comes to mind is the role of demand characteristics. The cue word procedure used is among the most open-ended in cognitive psychology, and so exactly what the subject takes the experimental task to be is not clear. The method produces reliable findings, but there are differences in distributions that have no clear cause. Thus, for instance, Jansari and Parkin's (1996) results, which are shown in Figure 8.3, have more early memories than other studies. To pursue this issue, a modification, or bias, in the standard instructions was made to favor earlier memories. Instead of asking for "events in a memory experiment," Rubin and Schulkind (1997c) asked for "memories in an autobiographical memory experiment." They also changed the content of their one example from a recent event to a childhood event. Figure 8.4 compares two groups of twenty 73-year-old subjects who, except for the differences just noted, performed the same task with the same 124 cue words. As can be seen, although the bump remains, the effects of such subtle biasing can be substantial.

Rubin and Schulkind (1997c) measured a host of other properties of autobiographical memories in the hope of distinguishing memories from the bump from memories from other periods. When memories for events from between age 10 and age 30 were compared with memories from other periods, there were no differences in reaction time, the properties of the cue words that evoked the memories (Rubin & Schulkind, 1997a), and rating scale measures including importance, vividness, emotionality, novelty, and number of times the memory was rehearsed. Because there are no simple obvious measures that distinguish memories in the bump from surrounding memories, it is difficult to know how, why, or even if memories from the bump differ from other memories.

In addition to the studies finding a bump when autobiographical memories were cued by words, several researchers found the bump when older adults were requested to provide either "important" or "vivid" autobiographical memories. Instead of cuing each memory with a single word as in the studies reviewed above, Fromholt and Larsen's (1991, 1992) 30 subjects were asked to spend 15 minutes recalling events that had been important in their lives. The volunteers were between age 71 and age 89 and had an average of 7 years of education. For their important memories, the bump occurred at the same general place and shape as it did in the studies reviewed above. The change in procedure, however, increased the bump at

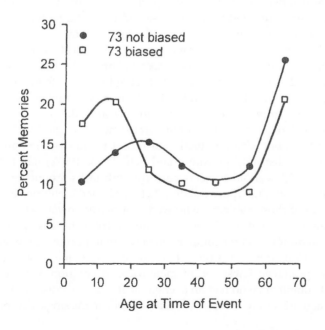

FIG. 8.4.
The distribution of autobiographical memories over the life span for older adults, half of whom were biased to have earlier memories. (Adapted with permission from Rubin & Schulkind, 1997c.)

the expense of memories from the most recent decade of life. In addition, there were slightly more memories in the 10 to 19-year-old decade than the 20 to 29-year-old decade. Thus, Fromholt and Larsen demonstrated that, at least for important memories, the bump's existence does not depend on the cuing technique or any details of its procedure and that the request for important memories produces relatively more bump memories. Similar results have been obtained with age-matched adults in the early stages of Alzheimer's dementia and with adults suffering from their first major depression (Fromholt, Larsen, & Larsen, 1995).

Fitzgerald (1988) asked individuals at an average age of almost 70 and an average of 12 years of education to record three "vivid" memories. The plots of the vivid memories corresponded more closely to Fromholt and Larsen's (1991, 1992) important memories than to the cue word studies reviewed above: the bump increased at the expense of recent memories. The bump peaked in the 16 to 20-year-old 5-year period, with fewer memories from the two surrounding 5-year periods and still fewer from the two 5-year periods surrounding them. In a later study, Fitzgerald (1996) found that adults between age 31 and 46 produced a clear peak in their distribution of vivid memories between age 16 and 25. Fitzgerald (1996) also demonstrated that younger and older adults both show a clear peak between age 6 and 25 in the distribution of memories that would go into a book about their lives. The inclusion of younger groups demonstrates that the bump for vivid and important memories exists fairly early in life and that the lack of a clear bump in 40-year-old subjects with word-cued memories may be due to the overshadowing by recent memories.

Two additional studies of vivid memories with older adults provided similar results. Benson et al. (1992) reported on studies in which 10 vivid memories were requested from Japanese and rural Midwestern American subjects. Both groups showed a bump: the Japanese in the 21- to 30-year-old decade of their lives and the Americans in the 11 to 20-year-old decade. Cohen and Faulkner (1988) requested six vivid memories from adults ranging from age 20 to 87. The bump was observed with the following exception. Subjects in the 40 to 59 and in the 60 to 87 age ranges recalled the most memories from when they were 0 to 10 years old.

In general, requests for vivid or important memories produce the bump in older adults, but with a reduction of recent memories compared with the word-cued distribution. Rubin and Schulkind (1997c) had the same forty 70- and 73-year-old subjects perform both tasks producing five important memories and approximately 124 word-cued memories each. The distribution of those subjects, who were not biased toward older memories, is shown in Figure 8.5. Here, memories from the past year are included to allow for a clearer comparison between important and word-cued memories. Consistent with the other studies, the request for important memories produced fewer recent memories. In addition, for the highly educated volunteers who had an average of 16 years of education, the important memories were reported as falling heavily in the single decade when

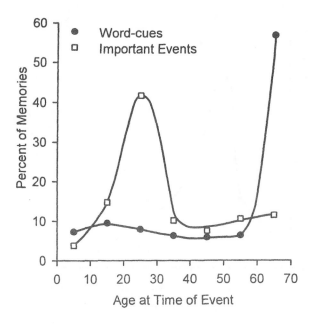

FIG. 8.5.
A comparison of word-cued and important memories obtained from the same older adults. (Adapted with permission from Rubin & Schulkind, 1997c.)

the subjects were in their twenties. Thus, the important memories have a different, narrower distribution than the word-cued memories. Comparisons with the other distributions of important memories indicated that the location and width of the peak changes with different populations and procedures, with a tendency for groups with less education to have earlier peaks. Nonetheless, the within-group comparison shown in Figure 8.5 clearly indicates that requests for memories of one kind or another can affect the period of the lifespan from which the memories originate.

The results reported so far are all from psychological laboratories, though not especially well controlled ones. Similar results have appeared outside the laboratory. Figure 8.6 presents the distribution of episodic and more extended events from the published intellectual autobiographies of famous psychologists (Mackavey, Malley, & Stewart, 1991). The same bump appears here as in the request for important memories from less famous subjects.

Memories for public events and general knowledge

The bump also appears when one asks for public, as opposed to private, events. Using telephone surveys, Schuman and his colleagues have shown that when people are asked for the most important event or change in the past half-century, they tend to report events or changes from when they were 10 to 30 years old (Belli, Schuman, & Jackson, 1997; Schuman, Akiyama, & Knäuper, 1997; Schuman, Belli, & Bischoping, 1997; Schuman & Rieger, 1992; Schuman, Rieger, & Gaidys, 1994; Schuman & Scott, 1989).

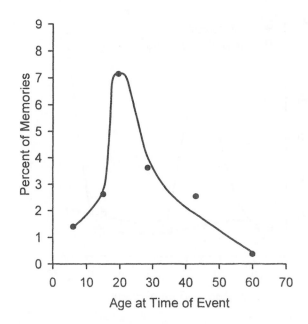

FIG. 8 6.
The distribution of
memories recorded in
published
autobiographical
sketches by famous
psychologists.
Memories for specific
events and those
extended over time
were combined,
weighted by their
relative frequency.
Adapted with
permission from
Mackavey, Malley, &
Stewart, 1991, Table 2.

Figure 8.7 shows the percentage of responses given as the most important public event of the past 50 years that was either World War II, John F. Kennedy's assassination, or the Vietnam War as a function of the age of the respondent at the time of the event. In the original studies, numerous plots of individual events showed the same pattern. The questions and methodology in the work of Schuman and his colleagues are different from the

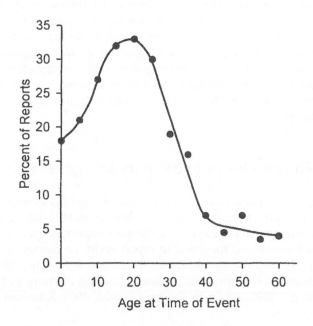

FIG. 8.7.
The percentage of people who judged either
World War II, the assassination of John F.
Kennedy, or the Vietnam War to be the most
important public event of the past 50 years
as a function of the age of the person at the
time of the event. The values reported are
the average percentages of these three
events for each 5-year period. For the first
periods and the periods over 40 years, the
averages are based on less than three
events because there were no respondents
who were of that age at the time of the
event. Adapted with permission from
Schuman & Scott, 1989.

other work reviewed here, but the basic results are the same, indicating that survey and experimental methods lead to the same results. Events judged as important by people are more likely to happen when those people are between 10 and 30 years old. Neisser (1982), in his discussion of flash-bulb memories, noted that the recall of one's personal circumstances at the time of a historical event ties one's autobiography to history. Having important personal and public memories peak at the same period of the life span makes this more likely to occur.

Having dealt at length with the distribution of episodic, autobiographical memories, the relation of such memories to more semantic memories should be considered. There are no studies for such semantic memories, or laboratory studies of any kind, that show the several-orders-of-magnitude drop shown in Figure 8.1, but it is argued here that for the limited range of the data available, such memories follow the same pattern as that presented above. The most well-known studies of very-long-term memory for factual material have been done by Bahrick and his colleagues (Bahrick, 1983, 1984; Bahrick, Bahrick, & Wittlinger, 1975). In these studies, there was a rapid drop in memory after initial learning, followed by a steady period of little observable drop that lasted a lifetime. Bahrick has described the existence of memories that decline little over decades as *permastore*. Bahrick found this permastore retention function in many domains, but always in studies in which the material initially was learned early in life, during high school or college, and then tested later at intervals of between a few days and 50 years. If the data in Figure 8.1 were plotted on a linear scale, they too would drop rapidly and then level off. To show the similarity, some permastore data from Bahrick is plotted in Figure 8.8 with a power function fit (for

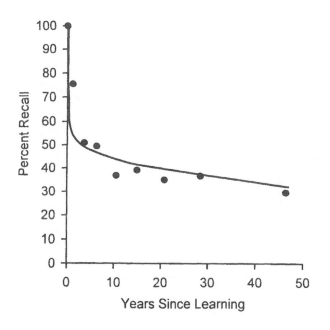

FIG. 8.8.
Retention data from an aggregation of six free-recall measures of knowledge of campus geography taken from Bahrick (1983). The level of initial learning was set equal to 100%. The curve shown is a power function. Adapted with permission from Rubin & Wenzel, 1996.)

more detail on this analysis, see Rubin & Wenzel, 1996). The power function and logarithmic function both fit Bahrick's data, as well as most data collected in the psychological laboratory (Rubin & Wenzel, 1996). If either the logarithmic or power function is used to describe retention, then ratios of time are what is important. The ratio of 3 years to 1 minute is 1,577,880. By comparison, the ratio of 60 years to 3 years is a meager 20. Thus, these functions and permastore make very similar predictions about the future loss of any information that still has a moderate level of recall after 3 years: It will show very little further loss.

Bahrick's studies (e.g. Bahrick, 1983) fit the retention component first discussed in this chapter, but have little to do with the bump. In the data presented here for the bump, the age of the acquisition of the memories varied across the life span, and the age at recall of the memories usually was held constant. That is, the x-axis was always age at time of learning. The exceptions are the data reported from Schuman (e.g. Schuman, Aikiyama, & Knäuper, 1997; Schuman, Belli, & Bischopins, 1997; Schuman & Rieger, 1992), which varied both in age at learning and age at test, but even here, the x-axis was age at time of learning. In contrast, in Bahrick's studies, the age at learning was always fixed and the retention interval could have been labeled in terms of the age of the subject at the time of the test. That is, in the data that produce the bump and in the data that produce permastore, different variables are confounded with retention interval. In contrast, when we test 70-year-old subjects for factual, semantic material learned at different points in the life span, the bump is still present.

Rubin, Rahhal, and Poon (1998) constructed multiple choice questions in a mechanical algorithmic fashion for each year data was available for

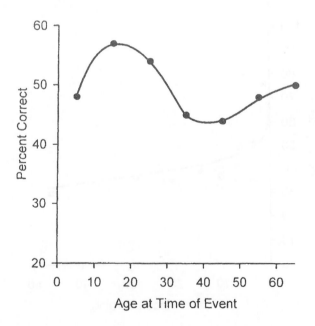

FIG. 8.9.
The percentage of correct answers of older subjects to five-alternative multiple choice questions as a function of their age at the time of the event questioned. The y-axis begins at 20%, which is chance.

each of the following five domains: what teams played in the World Series, what movie won the Academy Award, who won the Academy Award for best actor or actress, what was the most important news event according to the Associated Press, and who lost the presidential election. Thirty older adults were tested in 1984 and 30 other older adults were tested in 1994 to unconfound the particular questions from the subjects' ages at the time of the event queried. All topic areas showed better recall in the bump period than in later years. The combined data for all questions are shown in Figure 8.9, extending the autobiographical, episodic, free recall results from the studies presented above (which had answers that were not checked for correctness) to public, semantic recognition of verifiable responses.

References

Anderson, J. R., & Schooler, L. J. (1991). Reflections of the environment in memory. *Psychological Science, 2*, 396–408.

Bahrick, H. P. (1983). The cognitive map of a city: Fifty years of learning and memory. In G. H. Bower (Ed.), *The psychology of learning and motivation* (Vol. 17, pp. 125–163). New York: Academic Press.

Bahrick, H. P. (1984). Semantic memory content in permastore: Fifty years of memory for Spanish learned in school. *Journal of Experimental Psychology: General, 113*, 1–27.

Bahrick, H. P., Bahrick, P. O., & Wittlinger, R. P. (1975). Fifty years of memory for names and faces: A cross-sectional approach. *Journal of Experimental Psychology: General, 104*, 54–75.

Belli, R. F., Schuman, H., & Jackson, B. (1997). Autobiographical misremembering: John Dean is not alone. *Applied Cognitive Psychology, 11*, 187–209.

Benson, K. A., Jarvi, S. D., Arai, Y., Thielbar, P. R. S., Frye, K. J., & McDonald, B. L. G. (1992). Socio-historical context and autobiographical memories: Variations in the reminiscence phenomenon. In M. A. Conway, D. C. Rubin, H. Spinnler, & W. Wagenaar (Eds.), *Theoretical perspectives on autobiographical memory* (pp. 313–322). Utrecht, the Netherlands: Kluwer.

Brewer, W. F. (1996). What is recollective memory? In D. C. Rubin (Ed.), *Remembering our past: Studies in autobiographical memory* (pp. 19–66). Cambridge, England: Cambridge University Press.

Brown, N. R., Shevel, S. K., & Rips, L. J. (1986). Public memories and their personal context. In D. C. Rubin (Ed.), *Autobiographical memory* (pp. 137–158). Cambridge, England: Cambridge University Press.

Butler, R. N. (1964). The life review: An interpretation of reminiscence in the aged. In R. Kastenbaum (Ed.), *New thoughts on old age* (pp.265–280). New York: Springer-Verlag.

Butters, N., & Cermak, L. S. (1986). A case study of forgetting of autobiographical knowledge: Implications for the study of retrograde amnesia. In D. C. Rubin (Ed.), *Autobiographical memory* (pp. 253–272). Cambridge, England: Cambridge University Press.

Cohen, G., & Faulkner, D. (1988). Life span changes in autobiographical memory. In M. M. Gruenberg, P. E. Morris, & R. N. Sykes (Eds.), *Practical aspects of memory: Current research and issues: Vol. 1. Memory in everyday life* (pp. 277–282). New York: Wiley.

Conway, M. A. (1990). *Autobiographical memory: An introduction.* Milton Keynes, England: Open University Press.

Conway, M. A., & Rubin, D. C. (1993). The structure of autobiographical memory. In A. E. Collins, S. E. Gathercole, M. A. Conway, & P. E. Morris (Eds.), *Theories of memory* (pp. 103–137). Hove, England: Erlbaum.

Conway, M. A., Rubin, D. C., Spinnler, H., & Wagenaar, W. A. (Eds.). (1992). *Theoretical perspectives on autobiographical memory* (pp. 495–499). Dordrecht, The Netherlands: Kluwer.

Costa, P., & Kastenbaum, R. (1967). Some aspects of memories and ambitions in centenarians. *Journal of Genetic Psychology, 110,* 3–16.

Crovitz, H. F. (1970). *Galton's walk: Methods for the analysis of thinking, intelligence, and creativity.* New York: Harper & Row.

Crovitz, H. F., & Harvey, M. T. (1979). Early childhood amnesia: A quantitative study with implications for the study of retrograde amnesia after brain injury. *Cortex, 15,* 331–335.

Crovitz, H. F., Harvey, M. T., & McKee, D. C. (1980). Selecting retrieval cues for early-childhood amnesia: Implications for the study of shrinking retrograde amnesia. *Cortex, 16,* 305–310.

Crovitz, H. F., & Schiffman, H. (1974). Frequency of episodic memories as a function of their age. *Bulletin of the Psychonomic Society, 4,* 517–518.

Fitzgerald, J. M. (1988). Vivid memories and the reminiscence phenomenon: The role of a self narrative. *Human Development, 31,* 261–273.

Fitzgerald, J. M. (1996). Intersecting meanings of reminiscence in adult development and aging. In D. C. Rubin (Ed.), *Remembering our past: Studies in autobiographical memory* (pp. 360–383). Cambridge, England: Cambridge University Press.

Fitzgerald, J. M., & Lawrence, R. (1984). Autobiographical memory across the life span. *Journal of Gerontology, 39,* 692–699.

Franklin, H. C., & Holding, D. H. (1977). Personal memories at different ages. *Journal of Experimental Psychology, 29,* 527–532.

Friedman, W. J. (1993). Memory for the time of past events. *Psychological Bulletin, 113,* 44–66.

Fromholt, P., Larsen, P., & Larsen, S. F. (1995). Effects of late-onset depression and recovery on autobiographical memory. *Journal of Gerontology: Psychological Sciences, 50,* 74–81.

Fromholt, P., & Larsen, S. F. (1991). Autobiographical memory in normal aging and primary degenerative dementia (dementia of the Alzheimer type). *Journal of Gerontology: Psychological Sciences, 46,* 85–91.

Fromholt, P., & Larsen, S. F. (1992). Autobiographical memory and life-history narratives in aging and dementia (Alzheimer type). In M. A. Conway, D. C. Rubin, H. Spinnler, & W. Wagenaar (Eds.), *Theoretical perspectives on autobiographical memory* (pp. 413–426). Utrecht, The Netherlands: Kluwer.

Galton, F. (1879). Psychometric experiments. *Brain, 2,* 149–162.

Giambra, L. M., & Arenberg, D. (1993). Adult age differences in forgetting sentences. *Psychology and Aging, 8,* 451–462.

Hartley, A. A. (1992). Attention. In F. I. M. Craik & T. A. Salthouse (Eds.) *The handbook of aging and cognition* (pp. 3–50). Hillsdale NJ: Erlbaum.

Haug, H., & Eggers, R. (1991). Morphometry of the human cortex cerebri and corpus striatum during aging. *Neurobiology of Aging, 12,* 336–338.

Havighurst, R. J., & Glasser, R. (1972). An exploratory study of reminiscence. *Journal of Gerontology, 27*, 245–253.

Herz, R. S., & Cupchik, G. C. (1992). An experimental characterization of odor-evoked memories in humans. *Chemical Senses, 17*, 519–528.

Howes, J. L., & Katz, A. N. (1992). Remote memory: Recalling autobiographical and public events across the lifespan. *Canadian Journal of Psychology, 46*, 92–116.

Hulicka, I. M., & Weiss, R. L. (1965). Age differences in retention as a function of learning. *Journal of Consulting Psychology, 29*, 125–129.

Huttenlocher, J., Hedges, L., & Prohaska, V. (1988). Hierarchical organization in ordered domains: Estimating the dates of events. *Psychological Review, 95*, 471–484.

Hyland, D. T., & Ackerman, A. M. (1988). Reminiscence and autobiographical memory in the study of the personal past. *Journal of Gerontology: Psychological Sciences, 43*, 35–39.

Jansari, A., & Parkin, A. J. (1996). Things that go bump in your life: Explaining the reminiscence bump in autobiographical memory. *Psychology and Aging, 11*, 85–91.

Jobe, J. B., Tourangeau, R., & Smith, A. F. (1993). Contributions of survey research to the understanding of memory. *Applied Cognitive Psychology, 7*, 567–584.

Kemp, S., & Burt, C. D. B. (1998). The force of events: Cross-modality matching the recency of events. *Memory, 6*, 297–306.

Larsen, S. F., Thompson, C. P., & Hansen, T. (1996). Time in autobiographical memory. In D. C. Rubin (Ed.), *Remembering our past: Studies in autobiographical memory* (pp. 129–156). Cambridge, England: Cambridge University Press.

Mackavey, W. R., Malley, J. E., & Stewart, A. J. (1991). Remembering autobiographically consequential experiences: Content analysis of psychologists' accounts of their lives. *Psychology and Aging, 6*, 50–59.

Madden, D. J., Turkington, T. G., Provenzale, J. M., Denny, L. L. Hawk, T. C., Gottlob, L. R., & Coleman, R. E. (1999). Adult age differences in the functional neuroanatomy of verbal recognition memory. *Human Brain Mapping, 7*, 115–135.

Neisser, U. (1982). Snapshots or benchmarks? In U. Neisser (Ed.), *Memory observed: Remembering in natural contexts* (pp. 43–48). San Francisco: Freeman.

Neisser, U., & Fivush R. (1994). *The remembering self: Construction and accuracy of life narrative.* Cambridge, England: Cambridge University Press.

Prull, M. W., Gabrielli, J. D. E., & Bunge, S. A. (in press). Memory and aging: A cognitive neuroscience perspective. F. I. M. Craik & T. A. Salthouse (Eds.). *Handbook of aging and cognition–II.* Mahwah, NJ: Erlbaum.

Rabbitt, P., & Winthorpe, C. (1988). What do old people remember? The Galton paradigm reconsidered. In M. M. Gruenberg, P. E. Morris, & R. N. Sykes (Eds.), *Practical aspects of memory: Current research and issues: Vol. 1. Memory in everyday life* (pp. 301–307). New York: Wiley.

Ribot, T. (1882). *Diseases of memory: An essay in the positive psychology* (W. H. Smith, Trans.). New York: Appleton.

Robinson, J. A. (1976). Sampling autobiographical memory. *Cognitive Psychology, 8*, 578–595.

Robinson, J. A. (1996). Perspective, meaning, and remembering. In D. C. Rubin (Ed.), *Remembering our past: Studies in autobiographical memory* (pp. 199–217). Cambridge, England: Cambridge University Press.

Romaniuk, M. (1981). Reminiscence and the second half of life. *Experimental Aging Research, 7,* 315–336.

Rubin, D. C. (1982). On the retention function for autobiographical memory. *Journal of Verbal Learning and Verbal Behavior, 21,* 21–38.

Rubin, D. C. (Ed.). (1986). *Autobiographical memory.* Cambridge, England: Cambridge University Press.

Rubin, D. C. (Ed.). (1996). *Remembering our past: Studies in autobiographical memory.* Cambridge, England: Cambridge University Press.

Rubin, D. C. (1998). Beginnings of a theory of autobiographical remembering. In C. P. Thompson, D. J. Herrmann, D. Bruce, J. D. Reed, D. G. Payne, & M. P. Toglia (Eds.), *Autobiographical memory: Theoretical and applied perspectives* (pp. 47–67). Mahwah, NJ: Erlbaum.

Rubin, D. C., & Baddeley, A. D. (1989). Telescoping is not time compression: A model of dating autobiographical events. *Memory and Cognition, 17,* 653–661.

Rubin, D. C., Groth, L., & Goldsmith, D. (1984). Olfactory cuing of autobiographical memory. *American Journal of Psychology, 97,* 493–507.

Rubin, D. C., Rahhal, T. A., & Poon, L. W. (1998). Things learned in early adulthood are remembered best. *Memory and Cognition, 26,* 3–19.

Rubin, D. C., & Schulkind, M. D. (1997a). Properties of word cues for autobiographical memory. *Psychological Reports, 81,* 47–50.

Rubin, D. C., & Schulkind, M. D. (1997b). The distribution of autobiographical memories across the lifespan. *Memory and Cognition, 25,* 859–866.

Rubin, D. C., & Schulkind, M. D. (1997c). The distribution of important and word-cued autobiographical memories in 20-, 35-, and 70-year-old adults. *Psychology and Aging, 12,* 524–535.

Rubin, D. C., & Wenzel, A. E. (1996). One hundred years of forgetting: A quantitative description of retention. *Psychological Review, 103,* 734–760.

Rubin, D. C., Wetzler, S. E., & Nebes, R. D. (1986). Autobiographical memory across the adult lifespan. In D. C. Rubin (Ed.), *Autobiographical Memory* (pp. 202–221). Cambridge, England: Cambridge University Press.

Schacter, D. L. (1996). *Searching for memory: The brain, the mind, and the past.* New York: Basic Books.

Schrauf, R. W., & Rubin, D. C. (1998). Bilingual autobiographical memory in older adult immigrants: A test of cognitive explanations of the reminiscence bump and the linguistic encoding of memories. *Journal of Memory and Language, 39,* 437–457.

Schuman, H., Akiyama, H., & Knäuper, B. (1997. *Collective memories of Germans and Japanese about the past half century.* Unpublished manuscript.

Schuman, H., Belli, R. F., & Bischoping, K. (1997). The generational basis of historical knowledge. In J. W. Pennebaker, D. Paez, & Rime (Eds.), *Collective memory of political events: Social psychological perspectives* (pp. 47–77). Hillsdale, NJ: Erlbaum.

Schuman, H., & Rieger, C. (1992). Collective memory and collective memories. In M. A. Conway, D. C. Rubin, H. Spinnler, & W. A. Wagenaar (Eds.), *Theoretical perspectives on autobiographical memory* (pp. 323–336). Dordrecht, The Netherlands: Kluwer.

Schuman, H., Rieger, C., & Gaidys, V. (1994). Collective memories in the United States and Lithuania. In N. Schwartz & S. Sudman (Eds.), *Autobiographical memory and the validity of retrospective reports* (pp. 313–333). New York: Springer-Verlag.

Schuman, H., & Scott, J. (1989). Generations and collective memories. *American Sociological Review, 54*, 359–381.

Schwarz, N., & Sudman, S. (1994). *Autobiographical memory and the validity of retrospective reports*. New York: Springer-Verlag.

Shimamra, A. P., Janowsky, J. S., & Squire, L. R. (1990). Memory for temporal order of events in patients with frontal lobe lesions and amnesic patients. *Neuropsychologia, 28*, 803–813.

Squire, L. R., Chace, P. M., & Slater, P. C. (1975). Assessment of memory for remote events. *Psychological Reports, 37*, 223–234.

Thompson, C. P., Skowronski, J. J., Larsen, S. F., & Betz, A. (1996). *Autobiographical memory: Remembering what and remembering when*. Mahwah, NJ: Erlbaum.

Tulving, E. (1972). Episodic and semantic memory. In E. Tulving & W. Donaldson (Eds.), *Organization of memory* (pp. 382–403). New York: Academic Press.

Tulving, E. (1983). *Elements of episodic memory*. Oxford, England: Oxford University Press.

Waldfogel, S. (1948). The frequency and affective character of childhood memories. *Psychological Monographs: General and Applied, 62*(4, Whole No. 291).

Webster, J. D., & Cappeliez, P. (1993). Reminiscence and autobiographical memory: Complementary contexts for cognitive aging research. *Developmental Review, 13*, 54–91.

Wickelgren, W. A. (1975). Age and storage dynamics in continuous recognition memory. *Developmental Psychology, 11*, 165–169.

Winograd, E., & Neisser, U. (Eds.) (1992). *Affect and accuracy in recall: Studies of "flashbulb" memories*. New York: Cambridge University Press. Wixted, J. T., & Ebbesen, E. B. (1991). On the form of forgetting. *Psychological Science, 2*, 409–415.

Wixted, J. T., & Ebbesen, E. B. (1991). On the form of forgetting. *Psychological Science, 2*, 409–415.

Zola-Morgan, S., Cohen, N. J., & Squire, L. R. (1983). Recall of remote episodic memory in amnesia. *Neuropsychologia, 21*, 487–500.

Aging, circadian arousal patterns, and cognition 9

Carolyn Yoon, Cynthia P. May, Lynn Hasher

In the past few decades, human chronobiology research has documented circadian rhythms in a variety of biological and physiological functions, including body temperature, heart rate, and hormone secretions, reflecting regular peaks and declines across the day (Horne & Ostberg, 1976, 1977; Hrushesky, 1994). Circadian rhythms exhibit pronounced effects on important aspects of everyday life, including health and medical treatment (e.g., Hrushesky, 1989, 1994; Smolensky & D'Alonzo, 1993), as well as the ability to adapt to shift work (e.g., Monk, 1986; Moore-Ede & McIntosh, 1993). While extensive research addressing general circadian patterns exists, a far smaller literature concerns the extent to which there are individual differences in these patterns and, in turn, differences in performance at different times of day (e.g., Bodenhausen, 1990; Colquhoun, 1971; Folkard, Knauth, Monk, & Rutenfranz, 1976; Folkard, Weaver, & Wildgruber, 1983). This work has shown that individual patterns of circadian arousal are indeed correlated with performance on a variety of tasks (e.g., efficiency in reacting to stimuli, performing simple arithmetic, engaging in cognitive activity) such that performance peaks at a certain level of circadian arousal, a peak that occurs more or less regularly at a specific point in the day.

Within the field of cognition, awareness of the individual variation in circadian arousal patterns has been quite limited until recently. A few studies have demonstrated that this individual difference variable can significantly alter cognitive performance across the day (e.g., Bodenhausen, 1990; Horne, Brass, & Pettitt, 1980; Petros, Beckwith, & Anderson, 1990). A study by May, Hasher, and Stoltzfus (1993) further found clear age-group differ-

Much of the research reported in this chapter was supported by National Institute on Aging grants 12753 and 4306. This research was also supported in part by a grant from the Social Sciences and Humanities Research Council of Canada. We wish to thank the members of the Subject Registry at the Duke University Center for the Study of Aging and Human Development for their participation in many of the reported studies, and to acknowledge Fred Feinberg, Marcus Lee, Chad Massie, and Tammy Rahhal for their help.

ences in circadian arousal patterns, with older adults tending strongly toward a morningness pattern and with college students tending strongly away from this pattern of arousal. They also reported dramatic differences in memory performance across the day (from early morning to late afternoon) for both younger and older adults. However, the patterns of performance differences across the day were quite different for younger and older adults. Here, we report findings that differences in cognitive performance across the day are associated with age-related differences in circadian arousal, and that younger adults get better as the day progresses while older adults get worse. This pattern obtains across a number of tasks, although, as will be seen, there also are some very intriguing exceptions.

Age differences in morningness-eveningness tendencies

Measure

To assess individual and group differences in circadian patterns, we and others have used the Morningness-Eveningness Questionnaire (MEQ; Horne & Ostberg, 1976). The MEQ is a simple paper-and-pencil test consisting of 19 questions that address such issues as sleep-wake habits, subjective assessment of intellectual and physical peak times, and appetite and alertness over the day. Scores on the questionnaire delineate three main types of individuals: morning types, evening types, and neither types. This delineation has been validated by demonstrations of reliable differences between morning and evening types on both physiological (e.g., body temperature, heart rate, skin conductance, amplitude of evoked brain potentials; e.g., Adan, 1991; Horne, Brass, & Pettitt, 1980; Horne & Ostberg, 1976; Kerkhof, van der Geest, Korving, & Rietveld, 1981) and psychological measures of behavior (e.g., personality traits, sleep-wake behaviors, perceived alertness; Buela-Casal, Caballo, & Cueto, 1990; Horne & Ostberg, 1976; Mecacci, Zani, Rocchetti, & Lucioli, 1986; Webb & Bonnet, 1978; Wilson, 1990). In addition, the MEQ has high test retest reliability (e.g., Anderson, Petros, Beckwith, Mitchell, & Fritz, 1991; Kerkhof, 1984), and psychometric tests have indicated that it is a valid index of circadian rhythmicity (e.g., Smith, Reilly, & Midkiff, 1989).

Recent work on individual and group differences in morningness-eveningness tendencies has indicated a significant shift toward morningness with age (e.g., Adan & Almirall, 1990; Intons-Peterson, Rocchi, West, McLellan, & Hackney, 1998; Kerkhof, 1985; May et al., 1993; Mecacci & Zani, 1983; Vitiello, Smallwood, Avery, & Pascualy, 1986). The shift appears to begin around age 50 (Ishihara, Miyake, Miyasita, & Miyata, 1991), and occurs cross-culturally, as similar patterns have been obtained in Italy (Mecacci et al., 1986), Spain (Adan & Almirall, 1990), England (Wilson, 1990), Japan (Ishihara et al., 1991), Canada (Yoon & Lee, 1998), and the

United States (May & Hasher, 1998). We have now administered the MEQ to over 1,500 college students (age 18 to 23) and over 600 older adults (age 60 to 75) in different regions of North America and, as can be seen in Figure 9.1, the norms show clear age differences in the pattern of peak times across the day. Roughly 40% of younger adults (all of whom were college students) showed eveningness tendencies, with a large proportion of neither types and less than 10% morning-types. By contrast, less than 3% of older adults showed eveningness tendencies, and the majority (~75%) were morning types. These findings indicate that younger and older adults differ markedly in their circadian peaks over the day and suggest that, for those cognitive functions influenced by circadian arousal patterns, performance of many younger adults will improve across the day, while that of most older adults will deteriorate as the day progresses.

Differences in intellectual and physical behavior

Accounting for individual differences in circadian arousal thus is critical in aging studies involving intellectual and physical behavior that varies across the day. One set of findings which suggests real differences in behavior across the day comes from a study that addressed media and shopping patterns of older adults, compared with those of younger adults, and found them to be different across time of day (Yoon, 1997). In this study, a questionnaire was administered to younger and older adults regarding when they tended to read newspapers and magazines, watch television, and go shopping. More than 80% of the older subjects indicated that they read newspapers early in the morning, while only 14% of younger subjects reported doing so early in the morning. Magazines, on the other hand, were

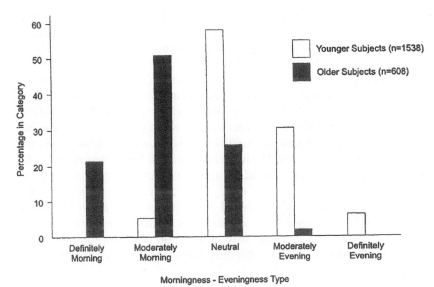

FIG. 9.1.
Time of day categories for older and younger adults.

read in the afternoon or evening by more than two thirds of both younger and older adults. About half of the older people indicated a clear preference for shopping in the morning or early afternoon, whereas younger people tended to do so in the late afternoon or evening. Older people's distinct preference to shop in the morning is consistent with their tendency to be mentally alert and energetic in the morning. They may reserve those hours to engage in tasks that pose a relatively greater cognitive or physical challenge.

Other studies have found intellectual and physical behavior to vary across age and time of day. One study found that prospective memory involving older adults' medication and appointment adherence was significantly greater in the morning than in the afternoon or evening (Leirer, Tanke, & Morrow, 1994). Another study conducted by Skinner (1985) with college students examined the relationship between grades and time of day when classes are held. The study involved a simple test comparing mean grades across morning, afternoon, and evening classes and found that grades in morning classes were significantly lower than those in afternoon and evening classes. Although these studies did not collect MEQ-type measures, they suggest real intellectual and behavioral differences across time of day that are quite consistent with circadian patterns reported elsewhere for these age groups (May et al., 1993; Yoon, 1997).

Changes in cognitive performance across the day

We have begun to explore the types of cognitive processes that are likely to be affected by the match between an individual's peak circadian arousal period and the time at which testing occurs, an influence referred to as the "synchrony effect" (May et al., 1993). Our goal is to identify those cognitive functions that demonstrate a synchrony effect as well as those that may be invariant over the day. To this end, our investigations have been guided by an inhibitory framework of attention and memory, positing that successful processing of information depends both on excitatory attentional mechanisms (Allport, 1989; Navon, 1989), which are responsible for the activation of relevant, goal oriented material, as well as on inhibitory mechanisms, which are responsible for the suppression of irrelevant, off-task information (Allport, 1989; Hasher, Zacks, & May, 1999; Navon, 1989). As discussed below, the bulk of data indicates that excitatory processing remains intact across optimal and nonoptimal times, but that inhibitory processing is impaired at individuals' off-peak times. The data also are consistent in confirming age-related impairments in inhibitory processes. We consider first the role of inhibition in information processing and then turn to the consequences of such inhibitory impairments for cognitive performance.

Inhibition

In taking an inhibitory view of attention and memory, we assume that, once familiar stimuli in the environment have established representations in memory, their reoccurrence will activate all linkages and associations to the existing representations, even though not all of them are necessarily relevant to the task at hand (Hasher & Zacks, 1988; Hasher et al., 1999). We further assume that among those representations that have received some degree of activation, conscious awareness is restricted to the most highly activated subset (cf., Cowan, 1988, 1993). This subset of representations is what we hereafter refer to as the *contents of working memory*. *Working memory* thus is assumed to be the contents of consciousness or ongoing mental workspace.

Inhibitory mechanisms are thought to be critical for three general functions, each of which is directed at controlling the contents of working memory so as to enable the efficient on-line processing and subsequent successful retrieval of target information (e.g., Hasher et al., 1999). First, inhibitory mechanisms prevent irrelevant, off-task information from entering working memory, thus limiting access to purely goal-relevant information. Inhibition also serves to delete or suppress from working memory information that is marginally relevant or that once was relevant but is no longer appropriate for current goals. Taken together, the access and deletion functions act to minimize competition from distracting material during both encoding and retrieval, thus increasing the likelihood that items activated concurrently in working memory are relevant to one another, and that target information will be successfully processed and retrieved. Finally, inhibition operates to restrain strong responses from being emitted before their appropriateness can be evaluated. The restraint function of inhibition thus allows for the appraisal and rejection of dominant responses when they are undesirable, so that a less probable, but more suitable, response can be produced.

There are both direct and indirect consequences of diminished inhibition. For example, individuals with impaired inhibitory functioning may be more susceptible to distracting, irrelevant information, whether that distraction is generated from external sources (e.g., speech from a radio or television that has been left on in the background) or internal sources (e.g., distracting thoughts about personal concerns or issues). In addition, the inability to clear away previously relevant, but currently inappropriate, information may lead to heightened interference between relevant and irrelevant information for poor inhibitors, resulting in difficulties in acquiring new material, comprehending questions, and retrieving stored memories. Poor inhibitors also may have difficulty disengaging from one line of thought or activity and switching to another, in addition to preventing the production of well-learned responses when those responses are inappropriate.

These direct impairments, produced by deficient inhibitory functioning, may lead to other, indirect cognitive consequences. Since control over working memory also ultimately reduces the efficiency of retrieval, diminished inhibition efficiency can further lead to an increased reliance on stereotypes, heuristics, or schemas in decision making, even in situations where detailed, analytical processing is clearly more appropriate (Bodenhausen, 1990; Yoon, 1997). For example, in social cognition studies involving perceptions of outgroup members' traits and behaviors, individuals are more likely to rely on stereotypic-based information, which often is negative, when responding at their nonoptimal compared to optimal time of day. This, in turn, may have implications for identifying important situations in which stereotyped groups may experience systematic disadvantages (e.g., personnel selection, law enforcement). Related to this is the possibility that inefficient inhibitors may be more susceptible to persuasion by weak arguments, particularly if those arguments contain material related to, but inconsequential for, the current topic (Rahhal, Abendroth, & Hasher, 1996; Yoon & Lee, 1998).

In the following sections, we first present direct evidence for on-line (i.e., current) failures of access, deletion, and restraint at off-peak times, failures that are attributed to deficient inhibition at nonoptimal times. We next discuss those tasks in which synchrony plays little or no role for either age group. We then present evidence for the subsequent downstream consequences of deficient inhibition at nonoptimal times. In each of the studies to be discussed, younger and older adults were tested at peak and off-peak times of day. All younger adults were evening types and all older adults were morning types, as assessed by the MEQ.[1]

Diminished inhibition at off-peak times

Access function of inhibition costs of distraction in problem solving. If individuals suffer inhibitory deficits at off-peak times, then distracting information should have a greater effect on their performance relative to participants tested at peak times. To test this prediction, we examined the impact of distraction on younger and older adults' ability to solve word problems at optimal and nonoptimal times of day (May, 1999). We used a modified version of the Remote Associates Test ([RAT]; Mednick, 1962), in which each problem consisted of three cue words (e.g., rat, blue, cottage) that all are remotely related to the same target word (e.g., cheese). The participants' task was to produce the target word that connected the three cue words. Our interest was in the effect of different types of distractors on individuals' ability to produce the targets by presenting distraction that led away from a solution versus distraction that led toward a solution.

Previous findings with this task indicated that target identification is impaired on the RAT when misleading distractors are placed next to each of the cue words (e.g., rat [cat], blue [red], cottage [cabin] = cheese; Smith & Blankenship, 1991). We expected that the cost of distraction would be greater for participants tested at off-peak relative to peak times, as they might be less able to suppress the irrelevant, misleading information. In addition, we explored the possibility that there might be situations in which the failure to suppress irrelevant information would be beneficial. To do so, we included a small proportion of test items in which the distractors presented with the cue trios were not misleading, but instead were "leading"; that is, they related the cues to the target (e.g., rat [eat], blue [dressing], cottage [diet] = cheese). Any benefits of distraction should be greater at nonoptimal times than at optimal times, when people have more control over distraction.

With all participants instructed to ignore distraction on all trials, we expected that, relative to individuals tested at optimal times, those tested at nonoptimal times would show greater deficits in solution production when misleading distractors were present, and greater benefit when leading distractors were present. The cost of misleading distractors and the benefit of leading distractors were calculated by subtracting the target identification rates for control trials (where no distraction was present) from the rates for misleading and leading trials, respectively. Table 9.1 shows the impact of distraction on problem solving for younger and older adults tested at peak and off-peak times of day. As expected, synchrony affected performance for both age groups, with those participants tested at off-peak times (i.e., younger adults tested in the morning and older adults tested in the evening) showing both greater costs of misleading distraction and greater benefits of leading distraction relative to age-mates tested at peak times. In addition, older adults generally showed a larger influence of distraction than younger adults, a finding consistent with an inhibitory-deficit model of aging (Hasher & Zacks, 1988).

Deletion function of inhibition: Sustained activation of no-longer-relevant material. In dynamic experiences, such as conversations, topics and locales change, and these shifts most often require that thought content also shifts. To simulate the need to stop thinking about one topic or idea and to start thinking about another, we assessed individuals' ability to suppress information that once was relevant, but is no longer suitable for current goals. To do this, May and Hasher (1998) used a garden path sentence completion task (Hartman & Hasher, 1991). In the first phase of this task, participants were presented with sentence frames that were missing highly predictable final words (e.g., "Before you go to bed, turn off the _____"), and

TABLE 9.1. Effect of distraction on problem solving for younger and older adults

Age and time	Cost	Benefit
Younger adults		
AM (nonpeak)	−11	17
PM (peak)	−2	1
Older adults		
AM (peak)	−10	8
PM (nonpeak)	−18	23

were asked to generate an ending for each frame (high-cloze sentences). Once participants generated an ending for a given frame (e.g., "lights" for the present example), a target word appeared, which participants were instructed to remember for a later, unspecified memory test. For half of the sentence frames (filler items), the participant-generated ending appeared; for the remaining sentence frames (critical items), the participant-generated ending was disconfirmed by the presence of a new, less probable, but nonetheless plausible, ending for the sentence (e.g., "stove"). Thus, for critical items, there was an implicit instruction to forget the generated ending (e.g., "lights"), as participants were informed that only the target endings (the ones presented by the experiment; e.g., "stove") would appear on the subsequent memory test.

Our aim was to determine, after a brief interval of 5 to 6 minutes, the accessibility of the target (e.g., "stove") and disconfirmed or no-longer-relevant (e.g., "lights") items from the critical sentence frames for younger and older participants who were tested at peak and off-peak times. On the premise that inhibition acts to delete from working memory those items that are no longer relevant for current goals, we expected efficient inhibitors (i.e., younger adults tested at peak times) to have access to target items only; disconfirmed items should be no more accessible than control items as a result of an active suppression operating to delete these items from working memory. By contrast, we expected inefficient inhibitors (i.e., older adults and those tested at asynchronous times) to have access to both target and disconfirmed items.

To assess these predictions, we used an indirect memory test, which enabled a comparison of production rates for target, disconfirmed, and control (i.e., words not presented in Phase 1) items. For this task, participants generated endings to sentence frames that had moderately predictable endings (medium cloze sentences) under the guise that they were helping create materials for a new experiment. Three types of frames were included: (a) frames that were moderately predictive of the target endings (e.g., "She remodeled her kitchen and replaced the old _____", for "stove"); (b) frames that were moderately predictive of the disconfirmed endings (e.g., "The baby was fascinated by the bright _____", for "lights"); and (c) frames that were moderately predictive of new, never-seen control endings (e.g., "The kitten slept peacefully on her owner's _____", for "lap"). We calculated priming scores for the target and disconfirmed endings by comparing completion rates for those items to the completion rate for control items[2]; positive priming indicates that the critical items were produced more often than control items, while negative priming indicates that the critical items were produced less often than control items. The priming data can be seen in Figure 9.2.

Consider first the pattern of priming for younger adults: at peak times, younger adults showed reliable priming of target endings and actually showed significant, below-baseline priming for the disconfirmed endings. These findings suggest that for younger adults at optimal times, the dele-

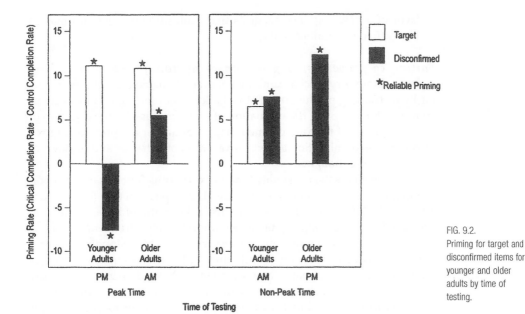

FIG. 9.2.
Priming for target and disconfirmed items for younger and older adults by time of testing.

tion function of inhibition is so efficient that the disconfirmed items actually are less accessible than items that were never presented. By contrast, younger adults tested at nonoptimal times showed positive priming for both target and disconfirmed items, indicating that they are impaired in their ability to delete from working memory no-longer-relevant information at down times of day.

Older adults also demonstrated strong synchrony effects on performance, but their overall pattern of priming was different from that of younger adults due to age-related inhibitory deficits. At their peak time, older adults closely resembled younger adults tested at nonoptimal times: they showed reliable positive priming for both target and disconfirmed items, suggesting that even at their best time of day, older adults are not efficient at deleting currently irrelevant information from working memory. At nonoptimal times, older adults were severely impaired in suppressing the self-generated but disconfirmed items, so much so that they showed marginally enhanced priming for those items relative to older adults tested at peak times, and actually failed to show any priming for experimenter-provided target items. It seems that inhibitory processing for older adults at nonoptimal times is so deficient that they are incapable of abandoning their self-generated, highly probable response, and as a consequence fail to show any priming at all for new target items. The patterns of priming for younger and older adults tested across the day are consistent with the suggestion that inhibitory functioning is diminished at off-peak relative to peak times, resulting in an inability to suppress or delete information that once was relevant, but is no longer appropriate for current goals. Note that the apparent inability of older adults to abandon their self-generated response in favor of a new response suggests that acquisition of new information will be difficult at nonoptimal times.

Failing to prevent strong responses at nonoptimal times: Stop signal. Inhibitory mechanisms are believed to enable control over behavior by restraining production of strong, dominant, or highly practiced responses, thus enabling the evaluation of and, if necessary, the rejection of those responses if they are deemed inappropriate for the present context. This function of inhibition allows for variation of behavior and retrieval of nondominating thoughts.

To investigate the possibility that the restraining function of inhibition is impaired at nonoptimal times, we used the stop signal task (e.g., Logan, 1983, 1985, 1994), in which participants had to withhold a very likely response whenever a stopping cue (which was relatively infrequent) occurred. The ability to prevent a response in the presence of the stopping cue provided a measure of restraint. In this study (May & Hasher, 1998), participants were trained to make category membership judgments (e.g., to say correctly that "yes, a chair is a piece of furniture" and "no, a stove is not a piece of furniture") as quickly as possible. On a small proportion of trials (stop-signal trials), participants heard a tone, which indicated that they were to stop or prevent their category judgment response. The proportion of stop-signal trials on which participants were successful at stopping their category response is displayed in Figure 9.3. Synchrony did affect stopping performance, such that both age groups were better able to stop when sig-

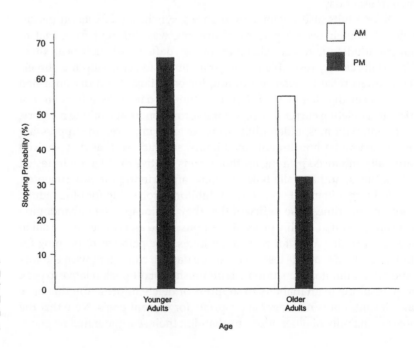

FIG. 9.3. Mean stopping probabilities for younger and older adults tested in the morning and in the evening.

naled to do so at peak relative to off-peak times. Thus, as with the access and deletion functions of inhibition, the restraint function of inhibition seems to be susceptible to synchrony effects for both younger and older adults. In addition, younger adults were generally better than older adults at withholding responses on stop-signal trials, again consistent with the suggestion that there are age-related declines in inhibitory efficiency.

Further evidence that individuals tested at off-peak times have difficulty controlling strong, well-practiced responses has come from a study examining general knowledge (May, Hasher, & Bhatt, 1994). In this study, participants were to answer simple trivia questions as quickly and accurately as possible (e.g., "What hero does Clark Kent become when he changes in a phone booth?"). Included in the list of questions however, were some "illusion" questions which, if taken literally, could not be answered (e.g., "How many animals of each kind did Moses take on the ark?" [Note that Noah, not Moses, built the ark.]). Participants were warned in advance of the presence of these illusion questions and were instructed not to produce the likely answer (e.g., two), but rather to respond "can't say." Thus, participants were asked to suppress the well-learned, highly probable verbal responses to the illusion questions and instead to answer with an alternative response. As illustrated in Figure 9.4, both younger and older adults showed an effect of synchrony on their ability to prevent strong, probable verbal responses: for illusion questions, participants tested at off-peak times were more likely to generate an inappropriate response (e.g., two) than age-mates tested at peak times.

When synchrony does not matter

Though the evidence we have reported thus far is consistent with the premise that inhibitory functioning is impaired at individuals' nonoptimal relative to optimal times, a number of findings also suggest that excitatory functioning does not vary across the day (see Table 9.2). First, scores on

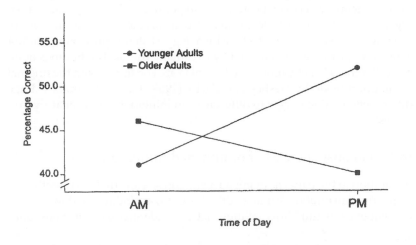

FIG. 9.4.
Percentage of correct answers on Moses illusion questions for younger and older adults by time of day.

TABLE 9.2. Tasks with no effect on synchrony on age

	Younger adults		Older adults	
	AM (Nonpeak)	PM (Peak)	AM (Nonpeak)	PM (Peak)
Vocabulary[a] (lap/bowl)	22	23	26	29
Vocabulary[b] (stop signal)	18	17	28	24
Moses trivia[c]	78%	78%	79%	81%
High-cloze rates[d]	89%	89%	88%	87%
Medium-cloze rates	52%	53%	49%	51%
Stop-signal categorization[c]	91%	92%	89%	91%
RAT control completion	36%	32%	33%	32%

Note. [a] ervt v4; max 48; [b] ervt v3; max 36; [c] percentage correct; [d] percentage of sentences completed with expected.

vocabulary tests (taken from several studies) did not change for either younger or older adults across the day, suggesting that retrieval of information from semantic or long-term memory is spared at nonoptimal times. Second, access to well-learned, familiar, or highly practiced responses was consistently preserved at nonoptimal times. We found spared performance on the trivia-type questions, into which illusion statements (e.g., Moses and the ark) were embedded. In the deletion experiment reported above (May & Hasher, 1998), both younger and older adults generated the expected ending for high-cloze sentence frames equally often at optimal and nonoptimal times. In addition, they were as fast and accurate in making category judgments about familiar categories across the day in the stop signal experiment. Finally, no effect of either synchrony or age on target production for control items was obtained for the RAT task in the May (1999) study, a finding which further supports the suggestion that activation processes are not impaired at nonoptimal times.

Thus, there is a growing number of findings that show that production of familiar, highly probable, or well-learned responses are not affected by the synchrony between peak circadian periods and testing times. Taken together, these findings are consistent with predictions of an inhibitory framework of synchrony effects, which suggest that suppression, but not activation, processes are affected by circadian arousal. The findings of no age differences in activation processes also are consistent with the original assumption made by Hasher and Zacks (1988) that attention-based age differences are due largely to differences in inhibition, not excitatory processes.

Indirect consequences of diminished inhibition

In addition to the patterns of impairment and sparing that are directly predicted from an inhibitory framework, there also are indirect or downstream consequences of inhibitory failures that are evident at asynchronous times of day. These deficits may be manifested in a number of ways, including memory impairments, particularly when tasks involve multiple trials and require the deletion of information from a previous trial in order to remember information from only the current trial. Other downstream consequences of diminished inhibition at nonpeak times of day include reliance on simple heuristic-based judgments, rather than more careful and effortful evaluations, and increased likelihood of being persuaded by weak arguments. Evidence of indirect consequences is provided in the sections that follow.

Heightened susceptibility to interference. As inhibitory control over no longer relevant information declines both at nonoptimal times of day and with age, it might be expected that all tasks that are performed best with no input from prior tasks will show circadian and age effects. One such family of tasks are multiple recall tasks in which the target items for each recall are at least partially different from preceding to-be-recalled sets. A classic example is the memory span task in which participants typically are given units of information to recall on multiple consecutive trials. Although the type of information tested in span experiments varies greatly from numbers to words to sentences, one common aspect of nearly all span experiments is that participants first receive small units of information (e.g., one or two words) and progressively advance to larger units (e.g., six or seven words). Span is determined by the largest unit size for which participants successfully recall all of the information; thus, those who recall the largest units have the highest span score. Note, however, that the largest units are also those that are most likely to be disrupted by unsuccessfully suppressed items from previous lists or trials and involve the greatest amount of proactive interference (disruption of performance on currently relevant target items brought about by material presented before these target items), as they are preceded by a number of trials with very similar information. For those such as older adults who cannot efficiently use inhibition to cut off access to previous information, the large units should be especially problematic; hence, span scores should be reduced. In addition, since inhibitory efficiency declines at nonoptimal times, span scores also should be reduced then, relative to optimal times.

Recent work by May, Hasher, and Kane (in press) has indicated that, indeed, span tasks do involve proactive interference, and that individuals who are particularly interference-prone are differentially disadvantaged by the standard administration of span tasks. To explore the possibility that synchrony impairs inhibitory functioning, thereby diminishing span performance, younger and older adults were administered a simple word span task, in which they read words on a computer screen and then had to repeat them aloud from memory. The words were presented in sets, beginning with set size 2 and progressing to set size 6. Each participant completed three trials at each set size, and span was calculated as the largest set size at which an individual was correct on two of the three trials. As can be seen in Figure 9.5, synchrony did affect span performance, with both age groups demonstrating higher span scores at peak relative to off-peak times.

Use of heuristics. Since research findings have seemed to suggest that both aging and performance at nonoptimal times can reduce access to details of information that are stored in memory, what is retrieved at nonoptimal times? Along with the evidence we have reviewed suggesting that strong responses are easily accessible, the work of Bodenhausen (1990) has suggested that heuristics (e.g., simple rules of thumb, shortcuts) and schemas, which Alba and Hasher (1983) argued are highly accessible relative to details of complex events, are also highly accessible at nonoptimal times and so are very likely to be used in evaluation situations. Below, we first discuss findings related to the role of synchrony in people's differential use of heuristics, and then consider further downstream consequences for persuasion in the following section.

During nonoptimal times of day, individuals appear to rely more on heuristics to process information than they do during optimal times of day. Bodenhausen (1990) found that people used stereotypes in making social judgments of individuals at nonoptimal times. Those who reached their mental peak early in the day were more likely to generate stereotypic responses in the afternoon and the evening, while those who reached their peak in the evening exhibited a greater tendency to generate stereotypic responses in the morning.

A study by Yoon (1997) provided further evidence that people rely more on heuristic or schema-based processing rather than detailed processing at nonoptimal times of day, and that this tendency is more pronounced in older than younger adults. In this study, participants were given a recognition task containing target and foil items. Consistent with a pattern of results suggestive of schema-based processing, older people at their nonoptimal time had relatively high hit rates and high false alarm rates for foils that were congruent and mildly incongruent (and, thus, likely to be mistakenly processed as a congruent item), but low false alarm rates for

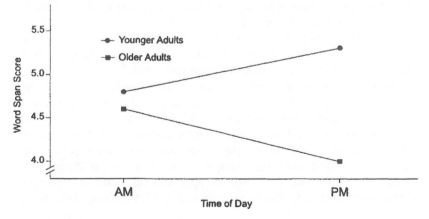

FIG. 9.5.
Word span scores for younger and older adults by time of day.

highly incongruent foils. However, at optimal times of day, older adults were as detailed in their processing as younger adults, evidenced by high hit rates and low false alarm rates (see Table 9.3).

The results of these two studies suggest the potential importance of considering the role of synchrony when investigating people's use of different types of processing strategies. For example, in social cognition studies involving perceptions of outgroup members' traits and behaviors, individuals may be more likely to rely on stereotype-based information, which often is negative, when responding at their nonoptimal compared to optimal time of day. This, in turn, may have implications for identifying important situations in which stereotyped groups may experience systematic disadvantages (e.g., personnel selection, law enforcement).

Persuasion. The notion that diminished inhibitory efficiency at nonpeak times can lead to an increased reliance on heuristic or schema-based, rather than more analytic, processing suggests further downstream consequences for persuasion. The elaboration likelihood model (Petty & Cacioppo, 1986) posits that there can be different routes to persuasion depending on an individual's ability and motivation to process information. In cases where the likelihood of elaboration is high (i.e., where ability and motivation to process are high), the attitude change process involves thoughtful scrutiny and detailed processing of persuasive communication (e.g., argument strength). This process is referred to as the "central route" to persuasion. On the other hand, when the individual lacks either the ability or the motivation to process information, a different process of attitude change occurs. This process, referred to as the "peripheral route" to persuasion, involves the use of simple rules of thumb, or heuristics, for evaluating the content of a persuasive message (e.g., peripheral cues). We thus might expect people who have neither the ability (e.g., at their nonoptimal time of day) nor the motivation to process incoming messages to be persuaded by cues that are not particularly diagnostic or informative, but nonetheless are appealing or relatively effortless to process.

TABLE 9.3. Effects of synchrony and age on recognition accuracy

| Age and time | Message items (Hit rates) | False alarm rates (FOILS) | | |
| | | | Incongruent | |
		Congruent	Low	High
Younger adults				
AM (nonpeak)	.81	.20	.06	.02
PM (peak)	.83	.08	.03	.06
Older adults				
AM (peak)	.93	.19	.04	.04
PM (nonpeak)	.77	.43	.37	.09

Adapted with permission from Yoon, 1997.

A study by Yoon and Lee (1998) found empirical support for such tendencies. The study examined how synchrony, age, and level of motivation might affect the extent to which people are persuaded by argument strength versus peripheral cues in an advertising setting. Persuasion was assessed by averaging four 9-point postmessage attitude ratings (semantic differential scales anchored by *bad/good, unsatisfactory/satisfactory, unfavorable/favorable, not worthwhile/worthwhile*). The results suggest that older adults, as well as younger adults, were persuaded by relatively strong arguments (i.e., a "central route"), as opposed to weak arguments, when highly motivated to process advertising messages during their respective peak times (see Table 9.4A). However, older adults also seemed to be persuaded by strong arguments, even when their motivation to process was low, as long as they were exposed to the information during their peak time of day. At the nonpeak time of day, the older adults appeared to be persuaded via a "peripheral route" (i.e., a peripheral cue operationalized as relevance of the picture to the product featured in the advertisement) under both low- and high-involvement conditions (see Table 9.4B). Thus, these results suggest that the ability to process incoming information depending on the time of day, not the level of motivation, is the critical determinant in the persuasibility of older adults. By contrast, younger adults who were highly motivated to process appeared to be persuaded by strong arguments even at their nonoptimal time of day (see Table 9.4A); they were persuaded by relevance of the picture (i.e., the peripheral cue) only when their motivation to process was low (see Table 9.4B).

Previous research involving younger adults has found that the degree to which people will agree with or be persuaded by the substance of an argument also may hinge on the degree to which people are distracted during the presentation of a message. In particular, Petty, Wells, and Brock (1976) demonstrated that weak arguments are particularly persuasive when people are distracted. In a study by Rahhal et al. (1996), the concern was with the degree to which distraction and persuasion effects are heightened at nonoptimal times. They conducted a study in which they created and normed two weak arguments (about abolishing home schooling and police

TABLE 9.4A. Persuasion of argument strength by age, time of day, and motivation

Argument strength	Low motivation		High motivation	
	Weak	Strong	Weak	Strong
Younger adults				
AM (nonpeak)	5.7	5.7	3.4	4.8
PM (peak)	5.6	5.8	3.5	5.2
Older adults				
AM (peak)	4.3	6.2	2.3	5.1
PM (nonpeak)	4.5	5.0	3.7	3.3

Note. Average of four postmessage attitude ratings on 9-point scales (1 = negative, 9 = positive).

TABLE 9.4B. Persuasion of picture relevance by age, time of day, and motivation

Picture relevance	Low motivation		High motivation	
	Weak	Strong	Weak	Strong
Younger adults				
AM (nonpeak)	5.2	6.3	4.1	3.7
PM (peak)	5.2	6.3	3.8	4.2
Older adults				
AM (peak)	4.8	5.4	3.1	3.4
PM (nonpeak)	4.3	5.7	3.0	4.2

Note. Average of four postmessage attitude ratings on 9-point scales (1 = negative, 9 = positive).

reassignment plans) which were presented in the presence versus absence of distraction to older adults who were tested in the morning or afternoon. The distraction task was extremely simple, and required participants to monitor where an X appeared on a computer screen. While doing this, participants listened to a message, and immediately afterward, their attitudes toward the message were assessed, using a series of 7-point rating scales. The data (see Figure 9.6) clearly show that distraction in the morning has little impact on attitude scores (how good, wise, favorable, and beneficial the arguments were). But, distraction at nonoptimal times has a major impact on older adults, such that the weak arguments were considerably more persuasive in the afternoon than in the morning.

Conclusion

The synchrony between circadian arousal periods really matters for some cognition- and social cognition–type tasks, but not for others. Moreover, the consequences of synchrony can be greater for older adults than for

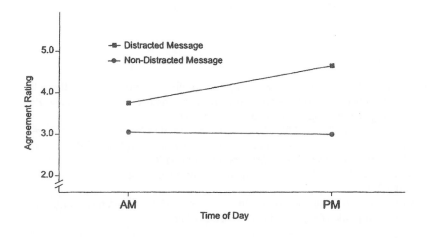

FIG. 9.6.
Agreement ratings for messages for older adults by time of day.

younger adults given the age-related deficits in inhibition. To the extent that changes in cognitive functioning at off-peak times do in fact stem from circadian related deficits in inhibition, performance at nonoptimal times reflects deficits such as heightened access to irrelevant information, failure to clear away or suppress information that is no longer useful, and difficulties in restraining or preventing the production of strong, dominant responses that are undesirable or inappropriate. In addition, downstream consequences of diminished inhibition include heightened susceptibility to proactive interference, impaired judgments resulting from retrieval failures, and increased reliance on stereotypes and heuristics.

On the other hand, performance appears to be spared over the day in some instances, such as when tasks simply require access to or production of familiar, well learned, or practiced material (e.g., vocabulary tests, simple trivia questions), or when strong, dominant responses produce correct answers (e.g., word associations, familiar category judgments).

Taken together, the evidence suggests that in investigations of age-related differences in cognitive performance, particularly those involving inhibitory functioning, it is important to guard against any potential biases by controlling for individual and group differences in circadian arousal patterns. Insomuch as we know that older adults tend to reach their mental peak in the morning while younger adults do so in the evening, studies failing to account for such differences in arousal patterns may otherwise produce results that reflect a systematic under- or over-estimation of relationships between age and other variables of interest.

Notes

1. Unfortunately, the fully crossed design of Age × Morningness-Eveningness was not possible because so few of the younger adults were morning types, and virtually none of the older adults was an evening type.

2. The control items for any given participant had served as presented items for another participant, via a counterbalancing scheme.

References

Adan, A. (1991). Influence of morningness-eveningness preference in the relationship between body temperature and performance: A diurnal study. *Personality and Individual Differences, 12,* 1159–1169.

Adan, A., & Almirall, H. (1990). Adaptation and standardization of a Spanish version of the morningness eveningness questionnaire: Individual differences. *Personality and Individual Differences, 11,* 1123–1130.

Alba, J. W., & Hasher, L. (1983). Is memory schematic? *Psychological Bulletin, 93,* 203–231.

Allport, A. (1989). Visual attention. In M. I. Posner (Ed.), *Foundations of cognitive science* (pp. 631–682). Cambridge, MA: MIT Press.

Anderson, M., Petros, T. V., Beckwith, B. E., Mitchell, W. W., & Fritz, S. (1991). Individual differences in the effect of time of day on long-term memory access. *American Journal of Psychology, 104*, 241–255.

Bodenhausen, G. V. (1990). Stereotypes and judgmental heuristics: Evidence of circadian variations in discrimination. *Psychological Science, 1*, 319–322.

Buela-Casal, G., Caballo, V. E., & Cueto, E. (1990). Differences between morning and evening types in performance. *Personality and Individual Differences, 11*, 447–450.

Colquhoun, W. P. (1971). Circadian variations in mental efficiency. In W. P. Colquhoun (Ed.), *Biological rhythms and human performance* (pp. 39–107). London: Academic Press.

Cowan, N. (1988). Evolving conceptions of memory storage, selective attention, and their mutual constraints within the human information processing system. *Psychological Bulletin, 104*, 163–191.

Cowan, N. (1993). Activation, attention, and short-term memory. *Memory and Cognition, 21*, 162–167.

Educational Testing Service. (1976). *Kit of factor-referenced tests*. Princeton, NJ.

Folkard, S., Knauth, P., Monk, T. H., & Rutenfranz, J. (1976). The effect of memory load on the circadian variation in performance efficiency under rapidly rotating shift system. *Ergonomics, 10*, 479–488.

Folkard, S., Weaver, R., & Wildgruber, C. (1983). Multi-oscillatory control of circadian rhythms in human performance. *Nature, 305*, 223–226.

Hartman, M., & Hasher, L. (1991). Aging and suppression: Memory for previously relevant information. *Psychology and Aging, 6*, 587–594.

Hasher, L., & Zacks, R. T. (1988) Working memory, comprehension, and aging: A review and new view. In G. H. Bower (Ed.), *The psychology of learning and motivation* (Vol. 22, pp. 193–225). New York: Academic Press.

Hasher, L., Zacks, R. T., & May, C. P. (1999). Inhibitory control, circadian arousal, and age. In D. Gopher & A. Koriat (Eds.), *Attention and performance: Vol. 17. Cognitive regulation of performance: Interaction of theory and application*. Cambridge, MA: MIT Press.

Horne, J., Brass, C., & Pettitt, S. (1980). Circadian performance differences between morning and evening types. *Ergonomics, 23*, 29–36.

Horne, J., & Ostberg, O. (1976). A self-assessment questionnaire to determine morningness-eveningness in human circadian rhythms. *International Journal of Chronobiology, 4*, 97–110.

Horne, J., & Ostberg, O. (1977). Individual differences in human circadian rhythms. *Biological Psychology, 5*, 179–190.

Hrushesky, W. (1989). Circadian chronotherapy: From animal experiments to human cancer chemotherapy. In B. Lemmer (Ed.), Chronopharmacology: Cellular and biochemical interactions (pp. 439–473). New York: Marcel Dekker.

Hrushesky, W. (1994, July/August). Timing is everything. *The Sciences, 34*, 32–37.

Intons-Peterson, M. J., Rocchi, P., West, T., McLellan, K., & Hackney, A. (1998). Aging, optimal testing times, and negative priming. *Journal of Experimental Psychology: Learning, Memory, and Cognition, 24*, 362–376.

Ishihara, K, Miyake, S., Miyasita, A., & Miyata, Y. (1991). Morningness-eveningness preference and sleep habits in Japanese office workers of different ages. *Chronobiologia, 18*, 9–16.

Kerkhof, G. A. (1984). A Dutch-language questionnaire for the selection of morn-

ing and evening type individuals. *Nederlands Tijdschrift voor de Psychologie,
39,* 281–294.

Kerkhof, G. A. (1985). Inter-individual differences in the human circadian system:
A review. *Biological Psychology, 20,* 83–112.

Kerkhof, G. A., van der Geest, W., Korving, H. J., & Rietveld W. J. (1981). Diurnal
differences between morning-type and evening-type subjects in some indices
of central and autonomous nervous activity. In A. Reinberg, N. Vieux, & P.
Andlauer (Eds.), *Night and shift work: Biological and social aspects* (pp. 457–
464). Oxford, England: Pergamon Press.

Leirer, V. O., Tanke, E. D., & Morrow, D. G. (1994). Time of day and naturalistic
prospective memory. *Experimental Aging Research, 20,* 127–134.

Logan, G. D. (1983). On the ability to inhibit simple thoughts and actions: I. Stop
signal studies of decision and memory. *Journal of Experimental Psychology: Learning, Memory, and Cognition, 9,* 585–606.

Logan, G. D. (1985). On the ability to inhibit simple thoughts and actions: II. Stop
signal studies of repetition priming. *Journal of Experimental Psychology: Learning, Memory, and Cognition, 11,* 675–691.

Logan, G. D. (1994). On the ability to inhibit thought and action: A users' guide to
the stop signal paradigm. In D. Dagenbach & T. Carr (Eds.), *Inhibitory mechanisms in attention, memory, and language* (pp. 189–239). New York: Academic
Press.

May, C. P. (1999). Synchrony effects in cognition: The costs and a benefit. *Psychological Bulletin and Review, 6,* 142–147.

May, C. P., & Hasher, L. (1998). Synchrony effects in inhibitory control over thought
and action. *Journal of Experimental Psychology: Human Perception and Performance, 24,* 363–379.

May, C. P., Hasher, L., & Bhatt, A. (1994, April). *Time of day affects susceptibility to
misinformation in younger and older adults.* Poster session presented at the Cognitive Aging Conference, Atlanta, GA.

May, C. P., Hasher, L., & Kane, M. J. (in press). The role of interference in memory
span measures. *Memory and Cognition.*

May, C. P., Hasher, L., & Stoltzfus, E. R. (1993). Optimal time of day and the
magnitude of age differences in memory. *Psychological Science, 4,* 326–330.

Mecacci, L., & Zani, A. (1983). Morningness-eveningness preferences and sleep-
waking diary data of morning and evening types in student and workers
samples. *Ergonomics, 26,* 1147–1153.

Mecacci, L., Zani, A., Rocchetti, G., & Lucioli, R. (1986). The relationships between morningness-eveningness, aging, and personality. *Personality and Individual Differences, 7,* 911–913.

Mednick, S. A. (1962). The associative basis of the creative process. *Psychological
Review, 69,* 220–232.

Monk, T. H. (1986). Advantages and disadvantages of rapidly rotating shift sched-
ules: A circadian viewpoint. *Human Factors, 28,* 553–557.

Moore-Ede, M., & McIntosh, J. (1993, October 1). Alert at the switch. *Technology
Review, 96,* 52–65.

Navon, D. (1989). The importance of being visible: On the role of attention in a
mind viewed as an anarchic intelligence system: I. Basic tenets. *European Journal of Cognitive Psychology, 1,* 191–213.

Petros, T. V., Beckwith, B. E., & Anderson, M. (1990). Individual differences in the effects of time of day and passage difficulty on prose memory in adults. *British Journal of Psychology, 81*, 63–72.

Petty, R. E., & Cacioppo, J. T. (1986). *Communication and persuasion: Central and peripheral routes to persuasion.* New York: Springer-Verlag.

Petty, R. E., Wells, G. L., & Brock, T. L. (1976). Distraction can enhance or reduce yielding to propaganda: Thought disruption versus effort justification. *Journal of Personality and Social Psychology, 34*, 874–884.

Rahhal, T. A., Abendroth, L. J., & Hasher, L. (1996, April). *Can older adults resist persuasion? The effects of distraction and time of day on attitude change.* Poster session presented at the Cognitive Aging Conference, Atlanta, GA.

Skinner, N. F. (1985). University grades and time of day of instruction. *Bulletin of the Psychonomic Society, 23*, 67.

Smith, C. S., Reilly, C., & Midkiff, K. (1989). Evaluation of the circadian rhythm questionnaires with suggestions for an improved measure of morningness. *Journal of Applied Psychology, 74*, 728–738.

Smith, S. M., & Blankenship, S. E. (1991). Incubation and the persistence of fixation in problem solving. *American Journal of Psychology, 104*, 61–87.

Smolensky, M., & D'Alonzo, G. (1993). Medical chronobiology: Concepts and applications. *American Review of Respiratory Disease, 147*, S2–S19.

Vitiello, M. V., Smallwood, R. G., Avery, D. H., & Pascualy, R. A. (1986). Circadian temperature rhythms in young adult and aged men. *Neurobiology of Aging, 7*, 97–100.

Webb, W. B., & Bonnet, M. H. (1978). The sleep of "morning" and "evening" types. *Biological Psychology, 7*, 29–35.

Wilson, G. D. (1990). Personality, time of day, and arousal. *Personality and Individual Differences, 11*, 153–168.

Yoon, C. (1997). Age differences in consumers' processing strategies: An investigation of moderating influences. *Journal of Consumer Research, 24*, 329–342.

Yoon, C., & Lee, M. (1998, April). *Age differences in processing of pictorial and verbal information across time of day.* Poster session presented at Cognitive Aging Conference, Atlanta, GA.

Language
and speech ‖‖

Speech perception and the comprehension of spoken language in adult aging

10

Arthur Wingfield

The ability to use rule-governed language appears early in childhood and is present in every society of the world. This universality of language is carried by specialized brain structures that are revealed by losses in specific language functions that occur following damage to certain areas of the brain, and by corresponding patterns of metabolic activity in these areas when language tasks are performed by neurologically healthy adults (Goodglass & Wingfield, 1998). In cases where oral communication cannot be conducted, sign languages have developed that are equally as rich in lexicon and syntax but with manual movements used to express objects, actions, and their syntactic relations (Meier, 1991).

The naturalness of language to the human family is reflected in the frequently noted observation that knowledge of linguistic rules, and the ability to use them in comprehension and production, remain strong even when aging takes a toll on other cognitive functions. This is the theme we develop in this chapter. We begin by examining speech perception, and the cognitive constraints that operate on spoken language comprehension, for both younger and older adults. We then highlight the sensory changes in audition that often accompany normal aging, and the impact these changes can have on spoken language comprehension. Finally, we discuss the cognitive constraints on language processing that are of special concern in older adulthood. These are the twin constraints of reduced effectiveness of working memory and a slowing in perceptual and cognitive

The author's research is supported by grants R37 AG04517 and R01 AG15852 from the National Institute on Aging. The author also gratefully acknowledges support from the W. M. Keck Foundation. Christine Koh, Kristen Prentice, Debra Titone, and Patricia Tun are thanked for their help and input in the preparation of this chapter.

operations. Throughout our presentation, the goal not only is to show how these constraints can affect older adults' ability to comprehend rapid spoken language, but also to show how spared knowledge and capabilities can ameliorate what might otherwise be more serious performance declines.

The perception of speech

One of the most salient features of natural speech is the rapid rate at which it arrives. It first should be said that there is no such thing as a "normal" speech rate. Speech rates can run from as slow as 90 words per minute (wpm) for individuals engaged in thoughtful conversation, to rates in excess of 210 wpm for a person attempting to read in a natural manner from a prepared script. On average, however, speech rates in ordinary conversation typically average between 140 and 180 wpm. To put this another way, successful comprehension requires that the words of a sentence be perceptually encoded, their linguistic relations determined, and a coherence (meaning) structure of the message constructed, all with the speech arriving at a rate of 2.3 to 3.0 words per second.

In Figure 10.1, we enumerate this challenge in terms of four operations, beginning from the acoustic waveform to the comprehension of the message at the discourse level. We refer to this sequence as processing the signal from the bottom up. We will address the other side of this issue, "top-down" processing, later in this section.

At the top of the left side of Figure 10.1, we show the speech waveform of a speaker who was asked to say in a clear way the phrase, "You talk and I'll listen." The speaker said these words into a microphone while a computer digitized the signal and displayed the utterance waveform on the computer screen as shown in the figure. The vertical displacements repre-

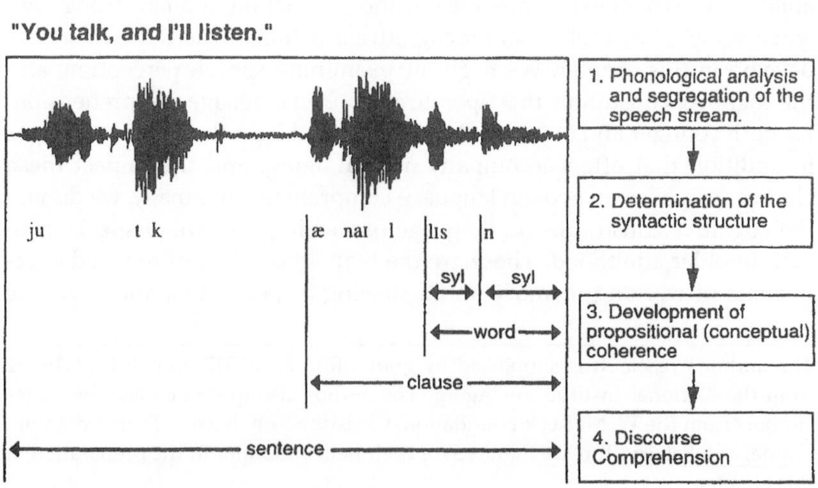

FIG. 10.1.
Bottom-up processing
from the acoustic
speech stream.

sent the sound energy, or amplitude, of the speech signal. The larger vertical displacements represent the speech sounds (phonemes) that have the
most sound energy. These typically are the vowels and the other voiced
sounds in the speech stream. (Voiceless phonemes such as the *s* in "whis-
per" or the *th* in "thin" are typical of the low-energy, high-frequency sounds
in English.) A flat area can be seen in the waveform between the words
"talk" and "and I'll." This space shows that the speaker paused for a moment between uttering the phrases, "You talk" and "and I'll listen." Below
the waveform we have indicated in phonetic script the individual speech
sounds of the utterance moving along the time base from left to right.

On the right side of the figure we have indicated four operations that
must be performed, from phonological analysis and segregation of the
speech stream to full discourse comprehension.

1. Phonological analysis and segregation of the speech stream. Unlike in writing, where words are separated on both sides by visible spaces,
in speech, words tend to run together without clear separations between
words. This is a natural property of the motor dynamics of the speech mechanism. We can see from inspection of the waveform that the words "and"
and "I'll" run together without any clear separation. It also is the case that
natural speech tends to be surprisingly underarticulated. For example, although a listener will perceptually "hear" a *d* at the end of the word "and,"
our speaker never actually articulated that sound. This is especially dramatic because our speaker was consciously attempting to speak the utterance especially clearly.

Careful analyses of natural speech utterances show that speakers tend
spontaneously to employ a functional adaptation in their production. That
is, we tend to articulate more clearly words that cannot be easily inferred
from context, and to articulate less clearly those that can (Lindblom,
Brownlee, Davis, & Moon, 1992). It is important to stress, however, that
these dynamic adjustments are not consciously applied by the speaker, any
more than listeners are consciously aware of using acoustic and linguistic
context in their perceptual operations.

2. Determination of syntactic structure. As we illustrate in Figure 10.1,
the listener's task includes identification of syllables and words, and also
recognition of how these words combine to form linguistic clauses and how
these clauses combine to form a sentence. In linguistic terms, the listener
must rapidly "parse" the input, or determine the syntactic function of the
incoming words.

3. Development of conceptual coherence. Determination of the main
nouns and verbs in the utterance has as its ultimate goal, of course, the
determination of the propositional content, or "ideas," represented in the
utterance and how these ideas are semantically related. This is referred to
as developing the conceptual coherence of an utterance, both within sentences and across sentences, as content derived from prior utterances and
the new information are integrated.

4. Discourse comprehension. Although most of psycholinguistics re-

search has focused on understanding perceptual processing at the sentence level, in actual practice, the listener's task includes assembling the semantic content of individual sentences in terms of the overall meaning of an utterance across many individual sentences that cross-refer to each other. At the discourse level, listeners not only must assemble the full meaning of a message based on the literal content of the utterances but also on inferences from information implied but not actually stated. If we heard as part of a narrative the sentence, "Asking the stranger for the time, he ran quickly to make his appointment," we would naturally assume that the stranger had a watch, that the stranger told the person the time, that the questioner was late for the appointment, and so forth. Indeed, when tested, listeners often will falsely remember having heard an item of information that had not been present in the message but that might reasonably be inferred given what had been heard (Bransford & Franks, 1971).

Top-down versus bottom-up processing

Drawing the directional arrows between the four operations enumerated on the right side of Figure 10.1 should not imply that comprehension moves in orderly steps from the analysis of the acoustic input to comprehension at the discourse level. Saying that a listener's perception of speech is facilitated by linguistic context already makes clear that lower levels of perception, such as perception at the syllable and word level, can be guided by knowledge derived from the sentence and discourse levels. Listeners also can develop useful expectations about probable word identity from real-world knowledge outside of any information contained in the particular utterance. As in the above example of asking a stranger for the time, speakers (and writers) assume shared knowledge as they organize their productions. The result is common omission of facts or information that can be reasonably inferred.

In the jargon of the literature, we refer to these as "bottom-up–top-down interactions." *Bottom-up processing* refers to moving from the physical signal of the acoustic input up through words, phrases, and sentences. *Top-down processing* refers to the use of information already available to a listener that produces context-driven expectations of what is about to be heard.

The fact that speech represents a continuous bottom-up–top-down interaction is one of the reasons why speech can be processed as rapidly as it is. That is, when a listener hears a word in a sentence, the listener has two sources of information. One of these is the bottom-up information supplied by the buildup of acoustic information as the uttered word unfolds over time. The second source comes from the top-down information of the sentence context. Because of this latter factor, words can be recognized in fluent speech long before their full acoustic duration has been completed (Marslen-Wilson, 1987).

An especially dramatic example of the importance of top-down information to speech processing comes from a demonstration offered many years ago by Pollack and Pickett (1963). They performed a simple experiment in which they recorded conversations and then spliced out individual words from the running discourse and presented them to listeners in isolation, without their surrounding context. Not only were these words often totally unrecognizable, but they sometimes barely sounded like words at all. To complete their demonstration, Pollack and Pickett played back the same recordings of the words, but this time reembedded in their original sentence contexts. The words now sounded crystal clear. Studies such as these have shown that speech perception is heavily context dependent on the linguistic and the acoustic contexts that precede a particular word, and also on the context that follows it (Grosjean, 1985; Pollack & Pickett, 1963; Wingfield, Alexander, & Cavigelli, 1994).

We thus may see that however effortless language comprehension may feel in our everyday experience, the operations that must be performed for effective comprehension are quite complex. Good reviews of processing models that attempt to capture this complexity can be found in Gernsbacher (1994).

Speech comprehension and working memory

In reading, the reader can use his or her eye movements to control the rate of input. The reader also can backtrack to an earlier part of the text if a region in a sentence is confusing or unclear. With a spoken message, the rate of speech is controlled by the speaker, and any "looking back" to an earlier part of the message must be done in memory.

Our earlier reference to functional adaptation at the level of articulatory clarity and the availability of facilitative context is an example of the natural partnership between speaker and listener. Another example of this partnership can be seen in differences between the characteristics of written and spoken discourse, in which planning constraints on the part of the speaker result in spoken sentences that tend to be shorter and syntactically less complex than their written counterparts. Long sentences with complex syntax that might be reasonable for comprehending written prose can place a greater memory and processing burden on a listener hearing the same text.

Most models of language processing assume that listeners analyze the syntax and semantic content of speech on-line, as the linguistic input is arriving. There are times, however, when processing lags behind or is conducted at a slower rate than the actual speech input. In such cases, the perceptual system must rely on a some form of transient memory system. For example, in the case of perceptual clarification from context that follows an unclear word, the acoustic form of the ambiguous word must be held in some form of memory representation pending the arrival of additional "downstream" context that will make clear what that word must have been.

Other cases where memory constrains language comprehension are second-pass operations in which we discover that we have misunderstood a sentence as we originally heard it. The most notable of these are so-called "garden path" sentences such as the sentence, "The old man the boats." A sentence like this is confusing because of the tendency on the part of listeners to interpreted the word "man" as a noun as part of the noun phrase, "the old man." This will lead us to expect a verb but, instead, we hear another noun phrase ("the boats"). The answer, of course, is that "man" in this sentence is being used as a verb (i.e., "to operate"). The ability to back up and reparse the sentence correctly demands the presence of a memory representation of the original utterance.

Although garden path sentences are somewhat extreme, substantial segments of speech input must be held in working memory whenever we have to deal with sentences that have embedded clauses, sentences that have left-branching constructions, or sentences that require the listener to identify the correct referents for several pronouns. Consider the sentence, "The man who sold the car to the woman had red hair." In order to know who had red hair, we must strip the clause "who sold the car to the woman" from the sentence and hold this clause in working memory while we process for meaning the overall sentence frame in which it is embedded ("The man had red hair"). This example is an interesting one because comprehension of the sentence requires that we not be distracted by the sequence "the woman had red hair." Such a strictly local analysis without access to a mental representation of the full sentence would give us the wrong answer.

In addition to correcting parsing errors and handling complex linguistic structures, a transient memory also is needed to allow temporary holding and integration of phrases and clauses that already have been heard with those that arrive later. This integration is necessary in order to develop full utterance meaning (van Dijk & Kintsch, 1983).

Sensory and cognitive change in adult aging

As we have tried to show in the above discussion, spoken language comprehension represents a complex process that may strain cognitive resources even for young adults whose memory capabilities and processing speed presumably are at their peak. In the following sections, we will examine three factors related to spoken language comprehension in the older listener. These three factors are changes in hearing acuity that can accompany normal aging, changes in the capacity of working memory, and, finally, age-related changes in the speed with which information can be processed.

Age and auditory acuity

Hearing acuity among older adults shows a wide range of individual differences, and it would be wrong to assume that speaking to an older adult automatically demands that one speak especially loud. Indeed, a very substantial proportion of noninstitutionalized older adults have no special problem with auditory acuity for speech. Within this background of caution, however, it certainly is the case that large-scale studies have shown that the incidence of clinically significant hearing loss increases across the adult life span (Morrell, Gordon-Salant, Pearson, Brant, & Fozard, 1996). Depending on the study, estimates of hearing impairment sufficient to affect speech comprehension have ranged between 24% and 30% for noninstitutionalized American adults between the age of 65 and 74, and between 30% and 48% for those 75 years and older (U.S. Congress, Office of Technology Assessment, 1986). Even those without clinically significant impairment, however, may have reduced auditory processing efficiency not necessarily detected in standard audiograms (Schneider, Pichora-Fuller, Kowalchuk, & Lamb, 1994).

The term *presbycusis* literally means "old hearing" and it has two features that are important to this discussion. The first is that the hearing losses associated with age are not uniform across the frequency range. We can see this in Figure 10.2, in which we have plotted data taken from a large-scale study by the National Center for Health Statistics showing the incidence of hearing loss at various sound frequencies for five different age groups (U.S. Congress, Office of Technology Assessment, 1986, p. 15). The figure is based on the ability of the listeners to hear tones that varied from 500 to 4000 Hz at an intensity level of 31 dB at least 50% of the time. This range, 500 to 4000 Hz, was chosen because it includes the general range of speech frequencies.

The data shown in Figure 10.2 clearly illustrate that although aging affects hearing at all frequencies, the effect is differentially greater at the higher frequencies. This is important for speech, as hearing loss at the higher frequencies will differentially affect the perception of high-frequency and low-energy sounds such as *p, k, s, t, sh, ch*, and the voiceless *th* (as in "thin").

Presbycusis, it should be noted, can include more than a high-frequency hearing loss. Not uncommon in older adults' hearing is *phonemic regression,* a lack of clarity for complex auditory signals such as speech. In testing, phonemic regression appears in the form of poorer speech discrimination than would be predicted from pure tone audiometry alone. Speech perception in older adults also can be especially vulnerable to the presence of background noise (Tun, 1998) and hearing speech in a room with poor reverberation characteristics (Gordon-Salant & Fitzgibbons, 1993). On the positive side, it can be shown that older adults, both those with presbycusis and older listeners with near-normal hearing, make better use of supporting context than younger listeners with normal hearing (e.g., Pichora-Fuller, Schneider, & Daneman, 1995; Wingfield, Aberdeen, & Stine, 1991; Wingfield et al., 1994). This is a powerful source of top-down compensation for bottom-up sensory decline. However, on the negative side, the allocation of processing resources for this top-down support of low-level auditory perception may reduce the resources available for higher-level

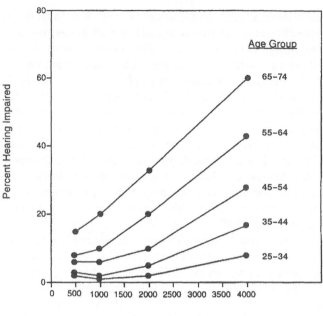

FIG. 10.2. The percentage of adults in five age groups showing a hearing impairment for tones presented at various sound frequencies representing the frequency range for speech. The data are taken from a large-scale study conducted by the National Center for Health Statistics (U.S. Congress, Office of Technology Assessment, 1986). Adapted with permission.

cognitive operations. It has been suggested that this could have a negative age-related impact on interpretive operations as well as on storage and retrieval functions in working memory (Pichora-Fuller et al., 1995).

The issue of sensory decline in cognitive aging has taken on renewed interest with reports that combined visual and auditory acuity account for a large measure of the age-related variance in performance on a range of cognitive tasks (Baltes & Lindenberger, 1997). This is, however, less likely to be a cause-and-effect relationship than it is a reflection of sensory change co-occurring with other areas of decline. A complicating factor in interpreting such results, of course, is that the accuracy with which sensory thresholds can be measured and defined far exceeds our precision in definition, and hence measurement, of higher-level cognitive mediators.

Age and the capacity of working memory

In the previous section, we cited the arguments for the necessity of some form of short-term memory for sentence processing. The memory system most commonly implicated has been called *working memory*. Working memory refers to the cognitive system that includes both the ability to temporarily hold recently received information and a limited-capacity "computation space," in which the materials in memory may be monitored and manipulated (Baddeley, 1986; Just & Carpenter, 1992). The essence of this memory capability is captured in the Daneman and Carpenter (1980) working memory span test. Although the best-known form of the Daneman and Carpenter test is a "reading span" version, because of our present interest in the role of memory in spoken language comprehension, we will focus on the spoken counterpart of the test.

In the spoken version of the Daneman and Carpenter test, the participant hears a list of sentences. Then, after all of the sentences have been presented, the participant is required to give from memory the last word in each sentence in the order in which they were presented. To ensure that the participant is comprehending the full sentences and not just listening for the final words, a simple expedient is to require the participant to say whether or not each sentence is true or false immediately after it is presented (Wingfield, Stine, Lahar, & Aberdeen, 1988). The number of sentences the subject hears in a set is progressively increased, and the estimate of the span of working memory is taken as the maximum number of sentences that still allow the subject to recall all of the final words. The Daneman and Carpenter span test thus is intended to capture the ability to hold information in memory while simultaneously performing comprehension operations. It is this combination of both holding and manipulation that distinguishes working memory from simple short-term memory storage that would be represented by, for example, verbatim recall of a list of digits or random words.

Figure 10.3 shows data taken from a study in which younger and older adults were given three span measures, each representing an increase in the mental load associated with the memory task (Wingfield et al., 1988). The older participants in this experiment were healthy, community-dwelling adults with good levels of education and verbal ability. On both of these

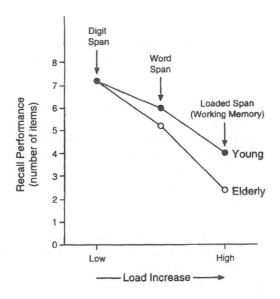

FIG. 10.3.
Younger and older adults were tested for their ability to recall lists of spoken digits (digit span), lists of words (word span), and the final words of sets of sentences presented for comprehension (loaded span). Adapted with permission from A. Wingfield, E. A. L. Stine, C. J. Lahar, and J. S. Aberdeen, 1988.

measures, the older participants were at least equal to the younger participants who were university undergraduates.

Moving from left to right along the x-axis in the figure, the first point represents the younger and older participants' mean digit spans, measured as the number of digits they could correctly repeat back immediately after one hearing. Age differences in simple digit span typically are small if they are present at all (Salthouse, 1991). Indeed, we can see in this sample that there was no age difference in simple digit span. The next set of points on the graph represent the younger and older participants' memory spans for lists of random words. Memory spans for words typically are smaller than digit spans (Cavanaugh, 1972), and this was the case here. We also can see that, for the word spans, there was a small but significant age difference. By far the greater difference, however, appears in the final set of points on the graph. These show the participants' scores on the spoken version of the Daneman and Carpenter span test referred to above, in which the participants had to listen to and comprehend the meaning of sets of sentences while holding in memory the last word of each of the sentences in that set. Consistent with the aging literature, this measure—which of the three measures best taps the capacity of working memory—shows a substantial age difference (Salthouse, 1991, 1994).

Working memory, age, and language comprehension

It has been well documented that cognitive resources, whether seen in terms of working memory capacity or the speed with which items can be encoded in working memory, account for a considerable amount of the variance in observed age differences in the recall of spoken (Stine & Wingfield, 1990) and written (Hartley, 1993) text. How does this limited working memory capacity impact language comprehension and memory for spoken and written language?

The earliest search for this relationship appeared not with contrasts between younger and older adults, but in terms of correlations between individual differences among young adults in comprehension ability and working memory capacity (Daneman & Carpenter, 1980). It was argued that mental operations such as syntactic parsing, integration of propositions, inference, and the assignment of reference, all of which are necessary for text comprehension, varied with individuals' working memory capacity. It thus was a reasonable step to assume that to the extent that older adults have a smaller working memory capacity than younger adults, one should see significant age differences in linguistic processes that require an especially heavy drain on working memory (Carpenter, Miyaki, & Just, 1994).

Studies in the aging literature would seem to support this suggestion. For example, when older adults hear short sentences with reasonably simple syntax, their comprehension and recall of speech content is generally quite good. However, as the length, and syntactic complexity of sentences increase, older adults have significantly more difficulty than younger adults in sentence comprehension and accuracy of recall (e.g., Norman, Kemper, Kynette, Cheung, & Anagnopoulos, 1991).

Older adults also can experience some difficulty when inferential processing and rapid gist extraction is required. This is more likely to be the case when anaphoric distances are especially great, as when a pronoun and its referent are separated by several sentences in a text (Light & Capps, 1986). This is true even for referent trace activation in on-line sentence comprehension (Zurif, Swinney, Prather, Wingfield, & Brownell, 1995). Finally, although older adults make excellent use of linguistic context to aid perception of an indistinct word when the context precedes the word (Wingfield et al., 1991), memory limitations put older adults at a disadvantage when attempting to use linguistic context for retrospective word recognition, as when the identity of a poorly articulated word is not recognized until several words of context are heard after that word (Wingfield et al., 1994).

Findings such as these usually are interpreted as resulting from age-related limitations in working memory capacity as distinct from a loss in linguistic knowledge or vocabulary. Except for cases of neuropathology, neither vocabulary nor procedural knowledge for the use of linguistic rules are thought to diminish with age (Kempler & Zelinski, 1994; Light, 1991). A good review of working memory and language comprehension, including data from both aphasia and normal aging, can be found in Carpenter et al. (1994; see also the review by Daneman & Merikle, 1996).

Although working memory serves as a descriptive convenience, we should recognize that the term refers less to a tangible construct than it does to the ability to perform well in tasks designed to measure this ability (generally, tasks that require one to do two things at one time, such as both holding and manipulating information in memory). The actual nature of the memory store(s) that support language comprehension remain a subject of study and debate. This debate has been especially marked in the neurolinguistics literature in studies of sentence comprehension by brain injured patients whose lesions to certain brain areas leave them with dramatically low span scores on traditional tests of short-term and working memory. From these diminished spans, one would expect them to have considerable difficulty with comprehension of sentences that we ordinarily think of as producing heavy demands on memory. Surprisingly, such patients can sometimes show good comprehension for sentences with complex relative clause constructions and even garden path sentences that require second-pass operations for correct comprehension. A review and an illustration can be found in Wingfield, Waters, and Tun (1998).

The data from these patients suggest strongly that the concept of working memory and the way it is measured only roughly tap a far more complex representational and processing system for speech comprehension. (A more complete discussion of these issues can be found in Waters & Caplan, 1996, and Wingfield et al., 1998). Much of the current literature in cognitive psychology and cognitive aging continues to treat working memory as a functional system with measurable capacity that carries, and hence constrains, language comprehension. In reality, however, it might be best to think of working memory as a placeholder term for a memory processing system yet to be fully specified (Baddeley, 1998; Waters & Caplan, 1996; Wingfield et al., 1998).

Age and speed of processing

Slowing is a virtual hallmark of the aging process. We cannot say whether slowing causes inefficient processing, or whether inefficient processing slows the system. Whether cause or consequence, we can say that perceptual and response slowing are an almost ubiquitous finding in the aging literature (Salthouse, 1991, 1994). Given the rapidity of normal speech rates, and hence the rate at which the necessary processing operations must be performed, one might expect "slowed" older adults to have special problems with speech comprehension. As we shall see in the following sections, this is certainly the case. We will also see, however, that the problem might be even more severe were it not for the excellent use older listeners routinely make of linguistic context and other top-down sources of information.

Studies of speech rate effects typically are conducted using computer algorithms that allow one to increase speech rates without disturbing the intonation pattern of the speech or the relative timing patterns of speech-to-silence or vowel durations tied to the linguistic structure of the sentences. The product of this operation is referred to as *time-compressed speech*. The most dramatic effects of age and speech rate are seen when time-compressed word lists are presented without the support of linguistic context. Although both younger and older adults show a decline in recall accuracy with increasing speech rates, such rates of decline can be five times greater for older adults than for younger adults (Konkle, Beasley, & Bess, 1977; Wingfield, Poon, Lombardi, & Lowe, 1985).

Available data suggest that older adults' special vulnerability to time-compressed speech is not simply a consequence of age-related differences in hearing acuity. That is, when younger and older adults are matched for hearing acuity (i.e., comparing younger adults with hearing losses that match those of an older group, or comparing normally hearing younger adults with older adults with no audiometric signs of presbycusis), older adults continue to show a differentially greater vulnerability to time-compressed speech as compared to younger adults (Gordon-Salant & Fitzgibbons, 1993; Konkle et al., 1977; Sticht & Gray, 1969).

It is well known that age differences in recall are dramatically reduced by the presence of environmental support, such as that offered by an individuals' real-world knowledge or supportive context (Craik & Jennings, 1992). It thus should not be surprising that an important factor in speech rate effects and age of the listener is the role played by linguistic context in helping younger and older adults overcome what otherwise would be very severe effects of overloading perceptual processing rates. Although older adults continue to show differentially greater difficulty with rapid speech than younger adults, age effects are significantly reduced when words are presented in a sentence context (Wingfield et al., 1985).

Older listeners also make especially good use of the prosodic pattern of normal speech to help comprehension at all times, but especially when listening conditions are difficult (Cohen & Faulkner, 1986; Wingfield, Lahar, & Stine, 1989). *Prosody* is a generic term that includes the intonation pattern, or pitch contour of speech. Prosody also includes word stress and variations in speech timing, such as the pauses that sometimes follow the ends of major linguistic elements or the lengthening of words that precede clause boundaries. It should be noted that although older adults can be shown to benefit from effective use of stress and other prosodic features to aid in speech comprehension (Cohen & Faulkner, 1986; Wingfield, Wayland, & Stine, 1992) and syntactic parsing (Kjelgaard, Titone, & Wingfield, 1999; Wingfield et al., 1989), exaggerated stress and intonation that crosses over the line to patronizing "elderspeak" will risk demeaning, and hence alienating, older listeners (cf., Ryan, Hummert, & Boich, 1995).

To get a sense of how older (and younger) listeners may get overloaded by receiving too much information too fast, one can refer to a study by Stine, Wingfield, and Poon (1986) in which younger and older participants listened to and recalled sentences that contained the same number of words (16 to 18 words) but that varied in the number of propositions, or idea units, they contained (4, 6, 8, or 10 propositions). The speech also was presented at three different speech rates: a fast normal rate of 200 wpm, and then time-compressed to two very rapid rates of 300 and 400 wpm. This allowed Stine et al. to measure speech rate, not simply in terms of words per minute or syllables per second, but in terms of the number of propositions delivered per unit time. This way of measuring input rate illustrates how one can increase speech processing load either by increasing the propositional (informational) density of the speech, increasing the speech rate, or both.

Figure 10.4 is taken from Wingfield and Stine (1992), which shows participants' recall for the content of spoken sentences plotted as a function of speech input rate expressed as propositions per second. The values shown on the abscissa are thus a compound product of the number of propositions contained in the sentences and the presentation rate of these sentences. The top curve in Figure 10.4 shows a best-fit linear function for the percentage of propositions recalled and the speech presentation rate for a group of university undergraduates ("young subjects"). Figure 10.4 also shows data for two groups of healthy older adults with good levels of education and vocabulary scores. The lowest curve shows data for a group of older adults matched with the younger adults for years of formal education and scores on a standard vocabulary test ("matched elderly"). We can clearly see by comparing the younger adults and this matched older group that

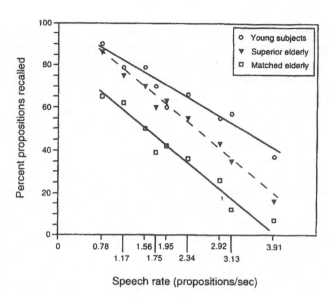

FIG. 10.4.
Mean percentage of propositions recalled as a function of speech input rate measured as propositions per second. Data are shown for a group of younger subjects and a group of older subjects who were matched for years of education and vocabulary scores (the upper and lower solid lines). The middle (dashed) line shows performance for a group of older subjects who were superior to the younger group and matched older group in years of education and vocabulary scores. From Figure. 7.1, R. L. West and J. D. Sinnot, 1992. Reprinted with permission.

the older participants had poorer recall performance than the younger group regardless of speech rate. It also can be seen, however, that the difference is smaller at the slower presentation rates (e.g., .78 propositions per second) than at the faster rates (e.g., 3.91 propositions per second). That is, the matched elderly's recall curve has a steeper slope than that of the younger participants. This was confirmed in an analysis of variance by a significant age-by-speech rate interaction for these two groups, along with main effects of age and of speech rate.

Of special note is a second group of older adults represented by the middle broken line in Figure 10.4. This group had the same age range as the first older group. They differed in that they had especially high verbal scores and levels of education that exceeded those of the younger participants and the matched elderly group. This group is labeled in Figure 10.4 as "superior elderly." The fact that the performance curve for this group comes closer to that of the younger participants is interesting, but it should not be surprising in view of the general finding that age differences in recall performance tend to be smaller for older adults with especially good levels of education and verbal ability (Hultsch & Dixon, 1990). Indeed, at the slowest rate of .78 propositions per second (a four-proposition sentence heard at 200 wpm) there was virtually no age difference at all. These data correspond well with the view that older adults with high vocabulary scores show a smaller decline in memory performance with advancing age than those with lower scores.

In spite of this difference in overall performance levels between the two older adult groups, however, the two older groups showed exactly the same rates of decline in recall performance with increasing input rates. That is, education and verbal ability may affect the overall level of recall performance (as measured by the y-intercepts of the performance curves), but not processing speed (as measured by the slopes of the lines). These data offer a good demonstration of an age-sensitive vulnerability to cognitive overload from too much being presented too rapidly. Indeed, when younger and older adults are allowed to adjust the speech rate of recorded passages for later recall, older adults adjust the speech to slower rates than the younger adults, and both groups are equally sensitive to the content complexity of the speech materials (Wingfield & Ducharme, 1999).

Does slowing speech help?

If older adults' comprehension is especially vulnerable to rapid speech, one is bound to ask whether slowing the speech input will help. The answer to this question is "yes," but only if the slowing is done in a principled way. For example, Schmitt and McCrosky (1981) slowed speech by resampling the speech signal and uniformly increasing the durations of all of the speech elements—words, syllables, and silent periods—by proportionally equal amounts. Their results were mixed. Although slowing the speech helped older adults' comprehension (Schmitt & McCrosky, 1981), slowing the speech by too much appeared to risk making the comprehension worse (Schmitt, 1983).

The reason for these apparently mixed findings is that how the speech is slowed is as important as how much the speech is slowed. We can illustrate this point with data taken from a study we recently conducted in which speech was time compressed from an original speaking rate of 165 wpm to a very rapid speech rate of 300 wpm. This was done by digitizing the speech and reiteratively removing small unnoticed segments of the speech signal equally across speech and silent intervals so as to reproduce the speech in 55% of its original playing time without disturbing the overall prosodic pattern. The participants' task was simply to listen to the speech passage and, when it was finished, to recall as much of the information from the passage as possible.

The goal of this study was to determine whether participants' performance with time-compressed speech would be improved if silent periods were inserted at positions in the speech passages that corresponded to natural linguistic constituents, such as after major clauses and between sentences. Studies with younger adults certainly would suggest that this would be so (e.g., Overmann, 1971). There were, however, two specific interests in this study. The first was to determine whether older listeners would benefit from time restoration in the same manner as younger adults, and the second was to determine the effects of where time was restored.

A subset of the data from this experiment are shown in Figure 10.5. The left panel shows results for a group of younger adults (university undergraduates) and the right panel shows results for a group of community-

FIG. 10.5.
Percent reduction in
recall performance for
time-compressed
speech heard at 300
wpm relative to a non-
compressed original
rate of 165 wpm, and
when processing time
was restored at random
points or at syntactic-
ally salient points in the
speech message for
younger (left panel) and
older (right panel)
adults. Adapted with
permission from A.
Wingfield, P. A. Tun, C.
K. Koh, and M. J.
Rosen, 1999.

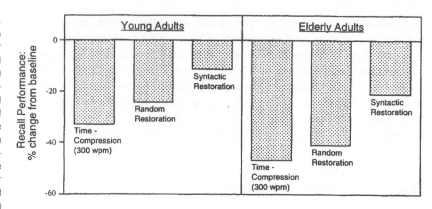

CONDITION

dwelling older adults with vocabulary scores and years of education equal to or superior to the younger adults. The first bar on the left in each of the two panels shows the percentage decline in the number of propositions participants were able to recall from the narrative passages presented at 300 wpm, relative to their performance for passages presented at the original recording rate of 165 wpm. We can see that the older participants showed a differentially greater proportional decline than the younger participants. This is a finding that would be expected from prior literature on age and speech rate effects previously cited (e.g., Gordon-Salant & Fitzgibbons, 1993; Konkle et al., 1977; Wingfield et al., 1985).

This study employed two schemes for time restoration. In one case, *syntactic restoration*, available processing time was restored by using a speech-editing computer program to insert silent periods into the 300 wpm speech at the ends of clauses and sentences. The total time restored was equivalent to the loss of processing time represented by the playing time difference between the original 165 wpm passages and the time-compressed 300 wpm versions. In the second restoration scheme, *random restoration*, pauses of exactly the same durations as in the syntactic restoration condition were introduced except that the pauses were inserted randomly with respect to linguistic content.

The results are shown in Figure 10.5, where it can be seen that restoring time at syntactic boundaries (syntactic restoration) brought both age groups closer to their normal speech rate baselines than restoring the same amount of time at random points relative to the linguistic content. We also can observe, however, that time restoration at syntactic points brought the younger participants closer to their baselines than was the case for the older participants. In fact, when a follow-up study was conducted in which the pause durations at syntactic points were increased to durations equivalent to restoring 125% of lost time, the younger adults performed at a level somewhat above their baseline levels for noncompressed speech. The older adults, although getting closer to their baseline performance, did not fully recover to that point.

A more complete account of these data is given in Wingfield, Tun, Koh, and Rosen (1999), along with an argument that these data illustrate a dramatic consequence of age-related slowing on comprehension and recall for rapid spoken language. These data show that making available additional processing time can improve both younger and older adults' recall, but that this will be most effective when the time is made available at major linguistic boundaries that are presumed to be the natural processing points for connected speech (Ferreira & Anes, 1994). That is, slowing speech is of benefit to older listeners as well as to younger listeners, but where processing time is supplied is as important as how much time is supplied.

It should be noted that our emphasis on higher-level slowing should not discount complex age differences in auditory processing that could negatively affect perception of time-compressed speech at lower levels of perceptual processing (cf., Schneider et al., 1994). Such age-related changes would be bound to place limits on recovery no matter how much processing time is made available to the listener. This is the negative side of the story. The positive side is that, although aging may take a toll on perceptual, bottom-up, processing and episodic recall, knowledge of the rules and structure of language is well preserved in normal aging, and this knowledge can be used as effectively by older adults as by younger adults.

Conclusion

Our goal in this presentation was to review recent research pertaining to the comprehension of spoken language by healthy older adults. In the course of this review, we have addressed several known areas of age-related decline. These included declines in auditory acuity, the capacity of working memory, and the rate at which speech input can be processed. These data highlight five important principles relating to adult aging and spoken language comprehension.

1. Adult aging often is accompanied by declines in auditory acuity that especially may affect sensory processing for speech. Except in cases of neuropathology, however, linguistic knowledge remains well preserved in older adulthood. This combination of areas of loss and preservation leads to a spontaneous use by older adults of top-down information drawn from linguistic context to supplement the impoverished bottom-up signal. This top-down–bottom-up interaction also characterizes natural language processing by younger adults under difficult listening conditions.
2. Unlike reading, where one can backtrack on the printed page to reread a sentence that was unclear in meaning, in speech percep-

tion, any such "look back" must be done in memory. Consistent with this principle, older adults can have greater difficulty than younger adults in comprehending speech with structures that place a heavy burden on memory capacity. These include very long sentences, sentences whose comprehension requires memory for referents that occurred far previously in the passage, and sentences with especially high propositional density or complex syntax.

3. The presence of normal prosody (intonation, timing, stress) has been shown to help older listeners by aiding in the rapid detection of the linguistic structure and the semantic focus of a question or statement. It is important, however, to avoid an exaggerated prosody that crosses the line into patronizing elderspeak.

4. Offering older adults additional time to process rapid speech input by pausing at periodic intervals produces a significant increase in recall performance relative to rapid speech heard without such processing time insertion. Where one pauses in a speech message, however, is as important as how long one pauses. Pausing is most effective when it follows natural processing units such as sentences and clauses.

5. Although one can form certain generalities regarding sensory and cognitive change in adult aging, individual differences in these respects can vary widely. For example, many older adults retain good hearing acuity for speech and relatively good capacity in tests of working memory. As such, the principles outlined above will take on more importance for some individuals than others. To one degree or another, however, these general principles have broad applicability to older and younger adults' ability to comprehend and recall natural language.

References

Baddeley, A. D. (1986). *Working memory*. Oxford, England: Oxford University Press.

Baddeley, A. D. (1998). The central executive: A concept and some misconceptions. *Journal of the International Neuropsychological Society, 4*, 523–526.

Baltes, P. B., & Lindenberger, U. (1997). Emergence of a powerful connection between sensory and cognitive functions across the adult life span: A new window to the study of cognitive aging? *Psychology and Aging, 12*, 12–21.

Bransford, J. D., & Franks, J. J. (1971). The abstraction of linguistic ideas. *Cognitive Psychology, 2*, 331–350.

Carpenter, P. A., Miyaki, A., & Just, M. A. (1994). Working memory constraints in comprehension: Evidence from individual differences, aphasia, and aging. In M. Gernsbacher (Ed.), *Handbook of psycholinguistics* (pp. 1075–1122). San Diego, CA: Academic Press.

Cavanaugh, J. P. (1972). Relation between the immediate memory span and the memory search rate. *Psychological Review, 79*, 525–530.

Cohen, G., & Faulkner, D. (1986). Does "elderspeak" work? The effect of intonation and stress on comprehension and recall of spoken discourse in old age. *Language and Communication, 6*, 91–98.

Craik, F. I. M., & Jennings, J. M. (1992). Human memory. In F. I. M. Craik & T. A. Salthouse (Eds.), *The handbook of aging and cognition* (pp. 51–110). Hillsdale, NJ: Erlbaum.

Daneman, M., & Carpenter, P. A. (1980). Individual differences in working memory and reading. *Journal of Verbal Learning and Verbal Behavior, 19*, 450–466.

Daneman, M., & Merikle, P. M. (1996). Working memory and language comprehension: A meta-analysis. *Psychonomic Bulletin and Review, 3*, 422–433.

Ferreira, F., & Anes, M.D. (1994). Why study spoken language processing? In M. Gernsbacher (Ed.), *Handbook of psycholinguistics* (pp. 35–56). San Diego, CA: Academic Press.

Gernsbacher, M. A. (Ed.). (1994). *Handbook of psycholinguistics.* San Diego, CA: Academic Press.

Goodglass, H., & Wingfield, A. (1998). The changing relationship between anatomic and cognitive explanation in the neuropsychology of language. *Journal of Psycholinguistic Research, 27*, 147–165.

Gordon-Salant, S., & Fitzgibbons, P. J. (1993). Temporal factors and speech recognition performance in young and elderly listeners. *Journal of Speech and Hearing Research, 36*, 1276–1285.

Grosjean, F. (1985). The recognition of words after their acoustic offset: Evidence and implications. *Perception and Psychophysics, 38*, 299–310.

Hartley, J. (1993). Aging and prose memory: Tests of the resource-deficit hypothesis. *Psychology and Aging, 8*, 538–551.

Hultsch, D., & Dixon, R. A. (1990). Learning and memory in aging. In J. E. Birren & K. W. Scheme (Eds.), *Handbook of the psychology of aging* (3rd ed., pp. 258–274). New York: Academic Press.

Just, M. A., & Carpenter, P. A. (1992). A capacity theory of comprehension: Individual differences in working memory. *Psychological Review, 99*, 122–149.

Kempler, D., & Zelinski, E. M. (1994). Language in dementia and normal aging. In F. A. Huppert, C. Brayne, & D. W. O'Connor (Eds.), *Dementia and normal aging* (pp. 331–365). New York: Cambridge University Press.

Kjelgaard, M. M., Titone, D., & Wingfield, A. (1999). The influence of prosodic structure on the interpretation of temporary syntactic ambiguity by young and elderly listeners. *Experimental Aging Research, 25*, 187–207.

Konkle, D. F., Beasley, D. S., & Bess, F. H. (1977). Intelligibility of time-altered speech in relation to chronological aging. *Journal of Speech and Hearing Research, 20*, 108–115.

Light, L. L. (1991). Memory and aging: Four hypotheses in search of data. *Annual Review of Psychology, 42*, 333–376.

Light, L. L., & Capps, J. L. (1986). Comprehension of pronouns in young and older adults. *Developmental Psychology, 22*, 580–585.

Lindblom, B., Brownlee, S., Davis, B., & Moon, S. J. (1992). Speech transforms. *Speech Communication, 11*, 357–368.

Marslen-Wilson, W. D. (1987). Functional parallelism in spoken word recognition. *Cognition, 25*, 71–102.

Meier, R. P. (1991). Language acquisition by deaf children. *American Scientist, 79*, 60–70.

Morrell, C. H., Gordon-Salant, S., Pearson, J. D., Brant, L. J., & Fozard, J. L. (1996). Age- and gender-specific reference ranges for hearing level and longitudinal changes in hearing level. *Journal of the Acoustical Society of America, 100,* 1949–1967.

Norman, S., Kemper, S., Kynette, D., Cheung, H., & Anagnopoulos, C. (1991). Syntactic complexity and adults' running memory span. *Journal of Gerontology: Psychological Sciences, 46,* 346–351.

Overmann, R. A. (1971). Processing time as a variable in the comprehension of time-compressed speech. In E. Foulke (Ed.), *Proceedings of the Second Louisville Conference on Rate and/or Frequency-Controlled Speech* (pp. 103–118). Louisville, KY: University of Louisville.

Pichora-Fuller, M. K., Schneider, B. A., & Daneman, M. (1995). How young and old adults listen to and remember speech in noise. *Journal of the Acoustical Society of America, 97,* 593–607.

Pollack, I., & Pickett, J. M. (1963). The intelligibility of excerpts from conversation. *Language and Speech, 6,* 165–171.

Ryan, E. B., Hummert, M. L., & Boich, L. H. (1995). Communication predicaments of aging: Patronizing behavior toward older adults. *Journal of Language and Social Psychology, 14,* 144–166.

Salthouse, T. A. (1991). *Theoretical perspectives on cognitive aging.* Hillsdale, NJ: Erlbaum.

Salthouse, T. A. (1994). The aging of working memory. *Neuropsychology, 8,* 535–543.

Schmitt, J. F. (1983). The effects of time compression and time expansion on passage comprehension by elderly listeners. *Journal of Speech and Hearing Research, 26,* 373–377.

Schmitt, J. F., & McCrosky, R. L. (1981). Sentence comprehension in elderly listeners: The factor of rate. *Journal of Gerontology, 36,* 441-445.

Schneider, B. A., Pichora-Fuller, M. K., Kowalchuk, D., & Lamb, M. (1994). Gap detection and the precedence effect in young and old adults. *Journal of the Acoustical Society of America, 95,* 980–991.

Sticht, T. G., & Gray, B. B. (1969). The intelligibility of time compressed speech as a function of age and hearing loss. *Journal of Speech and Hearing Research, 12,* 443–448.

Stine, E. A. L., & Wingfield, A. (1990). How much do working memory deficits contribute to age differences in discourse memory? *European Journal of Cognitive Psychology, 2,* 289–304.

Stine, E. A. L., Wingfield, A., & Poon, L. W. (1986). How much and how fast: Rapid processing of spoken language in later adulthood. *Psychology and Aging, 1,* 303–311.

Tun, P.A. (1998). Fast noisy speech: Age differences in processing rapid speech with background noise. *Psychology and Aging, 13,* 424–434.

U.S. Congress, Office of Technology Assessment. (1986, May). *Hearing impairment and elderly people—A background paper* (Publication No. OTA-BP-BA-30). Washington, DC: U.S. Government Printing Office.

van Dijk, T. A., & Kintsch, W. (1983). *Strategies of discourse comprehension.* New York: Academic Press.

Waters, G. S., & Caplan, D. (1996). The capacity theory of sentence comprehension: Critique of Just and Carpenter (1992). *Psychological Review, 103,* 761–772.

West, R. L., & Sinnott, J. D. (Eds). (1992). *Everyday memory and aging: Current research and methodology.* New York: Springer-Verlag.

Wingfield, A., Aberdeen, J. S., & Stine, E. A. L. (1991). Word onset gating and linguistic context in spoken word recognition by young and elderly adults. *Journal of Gerontology: Psychological Sciences, 46*, 127–129.

Wingfield, A., Alexander, A. H., & Cavigelli, S. (1994). Does memory constrain utilization of top-down information in spoken word recognition? Evidence from normal aging. *Language and Speech, 37*, 221–235.

Wingfield, A., & Ducharme, J. L. (1999). Effects of age and passage difficulty on listening-rate preferences for time-altered speech. *Journal of Gerontology: Psychological Sciences, 54B*, 199–202.

Wingfield, A., Lahar, C. J., & Stine, E. A. L. (1989). Age and decision strategies in running memory for speech. *Journal of Gerontology: Psychological Sciences, 44*, 106–113.

Wingfield, A., Poon, L. W., Lombardi, L., & Lowe, D. (1985). Speed of processing in normal aging: Effects of speech rate, linguistic structure, and processing time. *Journal of Gerontology, 40*, 579–585.

Wingfield, A., & Stine, E. A. L. (1992). Age differences in perceptual processing and memory for spoken language. In R. L. West & J. D. Sinnott (Eds.). *Everyday memory and aging: Current research and methodology* (pp. 101–123). New York: Springer-Verlag.

Wingfield, A., Stine, E. A. L., Lahar, C. J., & Aberdeen, J. S. (1988). Does the capacity of working memory change with age? *Experimental Aging Research, 14*, 103–107.

Wingfield, A., Tun, P. A., Koh, C. K., & Rosen, M. J. (1999). Regaining lost time: Adult aging and the effect of time restoration on recall of time-compressed speech. *Psychology and Aging, 14*, 122–132.

Wingfield, A., Waters, G. S., & Tun, P. A. (1998). Does working memory work in language comprehension?: Evidence from behavioral neuroscience. In N. Raz (Ed.), *The other side of the error term: Aging and development as model systems in cognitive neuroscience* (pp. 319–343). Amsterdam: Elsevier.

Wingfield, A., Wayland, S. C., & Stine, E. A. L. (1992). Adult age differences in the use of prosody for syntactic parsing and recall of spoken sentences. *Journal of Gerontology: Psychological Sciences, 47*, 350–356.

Zurif, E. B., Swinney, D., Prather, P., Wingfield, A., & Brownell, H. (1995). The allocation of memory resources during sentence comprehension: Evidence from the elderly. *Journal of Psycholinguistic Research, 24*, 165–182.

Aging and message production and comprehension 11

Susan Kemper, Karen Kemtes

Message production begins with the formulation of a message and includes steps of discourse planning, lexical selection, and syntactic encoding prior to the final step of phonological production. Message comprehension begins with a text, presented aurally or visually, and ends with the recovery of a representation of that text as ideas or propositions. Errors, reflecting attentional lapses, processing limitations, and execution problems can arise at any stage of production or comprehension. Normative aging processes, arising from general slowing of cognitive processes (Salthouse, 1992), reductions of working memory capacity (Light, 1991), or a breakdown of inhibitory processes (Hasher & Zacks, 1988), may exacerbate production or comprehension problems.

This chapter examines what is currently known about how normal aging affects message production and comprehension and examines how aging affects messages addressed to older adults. It must be noted at the outset that research on aging and message production, like the study of production processes in general, has lagged behind studies of message comprehension and memory because of the difficulties inherent in experimentally manipulating production processes. This chapter focuses on discourse production and comprehension since the effects of aging on syntactic and lexical encoding and processing recently have been reviewed (Kemper, 1992; Kemper & Hummert, 1997). It also reviews what is known about how Alzheimer's disease affects older adults' message production and comprehension. The chapter concludes with a dilemma raised by research in this field.

Changes in message production by older adults

Discourse encompasses a variety of communication skills, ranging from opening and closing conversations, maintaining and shifting topics, and

Preparation of this chapter was supported by grants AG09952 and AG00226 from the National Institute on Aging.

telling stories to establishing and modifying personal relationships, conveying individual and group identity, gaining and avoiding compliance, and being polite, saving face, or giving offense. To date, little research has examined older adults' discourse skills.

There is some evidence that discourse skills increase with age. Older adults create elaborate narrative structures that include hierarchically elaborated episodes with beginnings describing initiating events and motivating states, developments detailing the protagonists' goals and actions, and endings summarizing the outcomes of the protagonists' efforts; evaluative codas often are attached to older adults' narratives that assess the contemporary significance of these stories (Kemper, 1990; Kemper & Anagnopoulos, 1997; Kemper, Rash, Kynette, & Norman, 1990; Pratt, Boyes, Robins, & Manchester, 1989; Pratt & Robins, 1991). Narrative stories told by older adults are evaluated more positively, preferred by listeners, and more memorable than those told by younger adults (Kemper et al., 1990; Pratt & Robins, 1991; Pratt et al., 1989).

Other discourse skills appear to be vulnerable to aging. Older adults often have difficulty with referential communication tasks. In one such referential communication task, Hupet, Chantraine, and Nef (1993) tracked how dyads of younger and older adults formulated mutually acceptable labels for abstract drawings. The older adults benefited less from repetition of the task than the younger adults; whereas the younger adults added new information to previously used descriptions, the older adults tended to supply totally new labels. The older adults' problems with this task may have resulted from forgetting the old labels from trial to trial or from their inability to inhibit irrelevant thoughts or associations, including the new descriptions.

In a series of studies, Kemper and her colleagues (Kemper, Othick, Gerhing, Gubarchuk, & Billington, 1998; Kemper, Othick, Warren, Gubarchuk, & Gerhing, 1996; Kemper, Vandeputte, Rice, Cheung, & Gubarchuk, 1995b) have compared young-young, old-old, and young-old dyads on a referential communication task involving giving map directions. Whereas younger adults spontaneously adopted a simplified speech style when addressing older adults versus age-equivalent peers, older adults did not appear to code switch. This may be due to a number of factors, including: (a) older adults may not be sensitive to the same situational cues that elicit code switching from the younger adults; (b) older adults may not be able to vary their grammatical complexity or semantic content while simultaneously executing the complex task; (c) older speakers may have "optimized" their speech to peers as a result of extensive practice at communicating with other older adults and adults experiencing communicative problems; hence, shifting to a non-optimal speech style when addressing younger adults would not be an appropriate strategy; (d) older adults may be unwilling to shift to a simplified speech style when they are addressing peers since this form of speech may resemble patronizing talk (Ryan, Hummert, & Boich, 1995) or secondary baby talk (Caporael, 1981).

The discourse of younger and older adults differs in other ways. For instance, dyads of older adults mixed talk about the past along with talk about the present to achieve a shared sense of meaning and personal worth that was lacking in the discourse of younger adults (Boden & Bielby, 1986). In addition, conversations with older adults often are marked by "painful self-disclosures" of bereavement, ill health, immobility, and assorted personal and family problems (Coupland, Coupland, & Giles, 1991). Painful self-disclosures may serve several different goals for communicators (Coupland, Coupland, & Grainger, 1991; Shaner, 1996), for example, maintaining face by contrasting personal strengths and competencies with past problems and limitations, and coping with personal losses and difficulties. Yet, painful self-disclosures also maintain and reinforce negative age stereotypes about older adults as being weak and disabled (Shaner, 1996). Consequently, such self-disclosures can suppress conversational interactions and limit the quality of intergenerational communication (Nussbaum, Hummert, Williams, & Harwood, 1996).

Intergenerational communication also may be limited by other attributes of older adults' speech. Giles and Williams (1994) have observed that younger people often feel patronized by older adults who may adopt a "not-listening," "disapproving," or "overprotecting" style when interacting with younger adults. Age disclosure on the part of the older partner (also noted by Coupland, Coupland, & Grainger, 1991) may, like painful self-disclosures, lead to unsatisfactory intergenerational interactions by emphasizing the differences between older and younger partners. Collins and Gould (1994) noted, however, that younger and older women appeared to conform to the same norms regarding disclosures of negative and intimate life events and suggested that intergenerational communication may not conform to the stereotype that older adults dominate conversations with negative stories about the past.

A final discourse style often presumed to accompany aging is verbosity, or repetitive, prolonged, off-target speech. However, recent research (Arbuckle & Gold, 1993; Arbuckle, Gold, & Andres, 1986; Gold, Andres, Arbuckle, & Schwartzman, 1988; Gold & Arbuckle, 1992; Gold, Arbuckle, & Andres, 1994) has suggested that verbosity is not a general characteristic of older adults but is an extreme form of talkativeness that results from intellectual decline associated with frontal lobe impairments (see Arbuckle & Gold, 1993), for a review of these issues). Frontal lobe impairments disrupt inhibitory processes and lead to preservative behaviors on other tasks. Verbosity can be characterized as involving a loss of the ability to inhibit competing responses; hence, an age-related loss of frontal lobe function may lead to increased verbosity among older adults. Verbosity, like talk of the past, painful self-disclosures, and age disclosures, may disrupt social interactions and lead to a loss of interpersonal contact and social support. Unlike the other discourse practices of older adults, however, verbosity appears to reflect changes in message production processes that lie at the juncture between normal and pathological aging.

Changes in message comprehension by older adults

Discourse comprehension involves several steps, from decoding the auditory or visual stimulus to constructing a syntactic, semantic, and discourse representation of the message. The following sections review some of the recent research on studies of older adults' discourse comprehension, which have tended to focus separately on issues of auditory-based discourse and text-based discourse.

Auditory-based discourse

Stine and Wingfield (1990) noted that there is an apparent paradox of language processing in older adults. Older adults have difficulty with some effortful processes, such as semantic encoding, and are slower in many cognitive tasks, but normal older adults have relatively few difficulties in understanding everyday discourse. Wingfield and colleagues have focused on empirical investigations of how the semantic, syntactic, and prosodic structures of speech influence adults' discourse comprehension. Stine, Wingfield, and Poon (1986), for example, tested whether increased propositional density of text and increased presentation rates disrupt older adults' recall of auditorily presented text. Stine et al. (1986) found that older adults were not differentially influenced by the high propositionally dense text, though recall performance was poorer for speeded text presentation. In a related study, Wingfield and Stine (1986) found that older adults, like younger adults, segment auditory-based prose at syntactic boundaries and that recall performance did not decline as the rate of presentation increased. Stine and Wingfield (1988) found that while there are minimal quantitative age differences in the recall of propositionally dense speech, there are significant qualitative differences for older relative to younger adults.

Older adults' comprehension of everyday information, such as television newscasts, remains well preserved. Stine, Wingfield, and Myers (1990) examined younger and older adults' recall of information from a television newscast that was presented in auditory format, auditory format supplemented with a written transcript, or the original auditory and visual recording. Although the written transcript and visual presentation aided younger adults' recall of the information, older adults did not benefit.

Two recent studies are of interest in that both explored whether older adults' working memory limitations may affect text processing. Zurif, Swinney, Prather, Wingfield, and Brownell (1995) examined younger and older adults' on–line processing of object- and subject-relative sentences using a cross-modal priming task. In object–relative sentences, the object "moves" from the object position of the subordinate clause and leaves a "gap" or trace (e.g., "The tailor hemmed the cloak$_i$ that the actor from the studio needed (t_i) for the performance"). In subject–relative sentences, the gap is indexed by the object of the matrix clause (e.g., "The gymnast loved the professor$_i$ from the Northwestern city who (t_i) complained about the bad coffee"). The focus of their analysis was to determine whether reactivation of the antecedent occurs at the gap during sentence processing. Zurif et al. found that older adults evidenced priming for the subject- but not object-relative sentences (Experiment 1). In a second experiment, Zurif et al. reduced the distance between gap and antecedent in object-relative sentences from seven or eight intervening words to five and found a significant priming effect at the gap position. The authors concluded that older adults reactivate the antecedent when the distance between antecedent and gap is short. Zurif et al. did not report a direct comparison of young and old, but interpreted their results as showing that older adults' immediate syntactic analysis of a sentence is affected by working memory limitations.

This interpretation was challenged by a study by Kemtes and Kemper (1997) that also examined the relationship between younger and older adults' working memory and on-line syntactic processing. They used a word-by-word reading paradigm to assess younger and older adults' on-line comprehension of temporarily ambiguous sentences ("Several angry workers warned about low wages . . .") that were resolved either with a main verb (MV) interpretation (Several angry workers warned about low wages during the holiday season) or a reduced relative (RRC) clause interpretation ("Several angry workers warned about low wages decided to file complaints"). Kemtes and Kemper also assessed adults' off-line comprehension of the sentences by presenting a comprehension question immediately after each sentence had been read. The primary finding was that, while older adults' on-line reading times were slower than those of younger adults, the syntactic complexity did not differentially impair older adults' on-line comprehension of the sentences. Thus, there was no evidence that older adults' working memory limitations affected their ability to process the complex syntactic constructions. In contrast, older adults' off-line question comprehension was influenced by the syntactic ambiguity manipulation in that question comprehension was reliably poorer, relative to younger adults, for the syntactically ambiguous sentences.

Whether working memory limitations associated with age affect immediate or on-line processes currently is a subject of active debate. Caplan and Waters (1999) argued that immediate processing of semantic and syntactic information is automatic and is buffered from the effects of working memory limitations, whereas postcomprehension processes are not. Older adults' language performance does not show an inevitable decline under normal discourse conditions. Older adults' comprehension is compromised when the structure of the discourse is complex and presented at very rapid rates, and when assessed with tasks such as question answering, imitation, and recall.

Text-based discourse

The studies of older adults' text and prose processing largely have shown that text level characteristics, such as propositional content and syntactic complexity or whether the prose is narrative or expository, greatly influence older adults' text comprehension. For example, Zelinksi, Light, and Gilewski (1984) have found that older and younger adults recalled qualitatively similar features of the expository text, although older adults recalled less information than younger adults. In a study on younger and older adults' processing of narrative and expository texts, Tun (1989) found that recall was better for narrative rather than expository texts. Further, younger adults recalled more of the text than older adults irrespective of text type.

The syntactic and semantic content of prose also influences older adults' comprehension. Though overall recall of propositionally dense text may have been unimpaired, older adults tended to recall fewer main ideas relative to younger adults (Stine & Wingfield, 1988). Light and Capps (1986) found that older adults had more difficulty than younger adults in identifying pronominal referents as text processing load increased. Researchers also have documented deficits in older adults' ability to generate inferences from text (Cohen, 1979; Zacks, Hasher, Doren, Hamm, & Attig, 1987; but see Zelinski, 1988).

Recent research on text comprehension in aging has focused on the text- and reader-level variables that influence processing as it takes place, on-line. Hartley, Stojack, Mushaney, Kiku-Annon, and Lee (1994) compared younger and older adults' recall of prose that was presented in experimenter- and self-paced presentation tasks. They found that older adults recalled less than younger adults as the time available for processing increased. At the text level, Stine (1990) found that younger and older adults allocated word-by-word reading times similarly for word-level and more global phrase-level features of the text. Younger adults allocated additional reading time to the ends of phrases, clauses, and sentences, whereas older adults paused only at clause boundaries. A related study by Stine, Cheung, and Henderson (1995) extended this earlier research by showing that specific word-, phrase-, sentence-, and discourse-level features of text influenced older adults' word-by-word reading times and explicit recall of narrative texts such that, overall, older adults tended to allocate less reading time to processing new concepts. Stine-Morrow, Loveless, and Soederberg (1996) demonstrated that younger and older adults' on-line reading times were qualitatively similar in that both age groups allocated more reading time to text sectors with complex syntaxctic, new concepts, and longer words. However, older adults did allocate less reading time, relative to younger adults, to new concepts.

Changes in message production and comprehension due to Alzheimer's disease

Communication problems often are the first symptoms of a progressive dementia such as Alzheimer's dementia, and communication problems are frequently are noted by spouses and other family members (Bayles & Tomoeda, 1991; Orange, 1991; Rau, 1991). Clinical markers of the onset of Alzheimer's disease are difficult to distinguish from non-clinical age-related lapses of attention or memory, benign senescent forgetfulness or nonpathological age-associated memory impairments (Huppert, 1994; Kral, 1962). Distinguishing normative age-related changes to message production from nonnormative or pathological changes may be important for the early diagnosis (hence, possible treatment) of Alzheimer's disease and related disorders.

Many of the impairments to discourse that have been observed in adults with Alzheimer's dementia may stem from their gross word-finding problems, whereas other problems may stem from attentional deficits and cognitive confusions. The heavy use of deixtic terms such as "this" and "that," the loss of specific reference and loss of cohesion, the prevalence of vague terms and "empty speech," a loss of detail, an increase in repetition and redundancy, and confusing shifts in topic and focus all have been noted as characteristic of the speech of adults with Alzheimer's dementia (Bayles, Boone, Tomoeda, Slauson, & Kaszniak, 1989; Bayles & Kaszniak, 1987; Garcia & Joanette, 1994; Hier, Hagenlocker, & Shindler, 1985; Hutchinson & Jensen, 1980; Nicholas, Obler, Albert, & Helm-Esterbrooks, 1985; Ripich & Terrell, 1988; Ripich, Terrell, & Spinelli, 1983; Ulatowska, Allard, & Donnell, 1988; Ulatowska & Chapman, 1991).

Other discourse-level communication problems also have been linked to Alzheimer's dementia. Whereas healthy older adults follow a story grammar in telling personal narratives, relating setting information, complications, the protagonist's actions, and a resolution, the spontaneous narratives of adults with Alzheimer's dementia characteristically supply only setting information (Ulatowska & Chapman, 1991; Ulatowska et al., 1988), unless they are prompted by their conversational partner (Kemper, Lyons, & Anagnopoulos, 1995a). The ability to use or follow a familiar script, or a series of temporally and causally linked events such as eating in a restaurant, going to a movie, or holding a wedding, also is impaired by Alzheimer's dementia (Grafman, Thompson, Weingartner, Martinez, Lawlor, & Sunderland, 1991; Harrold, Anderson, Clancy, & Kempler, 1990), as are spontaneous turn taking, topic initiation, topic maintenance, topic shifting, conversational repairs, and speech acts such as requesting, asserting, clarifying, and questioning (Bayles & Kaszniak, 1987).

Some aspects of metalinguistic abilities appear to be preserved in individuals with Alzheimer's dementia. Saunders (1996) has noted that humor, reflecting metalinguistic awareness of cognitive problems, often is used by patients undergoing a neurological examination. Self-deprecatory remarks, making fun of memory lapses, and humorous remarks often are used by patients when they are unable to respond to the clinician's examination questions. A breakdown of self-awareness and metalinguistic skills may contribute to the discourse problems of adults with Alzheimer's dementia; Hamilton (1994a, 1994b) has suggested that the progression of

Alzheimer's dementia is indicated by an erosion of metalinguistic skills marked by declines in requests for clarification, references to memory problems, and self-evaluation of skills and abilities. By carefully tracing communication breakdowns during a series of conversations spanning 4 ½ years between herself and Elsie, a woman with Alzheimer's dementia, Hamilton was able to elucidate four stages to the deterioration of communication.

Stage 1. Elsie was an active participant in the conversations, but one who was bothered by word-finding problems as well as memory lapses; she was aware of her communication problems and attempted to deal with them through excuses, circumlocutions, and other metalinguistic comments. Turn taking, joking, and speech formalisms were preserved.

Stage 2. Elsie remained an active participant in the conversations, but her awareness of and responses to her memory lapses and word-finding problems had disappeared. Perseverations and excessive repetitions had begun to appear.

Stage 3. Elsie's participation in the conversations was markedly reduced, perseverations were common, and formulaic language (e.g., "ready-made" conversational routines) predominated, and neologisms frequently occurred. Politeness markers, expressions of appreciation, and joking routines had disappeared from Elsie's conversation.

Stage 4. Elsie had become a passive participant; lexical language was lost, replaced by a limited repertoire of nonverbal responses (e.g., uh-huh, mhn, mm-Hm, mmm, hmm?). Elsie was able to draw on this repertoire to request repetitions and clarifications, take a turn during the conversation, and indicate her interest in her surroundings.

As others have noted, end-stage Alzheimer's dementia often is characterized by mutism, inappropriate non-verbal vocalizations, and, frequently, failures to respond to others (Lamar, Obler, Knoefel, & Albert, 1994).

Changes in message production to older adults

A special speech register, sometimes termed "elderspeak," has been described as an accommodation to communicating with older adults. Elderspeak may be evoked by negative stereotypes of older adults as well as their actual communicative needs; hence, elderspeak is addressed to healthy older adults as well as those who are or are presumed to be cognitively impaired (Caporael, 1981; Caporael & Culbertson, 1986; Caporael, Lukaszewski, & Culbertson, 1983; Kemper, 1994; Ryan, Bourhis, & Knops, 1991; Ryan, Giles, Bartolucci, & Henwood, 1986). Elderspeak has been characterized as involving a simplified speech register with exaggerated pitch and intonation, simplified grammar, limited vocabulary, and slow rate of delivery. It appears to be a robust phenomenon that occurs in a wide range of settings involving older adults such as craft classes, legal seminars, and congregate meals as well as in nursing homes for older adults who have or do not have dementia (Kemper, 1994), although it most often is associated with nursing homes and other health care facilities (Ashburn & Gordon, 1981; Gibb & O'Brien, 1990; Gubrium, 1975; Lanceley, 1985; Ryan, Hummert, & Boich, 1995). Many of the characteristics of elderspeak, such as its slow rate, exaggerated prosody, and simplified syntax and vocabulary, resemble the characteristics of other speech registers such as those directed at young children, foreigners, and household pets (Warren & McCloskey, 1997). Elderspeak is assumed to have these special characteristics because it enhances or facilitates communication with older adults.

Kemper and her collaborators (Kemper et al., 1995b; Kemper et. al., 1996) have begun to examine this claim. They have shown that younger adults spontaneously adopted a simplified speech register when addressing older listeners during a referential communication task. The referential communication task used in these studies required the listener to reproduce a route drawn on a map, following directions given by a the speaker. Dyads of younger-younger, older-older, and younger-older adults alternated as speakers and listeners. Older adults showed little variation in their speech style whether they were addressing younger or older listeners. Younger adults, however, adopted a simplified speech style when instructing older listeners; the simplified style not only provided more information in terms of words, utterances, instructions, and location checks on the listener's progress but it also "packaged" this information differently. The younger adults paused more often, used shorter sentences, used few complex syntactic constructions, and reduced the informational content of individual utterances by lowering propositional density, a measure of how much information is packed in an utterance. These speech adjustments appeared to benefit the older listeners, who were able to reproduce the maps more accurately than when they were paired with older speakers.

The younger adults' use of elderspeak may have been triggered by beliefs about the communicative competence of older adults or by actual communicative problems of their older partners, as signaled by their older partners' behavior during the referential communication task. Older listeners frequently interrupted speakers to repeat the speakers' instructions, request clarification, or express confusion or difficulty with the task. These interruptions may have cued the younger adults to simplify their speech. In order to investigate this possibility, Kemper et al. (1996) replicated the study with one major change: listeners were prohibited from interrupting the speaker to request clarification or express confusion. In the second study, younger adults again spontaneously adopted a simplified speech register when addressing older listeners during the referential communication task. This speech register resembled other forms of elderspeak in that it was marked by reductions in speaking rate, sentence length, the use of complex syntactic constructions, and propositional density, and by increases in words, utterances, instructions, and repetitions. The younger adults' use of elderspeak in the second study was not cued by the actual behavior of the older listeners during the task, since listeners were prohibited from interrupting the speakers. Rather, the younger speakers were drawing upon a set of stereotypes of the communicative problems of older adults in order to modify their speech.

In both Kemper et al. (1995b, 1996) the younger adults' use of elderspeak improved the performance of the older adults on the referential communication task; older listeners performed more accurately when paired with younger speakers than when paired with other older adults. The younger speakers' decrease in sentence length, grammatical complexity, and propositional density, and their increase in words, utterances, instructions, repetitions, and location checks were associated with lower error scores by the older listeners. Working memory limitations appear to impair older adults' performance on the referential communication tasks, and it is likely that the younger adults' speech accommodations reduced working memory demands because they provided more information and packaged that information into shorter and simpler utterances (Kemper, 1992; Kemper, Anagnopoulos, Lyons, & Heberlein, 1994).

It is important to note that in these studies, the younger adults' use of elderspeak was not without cost. Although the older adults did better on the referential communication task when paired with younger partners, they reported more expressive and receptive communication problems. The older adults' self-reported communication problems with younger partners were associated with shorter sentences, slower speaking rate, higher pitch, greater pitch range, and more speaker repetitions. These stylistic factors appeared to trigger older adults' perceptions of themselves as communicatively impaired, leading to increased self-report of expressive and receptive problems. The older adults' self-reported expressive and receptive problems were not associated with the younger adults' grammatical complexity or other semantic content and repetitions.

Elderspeak also is modified by practice and task familiarity. When Kemper et al. (1998) gave younger adults extended practice on the same referential communication task with older partners, the younger adults adopted further simplifications to their speech, including further shortening their sentences, further increasing their production of sentence fragments, and shifting to a very slow speaking rate. This "streamlined" form of elderspeak appeared to result from an assessment of the communicative needs of their older partners. When partnered with other younger adults, extended practice led younger adults to shift to shorter, more fragmented speech, but speech that also was very terse, highly repetitive, and delivered at a very fast rate.

The use of elderspeak in these studies did enhance the performance of the older adults, but the older adults reported experiencing more expressive and receptive communication problems when they were paired with younger partners who used elderspeak. The use of elderspeak appeared to trigger older adults' perceptions of themselves as communicatively impaired and led to increased self-report of expressive and receptive problems by the older adults (Kemper et al., 1995b, 1996). The streamlined version of elderspeak that resulted from extended practice had an even more deleterious effect on the older adults' self-assessment of their communicative competence (Kemper et. al., 1998) than the spontaneous, unpracticed form. These findings have lent further support to the "communicative predicament of aging" (p. 6) model of Ryan et al. (1986; see below). In this case, the "communicative predicament of aging" is that elderspeak led to a decrease in the older adults' self-ratings of communicative competence, yet it also improved their performance on the referential communication tasks.

Conclusion

Only through systematic research will it be possible to show how which elderspeak or other discourse modifications will help older adults, especially those with Alzheimer's dementia, and which will hurt them. There is a danger that the inappropriate use of such elderspeak modifications may impair communication with older adults. Harwood, Giles, and Ryan (1995) argued that the use of elderspeak as well as other age-based behavioral modifications contributes to development of an ""old"" identity, reinforcing negative stereotypes of older adults, and lowering older adults' self-esteem. Following Ryan et. al. (1986), they further argued that a downward spiral can result such that elderspeak can contribute to the social isolation and cognitive decline of older adults, triggering further speech simplifications. As mentioned above, Ryan et al. (1986) termed this the "communicative predicament of aging." The predicament is that elderspeak can lead to a negative spiral of perceived and actual communicative impairments, but the failure to use appropriate speech accommodations for older adults also may lead to social isolation and cognitive decline. Other observational studies, as well as simulation studies using scripted interactions, have noted that elderspeak conveys a sense of disrespect toward its recipients, limits their conversational interactions, and implies that they are cognitively impaired (Edwards & Noller, 1993; Gubrium, 1975; Ryan, Hamilton, & Kwong See, 1994; Ryan, MacLean, & Orange, 1994; Ryan et al., 1991). O'Connor and Rigby (1996), following Ryan et al. (1991), suggested that older adults, especially those in nursing homes, adapt to situational demands by becoming more accepting of elderspeak.

The psychosocial consequences of the use of elderspeak are assumed to be offset by its positive benefits for enhancing communication with older adults. Although there is little empirical support for this assumption, caregivers and service providers commonly justify their use of elderspeak by claiming that it helps older adults' comprehension, especially that of older adults with dementia. One way to avoid the "communicative predicament of aging" would be to adopt appropriate speech modifications: to modulate the use and form of elderspeak based on the actual communicative needs of one's conversational partners rather than stereotypic assumptions about the cognitive impairments of older adults (Orange, Ryan, Meredith, & MacLean, 1995; Ryan, Meredith, MacLean, & Orange, 1995). The available descriptive and observational studies of elderspeak do not evaluate whether younger adults can or will tune their speech to the actual communicative needs of older adults. The studies by Kemper and her collaborators (1995b, 1996) suggested that younger adults simplify their speech as a result of extended practice with a task and on the basis of stereotypic assumptions about older adults' communicative needs rather than on the basis of actual behavioral cues and the performance of older adults. It may be necessary to disentangle those parameters of elderspeak that actually benefit older adults' performance from those that trigger older adults' negative self-assessments.

References

Arbuckle, T., & Gold, D. P. (1993). Aging, inhibition, and verbosity. *Journal of Gerontology: Psychological Sciences, 48,* 225–232.

Arbuckle, T. Y., Gold, D., & Andres, D. (1986). Cognitive functioning of older people in relation to social and personality variables. *Psychology and Aging, 1,* 55–62.

Ashburn, G., & Gordon, A. (1981). Features of a simplified register in speech to elderly conversationalists. *International Journal of Psycholinguistics, 7,* 31–43.

Bayles, K., Boone, D. R., Tomoeda, C., Slauson, T., & Kaszniak, A. W. (1989). Differentiating Alzheimer's patients from the normal elderly and stroke patients with aphasia. *Journal of Speech and Hearing Disorders, 54,* 74–87.

Bayles, K. A., & Kaszniak, A. W. (1987). *Communication and cognition in normal aging and dementia.* Boston: College-Hill.

Bayles, K. A., & Tomoeda, C. K. (1991). Caregiver report of prevalence and appearance order of linguistic symptoms in Alzheimer's patients. *The Gerontologist, 31,* 210–216.

Boden, D., & Bielby, D. D. (1986). The way it was: Topical organization in elderly conversation. *Language and Communication, 6,* 73–89.

Caplan, D., & Waters, G. (1999). Verbal working memory and sentence comprehension. *Behavioral and Brain Sciences.*

Caporael, L. (1981). The paralanguage of caregiving: Baby talk to the institutionalized aged. *Journal of Personality and Social Psychology, 40,* 876–884.

Caporael, L. R., & Culbertson, G. H. (1986). Verbal response modes of baby talk and other speech at institutions for the aged. *Language and Communication, 6,* 99–112.

Caporael, L. R., Lukaszewski, M. P., & Culbertson, G. H. (1983). Secondary babytalk: Judgments of institutionalized elderly and their caregivers. *Journal of Personality and Social Psychology, 44,* 746–754.

Cohen, G. (1979). Language comprehension in old age. *Cognitive Psychology, 11,* 412–429.

Collins, C. L., & Gould, O. N. (1994). Getting to know you: How own age and other's age relate to self-disclosure. *International Journal of Aging and Human Development, 39*, 55–66.

Coupland, J., Coupland, N., & Giles, H. (1991). My life in your hands: Processes of intergenerational self-disclosure. In N. Coupland, J. Coupland, & H. Giles (Eds.), *Language, society, and the elderly* (pp. 75–108). Oxford, England: Basil Blackwell.

Coupland, J., Coupland, N., & Grainger, K. (1991). Intergenerational discourse: Contextual versions of ageing and elderliness. *Aging and Society, 2*, 189–208.

Edwards, H., & Noller, P. (1993). Perceptions of overaccommodations used by nurses in communication with the elderly. *Journal of Language and Social Psychology, 1*, 207–223.

Garcia, L. J., & Joanette, Y. (1994). Conversational topic-shifting analysis in dementia. In R. L. Bloom, L. K. Obler, S. de Santi, & J. S. Ehrlich (Eds.), *Discourse analysis and applications: Studies of adult clinical populations* (pp. 161–184). Hillsdale, NJ: Erlbaum Associates.

Gibb, H., & O'Brien, B. (1990). Jokes and reassurances are not enough: Ways in which nurses related through conversation with elderly clients. *Journal of Advanced Nursing, 15*, 1389–1401.

Giles, H., & Williams, A. (1994). Patronizing the young: Forms and evaluations. *International Journal of Aging and Human Development, 39*, 33–54.

Gold, D., Andres, D., Arbuckle, T., & Schwartzman, A. (1988). Measurement and correlates of verbosity in elderly people. *Journal of Gerontology: Psychological Sciences, 43*, 27–33.

Gold, D. P., & Arbuckle, T. Y. (1992). Interactions between personality and cognition and their implications for theories of aging. In E. A. Lovelace (Ed.), *Aging and cognition: Mental processes, self-awareness, and interventions* (pp. 351–377). Amsterdam: North-Holland.

Gold, D. P., Arbuckle, T. Y., & Andres, D. (1994). Verbosity in older adults. In M. L. Hummert, J. M. Wiemann, & J. F. Nussbaum (Eds.), *Interpersonal communication in older adulthood: Interdisciplinary theory and research* (pp. 107–129). Thousand Oaks, CA: Sage.

Grafman, J., Thompson, K., Weingartner, H., Martinez, R., Lawlor, B. A., & Sunderland, T. (1991). Script generation as an indicator of knowledge representation in patients with Alzheimer's disease. *Brain and Language, 40*, 344–358.

Gubrium, J. F. (1975). *Living and dying at Murray Manor.* New York: St. Martin's Press.

Hamilton, H. (1994a). *Conversations with an Alzheimer's patient.* Cambridge, England: Cambridge University Press.

Hamilton, H. (1994b). Requests for clarification as evidence of pragmatic comprehension difficulty: The case of Alzheimer's disease. In R. L. Bloom, L. K. Obler, S. de Santi, & J. S. Ehrlich (Eds.), *Discourse analysis and applications: Studies in adult clinical populations* (pp. 185–200). Hillsdale, NJ: Erlbaum Associates.

Harrold, R. M., Anderson, E. S., Clancy, P., & Kempler, D. (1990). Script knowledge deficits in Alzheimer's disease. *Journal of Clinical and Experimental Neuropsychology, 12*, 397.

Hartley, J. T., Stojack, C. C., Mushaney, T. J., Kiku Annon, T. A., & Lee (1994). Reading speed and prose memory in older and younger adults. *Psychology and Aging, 9*, 216–223.

Harwood, J., Giles, H., & Ryan, E. B. (1995). Aging, communication, and intergroup theory: Social identity and intergenerational communication. In J. Nussbaum & J. Coupland (Eds.), *Handbook of communication and aging* (pp. 133–159). Hillsdale, NJ: Erlbaum Associates.

Hasher, L., & Zacks, R. T. (1988). Working memory, comprehension, and aging: A review and a new view. In G. H. Bower (Ed.), *The psychology of learning and motivation* (Vol. 22, pp. 193–226). New York: Academic Press.

Hier, D. B., Hagenlocker, D., & Shindler, A. G. (1985). Language disintegration in dementia: Effects of etiology and severity. *Brain and Language, 25*, 117–133.

Hupet, M., Chantraine, Y., & Nef, F. (1993). References in conversation between young and old normal adults. *Psychology and Aging, 8*, 339–346.

Huppert, F. A. (1994). Memory function in dementia and normal aging—dimension or dichotomy? In F. A. Huppert, C. Byrne, & D. W. O'Connor (Eds.), *Dementia and normal aging* (pp. 291–330). Cambridge: Cambridge University Press.

Hutchinson, J. M., & Jensen, M. (1980). A pragmatic evaluation of discourse communication in normal elderly and senile elderly in a nursing home. In L. K. Obler & M. L. Albert (Eds.), *Language and communication in the elderly* (pp. 59–73). Lexington, KY: D.C. Heath.

Kemper, S. (1990). Adults' diaries: Changes made to written narratives across the life-span. *Discourse Processes, 13*, 207–223.

Kemper, S. (1992). Language and aging. In F. I. M. Craik & T. A. Salthouse (Eds.), *Handbook of aging and cognition* (pp. 213–270). Hillsdale, NJ: Lawrence Erlbaum.

Kemper, S. (1994). "Elderspeak": Speech accommodations to older adults. *Aging and Cognition, 1*, 17–28.

Kemper, S., & Anagnopoulos, C. (1997). Linguistic creativity in older adults. In C. Adams-Price (Eds.), *Creativity and aging: Theoretical and empirical perspectives* (pp. 289–310). New York: Springer.

Kemper, S., Anagnopoulos, C., Lyons, K., & Heberlein, W. (1994). Speech accommodations to dementia. *Journal of Gerontology: Psychological Sciences, 49*, 223–230.

Kemper, S., & Hummert, M. L. (1997). New directions in research on aging and message production. In J. O. Greene (Ed.), *Message production: Advances in communication theory* (pp. 127–150). Mahwah, NJ: Erlbaum.

Kemper, S., Lyons, K., & Anagnopoulos, C. (1995a). Joint story-telling by Alzheimer's patients and their spouses. *Discourse Processes, 20*, 205–217.

Kemper, S., Othick, M., Gerhing, H., Gubarchuk, J., & Billington, C. (1998). Practicing speech accommodations to older adults. *Applied Psycholinguistics, 19*, 175–192.

Kemper, S., Othick, M., Warren, J., Gubarchuk, J., & Gerhing, H. (1996). Facilitating older adults' performance on a referential communication task through speech accommodations. *Aging, Neuropsychology, and Cognition, 3*, 37–55.

Kemper, S., Rash, S. R., Kynette, D., & Norman, S. (1990). Telling stories: The structure of adults' narratives. *European Journal of Cognitive Psychology, 2*, 205–228.

Kemper, S., Vandeputte, D., Rice, K., Cheung, H., & Gubarchuk, J. (1995b). Speech adjustments to aging during a referential communication task. *Journal of Language and Social Psychology, 14*, 40–59.

Kemtes, K. A., & Kemper, S. (1997). Younger and older adults on-line processing of syntactic ambiguities. *Psychology and Aging, 12*, 362–371.

Kral, V. A. (1962). Senescent forgetfulness: Benign and malignant. *The Canadian Medical Association Journal, 86,* 257–260.

Lamar, M. A. C., Obler, L. K., Knoefel, J. E., & Albert, M. L. (1994). Communication patterns in end-stage Alzheimer's disease: Pragmatic analyses. In R. L. Bloom, L. K. Obler, S. de Santi, & J. S. Ehrlich (Eds.), *Discourse analysis and applications: Studies in adult clinical populations* (pp. 216–236). Hillsdale, NJ: Erlbaum Associates.

Lanceley, A. (1985). Use of controlling language in the rehabilitation of the elderly. *Journal of Advanced Nursing, 10,* 125–135.

Light, L. L. (1991). Memory and aging: Four hypotheses in search of date. *Annual Review of Psychology, 42,* 333–376.

Light, L., & Capps, J. L. (1986). Comprehension of pronouns in younger and older adults. *Developmental Psychology, 22,* 580–585.

Nicholas, M., Obler, L. K., Albert, M. L., & Helm-Esterbrooks, N. (1985). Empty speech in Alzheimer's disease and fluent aphasia. *Journal of Speech and Hearing Research, 28,* 405–410.

Nussbaum, J. F., Hummert, M. L., Williams, A., & Harwood, J. (1996). Communication and older adults. In B. R. Burleson (Ed.), *Communication yearbook 19* (pp. 1–47). Newbury Park, CA: Sage.

O'Conner, B. P., & Rigby, H. (1996). Perceptions of baby talk, requency of receiving baby talk, and self-esteem among community and nursing home residents. *Psychology and Aging, 11,* 147–154.

Orange, J. B. (1991). Perspectives of family members regarding communication changes. In R. Lubinski (Ed.), *Dementia and communication* (pp. 168–187). Philadelphia, PA: Decker.

Orange, J. B., Ryan, E. B., Meredith, S. D., & MacLean, M. J. (1995). Application of the communication enhancement model for long-term care residents with Alzheimer's disease. *Topics in Language Disorders, 15,* 20–35.

Pratt, M. W., Boyes, C., Robins, S., & Manchester, J. (1989). Telling tales: Aging, working memory, and the narrative cohesion of storytellers. *Developmental Psychology, 25,* 628–635.

Pratt, M. W., & Robins, S. L. (1991). That's the way it was: Age differences in the structure and quality of adults' personal narratives. *Discourse Processes, 14,* 73–85.

Rau, M. T. (1991). Impact on families. In R. Lubinski (Ed.), *Dementia and Communication* (pp. 152–167). Philadelphia, PA: Decker.

Ripich, D. N., & Terrell, B. Y. (1988). Patterns of discourse cohesion and coherence in Alzheimer's disease. *Journal of Speech and Hearing Disorders, 53,* 8–15.

Ripich, D. N., Terrell, B. Y., & Spinelli, F. (1983). Discourse cohesion in senile dementia of the Alzheimer type. In R. H. Brookshire (Ed.), *Clinical Aphasiology Conference proceedings* (pp. 316–321). Minneapolis, MN: BRK.

Ryan, E. B., Bourhis, R. Y., & Knops, U. (1991). Evaluative perceptions of patronizing speech addressed to elders. *Psychology and Aging, 6,* 442–450.

Ryan, E. B., Giles, H., Bartolucci, G., & Henwood, K. (1986). Psycholinguistic and social psychological components of communication by and with the elderly. *Language and Communication, 6,* 1–24.

Ryan, E. B., Hamilton, J. M., & Kwong See, S. (1994a). Younger and older adult listeners' evaluations of baby talk addressed to institutionalized elders. *International Journal of Aging and Human Development, 39,* 21–32.

Ryan, E. B., Hummert, M. L., & Boich, L. H. (1995). Communication predicaments of aging: Patronizing behavior toward older adults. *Journal of Language and Social Psychology, 14,* 144–166.

Ryan, E. B., MacLean, M., & Orange, J. B. (1994b). Inappropriate accommodation in communication to elders: Inferences about nonverbal correlates. *International Journal of Aging and Human Development, 39,* 273–291.

Ryan, E. B., Meredith, S. D., MacLean, M. J., & Orange, J. B. (1995). Changing the way we talk with elders: Promotion health using the communication enhancement model. *International Journal of Aging and Human Development, 41,* 89–107.

Salthouse, T. A. (1992). *Mechanisms of aging–cognition relations in adulthood.* Hillsdale, NJ: Erlbaum.

Saunders, P. A. (1996). Humor and laughter as communication strategies between dementia patients and their clinicians. Presented at the annual meeting of the Gerontological Society of America, Washington, D.C.

Shaner, J. L. (1996). *Painful self-disclosures of older adults: Judgments of perceived motivations and discloser characteristics.* Unpublished doctoral dissertation, University of Kansas, Lawrence.

Stine, E. A. L. (1990). On-line processing of written text by younger and older adults. *Psychology and Aging, 5,* 68–78.

Stine, E. A. L., Chueng, H., & Henderson, D. (1995). Adult age differences in the on-line processing of new concepts in discourse. *Aging and Cognition, 2,* 1–18.

Stine, E. A. L., & Wingfield, A. (1988). Memorability functions as an indicator of qualitative age differences in text recall. *Psychology and Aging, 3,* 179–183.

Stine, E. A. L., & Wingfield, A. (1990). The assessment of qualitative age differences in discourse processing. In T. M. Hess (Ed.), *Aging and cognition: Knowledge organization and utilization* (pp. 33–91). Amsterdam: Elsevier.

Stine, E. L., Wingfield, A., & Myers, S. D. (1990). Age differences in processing information from television news: The effects of bisensory augmentation. *Journal of Gerontology, 45,* 1–8.

Stine, E. A. L., Wingfield, A., & Poon, L. W. (1986). How much and how fast: Rapid processing of spoken language in later adulthood. *Psychology and Aging, 1,* 303–311.

Stine-Morrow, E. A. L., Loveless, M. K., & Soederberg, L. M. (1996). Resource allocation in on-line reading by younger and older adults. *Psychology and Aging, 11,* 475–486.

Tun, P. A. (1989). Age differences in processing expository and narrative text. *Journal of Gerontology: Psychological Sciences, 44,* 9–15.

Ulatowska, H. K., Allard, L., & Donnell, A. (1988). Discourse performance in subjects with dementia of the Alzheimer type. In H. Whitaker (Ed.), *Neuropsychological studies of nonfocal brain damage* (pp. 108–131). New York: Springer-Verlag.

Ulatowska, H. K., & Chapman, S. B. (1991). Discourse studies. In R. Lubinski (Ed.), *Dementia and communication* (pp. 115–132). Philadelphia: Decker.

Warren, A., & McCloskey, L. A. (1997). Language in social contexts. In J. Berko Gleason (Ed.), *The development of language* (4th ed., pp. 210–258). Boston: Allyn & Bacon.

Wingfield, A., & Stine, E. L. (1986). Organizational strategies in immediate recall of rapid speech by young and elderly adults. *Experimental Aging Research, 12,* 79–83.

Zacks, R. T., Hasher, L., Doren, B., Hamm, F., & Attig, M. S. (1987). Encoding and memory of explicit and implicit information. *Journal of Gerontology, 42,* 418–422.

Zelinski, E. (1988). Integrating information from discourse: Do older adults show deficits? In L. Light & D. M. Burke (Eds.), *Language, memory, and aging* (pp. 133–160). New York: Cambridge University Press.

Zelinski, E. M., Light, L. L., & Gilewski, M. J. (1984). Adult age differences in memory for prose: The question of sensitivity to passage structure. *Developmental Psychology, 20*, 1181–1192.

Zurif, E., Swinney, D., Prather, P., Wingfield, A., & Brownell, H. (1995). The allocation of memory resources during sentence comprehension: Evidence from the elderly. *Journal of Psycholinguistic Research, 24*, 165–182.

Applications IV

VI Applications

Cognitive aging and everyday life 12

Denise C. Park, Angela Hall Gutchess

As described in many of the earlier chapters in this volume, it is clear that a variety of mental processes decline with age. In chapter 1, Park argues that declines in speed of processing, working memory function, and inhibitory processes likely are fundamental mechanisms that account for poorer memory function in late adulthood. Despite a wealth of laboratory evidence that these cognitive resources decline with age and are critically important in understanding performance on cognitive tasks, surprisingly little is known about their importance for function in everyday life. Interest in theory-driven applied research, however, is growing (Park, 1992). In this chapter, we examine the meaning of normal, age-related cognitive deficits for everyday life, drawing on work that has utilized what is known about age changes in basic cognitive processes to understand real-world problems of aging.

The global nature of the decline in speed of processing and working memory that occurs with age might lead one to expect that older adults would have substantial difficulties in managing the affairs of everyday life or maintaining a good level of performance on the job. There is considerable evidence, however, that older adults function well in many domains of everyday life, and that the cognitive declines of the considerable magnitude documented in the laboratory do not impact everyday domains of behavior as negatively as one might expect. The reasons for this are complex and not entirely understood, but will be a focus of discussion in this chapter.

Two important aspects of the aging cognitive system have been identified that likely play an important role in maintaining demanding cognitive behaviors in the everyday environment despite substantial declines in processing resource. The first is that there is considerable evidence knowl-

This work was supported by the National Institute on Aging through several grants. The Center for Applied Cognitive Research on Aging supported this research (grant P50AG11715), as did grant R01AGO62651, Effects of Context on the Aging Memory. The author gratefully acknowledges this assistance. A website with more information about related research is located at http://www.isr.umich.edu/rcgd/parklab/

edge is maintained across the lifespan or even continues to grow with age (see Park, chapter 1 in this volume). Thus, much of what has been learned throughout older adults' lives is preserved. This preserved learning provides older adults with access to an extensive knowledge base that can be useful in solving problems and addressing the needs of everyday life, thereby mitigating or compensating for declines in basic mechanisms of cognitive function. A second important element in maintaining performance of complex cognitive tasks in everyday life is the fact that frequent and familiar behaviors become automatized; that is, they require little cognitive resource or effort to perform. Jacoby (1991) developed a process dissociation procedure that allows separation of the effortful, resource-based components of memory from the effects of familiarity that control automatic cognitive processes. Automatic processes are cognitive processes that occur with no conscious awareness or effort and may be due to familiarity, practice, or the specific qualities of the stimulus being processed. Jacoby, Jennings, and Hay (1996) demonstrated that although the effortful component of memory declines with age, the familiarity-based, automatic component is age invariant. This finding suggests that in highly familiar situations where familiarity and automaticity contribute significantly to performance, older adults will be relatively unimpaired. However, in situations that demand controlled processing and mental effort, the age-related declines in processing resources will be of great importance and older adults will evidence impairment in their behavior.

Although everyday situations may superficially appear to be cognitively demanding, they often are based more on automatic processing than effortful processing. For example, consider an older woman who lives in the suburbs of a large city like Boston and has subscribed to the Boston Symphony for 20 years. She does not hesitate to drive into Boston to see the symphony on a Sunday afternoon. Automatic processes and acquired knowledge play a large role in her route selection and in finding her way. She simply knows how to get to the symphony with little thought and she easily negotiates complex traffic interchanges due to their high familiarity. Little controlled processing is required on her part to arrive at the destination, park the car, and find her way to the concert hall. Contrast this with another older woman who has flown into the same Boston suburb for a weekend to see friends who are busy on Sunday afternoon. She also would like to go to the symphony. For her, the task of driving to the symphony through Boston traffic is one that requires considerable engagement of processing resources and has a very small familiarity component. Age-related declines in cognitive function would play an important role in the everyday behavior of driving to the symphony in this second situation, but not the first. Driving to the symphony for the out-of-town guest would have a high working memory load in terms of keeping the directions in mind. Speeded processing also would be important in making rapid decisions about exit selection off the freeway and in deciding how to negotiate traffic circles in moving traffic. Acquired knowledge and familiarity would not contribute much to this drive. There are few elderly adults who would attempt the second drive described (as well as many younger adults who also would be daunted), based on the likely correct perception that the processing demands of driving in Boston exceed their level of cognitive resource.

In the remainder of this chapter, we will consider the impact of cognitive aging on three domains of everyday behavior that are important to older adults. We will assess the impact of cognitive aging on health behaviors, driving competence, and function in the workplace. In each case, we will examine how declines in cognitive function may be offset by the experience and knowledge that the older adult possesses.

Health

The domain of health behavior and cognitive aging is relatively unexplored. Older adults frequently must make complex health decisions and follow elaborate drug and treatment regimens that require a considerable amount of higher order cognitive processes. With the increased tendency to hospitalize only the most critically ill patients and also to discharge them as soon as possible, older adults frequently are expected to use complicated medical devices at home that require considerable training and expertise to use (Bogner, 1999). Declining cognitive resources likely play an important role in the older patient's ability to use medical equipment, take medications, and perform necessary steps to regulate an illness (Park, 1999). At the same time, it also is important to recognize that older adults have considerable experience with illness and health decisions and that their expertise and knowledge, particularly about chronic disorders that they have had for some time, may buffer them from the impact of declining cognitive resources in processing and managing information about their medical conditions.

Perhaps the most fundamental issue in understanding the medical behaviors of older patients is determining how much information they comprehend and what are the optimal methods for presenting this information. Considerable evidence from our laboratory has suggested that older adults have difficulty with comprehension. Morrell, Park, and Poon (1989, 1990) offered evidence that when presented with an array of prescription labels, older adults had more difficulty than younger adults in developing and remembering an accurate medication-taking plan. In other works, we examined how effectively older adults understood the information hospitals are required to present to patients about the development of advanced directives and living wills, as mandated by the 1990 Patient Self-Determination Act. Park, Eaton, Larson, and Palmer (1994) found that hospital administrators reported that the biggest perceived problem with implementing the law was the apparent difficulty patients had in comprehending the materials presented. In a later study, Zwahr, Park, Eaton, and Larson (1997) presented middle-aged and older adults with three versions of materials used by actual hospitals to explain living wills and advanced directives and how to go about completing them. They noted that middle-aged adults understood more than older adults and that the best predictors of comprehension were working memory function and verbal ability. The types of materials employed ranged from simple pictorial representations of the law to pages of complex documents. However, format and complexity of information had no effect on how much information patients acquired, regardless of age. In general, the literature suggests that there is evidence that normal older adults do have more trouble comprehending and remembering medical information than younger adults. There is interesting work to be done to explore whether older adults would show similar impairments when acquiring new information about medical conditions with which they are familiar, as they might even show superiority to young adults if they have well-elaborated knowledge structures about these conditions.

One critically important medical issue associated with cognitive aging is whether normal older adults are disadvantaged in making important medical decisions that require significant amounts of comprehension, memory, and judgment. (For information on the decision-making capacities of cognitively compromised older adults, see Marson & Harrell, 1999.) In general, the sparse literature available suggests that the limited cognitive capacity of normal older adults does affect the processes used to make medical decisions. However, the literature also shows that the types of decisions made about medical conditions do not differ for younger and older adults. Meyer, Russo, and Talbot (1995) and Zwahr, Park, and Shifren (1999) both reported evidence that cognitive factors affected the decisions made by older women when presented with medical scenarios. Meyer et al. (1995) found that when older and younger women had to make decisions about breast cancer treatment based on information presented to them, they made similar decisions about what treatment option to select (e.g, mastectomy, lumpectomy). The older women, however, made their decisions faster, requested less information to make the decision, and offered less complete rationales for their decisions than younger women. These findings are compatible with the notion that older adults recognize the limits on their information processing capacity and thus choose to examine less information. Their tendency toward rapid decision making compared to younger adults may be related to willingness to rely on physician suggestions in the face of limited cognitive resources (Cassileth, Zupkis, Sutton-Smith, & March, 1980), as well as knowledge of past medical experiences when information seeking did not prove to be too useful (Park, 1999).

Zwahr et al. (1999) reported similar findings when they studied the quality of decisions made by women who read lengthy materials regarding the pros and cons of estrogen replacement therapy for menopausal symptoms. Participants were then asked to make decisions about whether estrogen replacement therapy should be taken for menopausal symptoms. Older women perceived fewer options regarding choices about the therapy, made fewer comparisons among options, and exhibited less sophisticated reasoning as the basis for their decisions than did younger women. Path analyses indicated that cognitive variables predicted the age-related variance in both the number of options perceived and the number of comparative statements made in the decision process. Detailed discussions of adults' decision-making processes about medical events and diagnoses are included in Yates and Patalano (1999) and Zwahr (1999).

Thus far, we have largely considered the role that declines in controlled, effortful processes have on medical decisions. As mentioned above, it likely is important to recognize that older adults may be expert consumers of medical care and that some aspects of their health behaviors may be so highly practiced that they become automatic; that is, they require little effort or awareness to complete. One area where the controlled-automatic distinction may be of particular importance is in the area of medication adherence (Park, 1999; Park et al., 1999). Medication adherence is a behavior that has a substantial cognitive component, particularly when an individual is taking a complex medication regimen of four or more medications, as many older adults do. In order to adhere accurately to a complicated regimen, an older adult has to comprehend instructions on each medication, use working memory to integrate those instructions into a daily plan, use long-term memory to remember what the plan is, and, finally, engage prospective memory to remember to take the medication (Park, 1992; Park & Jones, 1996; Park & Kidder, 1996). Park, Morrell, Frieske, and Kincaid (1992) presented evidence that very old adults did show deficits in medication adherence compared to adults age 60 to 77, and that these deficits were remedied by providing the very old with medication organizers and charts designed to relieve the working memory burden associated with taking medications. The medication adherence was recorded via microelectronic monitors so that accurate data on medication usage was obtained. One surprising aspect of this work was that adults age 60 to 77 made almost no errors in their medication-taking behaviors, despite the fact that they were experiencing substantial age-related decline in cognitive function. The finding that older adults do not make many medication errors also was reported by Morrell, Park, Kidder, and Martin (1997). They found that, in a sample of hypertensive adults age 35 to 75, older adults from 65 to 75 years old made fewer errors than any other age group.

In a recent study, Park et al. (1999) reported a similar finding: adults age 60 to 75 with rheumatoid arthritis made the fewest medication errors of any age group. Forty-seven percent of the older adults, all of whom were taking four or more medications, made no errors at all with their medications over a 1-month period. Middle-aged adults made the most errors, despite strong evidence for markedly superior cognitive function in the middle-aged subjects. The use of individual difference measures that assessed not only cognitive function, but also socioemotional status and contextual variables, revealed that the best predictor of medication errors was self-report of a busy, highly engaged lifestyle. Such a lifestyle rarely characterized older adults. Moreover, older adults frequently had been taking medications for many years so that medication adherence behaviors were routine and highly familiar to them. Thus, the apparent high cognitive investment that medication adherence would seem to require was offset by highly practiced automatic behaviors, where the daily environment served as a cue for taking medications. In contrast, younger adults who led less habitual lives where context frequently was changing did not have the same environmental stimuli to serve as automatic cues for taking medications and, as a result, this group made more errors. One lesson to be learned from this pattern of findings is that even tasks that appear to be highly cognitive and resource driven, such as remembering to take medications, may operate very differently than one would expect in a real-world, everyday environment.

Driving

An everyday behavior of great importance to older adults is the ability to drive, as this plays a significant role in maintenance of the ability to live independently in contemporary society. Although older adults drive fewer miles than younger adults and overall are involved in fewer accidents, older adults are in the highest risk category when figures are based on number of accidents per mile driven. There has been frequent speculation in the literature on driving that some of the age-related increases in accident rates are due to decreased cognitive function in older adults (Arthur, Barrett, & Alexander, 1991; Staplin, Breton, Haimo, Farber, & Byrnes, 1986). However, few studies directly linked cognitive aging to driving errors. Because driving is a dynamic, contextual behavior where the cognitive requirements of the task can change in a matter of seconds, understanding the relationship of cognitive function to driving is challenging.

It also is important to recognize that, because driving is an expert, highly practiced behavior for most older adults, we must be cautious in concluding that observed declines in speed of processing or working memory function are necessarily the basis for their poorer driving records. Driving has many of the components of an effortless, automatic process under certain conditions. Many individuals have reported that they have no memory of the landmarks or the conditions under which they drove a familiar route, such as their daily drive to work, presumably because such a highly practiced task takes so little cognitive capacity. However, in a demanding traffic situation, we all have experienced as drivers a tendency to cease conversation, turn down the radio, or ask children to be quiet. This represents a shift to a controlled (effortful, resource-demanding) processing situation. Ackerman (1986, 1987) provided us with important data indicating that cognitive resource, as measured by high cognitive ability scores, is not important for automatized tasks but strongly predicts performance on controlled, effortful tasks. Because we know that cognitive ability scores decline with age, the Ackerman data suggest that older adults likely would be deficient in driving situations that require a high amount of controlled processing. In support of this conjecture, Holland and Rabbitt (1992) cited a study conducted by Moore, Sedgely, and Sabey (1982) that indicated that elderly drivers had a disproportionate number of accidents at complex junctions, a finding congruent with a cognitive explanation of accident rate. Also in keeping with the cognitive hypothesis, Lerner, Morrison and Ratte (1990) reported that older adults tended to be more likely to be involved in multivehicle crashes than other drivers, except on interstates where they were more likely to be involved in single-car accidents. It may be that the requirement for speeded responding on interstates results in cognitively demanding situations for older drivers.

The cognitive components of driving that perhaps are most important include attention, speed of processing, and working memory capacity. With respect to attention, Ball and colleagues (Ball, Beard, Roenker, Miller, & Griggs, 1988) demonstrated convincingly that older adults have a more limited useful field of view; that is, they are less able to attend to information and targets on the periphery of the visual field. In a series of studies, they demonstrated that older adults with more limited useful fields of view are more likely to be involved in crashes. In fact, the strongest predictor of crash involvement was performance on useful field of view measures (Owsley, Ball, Sloane, Roenker, & Bruni, 1991). The two factors of mental status (as measured by the Mattis Organic Mental Status Syndrome Examination [MOMSSE]) and the size of the useful field of view together account for 20% of accident variance and 29% of the variance for intersection accidents. Recent reports stated that over the 3 years following initial assessment, older drivers with at least a 40% decrease in useful field of view (found in 56.9% of the sample) are 2.2 times more likely to be crash involved (Owsley et al., 1998).

Although useful field of view has been reported to be a good predictor of accident involvement, it is a multifaceted construct requiring further research to determine which elements affect driving ability. Useful field of view is determined by three different components: decreased ability to divide attention, decreased ability to ignore distractors (e.g., selective attention), and reduced processing speed (Ball, Roenker, & Bruni, 1990). On examination of the contribution of each of these three mechanisms to useful field of view, divided attention impairments were associated with a 2.3 times increase in crashes, while decreased speed of processing and selective attention were not related to crash involvement (Owsley et al., 1998). The contribution of each of these three components to accident risk may be further clarified by current work on training techniques in the laboratory that can increase the useful field of view (Ball et al., 1988; Roenker, Cissel, & Ball, 1997). Of potentially great applied interest, trials currently are under way to determine if increasing the field of view decreases accident rates, as one would expect.

There also is evidence that measures of only selective attention (requiring subjects to attend to only one of two targets presented simultaneously) are correlated with accident rates (Kahneman, Ben-Ishai, & Lotan,

1973). Mihal and Barrett (1976) examined the relationship between auditory selective attention and accident data in younger and older drivers. They reported a stronger relationship for older drivers. Ranney and Pulling (1990) studied driving behavior of adults from age 30 to 83 on a driving course and reported lower driving performance and cognitive performance in the older adults, but did not find direct associations between the measures. They did note that although older drivers made more driving errors in decision speed, route selection, gap execution, vehicle control, and comprehension of instructions, the older drivers nevertheless performed as capably as the younger drivers in response to an emergency situation. It is fair to conclude that there appears to be a relationship between age, attentional variables, and driving function in some situations, but the exact conditions under which attentional variables are important remains unspecified.

The relationship of age-related declines in speed of processing to driving behavior also has been examined. Mihal and Barrett (1976) found that although simple and choice reaction times were not related to accidents in a simulator, complex reaction time had a modest relationship for the entire sample and a large correlation (.52) for the older adults. Ranney and Pulling (1989), however, found no association between simple reaction time or perceptual speed and driving performance. Finally, Olson and Sivak (1986) found that younger and older adults had equivalent perception-response times when they were required to notice and brake to an object in the road, using actual driving in an experimental vehicle to collect the data. In summary, the relationship of speed of processing deficits in older adults to driving function appears to be in question, requiring additional investigation.

The relationship of working memory to driving and aging has been studied using divided attention tasks. Working memory refers to the amount of cognitive resource available at a given moment to manipulate, retrieve, and store information (Baddeley, 1986, or see Park, chapter 1 in this volume). Due to age-related declines in working memory function (Park et al., 1996), older adults would appear to have fewer resources available to perform multiple operations that frequently are required when driving. However, there is considerable debate about whether older adults are disproportionately disadvantaged when performing two tasks at once (a divided attention situation). Hartley (1992) conducted a meta-analysis of all of the divided attention studies done with older adults. He stated that, although any simple conclusion probably is wrong, the "most plausible interpretation of the findings from dual-task studies is that younger and older adults do not differ in the ability to allocate attention across conditions" (p. 32).

Because of the particular concerns about aging and dual-task performance that occur in the context of driving, there actually are a number of studies on this topic. Ponds, Brouwer, and van Wolffelaar (1988) examined the ability to steer an automobile while performing a dot counting task. They reported the cost of dividing attention on steering was greater for older adults than younger adults. In a later study, they introduced a third task that required participants to monitor events in their peripheral field, in addition to steering and dot counting. They viewed the steering and peripheral tasks as typical of driving, and the dot-counting task as similar to the attention required by an in-vehicle navigational system. The older adults were most disadvantaged compared to younger adults when both the peripheral and dot-counting tasks were added to the steering task. Crook, West, and Larrabee (1993) conducted a simulated driving study where computer keys acted as an accelerator and as a brake pedal for a traffic scene depicted on the computer monitor. The secondary task was information about weather and traffic that the participant was asked to remember. Crook et al. (1993) reported that costs of the dual-task situation were higher for older adults for lift time (removing finger from the key), but not travel time (moving finger over to the other key). Although these studies do suggest disproportionate costs of divided attention to older adults in simulated driving situations, more realistic situations are needed to determine whether older adults are at particular risk in driving conditions that require high amounts of multitasking.

Work

The nature of work in contemporary society has shifted. In the past, workers often retired because aging had left them incapable of physically managing their work due to arthritis, heart conditions, or other physical ailments. The picture has changed today. Older people are healthier than they have been in the past, and contemporary work relies more on the ability to process and manage information than on physical strength. Because of the growing age of our workforce and the frequent desire to remain in the labor force into late adulthood, understanding the impact of age-related changes in cognitive function in workplace performance is becoming a matter of some urgency. Despite the growing importance of this issue as our society and workforce ages, there is a surprising dearth of information on this topic.

This is particularly surprising because there is a well-documented relationship between cognitive ability and work performance. Even the lowest level jobs show a positive relationship between cognitive function and rated excellence on the job (Hunter & Hunter, 1984; Schmidt, Hunter, & Outerbridge, 1986). The decline of cognitive abilities in older adults, combined with the finding that low ability workers perform more poorly, suggests that one would expect to find a negative relationship between aging and work performance. Meta-analyses, however, consistently have failed to find such a relationship (Rhodes, 1983; Waldman & Avolio, 1986). In general, there is a preponderance of evidence suggesting that there is no relationship between age and job performance.

Park (1994) hypothesized that there are four possibilities that can account for this relationship. One is that older adults have jobs for which they are highly experienced and that are characterized by maintenance functions. That is, older adults rarely encounter resource-demanding transition phases, described by Murphy (1989), where they must learn many new skills. As a result, age deficits in cognition are not very important in job performance. This hypothesis, in some ways, is an automatization hypothesis, since one of the reasons maintenance functions can be performed so effectively in the face of declining resources is the high familiarity component of such behaviors, which also are low in the effortful, controlled processing component. Salthouse, Hambrick, Lukas, and Dell (1996) reached a similar conclusion in their research on synthetic work time management situations. They suggested that older adults in the workforce may be less efficient than their younger colleagues, at least when beginning a job. Historically, the trend to remain in the same job throughout one's entire career may have masked transition difficulties for older workers. The recent trend toward changing companies, and even professions, throughout one's working years may reveal larger job performance deficits for older workers.

A second possibility is that experience protects against decline in the cognitive abilities used in the workplace. Meticulous work by Salthouse, Babcock, Mitchell, Skovronek, and Palmon (1990) on aging architects and by Salthouse (1984) on aging typists clearly shows that declines in component behaviors (such as spatial visualization in architects and interval to respond between key strokes in typists) do occur with age. In a laboratory-based training study that required participants to manage time among several simultaneous tasks, large age differences were maintained across a 2-hour performance interval (Salthouse et al., 1996). Thus, there is little evidence that practice protects against declines in the basic cognitive mechanisms underlying the work behavior.

A third possibility is that complex knowledge structures about a job increase with age and compensate for decline in basic cognitive abilities. A number of studies have shown that older workers in various professions have as much or more domain-specific knowledge about aspects of their job than younger workers (Baltes & Smith, 1990; Stumpf & Rabinowitz, 1981; Taylor, 1975), so there is some legitimacy to this hypothesis.

Finally, a fourth reason that the relationship between age and job performance may be null is that older adults increasingly use environmental supports to compensate for declining cognition (Park, 1994). There is evidence that older adults consult with younger colleagues, collaborate extensively, and gravitate toward positions that require knowledge and judgment while moving away from positions that have high cognitive resource requirements. (For example, a position as a university administrator, which is typical for older academics, requires more judgment and less intensive processing resource compared to that of a bench scientist, which is more typical of younger academics. Similar analogies exist in the legal and corporate world.)

Tacit knowledge of a job is a type of procedural knowledge that is useful for solving everyday problems associated with a job, but that usually is not explicitly verbalized in job training. There is evidence that tacit knowledge of a job may also be relatively preserved with age and may serve as a determinant of job success with age. A recent study of 200 bank managers by Colonia-Willner (1998) found that tacit knowledge (as measured by the Tacit Knowledge Inventory for Managers [TKIM]) decreased less with age than did psychometric reasoning ability (as measured by Raven's Advanced Progressive Matrices and the Verbal Reasoning subtest of the Differential Aptitude Test [DAT]). Age, Raven's performance, and DAT performance failed to predict managerial skill as assessed by job performance ratings, salary, and management span (a count of the number of personnel supervised, both directly and indirectly). However, tacit, job-related knowledge in dealing with others did appear to be related to managerial skill. Because tacit knowledge is relatively preserved with age, and experts appear to possess more of it than nonexperts, perhaps tacit knowledge mitigates the relationship between age and expected declines in job performance.

The data on aging, work, and cognition point to the fact that, although basic declines in cognitive function would appear to be critical obstacles to performing a demanding job, the environmental supports, elaborated knowledge structures, tacit knowledge, and experiences of older workers may serve as compensatory mechanisms in familiar, everyday environments.

A final important issue with respect to the aging workforce is how able and willing older workers will learn and use new technology. Given the rapid pace of technology changes in the workplace, this has become a critically important issue. There is evidence that older workers are perceived more negatively and thus have less potential for development (Rosen & Jerdee, 1976), and that they are less likely to be selected for continuing job training (Fossum, Arvey, Paradise, & Robbins, 1986; Lee & Clemons, 1985).

Evidence has suggested that older workers do perform computer entry tasks more slowly and that cognitive abilities underlie the performance difference (Czaja & Sharit, 1998; Czaja, Sharit, Nair, & Rubert, 1998). Other research has indicated that older adults acquire computer skills more slowly than younger adults (Elias, Elias, Robbins, & Gage, 1987; Kelley & Charness, 1995; Zandri & Charness, 1989). There also is evidence that age-related differences in acquisition ability of computer tasks are controlled by measures of speed and working memory (Echt, Morrell, & Park, 1998; Morrell, Park, Mayhorn, & Kelley, in press), and perhaps spatial ability (Kelley & Charness, 1995). Although these studies consistently have demonstrated learning advantages and better performance on the part of younger adults for important technical workplace skills, the studies also consistently have indicated that older adults do learn and perform with a high degree of accuracy. Because it is clear that continuous and gradual cognitive decline begins in early adulthood (see Park, chapter 1 in this volume), it is important that, as workers age, they keep abreast of changes in technology and job requirements. A middle-aged worker who updates skills in a continuous and gradual fashion will not have to make large adaptations to learn new workplace functions. An older worker, however, who perhaps has never used a computer and suddenly is required to learn many new functions simultaneously as a new job requirement would be much more disadvantaged than a middle-aged worker who had to learn only an updated version of a software package as a new job function. Data suggest that the failure to invest in training in middle-aged and older workers will severely disadvantage these sectors of the workforce.

Summary

An increasing understanding of age-related changes in the basic mechanisms of cognitive function has resulted in a growing understanding of the meaning of these changes for the function of older adults in their everyday environments. Although the declines in speed of processing and working memory that occur with age result in some decrements in performance in everyday behaviors, the decrements tend to be less pronounced than one might expect, or may not be evident at all. There is a wealth of evidence suggesting that older adults perform well when they are performing behaviors at which they are expert or when they are in familiar environments. The impact of cognitive deficits on everyday behaviors is most pronounced when older adults are in unfamiliar environments and must perform tasks that are novel to them.

References

Ackerman, P. L. (1986). Individual differences in information processing: An investigation of intellectual abilities and task performance during practice. *Intelligence, 10*, 101–139.

Ackerman, P. L. (1987). Individual differences in skill learning: An integration of psychonomic and information processing perspectives. *Psychological Bulletin, 102*, 3–27.

Arthur, W., Jr., Barrett, G. V., & Alexander, R. A. (1991). Prediction of vehicular accident involvement: A meta-analysis. *Human Performance, 4*, 89–105.

Baddeley, A. (1986). *Working memory*. Oxford, England: Clarendon Press.

Ball, K. K., Beard, B. L., Roenker, D. L., Miller, R. L., & Griggs, D. S. (1988). Age and visual search: Expanding the useful field of view. *Journal of the Optical Society of America A*, 2210–2219.

Ball, K., Roenker, D. L., & Bruni, J. R. (1990). Developmental changes in attention and visual search throughout adulthood. In J. Enns (Ed.), *Advances in Psychology* (Vol. 69, pp. 489–508). Amsterdam: North-Holland-Elsevier Science.

Baltes, P. B., & Smith, J. (1990). The psychology of wisdom and its ontogenesis. In R. J. Sternberg (Ed.), *Wisdom: Its nature, origins, and development* (pp. 87–120). Cambridge, England: Cambridge University Press.

Bogner, M. S. (1999). How do I work this thing? Cognitive issues in home medical equipment use and maintenance. In D. C. Park, R. W. Morrell, & K. Shifren

(Eds.), *Processing of medical information in aging patients: Cognitive and human factors perspectives* (pp. 223–232). Mahwah, NJ: Erlbaum.

Cassileth, B. R., Zupkis, R. V., Sutton-Smith, K., & March, V. (1980). Information and participation preferences among cancer patients. *Annals of Internal Medicine, 92,* 832–836.

Colonia-Willner, R. (1998). Practical intelligence at work: Relationship between aging and cognitive efficiency among managers in a bank environment. *Psychology and Aging, 13,* 45–57.

Crook, T. H., West, R. L., & Larrabee, G. J. (1993). The driving-reaction time test: Assessing age declines in dual-task performance. *Developmental Neuropsychology, 9,* 31–39.

Czaja, S. J., & Sharit, J. (1998). Ability-performance relationships as a function of age and task experience for a data entry task. *Journal of Experimental Psychology: Applied, 4,* 332–351.

Czaja, S. J., Sharit, J., Nair, S., & Rubert, M. (1998). Understanding sources of user variability in computer-based data entry performance. *Behaviour and Information Technology, 17,* 282–293.

Echt, K. V., Morrell, R. W., & Park, D. C. (1998). Effects of age and training formats on basic computer skill acquisition in older adults. *Educational Gerontology, 24,* 3–25.

Elias, P. K., Elias, M. F., Robbins, M. A., & Gage, P. (1987). Acquisition of word-processing skills by younger, middle-age, and older adults. *Psychology and Aging, 2,* 340–348.

Fossum, J. A., Arvey, R. D., Paradise, C. A., & Robbins, N. E. (1986). Modeling the skills obsolescence process: A psychological/economic integration. *Academy of Management Review, 11,* 362–374.

Hartley, A. A. (1992). Attention. In F. I. M. Craik & T. A. Salthouse (Eds.), *The handbook of aging and cognition* (pp. 3–49). Hillsdale, NJ: Erlbaum.

Holland, C. A., & Rabbitt, P. M. A. (1992). People's awareness of their age-related sensory and cognitive deficits and the implications for road safety. *Applied Cognitive Psychology, 6,* 217–231.

Hunter, J. E., & Hunter, R. F. (1984). Validity and utility of alternative predictors of job performance. *Psychological Bulletin, 96,* 72–98.

Jacoby, L. L. (1991). A process dissociation framework: Separating automatic from intentional uses of memory. *Journal of Memory and Language, 30,* 513–541.

Jacoby, L. L., Jennings, J. M., & Hay, J. F. (1996). Dissociating automatic and con-sciously-controlled processes: Implications for diagnosis and rehabilitation of memory deficits. In D. J. Hermann, C. L. McEvoy, C. Hertzog, P. Hertel, & M. K. Johnson (Eds.), *Basic and applied memory research: Theory in context* (Vol. 1, pp. 161–193). Hillsdale, NJ: Erlbaum.

Kahneman, D., Ben-Ishai, R., & Lotan, M. (1973). Relation of a test of attention to road accidents. *Journal of Applied Psychology, 58,* 113–115.

Kelley, C. L., & Charness, N. (1995). Issues in training older adults to use computers. *Behavior and Information Technology, 14,* 107–120.

Lee, J. A., & Clemons, T. (1985). Factors affecting employment decisions about older workers. *Journal of Applied Psychology, 70,* 785–788.

Lerner, N. D., Morrison, M. L., & Ratte, D. J. (1990). *Older drivers' perceptions of problems in freeway use.* Silver Spring, MD: Comsis Corporation. (Available from AAA Foundation for Traffic Safety, 1440 New York Avenue NW, Suite 201, Washington, DC 20005.)

Marson, D., & Harrell, L. (1999). Neurocognitive changes associated with loss of capacity to consent to medical treatment in patients with Alzheimer's disease. In D. C. Park, R. W. Morrell, & K. Shifren (Eds.), *Processing of medical information in aging patients: Cognitive and human factors perspectives* (pp. 109-126). Mahwah, NJ: Erlbaum.

Meyer, B. J. F., Russo, C., & Talbot, A. (1995). Discourse comprehension and problem solving: Decisions about the treatment of breast cancer by women across the life span. *Psychology and Aging, 10*, 84–103.

Mihal, W. L., & Barrett, G. V. (1976). Individual differences in perceptual information processing and their relation to automobile accident involvement. *Journal of Applied Psychology, 61*, 229–233.

Moore, R. L., Sedgely, I. P., & Sabey, B. E. (1982). *Ages of car drivers involved in accidents, with special references to junctions* (RR Supplementary Rep. No. 718). Transport and Road Research Laboratory Crowthorne, Berkshire UK.

Morrell, R. W., Park, D. C., Kidder, D. P., & Martin, M. (1997). Adherence to antihypertensive medications over the lifespan. *The Gerontologist, 37*, 609–619.

Morrell, R. W., Park, D. C., Mayhorn, C. B., & Kelley, C. L. (in press). The effects of age and instructions on teaching older adults how to use ELDERCOMM: An electronic bulletin board system. *Educational Gerontology*.

Morrell, R. W., Park, D. C., & Poon, L. W. (1989). Quality of instructions on prescription drug labels: Effects on memory and comprehension in young and old adults. *The Gerontologist, 29*, 345–354.

Morrell, R. W., Park, D. C., & Poon, L. W. (1990). Effects of labeling techniques on memory and comprehension of prescription information in young and old adults. *Journals of Gerontology, 45*, 166–172.

Murphy, K. R. (1989). Is the relationship between cognitive ability and job performance stable over time? *Human Performance, 2*, 183–200.

Olson, P. L., & Sivak, M. (1986). Perception-response time to unexpected roadway hazards. *Human Factors, 28*, 91–96.

Owsley, C., Ball, K., McGwin, G., Jr., Sloane, M. E., Roenker, D. L., White, M. F., & Overley, E. T. (1998). Visual processing impairment and risk of motor vehicle crash among older adults. *Journal of the American Medical Association, 279*, 1083-1088.

Owsley, C., Ball, K., Sloane, M. E., Roenker, D. L., & Bruni, J. R. (1991). Visual/cognitive correlates of vehicle accidents in older drivers. *Psychology and Aging, 6*, 403-415.

Park, D. C. (1992). Applied cognitive aging research. In F. I. M. Craik & T. A. Salthouse (Eds.), *The handbook of cognition and aging* (pp. 449–493), Mahwah, NJ: Erlbaum.

Park, D. C. (1994). Aging, cognition, and work. *Human Performance, 7*, 181–205.

Park, D. C. (1999). Aging and the controlled and automatic processing of medical information and medical intentions. In D. C. Park, R. W. Morrell, & K. Shifren (Eds.), *Processing of medical information in aging patients: Cognitive and human factors perspectives* (pp. 3–22). Mahwah, NJ: Erlbaum.

Park, D. C., Eaton, T. A., Larson, E. J., & Palmer, H. T. (1994). Implementation and impact of the patient self-determination act. *Southern Medical Journal, 87*, 971–977.

Park, D. C., Hertzog, C., Leventhal, H., Morrell, R. W., Leventhal, E., Birchmore, D., Martin, M., & Bennett, J. (1999). Medication adherence in rheumatoid arthitis patients: Older is wiser. *Journal of the American Geriatrics Society, 47,* 172–183.

Park, D. C., & Jones, T. R. (1996). Medication adherence and aging. In A. D. Fiske & W. A. Rogers (Eds.), *Handbook of human factors and the older adult* (pp. 257–288). San Diego, CA: Academic Press.

Park, D. C., & Kidder, D. (1996). Prospective memory and medication adherence. In M. Brandimonte, G. Einstein, & M. McDaniel (Eds.), *Prospective memory: theory and applications* (pp. 369–390). Mahwah, NJ: Erlbaum.

Park, D. C., Morrell, R. W., Frieske, D., & Kinkaid, D. (1992). Medication adherence behaviors in older adults: Effects of external cognitive supports. *Psychology and Aging, 7,* 252–256.

Park, D. C., Smith, A. D., Lautenschlager, G., Earles, J., Frieske, D., Zwahr, M., & Gaines, C. (1996). Mediators of long-term memory performance across the life span. *Psychology and Aging, 11,* 621–637.

Ponds, R. W. H. M., Brouwer, W. H., & van Wolffelaar, P. C. (1988). Age differences in divided attention in a simulated driving task. *Journal of Gerontology: Psychological Science, 43,* 151–156.

Ranney, T. A., & Pulling, N. H. (1989). Relation of individual differences in information-processing ability to driving performance. *Proceedings of the Human Factors Society 33rd Annual Meeting* (pp. 965–969). Santa Monica, CA: Human Factors Society.

Ranney, T. A., & Pulling, N. H. (1990). Performance difference on driving and laboratory tasks between drivers of different ages. *Transportation Research Record, 1281,* 3–10.

Rhodes, S. R. (1983). Age-related differences in work attitudes and behavior: A review and conceptual analysis. *Psychological Bulletin, 93,* 328–367.

Roenker, D. L., Cissel, G. M., & Ball, K. K. (1997). The effects of visual attention training on driving performance. *Investigative Ophthalmology & Visual Science, 38,* 871.

Rosen, B., & Jerdee, T. H. (1976). The nature of job-related age stereotypes. *Journal of Applied Psychology, 61,* 180–183.

Salthouse, T. A. (1984). Effects of age and skill in typing. *Journal of Experimental Psychology: General, 113,* 345–371.

Salthouse, T. A., Babcock, R. L., Mitchell, D. R., Skovronek, E., & Palmon, R. (1990). Age and experience effects in spatial visualization. *Developmental Psychology, 26,* 128–136.

Salthouse, T. A., Hambrick, D. Z., Lukas, K. E., & Dell, T. C. (1996). Determinants of adult age differences on synthetic work performance. *Journal of Experimental Psychology: Applied, 2,* 305–329.

Schmidt, F. L., Hunter, J. E., & Outerbridge, A. N. (1986). Impact of job experience and ability on job knowledge, work sample performance, and supervisory ratings of job performance. *Journal of Applied Psychology, 71,* 432–439.

Staplin, L. K., Breton, M. E., Haimo, S. F., Farber, E. I., & Byrnes, A. M. (1986). *Age-related diminished capabilities and driver performance.* Submitted by Ketron, Inc., Malvern, PA, to the Federal Highway Administration, McLean, VA.

Stumpf, S. A., & Rabinowitz, S. (1981). Career stage as a moderator of performance relationships with facets of job satisfaction and role perceptions. *Journal of Vocational Behavior, 18,* 202–218.

Taylor, R. N. (1975). Age and experience as determinants of managerial information processing and decision making performance. *Academy of Management Journal, 18,* 74–81.

Waldman, D. A., & Avolio, B. J. (1986). A meta-analysis of age differences in job performance. *Journal of Applied Psychology, 71,* 33–38.

Yates, J. F., & Patalano, A. L. (1999). Decision making and aging. In D. C. Park, R. W. Morrell, & K. Shifren (Eds.), *Processing of medical information in aging patients: Cognitive and human factors perpectives* (pp. 31–54). Mahwah, NJ: Erlbaum.

Zandri, E., & Charness, N. (1989). Training older and younger adults to use software. *Educational Gerontology, 15,* 615–631.

Zwahr, M. D. (1999). Cognitive processes and medical decisions. In D. C. Park, R. W. Morell, & K. Shifren (Eds.), *Processing of medical information in aging patients: Cognitive and human factors perspectives* (pp. 55–68). Mahwah, NJ: Erlbaum.

Zwahr, M. D., Park, D. C., Eaton, T. A., & Larson, E. J. (1997). Implementation of the patient self-determination act: A comparison of nursing homes to hospitals. *Journal of Applied Gerontology, 16,* 190–207.

Zwahr, M. D., Park, D. C., & Shifren, K. (1999). The role of age, cognitive abilities, and beliefs. *Psychology and Aging, 14,* 179–191.

Cognition, aging, and self-reports 13

Norbert Schwarz, Bärbel Knäuper

Much of what we know about age-related differences in individuals' behaviors and opinions is based on self-reports obtained from older and younger respondents. Unfortunately, self-reports are a fallible source of data, and researchers have long been aware that minor changes in question wording, question format, or question order may profoundly influence the answers that research participants provide (for reviews see Schuman & Presser, 1981; Schwarz, 1999a; Sudman, Bradburn, & Schwarz, 1996; Tourangeau & Rasinski, 1988). Complicating things further, recent research has suggested that older and younger respondents may be differentially affected by features of the research instrument (for reviews, see the contributions in Schwarz, Park, Knäuper, & Sudman, 1999). Hence, it often is difficult to tell the extent that age-related differences in self-reports reflect (a) age-related differences in respondents' actual attitudes or behaviors or (b) age-related differences in the emergence of context effects. At present, this possibility has received limited attention in the methodological literature, which instead focused on methods that allow us to determine whether any observed age differences reflect developmental changes or cohort effects (cf., Baltes, Reese, & Nesselroade, 1977). If older and younger respondents are differentially influenced by the research instrument, however, the self-reports we obtain may result in misleading conclusions about either developmental changes or cohort differences, rendering it important that we understand age-related differences in the response process in the first place. As a first step toward this goal, this chapter introduces readers to the cognitive and communicative processes underlying self-reports and highlights how age-related changes in cognitive and communicative functioning influence these processes.

Respondents' tasks

From a cognitive perspective, answering a question posed in a research setting requires that respondents solve several tasks. First, they need to

Preparation of this chapter was supported by grant AG14111-01 from the National Institute of Aging to N. Schwarz, D. Park, and B. Knäuper.

interpret the question to understand what is meant. If the question is an opinion question, they either may retrieve a previously formed opinion from memory, or they may "compute" an opinion on the spot. While researchers typically hope for the former, the latter is far more likely. Even when respondents have previously formed a judgment accessible in memory, this previous judgment is unlikely to match the specifics of the question asked, forcing respondents to compute a new judgment. To do so, they need to retrieve relevant information from memory to form a mental representation of the target that they are to evaluate. In most cases, they also will need to retrieve or construct some standard against which the target is evaluated. Once a "private" judgment is formed in their mind, respondents have to communicate it to the researcher. To do so, they may need to format their judgment to fit the response alternatives provided as part of the question. Moreover, respondents may wish to edit their response before they communicate it, due to influences of social desirability and situational adequacy.

Similar considerations apply to behavioral questions. Again, respondents first need to understand what the question refers to, and which behavior they are supposed to report on. Next, they have to recall or reconstruct relevant instances of this behavior from memory. If the question specifies a reference period, they also must determine if the recalled instances occurred during this reference period or not. Similarly, if the question refers to their "usual" behavior, respondents have to determine if the recalled or reconstructed instances are reasonably representative or if they reflect a deviation from their usual behavior. If they cannot recall or reconstruct specific instances of the behavior, or are not sufficiently motivated to engage in this effort, respondents may rely on their general knowledge or other salient information that may bear on their task to compute an estimate. Finally, respondents have to provide their estimate to the researcher. They may need to map their estimate onto a response scale provided to them, and they may want to edit it for reasons of social desirability.

Accordingly, interpreting the question, generating an opinion or a representation of the relevant behavior, formatting the response, and editing the answer are the main psychological components of a process that starts with the respondents' exposure to a survey question and ends with their overt report (Strack & Martin, 1987; Tourangeau, 1984). Although it is useful to present these tasks in a sequential order, respondents may not always follow this sequence, as we shall see below. Next, we address each of these steps in more detail.

Question comprehension

The key issue at the question comprehension stage is whether the respondent's understanding of the question does or does not match what the researcher had in mind: is the attitude object, or the behavior, that the respondent identifies as the target of the question the one that the researcher intended? Does the respondent's understanding tap the same facet of the issue and the same evaluative dimension? From a psychological point of view, question comprehension reflects the operation of two intertwined processes.

The first refers to the semantic understanding of the utterance. Comprehending the *literal meaning* of a sentence involves the identification of words, the recall of lexical information from semantic memory, and the construction of a meaning of the utterance, which is constrained by its context. Not surprisingly, methodology textbooks urge researchers to write simple questions and to avoid unfamiliar or ambiguous terms (e.g., Sudman & Bradburn, 1983). However, understanding the words is not sufficient to answer a question. For example, when respondents are asked, "What have you done today?" they are likely to understand the meaning of the words. Yet, they still need to determine what kind of activities the researcher is interested in. Should they report, for example, that they took a shower or not? Hence, understanding a question in a way that allows an appropriate answer requires not only an understanding of the literal meaning of the question, but involves inferences about the questioner's intention to determine the pragmatic meaning of the question.

To infer the *pragmatic meaning* of a question, respondents draw on contextual information, including the content of preceding questions and the nature of the response alternatives presented by the researcher. Their use of this information is licensed by the tacit assumptions that govern the conduct of conversation in daily life, as described in Grice's (1975) logic of conversation. These tacit assumptions entail that all contributions of a speaker are relevant to the goals of the ongoing conversation, unless otherwise indicated. In a research setting, the researcher's contributions include the content of preceding questions as well as apparently formal features of the questionnaire, rendering them a relevant source of information for respondents (for comprehensive reviews of conversational processes in research situations, see Clark & Schober, 1992; Hilton, 1995; Schwarz, 1994, 1996; Strack, 1994).

Formal features of questionnaires. Open versus closed question formats. Suppose respondents are asked in an open response format, "What have you done today?" To give a meaningful answer, respondents have to determine which activities may be of interest to the researcher. In an attempt to be informative, respondents are likely to omit activities of which the researcher is obviously aware (e.g., "I gave a survey interview") or may take for granted anyway (e.g., "I took a shower"). If respondents were given a list of activities that included giving an interview and taking a shower, most respondents would endorse them. At the same time, however, such a list would reduce the likelihood that respondents would report activities that are not represented on the list (see Schuman & Presser, 1981; Schwarz & Hippler, 1991, for reviews). Both of these question form effects reflect that response alternatives can clarify the intended meaning of a question, in the present example by specifying the activities that the researcher is interested in, and may remind respondents of activities they otherwise may not consider. Whereas this example may seem rather obvious, more subtle influences frequently are overlooked.

Frequency scales. Suppose that respondents are asked how frequently they felt "really irritated" recently. To answer this question, they again have to determine what the researcher means with "really irritated." Does this term refer to major or to minor annoyances? To identify the intended meaning of the question, they may consult the response alternatives provided by the researcher. If the response alternatives present low-frequency categories (e.g., ranging from "less than once a year" to "more than once a month"), they may conclude that the researcher has relatively rare events in mind and that the question cannot refer to minor irritations, which are likely to occur more often. In line with this assumption, Schwarz, Strack, Müller, and Chassein (1988) observed that respondents who had to report the frequency of irritating experiences on a low-frequency scale assumed that the question referred to major annoyances, whereas respondents who had to give their report on a high frequency scale assumed that the question referred to minor annoyances. Thus, respondents identified different experiences as the target of the question, depending on the frequency range of the response alternatives provided to them (see also Winkielman, Knäuper, & Schwarz, 1998).

The numeric values of rating scales. Similarly, Schwarz and Hippler (1995a; see also Schwarz, Knäuper, Hippler, Noelle-Neumann, & Clark, 1991) observed that respondents may use the specific numeric values provided as part of a rating scale to interpret the meaning of the scale's verbal endpoints. In their study, German adults were asked to evaluate politicians along an 11-point rating scale, ranging from 0 or –5 (*don't think very highly of this politician*) to 11 or +5 (*think very highly of this politician*). To answer this question, respondents have to determine the meaning of "don't think very highly of this politician." Does this imply the absence of positive thoughts or the presence of negative thoughts? To do so, respondents draw on the numeric values of the rating scale, inferring that the label pertains to the presence of negative thoughts ("I have unfavorable thoughts about him") when accompanied by the numeric value –5, but to the absence of positive thoughts ("I have no particularly favorable thoughts about him") when accompanied by the numeric value 0. These differential interpretations of the verbal scale anchor are reflected in markedly different ratings: Whereas only 29.3% reported a rating below the midpoint along the –5 to +5 scale, 40.2% did so along the 0 to 10 scale. Obviously, politicians interested in high approval ratings would fare much better on the former scale.

Age-related differences. In combination, the above findings demonstrate that respondents use the response alternatives in interpreting the meaning of a question. In doing so, they proceed on the tacit assumption that every contribution is relevant to the aims of the ongoing conversation. In research situations, the researcher's contributions include apparently formal features of questionnaire design, such as the numeric values given on a rating scale. Hence, identically worded questions may acquire different meanings, depending on the response alternatives by which they are accompanied (see Schwarz, 1996, for a more extended discussion).

Are these processes likely to be affected by age-related changes in cognitive functioning? On the one hand, we safely can assume that older respondents share the tacit assumptions that underlie the conduct of conversation and hence are likely to draw on formal features of the questionnaire in much the same way as younger respondents. On the other hand, using these features to disambiguate the meaning of a question requires that respondents relate the text presented in the body of the question to the accompanying response alternatives, potentially requiring considerable cognitive resources. Given age-related decline in cognitive resources (see Park, chapter 1 in this volume), older respondents therefore may be less likely to arrive at an interpretation that reflects the integration of question wording and response alternatives.

Some preliminary data (Schwarz, Park, Knäuper, Davidson, & Smith, 1998) support the latter possibility. In a replication of Schwarz and Hippler's (1995a) experiment on the numeric values of rating scales, younger and older respondents were asked to rate Bob Dole, the Republican candidate in the 1996 U.S. presidential election. Replicating the previous findings, younger respondents rated Bob Dole more positively when the verbal label *don't think very highly of this politician* was accompanied by the numeric value –5 rather than the numeric value 0. Respondents age 70 and older, however, provided the same ratings independent of the type of numeric values offered. This suggests that they did not draw on the numeric values in interpreting the meaning of the verbal labels, presumably because their limited cognitive resources did not allow them to relate the wording of the question and the numeric values to one another. Supporting this interpretation, we observed that the impact of numeric values varied as a function of respondents' reading span, a measure of cognitive resource. As expected, respondents high in cognitive resource related the text to the numeric values, whereas respondents low in cognitive resource did not.

Preceding questions.   Respondents' interpretation of a question's intended meaning is further influenced by the context in which the question is presented. Not surprisingly, this influence is more pronounced when the wording of the question is more ambiguous because ambiguous questions force respondents to rely on contextual information to infer the intended meaning (e.g., Strack, Schwarz, & Wänke, 1991). Using the content of a preceding question in interpreting a subsequent one, however, requires that the preceding question still be accessible in memory. Secondary analyses of question order experiments (Knäuper, 1998), reviewed in the section on attitude questions, indicate that this often may not be the case for older respondents. Hence, older respondents may be less likely to draw on preceding questions than younger respondents, resulting in differential interpretations of subsequent questions, much as we have observed above for the numeric values of rating scales (Schwarz et al., 1998). This should be particularly likely in face-to-face and telephone interviews, where respondents cannot go back to earlier questions. In contrast, such age differences may be less pronounced in self-administered questionnaires, where respondents can deliberately return to previous questions when they encounter an ambiguous one (Schwarz & Hippler, 1995b). Accordingly, the emergence of age-related differences in context-dependent question interpretation may to some extent depend on the mode of data collection (see Schwarz, Strack, Hippler, & Bishop, 1991, for a comparison of self-administered questionnaires and face-to-face and telephone interviews).

Answering "don't know." In general, respondents are more likely to answer "don't know" when this answer is offered as part of the response alternatives than they are to volunteer it when not offered (see Schwarz & Hippler, 1991, for a review). Although this question form effect also holds for older respondents, researchers repeatedly have observed that older respondents generally are more likely to offer a "don't know" response than younger respondents (e.g., Colsher & Wallace, 1989; Gergen & Back, 1966; Rodgers & Herzog, 1987). This may, in part, reflect that older respondents are less likely to draw on contextual information that could help them in arriving at an answer to ambiguous questions. Moreover, they may find it more legitimate that they "don't know" and hence not only may be more likely to volunteer this response, but also may be less motivated to invest considerable effort in drawing on contextual information. Not surprisingly, older respondents are particularly likely to answer "don't know" to questions that are very complex, either semantically, syntactically, or both (Knäuper, Belli, Hill, & Hertzog, 1997). Finally, the hypothesis that older adults are more "cautious" (Botwinick, 1984) in their inferences and behavior suggests that they also may employ higher thresholds of certainty before they offer an opinion. The relative contribution of these factors to older adults' response behavior awaits empirical analysis.

Summary. As the preceding examples illustrate, question comprehension is not primarily an issue of understanding the literal meaning of an utterance. Rather, question comprehension involves extensive inferences about the speaker's intentions to determine the pragmatic meaning of the question. To make these inferences, respondents draw on the nature of preceding questions as well as the response alternatives. The limited available evidence suggests that older respondents may be less likely to make use of contextual information than younger respondents, resulting in systematic age-related differences in question interpretation—a possibility that renders the comparison of answers across age groups fraught with uncertainty.

Recalling or computing a judgment

Once respondents determine what the researcher is interested in, they need to recall relevant information from memory. In some cases, respondents may have direct access to a previously formed relevant judgment that they can offer as an answer. In most cases, however, they will not find an appropriate answer readily stored in memory and will need to compute a judgment on the spot. The processes involved in doing so are somewhat different for behavioral questions and attitude questions, and will be discussed in the respective sections below.

Formatting the response

After respondents have formed a judgment, they typically cannot report it in their own words. Rather, they are supposed to report it by endorsing one of the response alternatives provided by the researcher. This requires that they format their response in line with the options given. Accordingly, the researcher's choice of response alternatives may strongly affect the obtained results (see Schwarz & Hippler, 1991, for a review): First, respondents are more likely to endorse a response alternative presented in a closed-response format than to volunteer it in an open-response format, as discussed in the section on question comprehension. Second, the order in which response alternatives are presented affects the likelihood of their endorsement (Knäuper, in press), as we will review in our discussion of attitude questions below.

Finally, the context in which a stimulus is rated influences respondents' use of rating scales (e.g., Ostrom & Upshaw, 1968; Parducci, 1983). Specifically, respondents use the most extreme stimuli to anchor the endpoints of a rating scale. As a result, a given stimulus will be rated as less extreme if presented in the context of a more extreme one than if presented in the context of a less extreme one. In Parducci's model, this impact of the range of stimuli was referred to as the "range effect." In addition, if the number of stimuli to be rated is sufficiently large, respondents attempt to use all categories of the rating scale about equally often. Accordingly, the specific ratings given also depend on the frequency distribution of the presented stimuli, an effect that is referred to as the "frequency effect."

At present, the data bearing on age-related differences in response formatting are limited to the emergence of response order effects. It seems likely, however, that the impact of contextual stimuli on the use of rating scales is also age dependent. Specifically, older respondents may be less likely to keep track of numerous stimuli presented to them, and of the ratings they assigned to each one. If so, we may expect that range as well as frequency effects are attenuated for older respondents, again raising the possibility that researchers may misinterpret differences in scale use as differences in the substantive opinion reported. In addition, some findings suggest that very old respondents (age 80 and higher) discriminate less between categories of response scales, thus reducing the predictive power of their ratings (Knäuper & Seibt, 1999).

Editing the response

Finally, respondents may want to edit their response before they communicate it, reflecting considerations of social desirability and self-presentation. DeMaio (1984) reviewed the survey literature on this topic. Not surprisingly, the impact of self-presentation concerns is more pronounced in face-to-face interviews than in self-administered questionnaires. It is important to emphasize, however, that influences of social desirability are limited to potentially threatening questions and typically are modest in size.

Age-related differences. The observation that older respondents receive higher scores on social desirability scales (e.g., Gove & Geerken, 1977; Lewinsohn, Rohde, Seeley, & Fischer, 1993) suggests that socially desirable responding may increase with age. If so, this would have important methodological implications. Specifically, it suggests that differences in the obtained substantive responses to some extent may depend on the specific technique of data collection used: older respondents may provide more socially acceptable answers in face-to-face interviews, but this difference may disappear under more anonymous modes of data collection. In the latter respect, survey researchers have developed a number of different techniques designed to ensure the confidentiality of respondents' reports, to reduce respondents' concerns about their self-presentation, or both. These procedures range from appropriate question wordings and sealed envelopes to complicated randomized response procedures, which allow the researcher to estimate the frequency of an undesirable behavior in the population without linking a given response to a given individual. Sudman and Bradburn (1983) reviewed the various procedures in their chapter on threatening questions and provided detailed advice on how to use them. To what extent the use of such procedures affects age differences in the obtained reports, however, is an open issue.

Summary

This section reviewed what respondents must do to answer a question. For ease of exposition, respondents' tasks were presented in a sequential order. Although this order is plausible, respondents obviously may go back and forth between different steps revising, for example, their initial question interpretation once the response alternatives suggest a different meaning. In any case, however, they have to determine the intended meaning of the question, recall relevant information from memory, form a judgment, and format the judgment to fit the response alternatives provided to them. Moreover, they may want to edit their private judgment before they communicate it. Next, we turn to specific considerations that pertain to behavioral reports and attitude questions.

Answering questions about behaviors

Many questions about respondents' behavior are frequency questions pertaining, for example, to how often the respondent has bought something, has seen a doctor, or has missed a day at work during some specified period of time. Researchers who ask these questions ideally would like the respondent to identify the behavior of interest, to scan the reference period, to retrieve all instances that match the target behavior, and to count these instances to determine the overall frequency of the behavior. This, however, is the route that respondents are least likely to take.

In fact, except for rare and very important behaviors, respondents are unlikely to have detailed representations of numerous individual instances of a behavior stored in memory. Rather, the details of various instances of closely related behaviors blend into one global representation (Linton, 1982; Neisser, 1986). Thus, many individual episodes become indistinguishable or irretrievable, due to interference from other similar instances (Baddeley & Hitch, 1977; Wagenaar, 1986), fostering the generation of knowledge-like representations that "lack specific time or location indicators" (Strube, 1987, p. 89). The finding that a single spell of unemployment is more accurately recalled than multiple spells (Mathiowetz, 1986), for example, suggests that this phenomenon not only applies to mundane and unimportant behaviors, but also to repeated experiences that profoundly affect an individual's life. Accordingly, a "recall and count" model does not capture how people answer questions about frequent behaviors or experiences. Rather, their answers are likely to be based on some fragmented recall and the application of inference rules to compute a frequency estimate (see Bradburn, Rips, & Shevell, 1987; Schwarz, 1990; Sudman et al., 1996, for extensive reviews, and the contributions in Schwarz & Sudman, 1994, for research examples).

Estimation strategies

The most important estimation strategies involve the decomposition of the recall problem into subparts, reliance on subjective theories of stability and change, and the use of information provided by the response alternatives.

Decomposition strategies. Many recall problems become easier when the recall task is decomposed into several subtasks (e.g., Blair & Burton, 1987). To estimate how often she has been eating out during the past 3 months, for example, a respondent may determine that she eats out about every weekend and had dinner at a restaurant this Wednesday, but apparently not the week before. Thus, she may infer that this makes 4 times a month for the weekends, and let us say twice for other occasions, resulting in about "18 times during the past 3 months." Estimates of this type are likely to be accurate if the respondent's inference rule is adequate, and if exceptions to the usual behavior are rare.

In the absence of these fortunate conditions, however, decomposition strategies are likely to result in overestimates. This reflects that people usually overestimate the occurrence of low-frequency events and underestimate the occurrence of high frequency events (see Fiedler & Armbruster, 1994). As a result, asking for estimates of a global, and hence frequent, category (e.g., "eating out") is likely to elicit an underestimate, whereas asking for estimates of a narrow, and hence rare, category (e.g., "eating at a Mexican restaurant") is likely to elicit an overestimate. The observation that decomposition usually results in higher estimates therefore does not necessarily reflect better recall (see Belli, Schwarz, & Singer, in press). To what extent the use of decomposition strategies is age dependent is currently unknown.

Subjective theories. A particularly important inference strategy is based on subjective theories of stability and change (see Ross, 1989, for a review). In answering retrospective questions, respondents often use their current behavior or opinion as a benchmark and invoke an implicit theory of self to assess whether their past behavior or opinion was similar to, or different from, their present behavior or opinion. Assuming, for example, that one's political beliefs become more conservative over the life span, older adults may infer that they held more liberal political attitudes as teenagers than they do now (Markus, 1986). The resulting reports of previous opinions and behaviors are correct to the extent that the implicit theory is accurate.

In many domains, individuals assume a rather high degree of stability, resulting in underestimates of the degree of change that has occurred over time. Accordingly, retrospective estimates of income (Withey, 1954) or of tobacco, marijuana, and alcohol consumption (Collins, Graham, Hansen, & Johnson, 1985) were found to be influenced heavily by respondents' income or consumption habits at the time of interview. On the other hand, when respondents have reason to believe in change, they will detect change, even though none has occurred. For example, participants in a study skills training inferred that their skills prior to training were much poorer than after training, even though the training had no measurable effect on actual performance (see Ross, 1989).

As this discussion indicates, retrospective reports of changes across the lifespan will depend crucially on respondents' subjective theories. At present, we know relatively little about these subjective theories, nor do we know how these theories themselves change across the lifespan. This provides a promising avenue for future research, which may greatly improve our understanding of retrospective reports.

Response alternatives. A particularly important source of information that respondents use in arriving at an estimate is provided by the questionnaire itself. In many studies, respondents are asked to report their behavior by checking the appropriate alternative from a list of response alternatives of the type shown in Table 13.1. While the selected alternative is assumed to inform the researcher about the respondent's behavior, it frequently is overlooked that a given set of response alternatives may be far more than a simple "measurement device." Rather, it also may constitute a source of information for the respondent (see Schwarz, 1996; Schwarz & Hippler, 1991, for reviews), as we have already seen in the section on question comprehension.

Specifically, respondents assume that the range of the response alternatives provided to them reflects the researcher's knowledge of, or expectations about, the distribution of the behavior in the "real world." Accordingly, they assume that the values in the middle range of the scale reflect the "average" or "usual" behavioral frequency, whereas the extremes of the scale correspond to the extremes of the distribution. Given this assumption, respondents can use the range of the response alternatives as a frame of reference in estimating their own behavioral frequency.

This strategy results in higher estimates along scales that present high- rather than low-frequency response alternatives, as shown in Table 13.1. In this study (Schwarz, Hippler, Deutsch, & Strack, 1985), only 16.2% of a sample of German respondents reported watching TV for more than 2 ½ hours a day when the scale presented low-frequency response alternatives, whereas 37.5% reported doing so when the scale presented high frequency response alternatives. Similar results have been obtained for a wide range of different behaviors (see Schwarz, 1990, 1996, for reviews).

Age-related differences. Not surprisingly, the impact of response alternatives is more pronounced the less well the behavior is represented in memory, thus forcing respondents to rely on an estimation strategy (Menon, Rhagubir, & Schwarz, 1995). This suggests that the impact of response al-

TABLE 13.1. Reported daily TV consumption as a function of response alternatives

Low frequency alternatives		High frequency alternatives	
Up to ½ hr	7.4%	Up to 2½ hr	62.5%
½ hr to 1hr	17.7%	2½ hr to 3hr	23.4%
1 hr to 1½ hr	26.5%	3 hr to 3½ hr	7.8%
1½ hr to 2 hr	14.7%	3½ hr to 4 hr	4.7%
2 hr to 2½ hr	17.7%	4 hr to 4½ hr	1.6%
More than 2½ hr	16.2%	More than 4½ hr	0.0%

Note. N = 132. Adapted with permission from Schwarz et al. (1985).

ternatives typically may be more pronounced for older than for younger respondents. The available data support this prediction with some qualifications. As shown in Table 13.2, Schwarz, Park, and Knäuper (reported in Schwarz, 1999b) observed that older respondents were more affected by the frequency range of the response scale when asked to report the frequency of mundane events, such as buying a birthday present. On the other hand, older respondents were less affected than younger respondents when the question pertained to the frequency of physical symptoms. In combination, these findings suggest that respondents of all ages draw on the response alternatives when they need to form an estimate. Yet, the need to form an estimate depends on how much attention they pay to the respective behavior, which itself is age-dependent.

Importantly, we would again draw different conclusions about age-related differences in actual behavior from these reports, depending on the scale format used. We would conclude, for example, that age differences in red meat consumption (a health-relevant dietary behavior) or the purchase of birthday presents (an indicator of social integration) are minor when a low frequency scale is used, but rather pronounced when a high frequency scale is used. To avoid systematic influences of response alternatives, and the age-related differences in their impact, it is advisable to ask frequency questions in an open response format such as, "How many hours a day do you watch TV? ___ hours per day." Note that such an open format needs to specify the relevant units of measurement (e.g., "hours per day")

TABLE 13.2. The impact of response alternatives on behavioral reports as a function of content and respondents' age

	Frequency scale		
	Low	High	Difference
Mundane behaviors			
Eating red meat			
Young	24	43	19
Old	19	63	44
Buying birthday presents			
Young	42	49	7
Old	46	61	15
Physical symptoms			
Headaches			
Young	37	56	19
Old	11	10	1
Heartburn			
Young	14	33	19
Old	24	31	7

Note. Younger respondents are age 29 to 40, older respondents age 60 to 90. Shown is the percentage of respondents reporting eating red meat 10 times a month or more, buying birthday presents 5 times a year or more, and having headaches or heartburn twice a month or more. Adapted with permission from Schwarz (1999b).

to avoid answers like "a few." While the reports obtained under an open format are far from error-free, they at least are not systematically biased by the instrument (see Schwarz, 1990, for a discussion).

Summary

The findings reviewed in this section emphasize that retrospective behavioral reports rarely are based on adequate recall of relevant episodes. Rather, the obtained reports, to a large degree, are theory driven: respondents are likely to begin with some fragmented recall of the behavior under study and to apply various inference rules to arrive at a reasonable estimate. Moreover, if quantitative response alternatives are provided, they are likely to use them as a frame of reference, resulting in systematic biases. Although researchers have developed a number of strategies to facilitate recall (which are described in Sudman et al., 1996, and the contributions in Schwarz & Sudman, 1994), it is important to keep in mind that the best we can hope for is a reasonable estimate, unless the behavior is rare and of considerable importance to respondents.

Answering attitude questions

Like retrospective behavioral reports, respondents' answers to attitude questions are highly context dependent. As seen in the discussion of respondents' tasks, respondents' interpretation of a question or the information they draw on in forming a judgment may be strongly influenced by the specific wording of the question or by the content of preceding questions (see Schuman & Presser, 1981; Schwarz, 1999a; Schwarz & Sudman, 1992; Tourangeau & Rasinski, 1988, for research examples and reviews). Sudman et al. (1996, chap. 3–6) provided a detailed discussion of different sources of context effects in the light of psychological theorizing. Here, we focus on two key issues; namely, the emergence of question order effects and response order effects.

Question order effects

As many psychological experiments have documented, individuals are unlikely to retrieve all information that may potentially bear on a judgment, but truncate the search process as soon as enough information has come to mind to form a judgment with sufficient subjective certainty (see Bodenhausen & Wyer, 1987; Higgins, 1996; Schwarz, 1995, for reviews). Accordingly, their judgments strongly reflect the impact of the information that is most accessible in memory at the time of judgment. This usually is the information that has been used most recently (e.g., for the purpose of answering a preceding question). Given age-related declines in short term memory (see Park, chapter 1 in this volume), however, the information brought to mind by preceding questions may fade more quickly from older respondents' memory. Accordingly, we may expect that question order effects decrease with increasing age. Secondary analyses reported by Knäuper (1998) confirmed this prediction.

As an example, consider an experiment reported by Schuman and Presser (1981). These researchers asked respondents, "Do you think that it should be possible for a pregnant woman to obtain a legal abortion if she is married and does not want any more children?" The answers to this general question depended on whether or not it was preceded by a more specific one which read, "Do you think it should be possible for a pregnant woman to obtain a legal abortion if there is a strong chance of a serious defect in the baby?" When this specific question preceded the general one, support for abortion in response to the general question decreased significantly in the sample as a whole. This presumably reflects that "not wanting any more children" appears as a less legitimate reason for an abortion when contrasted with "serious defects in the baby." A breakdown by age, however, indicated that this order effect is limited to younger respondents, as shown in Figure 13.1.

Specifically, the under-55-year-olds reported significantly more support for legal abortions when the general question was asked first than when it was preceded by the specific question, resulting in a difference of 19.5%. This question order effect decreases with age, as shown in Figure 13.1, and is no longer reliably obtained for those over age 60. Based on

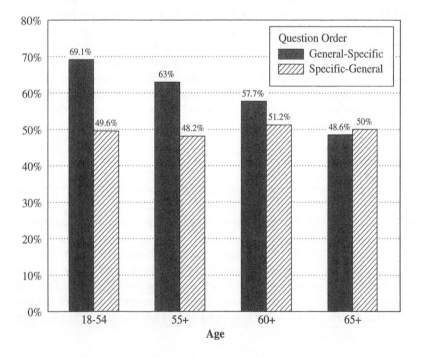

FIG. 13.1
Age and question order percent supporting abortion.

these data, we would conclude that older adults are less supportive of legalized abortion when the general question is asked first, but that attitudes toward abortion are thoroughly independent of age when the general question is preceded by the specific one. Thus, the age dependency of question order effects would lead us to draw different substantive conclusions, much as we have seen for the age dependency of the use of contextual information at the question comprehension stage.

Response order effects

So far, the bulk of the reported findings have indicated that context effects decrease with age. Considered in isolation, findings of this type are theoretically ambiguous. On the one hand, they may indicate that older respondents' limited resources undermine their ability to draw on contextual information, as we have suggested. On the other hand, they may reflect that older respondents' attitudes are more crystallized than younger respondents' attitudes and hence are less subject to contextual influences, as Sears (1987) suggested.

Analyses of response order effects bear on this theoretical issue. Specifically, answering a question that presents several substantively different response alternatives requires that respondents (a) hold the question and the response alternatives in mind, (b) evaluate the implications of each response alternative, and (c) select the one that they find most agreeable. (See Schwarz, Hippler, & Noelle-Neumann, 1992; Sudman et al., 1996, chap. 6, for more detailed discussions of the underlying processes.) This sequence of tasks poses a high demand on working memory, particularly when the response alternatives are read to respondents, as is the case in telephone interviews. Accordingly, a cognitive resource account of age differences in self-reports predicts that older respondents, are more likely to be influenced by the order in which response alternatives are presented than are younger respondents. In contrast, the assumption that older respondents' attitudes are more crystallized predicts that older respondents should be less likely to show response order effects than younger respondents.

The available data strongly support the cognitive resource prediction (see Knäuper, in press, for a comprehensive review and meta-analysis). For example, Schuman and Presser (1981) asked respondents in a telephone interview, "Should divorce in this country be easier to obtain, more difficult to obtain, or stay as it is now?" Depending on conditions, the response alternative "more difficult" was read to respondents as the second or as the last alternative. Overall, respondents were somewhat more likely to select the response alternative "more difficult" when presented last, a so called recency effect. However, secondary analyses reported by Knäuper (1998, in press) indicated a dramatic age difference: As shown in Figure 13.2, the size of the recency effect increased with respondents' age, ranging from an insignificant 5% for age 54 and younger to a whopping 36.3% for age 70 and older. Note again that we would draw different substantive conclu-

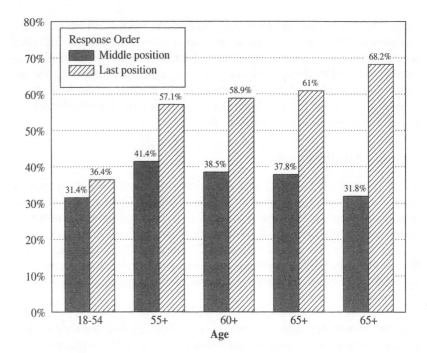

FIG 13.2.
Age and response
order percent
endorsing "more
difficult."

sions about the relationship of age and attitudes toward divorce, depending on the order in which the response alternatives are presented. While attitudes toward divorce seem to become much more conservative with age under one order condition, no reliable age differences are obtained under the other order condition.

Summary

In sum, the reviewed findings suggest that question order effects are likely to decrease with age, whereas response order effects are likely to increase with age. Both of these effects can be traced to age-related declines in cognitive resources, which make it more difficult for older respondents to hold large amounts of relevant information in short term memory. As a result, self-reports of attitudes not only are context dependent, but the size of the emerging context effects itself is age-sensitive, rendering comparisons across age groups fraught with uncertainty.

Conclusions

As the reviewed examples illustrate, minor differences in question wording, question format, and question order may greatly influence the obtained results in representative sample surveys as well as in the psychological laboratory. Over the past decade, researchers have made considerable progress in understanding the cognitive and communicative processes underlying the emergence of context effects in self-reports of behaviors and attitudes (see Sudman et al., 1996, for a comprehensive review). Despite this progress, however, we know little about the impact of age-related changes in cognitive and communicative functioning on the question answering process, nor do we understand how age-related effects in this domain may be influenced by individuals' educational attainment and related variables. The little we do know, however, is cause for considerable concern: not surprisingly, age-related differences in cognitive resources, memory, text comprehension, speech processing, and communication can have a profound impact on the components of the question answering process, resulting in differential context effects for older and younger respondents. The reviewed research examples illustrate that age-sensitive context effects may lead us to conclude that older and younger respondents differ in their attitudes or behaviors under one question format or question order. Yet, we would conclude that no age difference exists under another question format or question order. If we want to avoid the misinterpretation of age-sensitive methods effects as substantive findings, we need to understand how age-related changes in cognitive and communicative functioning interact with the features of our research instruments in shaping respondents' reports. Exploring this thorny issue provides a challenging avenue for future interdisciplinary research that promises to advance our theoretical understanding of human cognition and communication across the lifespan and to improve the methodology of social research.

References

Baddeley, A. D., & Hitch, G. J. (1977). Recency reexamined. In S. Dornic (Ed.), *Attention and performance* (Vol. 6, pp. 647–667). Hillsdale, NJ: Erlbaum.

Baltes, P. B., Reese, H. W., & Nesselroade, J. R. (1977). *Life-span developmental psychology: Introduction to research methods.* Pacific Grove, CA: Brooks/Cole.

Belli, R., Schwarz, N., & Singer, E. (in press). Decomposition can harm the accuracy of retrospective behavioral reports. *Applied Cognitive Psychology.*

Blair, E., & Burton, S. (1987). Cognitive processes used by survey respondents to answer behavioral frequency questions. *Journal of Consumer Research, 14,* 280–288.

Bodenhausen, G. V., & Wyer, R. S. (1987). Social cognition and social reality: Information acquisition and use in the laboratory and the real world. In H. J. Hippler, N. Schwarz, & S. Sudman (Eds.), *Social information processing and survey methodology* (pp. 6–41). New York: Springer Verlag.

Botwinick, J. (1984). *Aging and behavior* (3rd ed.). New York: Springer.

Bradburn, N. M., Rips, L. J., & Shevell, S. K. (1987). Answering autobiographical questions: The impact of memory and inference on surveys. *Science, 236,* 157–161.

Clark, H. H., & Schober, M. F. (1992). Asking questions and influencing answers. In J. M. Tanur (Ed.), *Questions about questions* (pp. 15–48). New York: Sage.

Collins, L. M., Graham, J. W., Hansen, W. B., & Johnson, C. A. (1985). Agreement between retrospective accounts of substance use and earlier reported substance use. *Applied Psychological Measurement, 9,* 301–309.

Colsher, P. L., & Wallace, R. B. (1989). Data quality and age. *Journal of Gerontology: Psychological Sciences, 44,* 45–52.

DeMaio, T. J. (1984). Social desirability and survey measurement: A review. In C. F. Turner & E. Martin (Eds.), *Surveying subjective phenomena* (Vol. 2, pp. 257–281). New York: Sage.

Fiedler, K., & Armbruster, T. (1994). Two halves may be more than one whole: Category-split effects on frequency illusions. *Journal of Personality and Social Psychology, 66,* 633–645.

Gergen, K. J., & Back, K. W. (1966). Communication in the interview and the disengaged respondent. *Public Opinion Quarterly, 30,* 385–398.

Gove, W. R., & Geerken, M. R. (1977). Response bias in surveys of mental health: An empirical investigation. *American Journal of Sociology, 82,* 1289–1317.

Grice, H. P. (1975). Logic and conversation. In P. Cole, & J. L. Morgan (Eds.), *Syntax and semantics: Vol.3. Speech acts* (pp. 41–58). New York: Academic Press.

Higgins, E. T. (1996). Knowledge activation: Accessibility, applicability, and salience. In E. T. Higgins & A. Kruglanski (Eds.), *Social psychology: Handbook of basic principles* (pp. 133 –168). New York: Guilford Press.

Hilton, D. J. (1995). The social context of reasoning: Conversational inference and rational judgment. *Psychological Bulletin, 118,* 248-271.

Knäuper, B. (1998). Age differences in question and response order effects. In N. Schwarz, D. Park, B. Knäuper, & S. Sudman (Eds.), *Cognition, aging, and self-reports* (pp. 341–363). Philadelphia, PA: Psychology Press.

Knäuper, B. (1999). The impact of age and education on response order effects in attitude measurement. *Public Opinion Quarterly, 63,* 347–370.

Knäuper, B., Belli, R. F., Hill, D. H., & Herzog, A. R. (1997). Question difficulty and respondents' cognitive ability: The impact on data quality. *Journal of Official Statistics, 13,* 181–199.

Knäuper, B., & Seibt, B. (1999). *Rating scales: Limited discrimination between categories among the oldest old.* Unpublished manuscript, Free University of Berlin.

Lewinsohn, P. M., Rohde, P., Seeley, J. R., & Fischer, S. A. (1993). Age-cohort changes in the lifetime occurence of depression and other mental disorders. *Journal of Abnormal Psychology, 102,* 110–120.

Linton, M. (1982). Transformations of memory in everyday life. In U. Neisser (Ed.), *Memory observed: Remembering in natural contexts* (pp. 77–91). San Francisco: Freeman.

Markus, G. B. (1986). Stability and change in political attitudes: Observed, recalled, and explained. *Political Behavior, 8,* 21–44.

Mathiowetz, N. A. (1986, June). *Episodic recall and estimation: Applicability of cognitive theories to survey data.* Paper presented at the Social Science Research Council Seminar on Retrospective Data, New York.

Menon, G., Raghubir, P., & Schwarz, N. (1995). Behavioral frequency judgments: An accessibility-diagnosticity framework. *Journal of Consumer Research, 22,* 212–228.

Neisser, U. (1986). Nested structure in autobiographical memory. In D. C. Rubin (Ed.), *Autobiographical memory* (pp. 71–88). Cambridge, England: Cambridge University Press.

Ostrom, T. M., & Upshaw, H. S. (1968). Psychological perspective and attitude change. In A. C. Greenwald, T. C. Brock, & T. M. Ostrom (Eds.), *Psychological foundations of attitudes*. New York: Academic Press.

Parducci, A. (1983). Category ratings and the relational character of judgment. In H. G. Geissler, H. F. J. M. Bulfart, E. L. H. Leeuwenberg, & V. Sarris (Eds.), *Modern issues in perception* (pp. 262–282). Berlin: VEB Deutscher Verlag der Wissenschaften.

Rodgers, W. L., & Herzog, A. R. (1987). Interviewing older adults: The accuracy of factual information. *Journal of Gerontology, 42*, 387–394.

Ross, M. (1989). The relation of implicit theories to the construction of personal histories. *Psychological Review, 96*, 341–357.

Schuman, H., & Presser, S. (1981). *Questions and answers in attitude surveys*. New York: Academic Press.

Schwarz, N. (1990). Assessing frequency reports of mundane behaviors: Contributions of cognitive psychology to questionnaire construction. In C. Hendrick & M. S. Clark (Eds.), *Review of personality and social psychology: Vol. 11. Research methods in personality and social psychology* (pp. 98–119). Beverly Hills, CA: Sage.

Schwarz, N. (1994). Judgment in a social context: Biases, shortcomings, and the logic of conversation. In M. Zanna (Ed.), *Advances in experimental social psychology* (Vol. 26). San Diego, CA: Academic Press.

Schwarz, N. (1995). Social cognition: Information accessibility and use in social judgment. In D. N. Osherson & E. E. Smith (Eds.), *Thinking: An invitation to cognitive science* (Vol. 3, 2nd ed., pp. 345–376). Cambridge, MA: MIT Press.

Schwarz, N. (1996). *Cognition and communication: Judgmental biases, research methods and the logic of conversation*. Hillsdale, NJ: Erlbaum.

Schwarz, N. (1999a). Self-reports: How the questions shape the answers. *American Psychologist, 54*, 93–105.

Schwarz, N. (1999b). Frequency reports of physical symptoms and health behaviors: How the questionnaire determines the results. In Park, D. C., Morrell, R. W., & Shifren, K. (Eds.), *Processing medical information in aging patients: Cognitive and human factors perspectives* (pp. 93–108). Mahwah, NJ: Erlbaum.

Schwarz, N., & Hippler, H. J. (1991). Response alternatives: The impact of their choice and ordering. In P. Biemer, R. Groves, N. Mathiowetz, & S. Sudman (Eds.), *Measurement error in surveys* (pp. 41–56). Chichester, England: Wiley.

Schwarz, N., & Hippler, H. J. (1995a). The numeric values of rating scales: A comparison of their impact in mail surveys and telephone interviews. *International Journal of Public Opinion Research, 7*, 72–74.

Schwarz, N., & Hippler, H. J. (1995b). Subsequent questions may influence answers to preceding questions in mail surveys. *Public Opinion Quarterly, 59*, 93–97.

Schwarz, N., Hippler, H. J., Deutsch, B. & Strack, F. (1985). Response categories: Effects on behavioral reports and comparative judgments. *Public Opinion Quarterly, 49*, 388–395.

Schwarz, N., Knäuper, B., Hippler, H. J., Noelle-Neumann, E., & Clark, F. (1991). Rating scales: Numeric values may change the meaning of scale labels. *Public Opinion Quarterly, 55*, 570–582.

Schwarz, N., Park, D. C., Knäuper, B., Davidson, N., & Smith, P. (1998, April). *Aging, cognition, and self-reports: Age-dependent context effects and misleading conclusions about age-differences in attitudes and behavior*. Cognitive Aging Conference, Atlanta, GA.

Schwarz, N., Strack, F., Hippler, H. J., & Bishop, G. (1991). The impact of administration mode on response effects in survey measurement. *Applied Cognitive Psychology, 5,* 193–212.

Schwarz, N., Strack, F., Müller, G., & Chassein, B. (1988). The range of response alternatives may determine the meaning of the question: Further evidence on informative functions of response alternatives. *Social Cognition, 6,* 107–117.

Schwarz, N., & Sudman, S. (Eds.). (1992). *Context effects in social and psychological research.* New York: Springer-Verlag.

Schwarz, N., & Sudman, S. (1994). *Autobiographical memory and the validity of retrospective reports.* New York: Springer-Verlag.

Sears, D. O. (1987). Implications of the life-span approach for research on attitudes and social cognition. In R. P. Abeles (Ed.), *Life-span perspectives and social psychology* (pp. 17–60). Hillsdale, NJ: Erlbaum.

Strack, F. (1994). *Zur Psychologie der Standardisierten Befragung.* Heidelberg, Germany: Springer-Verlag.

Strack, F., & Martin, L. (1987). Thinking, judging, and communicating: A process account of context effects in attitude surveys. In H. J. Hippler, N. Schwarz, & S. Sudman (Eds.), *Social information processing and survey methodology* (pp. 123–148). New York: Springer Verlag.

Strack, F., Schwarz, N., & Wänke, M. (1991). Semantic and pragmatic aspects of context effects in social and psychological research. *Social Cognition, 9,* 111–125.

Strube, G. (1987). Answering survey questions: The role of memory. In H. J. Hippler, N. Schwarz, & S. Sudman (Eds.), *Social information processing and survey methodology* (pp. 86–101). New York: Springer-Verlag.

Sudman, S., & Bradburn, N. M. (1983). *Asking questions.* San Francisco: Jossey-Bass.

Sudman, S., Bradburn, N., & Schwarz, N. (1996). *Thinking about answers: The application of cognitive processes to survey methodology.* San Francisco, CA: Jossey-Bass.

Tourangeau, R. (1984). Cognitive science and survey methods: A cognitive perspective. In T. Jabine, M. Straf, J. Tanur, & R. Tourangeau (Eds.), *Cognitive aspects of survey methodology: Building a bridge between disciplines* (pp. 73–100). Washington, DC: National Academy Press.

Tourangeau, R., & Rasinski, K. A. (1988). Cognitive processes underlying context effects in attitude measurement. *Psychological Bulletin, 103,* 299–314.

Wagenaar, W. A. (1986). My memory: A study of autobiographical memory over six years. *Cognitive Psychology, 18,* 225–252.

Winkielman, P., Knäuper, B., & Schwarz, N. (1998). Looking back at anger: Reference periods change the interpretation of (emotion) frequency questions. *Journal of Personality and Social Psychology, 75,* 719–728.

Withey, S. B. (1954). Reliability of recall of income. *Public Opinion Quarterly, 18,* 31–34.

Judgment and decision making across the adult life span: A tutorial review of psychological research

Alan G. Sanfey, Reid Hastie

The abilities to judge and decide are fundamental higher-order cognitive capacities. They frequently are cited at the top of the list of critical survival functions in ancestral environments and in everyday life. Even in the modern world, life quality and longevity are directly contingent on decisions about diet, health care, transportation, and living situations.

In recent years, the amount of theoretical and practical research on decision making has grown, and this topic is now a substantial subfield within the field of psychology. But, decision processes have been neglected in research on aging. This neglect is surprising because there are several standard, well-understood, externally valid research paradigms to study decision making processes. Clearly, the types of decisions and judgments that we are required to make change over the course of the lifespan. It is obvious that the decisions facing a person at age 20 are different from the decisions a 70-year-old needs to make. For example, decisions about medical and financial matters tend to increase in frequency and importance as we get older. But, what about the fundamental decision-making process? Do we decide and judge in the same way as we advance in years? Or, is there an essential difference to the way our decisions are made as we get older? This question is still largely unanswered due to the dearth of studies in this area. The goal of the present chapter is to review those few studies that have been conducted on the topic of aging and decision making.

While there is surprisingly little past research on judgment and decision making across the lifespan, there is a substantial base of empirical knowledge of the effects of aging on elementary processes that are components of the higher-level cognitive achievements in the tasks we will review. For example, there is an informative literature on frequency estimation, recognition (identification of previously experienced individuals and events), and recall memory across the lifespan. There are five currently popular hypotheses to explain the effects of aging on higher order cognitive performances: global changes in brain function that produce both sensory and intellectual system declines (Baltes & Lindenberger, 1997), decrements in storage capacity (or storage processes; Parkinson, Lindholm, & Inman, 1982), decreasing ability to inhibit the activation and processing of task-irrelevant, interfering information in working memory (Stoltzfus, Hasher, & Zacks, 1996), decrements in the ability to link goals to complex plans for cognitive or behavioral performance (Craik, 1994; Kirchner, 1958), and slowdowns in the activation of information in working memory (Cerella, 1990; Salthouse, 1996; cf., Morris, Gick, & Craik, 1988). Based on these hypotheses, it is possible to speculate as to the degree to which decision processes are affected by aging.

Choosing a financial institution to handle one's money or deciding to have an operation to remove a possibly cancerous growth clearly meet the criteria to be considered a "decision." But, what about less clear-cut examples of decisions? When we go off to work every morning, does this count as a decision? After all, we could have done a number of different things with our day, but on the other hand, we probably never made a conscious decision as whether to go to our job or not. Our focus in the present review is on cognitive processes in deliberate decision tasks. Within the field of judgment and decision making there are three primary types of tasks which are grouped under the category of "judgment and decision making." The first of these tasks, judgment and estimation, involves integrating the information from several sources into a single estimate or judgment. For example, we might review several of our own symptoms to infer a judgment of the severity of an illness or disability, or we might study several aspects of a property to make an estimate of the price we expect it will sell for on a real estate market. The second task is choice among multiattribute "commodities" such as health care plans or automobiles, where we examine the characteristics of several options or commodities and make a choice of which one to purchase or commit to. The third task concerns risky decisions such as preferences for medical treatment options. The word *risky* is used here in a technical sense to refer to the fact that the possible consequences contingent on a decision are uncertain. Usually, but not always, there is the further implication that at least some of the consequences are negative and could reduce our personal capital, health, or happiness below its current "status quo" level.

It is these tasks that will be examined in the course of the present review with reference to describing ways in which they can be studied across the lifespan. We should note that, while there is a reasonably large body of research devoted to the topic of expertise and judgment, we do not equate aging with expertise per se and, hence, we do not review these studies. While experts tend most definitely to be older than novices, there are numerous confounding factors which obscure raw aging effects. Our discussion starts with a detailed description of each of the three tasks mentioned above, accompanied by a review of previous studies relevant to aging. We also suggest some possible directions for future research to help clarify the relationship between aging and each of the three fundamental decision tasks.

Basic judgment and decision-making tasks

Judgment and estimation

Many everyday judgment tasks involve reasoning from items of information to estimate a magnitude, quantity, or condition (Fischhoff, 1988, provides a good introductory overview). We make dozens of these quantitative judgments every day: how much will the groceries cost? What time will the meeting end? What will the temperature be tomorrow? How many guests will show up for the party? And, many important judgments also are of quantities or magnitudes: what will the interest rate be on the mortgage? How long will the patient live? How many citizens will move into the new suburb? What will my monthly income be if I change jobs or retire? Will the rate of violent crime in my neighborhood continue to increase?

Research methods.   Most judgment research of this type looks at situations where the outcome is signaled by a number of factors or cues. Typically, each cue has a value on some dimension and will have a high and a low end with respect to the goal; for example, in predicting academic ability, high test scores are better than low scores. The judge's task usually is to evaluate the outcome or predict a value based on these cues. For example, a judge might try to assess a number of applicants for graduate school based on cues such as previous research experience, Graduate Record Examination (GRE) scores, and quality of recommendations. Or, in a medical judgment task, participants might be asked to predict the severity of a particular medical condition based on information about various symptoms presented by each patient, such as, blood pressure level, presence or absence of headaches, stomach acidity levels (see Figure 14.1 for an example display). Cue information usually is summarized numerically for the judge, although virtually any imaginable stimulus format (from radiographs to face-to-face interviews) has been employed in research (Cooksey, 1996).

The most popular approach to the analysis of the multiple cue judgment process, the lens model, was developed by Brunswik (1952) and his student Hammond (1955). The environmental variable to be estimated, whether it is the cost of the groceries or how well a potential graduate student will do if admitted to the program, is inferred by the judge based on the values of a set of components (cues). The predictive importance of these cues to the real state of the world (how much the groceries actually

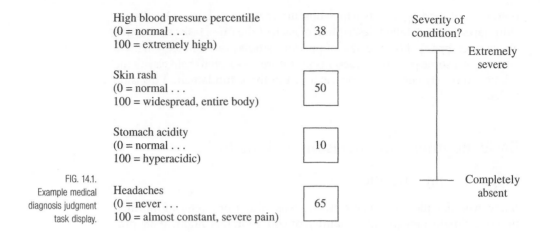

High blood pressure percentille
(0 = normal . . .
100 = extremely high)

38

Severity of
condition?

Extremely
severe

Skin rash
(0 = normal . . .
100 = widespread, entire body)

50

Stomach acidity
(0 = normal . . .
100 = hyperacidic)

10

FIG. 14.1.
Example medical
diagnosis judgment
task display.

Headaches
(0 = never . . .
100 = almost constant, severe pain)

65

Completely
absent

cost; how well the student actually did) can be expressed by numerical coefficients, as can the association between the cue values and the judge's estimates.

In an experiment based on this method, a subject would make several of the judgments outlined above and, through the statistical process of multiple regression, the judgment policy of the subject can then be "captured." This is carried out by regressing the judgments on the values of the cues, producing a judgment "cue weight profile" for each subject. One of the most useful results of this policy capturing approach (Stewart, 1988) is a summary description of the subject's judgment habits in an algebraic equation.

Central to this policy capturing approach is the notion of quantifying the accuracy of the subject's judgments. This is a particularly relevant aspect of the judgment process, especially in cases where it is of great importance that the judgment be as accurate as possible, such as in medical diagnosis and financial forecasting. When there is a known to-be-judged target value, the typical measure of accuracy is a correlation computed between the judge's estimate of the variable in question and the actual observed or measured value of it. To refer to our medical judgment task described above, accuracy would be assessed by comparing the various patients' actual conditions with the estimates provided by the judge. It is evident that accuracy involves the art of knowing which cues to use and to what extent to rely on them. It should be noted, though, that while an experimental setting for judgment provides many reasonably clear examples, usually with some element of feedback to "fine tune" one's judgment strategy, nature is rarely as kind, giving us as it does incomplete information, long time lags between prediction and the actual event, and noisy cue-criterion relationships.

Another important aspect of performance in these judgment tasks is consistency of the judge's behavior, which involves how well the judge follows a consistent pattern in his or her estimates and predictions; consistent judges use the same cues to the same degree in each of their estimates.

Again referring to our medical example, if a judge put most credence in blood pressure levels and paid no attention to the presence or absence of a skin rash in trying to estimate the severity of the patient's condition, and he or she did this across all judgments, we would categorize this judge as consistent.

This judgment profile is a list of *cue impact weights* for each of the cues presented for the judgment. Standardized ß-weights provide a measure of the relative contributions of each cue to the judgment of the subject, and by comparing these weights to each other, it is possible to make inferences about the importance of each cue with regard to the judgment (Stewart, 1988). This yields useful information regarding the extent to which the judges used all or some of the cues in coming to their estimate. Further, in a controlled experimental situation, cues can be constructed or selected so as to be either directly or inversely predictive, to be linearly or nonlinearly related to the outcome, and to interact with other cues (or not) in predicting the criterion. This allows for the analysis of the types and patterns of cues to which people are sensitive. Cue impact weight profiles can be summarized to yield various indexes of judgment strategies, such as complexity in terms of number of cues to which the judge was sensitive and in terms of the mathematical properties of the policy, for example, the degree to which nonlinear or configural relationships characterize the cue utilization process. It also is possible to calculate a summary "matching" index of the similarity between the cue impact profile and the best comparable regression equation that predicts the to-be-judged criterion (not the judgment itself) from the cues (Castellan, 1992). This can be interpreted (with caution) as a measure of the extent to which the general structure of the environment (criterion-to-cue relationships) is reflected in the mind of the judge (cue-to-judgment relationships).

The lens model, in combination with multiple cue learning and judgment experimental tasks, can be used to study two general characteristics of human judges that are especially relevant to research on aging. First, the lens model framework can be used to study the process of learning to make a judgment. In most studies, the subject is presented with a series of cases, makes a judgment for each case, and then receives feedback in the form of the correct "answer" for each case. To the best of our knowledge, learning involves an active hypothesis-testing process (Brehmer, 1980; Klayman & Ha, 1989). Obviously, any of the statistics summarizing behavior can be calculated separately for blocks of learning-from-feedback trials and the course of learning (changes in accuracy, consistency, and judgment policies) can be tracked across trials. Another temporally extended adaptive process that might be of special interest in research on aging concerns people's reactions to changes in the environment that demand revisions of belief about the nature of the world. The lens model framework provides a natural procedure to study the effects of changes in the criterion-cue relationships reflected in the judgment policy. So, for example, the experimenter can manipulate the criterion-cue relationship to make a previously valid cue no longer informative or to make a previously uninformative cue predictive of the criterion and then observe the judge's adaptation to this change, reflected in changes in the weighting of cues in the judgment policy. Many hypotheses about the aging of cognitive processes lead to predictions that older people will be slower to learn and slower to revise judgment policies than younger people.

Previous research. In terms of how people perform across the lifespan, one relevant study was carried out by Chasseigne, Mullet, and Stewart (1997). These investigators conducted a study of multiple cue probability learning in which three age groups (20–30, 65–75, 76–90 years old) of participants made approximately 150 estimates of a numerical quantity. On each trial, the participant saw three cues (presented as vertical bars, where height indicated amount), which they were told represented settings on a water heater, and their task was to learn to estimate the water temperature (criterion) from the settings. The experimenters varied whether or not feedback (the "correct" answer) was presented, whether or not the cue-criterion relationships either were explicitly stated or had to be learned inductively from the experience of making judgments, and also the form of the probabilistic relationship between each cue and the to-be-predicted criterion temperature. The data were analyzed using multiple regression "policy capturing" equations as described above. Older and younger participants performed at similar levels of accuracy when the cue-criterion relationship was simple (linear, direct), but older participants were much less accurate when important cue-criterion relationships were difficult to comprehend (indirect). Further, they found that the oldest participants (age 76 to 90) did not utilize the indirect cue-criterion relationship, even when they were given explicit instructions as to the form of the relationship.

While decreased working memory processing often is cited as a reason why older adults perform more poorly at a task than younger adults, in this case, the direct and indirect conditions have the same working memory load. The authors therefore interpreted their result as a gradual decrease of cognitive flexibility in older adults. The younger group was highly flexible in terms of adapting to different types of cue-criterion relationships (direct and indirect), while the intermediate group (65–75 years old) had lost this flexibility in regard to the indirect relationship, although group members were able to utilize this relationship when explicitly instructed as to the nature of the relationship. The oldest group had even more restricted flexibility and could not use the instructional information to modify their judgments. Although the concept of "cognitive flexibility" varies in meaning from researcher to researcher, these results suggest that that the ability to think in a flexible, self-initiated fashion declines as one gets older.

In a related study, Mutter and Pliske (1994) examined age differences in covariation judgments; that is, assessing to what extent values on one variable predict values on another. Obviously, the ability to infer correlational relationships plays a central role in people's ability to learn to make judgments from feedback, as in the Chasseigne et al. (1997) study. For example, for a weather forecaster, the covariation between amount of cloud cover and rainfall is one basis for judgments of precipitation. Past research (e.g., Chapman & Chapman, 1967) has demonstrated that people often perceive "illusory correlations," which occur when they "observe" a relationship between two uncorrelated variables. The usual interpretation is that the "data" are overshadowed by previous associations between the variables. For example, clinicians and laypeople tend to "see" relationships between symptoms and mental illness that they expect on the basis of folk theories of personality, even when there is no objective association between symptoms and psychopathological condition.

Mutter and Pliske (1994) presented subjects with a collection of cases, each of which described a characteristic of a psychiatric patient and gave an account of that patient's interpretation of a Rorschach card. The subjects were then asked to judge any association between the patients' Rorschach interpretations and their psychiatric characteristics. As is typical in these studies, subjects generally reported "illusory correlations" that had no statistical foundation based on the data they saw, but that were consistent with some intuitive associations (cf., Alloy & Tabachnik, 1984). Of more interest than this well-documented finding is the observation that older adults (age 62 to 76) were just as susceptible to the illusory correlation effect as younger subjects (age 18 to 24). However, in line with the cognitive flexibility hypothesis outlined above, when presented with information which contradicted the intuitive association, the younger adults showed less evidence of a bias than the older subjects.

The studies by Chasseigne et al. and by Mutter and Pliske suggest that there are age-related effects in judgment and estimation tasks and both can be interpreted in terms of decreased cognitive flexibility in aging adults. However, cognitive flexibility is not uniquely singled out as the best explanation. Yates and Patalano (1999) offered some alternative interpretations of these results, including an account in terms of a normative (Bayesian) reasoning process and an account based on psychological association strength.

One special kind of judgment, estimations or expressions of uncertainty, confidence, or probability, has received a great deal of attention from judgment researchers. This surely is because of the central role of probability measures in formal decision theories (Dawes, 1998), but we often refer to these concepts in everyday talk about judgments: "I think that," "chances are," "it's likely that." There is considerable evidence that our conceptions of the nature of probability change dramatically during childhood development (e.g., Byrnes, 1998; Piaget & Inhelder, 1975). Still, there is little research on changes in probability judgment or reasoning across the adult lifespan. However, estimates and impressions of frequency are likely to be the basis for many kinds of probability judgments, where notions of relative frequency are pertinent. There is a useful collection of studies of frequency estimation across the lifespan. The conclusion from this research is that frequency estimation is a fundamental skill, perhaps heavily determined by evolution and "wired-in" to our brains as a basic cognitive capacity (along with the abilities to judge similarity, recognition-identity, and perhaps causal strength). Hasher and Zacks (1984) concluded that past the age of 4 or 5, sensitivity to frequency is fairly immutable across the lifespan (Attig & Hasher, 1980; Kausler & Puckett, 1980).

Discussion. To date, there are only a few findings to interpret that describe judgment processes across the adult lifespan. Older adults may be a bit less flexible than younger in learning new judgment habits and in learning more complex relationships (e.g., slower to learn nonlinear relationships). These initial findings suggest it might be especially interesting to study the ability to notice changed cue-criterion relationships and to adapt to the change by learning the new relationships across the lifespan (e.g., Knowlton, Squire, & Gluck, 1994, used a similar, "changed prediction rule" task to study flexibility of judgment in amnesia patients). We are surprised that other working memory–related phenomena have not been observed. For example, if we can generalize from research that concludes that working memory capacity or processing speeds diminish across the lifespan, we would expect that older adults would exhibit simpler judgment policies (e.g., rely on fewer cues) than younger adults. Similarly, if a judgment task is studied in which part of the "problem" for the judge is to ignore associated, but irrelevant (even misleading) information (cues), older judges would be expected to perform more poorly than younger judges, if the hypothesis of working memory inhibition failures is a correct depiction of cognitive aging. But, at the moment, these interesting possibilities are open for future empirical research.

Choice

The second popular class of tasks studied by judgment and decision researchers concerns the manner in which people choose among a set of multiattribute alternatives (Slovic, 1990, provides an excellent tutorial introduction). This task is sometimes called "choice under certainty," because the objective choice set is fixed, and the decision to choose an option is assumed to be followed by the reception of that option. But, of course, there still may remain much subjective uncertainty about how satisfying the experience of the chosen option will be. For example, how do people choose which car to buy when faced with many alternatives, varying on a host of attributes relevant to price, reliability, safety, fuel economy, prestige, and so on? Do people pick one particularly important attribute and analyze all alternatives on that dimension? Or, do they look at all the attributes of each alternative in turn and use all of the information in order to make a decision? Or, as seems at least intuitively more likely, do they use a mix of these strategies?

It should be noted that, unlike the judgment and estimation tasks outlined in the previous section, in choice tasks there rarely is a method for ascertaining the accuracy of a particular choice. The car that is ideal for one person may be unsuitable for a friend, and vice versa. Furthermore, people seem to be far from perfect at predicting today the outcomes they will most enjoy in the future or in estimating the degree of their experienced pleasures and pains in the future (see Kahneman & Diener, 1999). Therefore, while we can measure and describe many aspects of choice behavior, accuracy is not a factor we usually can talk about. Payne, Bettman, and Johnson (1988) studied choices of monetary payoff gambles and constructed a measure of "relative accuracy" based on the assumption that the gamble with the highest expected value was the "correct" choice.

Research methods. Laboratory tasks used to investigate this type of choice behavior traditionally have used a choice board procedure (or, in its automated form, the MouseLab process-tracing system described by Payne, Bettman, & Johnson, 1993; see Figure 14.2 for an example display). In these tasks, participants are presented with a number of possible alternatives and asked to choose the single alternative they would most prefer to receive. The alternatives might be which of a number of insurance policies to take out, apartments to rent, gambles to play, or college courses to take, for example. Each of the alternatives is described by a number of attributes—in the apartment scenario, the various alternatives might be described in terms of their rent, location, spaciousness, and so forth.

The usual method of displaying these choices is in the form of a matrix of alternatives ("rows," e.g., insurance policies, apartments to rent, gambles to play, college courses in which to enroll) by attributes ("columns," e.g., cost, hospitalization coverage for the policies; rent, location, roominess for the apartments; probabilities and payoffs for the gambles; grading curve, instructor appeal for the courses), a display format that is used frequently in the familiar *Consumer Reports* magazine articles. The task of the chooser is straightforward: to decide, based on personal preferences which alternative to select. The information in each cell is hidden, however, so in

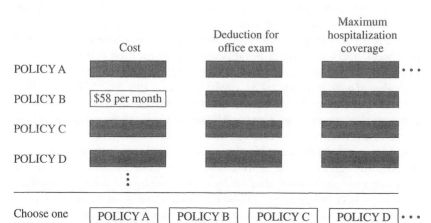

FIG. 14.2. Example MouseLab information search display that would be presented to experimental participants choosing among medical insurance policies. (Hartley, 1989, used a display like this to study choice among Medicare supplement insurance policies.)

order to find out the cost of policy B, the chooser must uncover that cell and read the information. The information search pattern, as the chooser uncovers cells in the matrix, is recorded by the experimenters. This data yields direct measures of thoroughness and uncertainty, and indirect measures of choice strategy based on the amount, sequence, and timing of information acquisition (see Payne et al., 1988, for examples of a typical analysis of choice strategy and efficiency).

Experiments of this nature have greatly clarified the means by which people undertake this type of choice task. Questions of interest that can be answered involve whether choosers adopt a primarily alternative-based or attribute-based strategy, whether they search sequentially or nonsequentially, and how much and what types of information they use. Generally, participants are typed according to their search patterns into one or more of approximately eight choice strategies which have been identified: weighted additive rule, weighted difference rule, equal weight, satisficing, lexicographic, elimination by aspects, majority of confirming dimensions, frequency of bad features, and some additional combinatorial strategies (Payne et al., 1993, provide a comprehensive discussion). These strategies have been extensively studied and their optimality, efficiency, and the conditions under which they both are likely to be exhibited and likely to fail are well established.

Information search processes can be divided into two categories of *compensatory* and *noncompensatory* strategies. In terms of cognitive load, compensatory strategies typically require more processing. These strategies utilize rules whereby information is summed, weighted, or averaged for each alternative. A good example of a compensatory strategy is a weighted additive model. Using this particular strategy, the chooser weights the various attributes according to their perceived importance and then adds up these weighted values across the attributes (n.b., this is essentially the same process as that captured by the linear regression models for judgment that are used in the lens model analysis, see above). The alternative with the highest overall value is then chosen.

For example, if the task is to choose between a number of health insurance policies, the chooser who follows this strategy will first look at the choice attributes (e.g., monthly fee, deduction for an office exam, hospital coverage), and assign them weights depending on their relative personal importance. For each alternative, a total is then calculated by multiplying the value of each attribute by its weight (e.g., monthly fee = $58, deduction for an office exam = $15, but note that these values must be rescaled on a psychologically meaningful metric). By summing up these weighted values for each alternative, it is relatively easy to determine which option is expected to yield the most satisfaction. These approaches are compensatory in that, through averaging or weighting, a low (unattractive) value on one attribute may be compensated for by a high (desirable) value on another. So, a expensive policy might still be most attractive because its coverage is so comprehensive. Noncompensatory strategies, on the other hand, usually economize processing loads and tend to yield a final choice based on an incomplete search, because alternatives are eliminated from consideration after they have been only partially examined. For example, in a noncompensatory strategy, such as elimination by aspects, a low value on a single attribute often will eliminate that alternative from future consideration. In the insurance policy choice task, we might set a cutoff whereby we do not want to pay more than $50 a month in fees, or will not consider any policy with less than $10,000 in hospitalization coverage. Therefore we can quickly rule out any alternative which possesses attribute values outside these criteria.

The typical pattern observed in a consumer choice (e.g., which apartment to rent, which television to purchase) is an initial winnowing process exhibiting a cursory noncompensatory attribute-based strategy, like satisficing or elimination by aspects, which continues until the choice set retains only two or three alternatives. Damasio (1994) has argued that such preliminary winnowing stages are essential for adaptive decision making and even that primitive emotional reaction-based elimination processes may be fundamental to effective choice. While not optimal, this initial process does eliminate obviously unsuitable alternatives, and reflects the tendency of the chooser to reduce the choice set to a more manageable level numerically, and hence cognitively, before embarking on the second stage. At this point, when the choice set is small, a more thorough compensatory, alternative-based strategy is generally followed. One of the weighted additive strategies is a good example of this kind of almost optimal strategy (Onken, Hastie, & Revelle, 1985). Measures of strategy and thoroughness also can be related to summary indexes of cognitive load and risk aversion–risk seeking.

Previous research. While these types of choice tasks have been extensively researched in college students and adults, once again there are few studies that look at choice strategies in relation to age. Johnson (1990) presented two age groups of participants (college, mean age = 19, versus retired, mean age = 66) a six automobile choice set and asked them to select the car they would purchase for their own use. The information about the cars was presented on an information board as described above, so the experimenter could trace the choosers' search paths as they examined information describing each car on nine attributes (e.g., price, safety record, handling). Although both groups reached their decisions in approximately the same amount of time, college students searched through more information and were more likely to use a compensatory choice strategy, compared to retired participants. Johnson (1993) provided a systematic replication of the basic experiment, this time asking participants to choose the most desirable apartment to rent. This study also compared think-aloud with silent choice processes and found that the process was slower, but not otherwise different under think-aloud conditions.

The finding that older adults review less information before rendering a choice is consistent with the many indications that older adults' working memory capacity and fluency is reduced compared to younger people's (Park et al., 1996). Although it is possible, as the author suggested, that factors such as experience in the domain and motivation may have influenced the choice strategies, we think is that it is likely that the older adults adopted strategies to minimize working memory load. Such strategies would mean they looked at fewer pieces of information, took more time on each piece of information, and engaged in less averaging and weighting. Of course, this reliance on a less cognitively demanding strategy does not necessarily imply that the decision was poorer. As we have noted, accuracy in judgment tasks is difficult to assess, and it is possible that the presumably greater experience of older adults in automobile purchase choice would allow them to choose competently with less information.

Discussion. One major hypothesis concerning the performance of older adults on choice tasks is based on the assumption that working memory abilities decline with age. Thus, older people would be more likely to exhibit choice strategies that have reduced "cognitive load" requirements. The findings from Johnson (1990) are certainly consistent with this hypothesis, but further research is needed to provide a detailed picture of choice strategies across the lifespan. It might be especially instructive to study the effects of choice time deadlines on the performance of people across the adult lifespan. One pessimistic possibility is that under some conditions, older people both would lack processing capacity and be inflexible, leaving them exercising demanding choice strategies but doing so badly.

Risky decisions

The final popular laboratory judgment and decision making task involves making risky decisions. By risky decisions, we mean choosing one course of action from a set of two or more, where there is uncertainty (usually expressed as a numerical probability) about what objective consequences will occur contingent on the decision (under the traditional definition, only decisions where probabilities are known should be properly called "risky decisions"). These decision tasks require decision makers to integrate judgments, under uncertainty with assessments of the personal value and consequences, and to choose the course of action that is most likely to achieve the decision maker's goals (Dawes, 1998, provides a comprehensive review of research and theory on behavioral decision making). Many important and difficult decisions fall into this category. The decision of whether to invest money in the unpredictable stock market or instead to invest it in a less "risky" option such as a treasury bond; the decision about which therapy to choose for a serious illness or disability, where any of the options have uncertain results; or consequential social decisions about marriage and child rearing. The situation that is considered the prototype risky decision in laboratory research involves betting in the games of chance (roulette, blackjack, craps) as in a commercial casino.

Measuring accuracy is difficult in risky decision problems although, as in simple choice, we can use expected value as one standard of correctness. However, even in the context of casino-style gambles, it might be rational to choose a gamble with a high possible outcome even though it has a relatively low expected value. Consider a situation in which you need a minimum of $500 in order to purchase something you desperately need (perhaps a bus ticket home). Then you would play low expected value bets because they are the only options available that might achieve your aspiration level. Or, consider the reverse situation in which you cannot afford to lose more than $100 because that is all you have in your pocket. Again you might choose to play bets with relatively low expected values, and low maximum losses, to insure against a catastrophic loss. While economic theory has provided us with yardsticks in the form of ideally rational models such as utility theory, which seek to define what a "normative" or optimal decision would be (usually under the assumption that expected value is to be maximized across repeated plays of the gamble), there is much controversy within the field of judgment and decision making regarding the descriptive validity of these models (see Dawes, 1998, for a thorough review of these issues concerning rationality).

Research methods. The classic laboratory risky decision making tasks involve situations where research participants are offered the chance to play monetary gambles of various types. A typical gamble might consist of two options: a "sure thing" choice and a risky choice. For example, a subject might be offered the choice of either a sure $50 or a chance to flip a coin, where "heads" means they receive $100, but "tails" means they get nothing (see Figure 14.3 for an example). Although both options in the this example have the same positive expected value ($50), the majority of college student participants take the safe option in this instance and select the sure $50, typing people as generally risk averse where gains are concerned. In contrast, however, if the same gamble is presented to participants, but instead framed as a loss (either a sure $50 loss or the chance to lose either nothing or $100), people usually take the risky option, indicating that they are risk seeking for losses.

Another method of eliciting preferences for gambles with a positive expected value is to ask subjects how much money they would need to receive in order to sell the chance to play the gamble (or conversely, how much they would pay for the opportunity to play the gamble). Similarly for negative gambles, subjects can be asked what is the highest price they would pay to avoid having to play the particular gamble. In the course of an experiment, a subject usually is presented with many gambles, varying in both magnitude and probability of gain and loss. Based on preferences among these gambles, the risk propensity of subjects can be established. Although there are well-described limits on traditional subjective expected

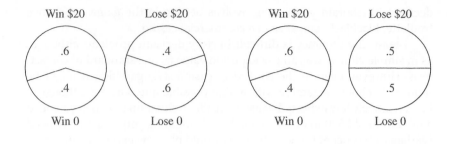

Win $20   Lose $20   Win $20   Lose $20

.6   .4   .6   .5

.4   .6   .4   .5

Win 0   Lose 0   Win 0   Lose 0

Different distributions   Same distributions
but same stated   but different stated
probabilities   probabilities
and payoffs   and payoffs

FIG. 14.3.
Example duplex bets
displayed as wheel of
fortune spinners. (The
duplex and simple bets
in the right hand
column have equal
expected values
[Expected Value = $4],
but different variances:
Variance [Duplex Bet] =
$192 versus Variance
[Simple Bet] = $384.)

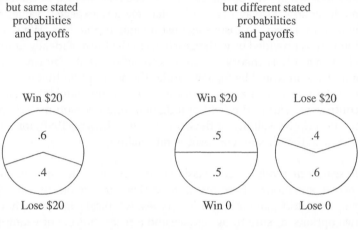

Win $20   Win $20   Lose $20

.6   .5   .4

.4   .5   .6

Lose $20   Win 0   Lose 0

utility theory, subjects' results usually are summarized by best-fitting subjective probability and utility functions. Parameters of the typical subjective probability or "decision weight" functions (relating objective probabilities to subjective scales) can be interpreted as indicating a tendency to overestimate the probabilities of low probability events (or to overweight unlikely outcomes) and to underestimate the probabilities of high-probability events (e.g., prospect theory's modal S-shaped decision weight function: Gonzalez & Wu, 1999; Tversky & Fox, 1995; Tversky & Kahneman, 1992). But, other patterns are observed and can be interpreted as reflecting individual differences in security-risk orientations or differential sensitivities to outcomes or decision-relevant information (Weber, 1994). Similarly, most of the theories in the (non)expected utility family provide methods to estimate and interpret the functions relating objective outcome values and subjective values (often called utilities). A common finding is that the curves for positive gain outcomes are concave, indicating a tendency for gains to diminish in impact as the net amount gained increases (the first $10 gained "feels" like a dramatic change, the gain of $10 from $1,000 to $1,010 "feels" like a miniscule change). Similarly, for losses, a convex function applies, suggesting that loss amounts also show a diminishing impact subjectively (the first $10 loss "hits" much harder than an additional $10 loss after $1,000 has just been lost). The overall slope of the function also provides a measure of sensitivity, for example, losses are usually associated with steeper curves than gains, implying that losses hurt more than equal gains "feel good" (the negative experience of losing $100 is more intense than the positive experience of winning $100). Other theoretical frameworks provide for additional parameter-based measures of individual decision making habits; for example, security-potential/aspiration theory includes measures of decision weight and utility functions plus an estimate of "level of aspiration," an outcome with a special significance in choice among risky options (and the personal value of an uncertain option is determined partly by the chances it will satisfy the decision maker's aspiration level or situational goal; Lopes & Oden, 1999).

Previous research.   Dror, Katona, and Mungur (1998) asked two age groups (younger, mean age = 19, versus older, mean age = 74) to play a card game modeled on blackjack. Participants were shown their hands, their opponents' hands, and then made a decision to take another card or not (trying to form a hand as close in value to "21 points" as possible, without exceeding "21"). There were no payoffs and the participants were not told the results of any of their decisions. No age differences in speed, quality, or riskiness in playing the game were observed (although an examination of the displayed results showed a clear and nearly significant pattern of slower responding at all levels of risk for the older adults).

Hershey and Wilson (1997) studied retirement investment decisions by two groups of participants, a younger group (mean age = 19) and an old group (mean age = 71). The participants solved six investment problems which involved decisions about how much money an individual should allocate to an employer-sponsored retirement fund. The quality of the allocation decisions did not differ reliably between the two age groups, though younger participants appeared to profit more from an investment training course (although the effect was not reported to be reliable). Younger participants who had not had training were distinctively overconfident in their decisions, although all participants appeared to exhibit some degree of overconfidence.

Green, Fry, and Myerson (1994) conducted a study of discounting of delayed monetary payoffs in three age groups, sixth grade students (mean age = 12), college students (mean age = 20), and older adults (mean age = 68). All three age groups showed delay discounting, such that the amount of an immediate reward judged to be of value equal to a delayed reward decreased as a function of delay. The rate of discounting was highest for the sixth graders and lowest for the oldest participants. This may be interpretable as a lifespan trend toward increased self-control or decreased impulsiveness (cf., Mischel, Shoda, & Rodriguez, 1989).

Curley, Eraker, and Yates (1984) presented subjects with a scenario in which they were to imagine themselves with a medical complaint which made it very difficult to walk more than a couple of blocks at a time. They were told that a treatment was available for this illness, but that it was risky. There was a chance that the treatment would mean they could walk twice as far as before, but there also was a chance that the treatment would leave them in worse shape than they were originally. The odds given for a successful treatment were manipulated by the experimenters. The task for the subjects was to decide whether to opt for the treatment or not. There were no clear age-related differences in the options selected. An interesting result of the study was that there was a much stronger tendency (45% vs. 20%) for older subjects to let the doctor decide what course of action to take.

Meyer, Russo, and Talbot (1995) conducted a similar study in which women were presented with a realistic unfolding health scenario involving breast cancer. The women, ranging in age from 18 to 88, were grouped into younger (18–39), middle-aged (40–64), and older (65–88) age groups and presented with text material describing a scenario which starts when a lump is discovered in a woman's breast. They then received additional information and made a sequence of decisions concerning exploratory tests and treatments. Older women sought less information and made faster treatment decisions than younger women, although the ultimate decisions did not differ across age groups.

There have been many efforts to assess age differences in risk attitudes, the preference for riskier versus more secure uncertainty options. The interest in risk taking and age may derive from the common stereotype, supported by statistics, that adolescence is a time of heightened risk taking in everyday behaviors (e.g., higher rates of traffic accidents and sexually transmitted diseases). One explanation for this nonmonotonic relationship is that adolescents, compared to other age groups, perceive themselves as relatively invulnerable to risks. However, questionnaire studies asking about everyday (e.g., automobile, substance abuse, medical, accident) risk perceptions have failed to consistently support the "adolescent invulnerability hypothesis" (Quadrel, Fischhoff, & Davis, 1993, found that most respondents overestimated their personal invulnerability, but this tendency was not greater for adolescents; although Glik, Kronenfeld, Jackson, & Zhang, 1999, found that young men unrealistically did not see themselves as at greater risk for traffic accidents). There also is a suggestion that adolescents may be biologically predisposed to prefer intense, novel experiences that are associated with riskier courses of action. Adolescents score higher than older or younger respondents on measures of sensation seeking habits (Zuckerman, Eysenck, & Eysenck, 1978), although it is possible that adolescents simply value different activities and that their risk-seeking behavior is a byproduct of their higher values for sexual, athletic, criminal, and other outcomes.

Okun (1976; see also Botwinick, 1969; Calhoun & Hutchison, 1981) reviewed several questionnaire studies of risk taking in hypothetical situations (mostly using Wallach & Kogan's, 1961, Choice Dilemmas Questionnaire). Vroom and Pahl (1971) provide a representative example study, in which they administered the Choice Dilemmas Questionnaire to 1,484 managers and observed a significant relationship such that older respondents were more conservative, more risk averse than younger respondents.

Okun and his colleagues also conducted several studies of people's preferences for problems to solve at various levels of difficulty (cf., Atkinson, 1957), where the difficulty level selected is interpreted as willingness to take the risk of failing an intellectual task (e.g., Okun & Siegler, 1976; Okun, Stock, & Ceurvorst, 1980). These results could be interpreted simply as an increasing reluctance to respond, as easily as evidence for cautiousness or risk aversion (cf., Salthouse, 1982, especially pp. 83–102). A further problem with simple versions of this task is that the intrinsic and extrinsic incentives contingent on success and failure are unclear. In natural versions of the task, there usually are greater rewards associated with less probable (greater difficulty) outcomes. In two studies in which an attempt was made to control expected value (Reward × Probability of Success = Constant), older participants (in their sixties and seventies) selected less difficult problems than younger participants (teens and twenties; Okun & DiVesta, 1976; Okun & Siegler, 1976). However, when expected values varied across problems, so that the expected values for attempting more difficult problems were higher, no age differences were observed (Okun & Elias, 1977). Holliday (1988) also found no significant effect of age on riskiness, and found that older adults chose certain and uncertain options at the same rates as younger adults.

Perhaps the most demanding decision making task that has been used to study the effects of aging involved asking managers to play the role of members of the four-person national security council of a fictitious nation (Streufert, Pogash, Piasecki, & Post, 1990). The simulation required the participants to study background materials about the nation and then to "manage" the country for several hours that simulated on a compressed timescale the events occurring over a several month time span. Three age groups were recruited: younger teams with members age 28 to 35, middle-aged teams (age 45 to 55), and older teams (age 65 to 75). The simulation task posed several complex management, governance, and diplomacy problems to each team. The teams made decisions about political and economic actions and then reacted to the outcomes of those actions in a dynamic fashion. Older teams considered less information, made fewer decisions, and were less responsive to incoming information compared to younger teams. However, older teams responded to unexpected positive opportunities and negative emergencies as effectively as younger teams.

Discussion.   There seems to be a tendency for older people to search for and consider less decision-relevant information, and to decide more slowly than younger people. Older people also seem to discount future money payoffs at a lower rate than do younger people, perhaps indicating less impulsive decision-making habits. We can discern no consistent changes in risk-attitudes or actual risk taking habits across the adult, postadolescent lifespan (see also Botwinick, 1984, chap. 10).

Conclusion

Obviously, we do not have many behavioral research findings that tell us about changes in judgment and decision making capacities or habits. The few studies we have suggest that older adults are less flexible in learning and revising judgment and choice strategies, that they prefer less cognitively demanding strategies, and that they are slower and perhaps more cautious than younger adults, although they consider less decision-relevant information than younger decision makers. However, the good news is that there are several well-established research paradigms that easily can be applied to study age-related changes. And, the major hypotheses about cognitive aging support many predictions (albeit, perhaps not predictions that discriminate among the hypotheses) about the performance of judgment, choice, and decision tasks.

References

Alloy, L. B., & Tabachnik, N. (1984). Assessment of covariation by humans and animals: The joint influence of prior expectation and current situational information. *Psychological Review, 91,* 112–149.

Atkinson, J. W. (1957). Motivational determinants of risk-taking behavior. *Psychological Review, 64,* 359–372.

Attig, M. S., & Hasher, L. (1980). The processing of frequency of occurrence information in adults. *Journal of Gerontology, 35,* 66–69.

Baltes, P. B., & Lindenberger, U. (1997). Emergence of a powerful connection between sensory and cognitive functions across the adult lifespan: A new window to the study of cognitive aging? *Psychology and Aging, 12,* 12–21.

Botwinick J. (1969). Disinclination to venture response versus cautiousness in responding: Age differences. *Journal of Genetic Psychology, 115,* 55–62.

Botwinick, J. (1984). *Aging and behavior: A comprehensive integration of research findings* (3rd ed.). New York: Springer.

Brehmer, B. (1980). In one word: Not from experience. *Acta Psychologica, 45,* 223–241.

Brunswik, E. (1952). The conceptual framework of psychology. In *International encyclopedia of unified science* (Vol. 1, pp. 4–102). Chicago: University of Chicago Press.

Byrnes, J. P. (1998). *The nature and development of decision making: A self-regulation model.* Mahwah, NJ: Erlbaum.

Calhoun, R. E., & Hutchison, S. L., Jr. (1981). Decision-making in old age: Cautiousness and rigidity. *International Journal of Aging and Human Development, 13,* 89–98.

Castellan, N. J. (1992). Relations between linear models: Implications for the lens model. *Organizational Behavior and Human Decision Processes, 51,* 364–381.

Cerella, J. (1990). Aging and information processing rates in the elderly. In J. E. Birren & K. W. Schaie (Eds.), *Handbook of the psychology of aging* (3rd ed., pp. 201–221). New York: Academic Press.

Chapman, L. J., & Chapman, J. P. (1967). Genesis of popular but erroneous psychodiagnostic observations. *Journal of Abnormal Psychology, 74,* 271–280.

Chasseigne, G., Mullet, E., & Stewart, T. R. (1997). Aging and multiple cue probability learning: The case of inverse relationships. *Acta Psychologica, 97,* 235–252.

Cooksey, R. W. (1996). *Judgment analysis: Theory, methods, and applications.* San Diego: Academic Press.

Craik, F. I. M. (1994). Memory changes in normal aging. *Current Directions in Psychological Science, 3,* 155–158.

Curley, S. P., Eraker, S. A., & Yates, J. F. (1984). An investigation of patients' reactions to therapeutic uncertainty. *Medical Decision Making, 4,* 501–511.

Damasio, A. R. (1994). *Descartes' error: Emotion, reason, and the human brain.* New York: Putnam.

Dawes, R. M. (1998). Behavioral decision making and judgment. In D. T. Gilbert, S. T. Fiske, & G. Lindzey (Eds.), *The handbook of social psychology* (4th ed., Vol. 1, pp. 497–548). New York: McGraw-Hill.

Dror, I. E., Katona, M., & Mungur, K. (1998). Age differences in decision making: To take a risk or not? *Gerontology, 44,* 67–71.

Fischhoff, B. (1988). Judgment and decision making. In R. J. Sternberg & E. E. Smith (Eds.), *The psychology of human thought* (pp. 153–187). New York: Cambridge University Press.

Glik, D. C., Kronenfeld, J. J., Jackson, K., & Zhang, W. (1999). Comparison of traffic accident and chronic disease risk perceptions. *American Journal of Health Behavior, 23,* 198–209.

Gonzalez, R., & Wu, G. (1999). On the shape of the probability weighting function. *Cognitive Psychology, 38,* 129–166.

Green, L., Fry, A. F., & Myerson, J. (1994). Discounting of delayed rewards: A lifespan comparison. *Psychological Science, 5,* 33–36.

Hammond, K. R. (1955). Probabilistic functioning and the clinical method. *Psychological Review, 62,* 255–262.

Hartley, A. A. (1989). The cognitive ecology of problem solving. In L. W. Poon, D. C. Rubin, & B. A. Wilson (Eds.), *Everyday cognition in adulthood and late life* (pp. 300–329). New York: Cambridge University Press.

Hasher, L., & Zacks, R. (1984). Automatic processing of fundamental information: The case of frequency of occurrence. *American Psychologist, 39,* 1372–1388.

Hershey, D. A., & Wilson, J. A. (1997). Age differences in performance awareness of a complex financial decision-making task. *Experimental Aging Research, 23,* 257–273.

Holliday, S. G. (1988). Risky-choice behavior: A life-span analysis. *International Journal of Aging and Human Development, 27,* 25–33.

Johnson, M. M. S. (1990). Age differences in decision making: A process methodology for examining strategic information processing. *Journal of Gerontology: Psychological Sciences, 45*(2), 75–78.

Johnson, M. M. S. (1993). Thinking about strategies during, before, and after making a decision. *Psychology and Aging, 8,* 231–241.

Kahneman, D., & Diener, E. (Eds.). (1999). *Well-being: The foundations of hedonic psychology.* New York: Russell Sage.

Kausler, D. H., & Puckett, J. M. (1980). Frequency judgments and correlated cognitive abilities in young and elderly adults. *Journal of Gerontology, 35,* 376–382.

Kirchner, W. K. (1958). Age differences in short-term retention of rapidly changing information. *Journal of Experimental Psychology, 55,* 352–358.

Klayman, J., & Ha, Y.-W. (1989). Hypothesis testing in rule discovery: Strategy, structure, and content. *Journal of Experimental Psychology: Learning, Memory, and Cognition, 15,* 596–604.

Knowlton, B. J., Squire, L. R., & Gluck, M. A. (1994). Probabilistic classification learning in amnesia. *Learning and Memory, 1,* 106–120.

Lopes, L. L., & Oden, G. C. (1999). The role of aspiration level in risky choice: A comparison of cumulative prospect theory and SP/A theory. *Journal of Mathematical Psychology, 43,* 286–313.

Meyer, B. J. F., Russo, C., & Talbot, A. (1995). Discourse comprehension and problem solving: Decisions about the treatment of breast cancer by women across the lifespan. *Psychology and Aging, 10,* 84–103.

Mischel, W., Shoda, Y., & Rodriguez, M. (1989, May). Delay of gratification in children. *Science, 244,* 933–938.

Morris, R. G., Gick. M. L., & Craik, F. I. M. (1988). Processing resources and age differences in working memory. *Memory and Cognition, 16,* 362–366.

Mutter, S. A., & Pliske, R. M. (1994). Aging and illusory correlation in judgments of co-occurrence. *Psychology and Aging, 9,* 53–63.

Okun, M. A. (1976). Adult age and cautiousness in decision. *Human Development, 19,* 220–233.

Okun, M. A., & DiVesta, F. J. (1976). Cautiousness in adulthood as a function of age and instructions. *Journal of Gerontology, 31,* 571–576.

Okun, M. A., & Elias, C. S. (1977). Cautiousness in adulthood as a function of age and payoff structure. *Journal of Gerontology, 32,* 451–455.

Okun, M. A., & Siegler, I. C. (1976). Relation between preference for immediate risk and adult age in men: A cross-cultural validation. *Developmental Psychology, 12,* 565–566.

Okun, M. A., Stock, W. A., & Ceurvorst, R. W. (1980). Risk taking through the adult lifespan. *Experimental Aging Research, 6,* 463–473

Onken, J., Hastie, R., & Revelle, W. (1985). Individual differences in the use of simplification strategies in a complex decision making task. *Journal of Experimental Psychology: Human Perception and Performance, 11,* 14–27.

Park, D. C., Smith, A. D., Lautenschlager, G., Earles, J., Frieske, D., Zwahr, M., & Gaines, C. (1996). Mediators of long-term memory performance across the life-span. *Psychology and Aging, 11,* 621–637.

Parkinson, S. R., Lindholm, J. M., & Inman, V. W. (1982). An analysis of age differences in immediate recall. *Journal of Gerontology, 37,* 425–431.

Payne, J. W., Bettman, J. R., & Johnson, E. J. (1988). Adaptive strategy selection in decision making. *Journal of Experimental Psychology: Learning, Memory, and Cognition, 14,* 534–552.

Payne, J. W., Bettman, J. R., & Johnson, E. J. (1993). *The adaptive decision maker.* New York: Cambridge University Press.

Piaget, J., & Inhelder, B. (1975). *The origin of the idea of chance in children.* New York: Norton.

Pliske, R. M., & Mutter, S. A. (1996). Age differences in accuracy of confidence judgments. *Experimental Aging Research, 22,* 199–216.

Quadrel, M. J., Fischhoff, B., & Davis, W. (1993). Adolescent (in)vulnerability. *American Psychologist, 48,* 102–116.

Salthouse, T. A. (1982). *Adult cognition: An experimental psychology of human aging.* New York: Springer-Verlag.

Salthouse, T. A. (1996). The processing-speed theory of adult age differences in cognition. *Psychological Review, 103,* 403–428.

Slovic, P. (1990). Choice. In D. N. Osherson & E. E. Smith (Eds.), *Thinking: An invitation to cognitive science* (Vol. 3, pp. 89–116). Cambridge, MA: MIT Press.

Stewart, T. R. (1988). Judgment analysis: Procedures. In B. Brehmer & C. R. B. Joyce (Eds.), *Human judgment: The SJT view* (pp. 41–74). Amsterdam: Elsevier.

Stoltzfus, E. R., Hasher, L., & Zacks, R. T. (1996). Working memory and aging: Current status of the inhibitory view. In J. T. E. Richardson, R. W. Engle, L. Hasher, R. H. Logie, E. R. Stoltzfus, & R. T. Zacks (Eds.), *Working memory and human cognition* (pp. 66–88). New York: Oxford University Press.

Streufert, S., Pogash, R., Piasecki, M., & Post, G. M. (1990). Age and management team performance. *Psychology and Aging, 5,* 551–559.

Tversky, A., & Fox, C. R. (1995). Weighing risk and uncertainty. *Psychological Review, 102,* 269–283.

Tversky, A., & Kahneman, D. (1992). Advances in prospect theory: Cumulative representation of uncertainty. *Journal of Risk and Uncertainty, 5,* 297–323.

Vroom, V. H., & Phal, B. (1971). Relationship between age and risk taking among managers. *Journal of Applied Psychology, 55,* 399–405.

Wallach, M. A., & Kogan, N. (1961). Aspects of judgment and decision making: Interrelationships and changes with age. *Behavioral Science, 6,* 23–36.

Weber, E. U. (1994). From subjective probabilities to decision weights: The effects of asymmetric loss functions on the evaluation of uncertain outcomes and events. *Psychological Bulletin, 114,* 228–242.

Yates, J. F., & Patalano, A. L. (1999). Decision making and aging. In D. C. Park, R. W. Morrell, & K. Shifren (Eds.), *Processing of medical information in aging patients: Cognitive and human factors perspectives* (pp. 31–54). Mahwah, NJ: Erlbaum.

Zuckerman, M., Eysenck, S. B. G., & Eysenck, H. J. (1978). Sensation seeking in England and America: Cross-cultural, age, and sex comparisons. *Journal of Consulting and Clinical Psychology, 46,* 139–149.

Author Index

A

Abendroth, L. J., 156, 166
Aberdeen, J. S., 81, 181, 183, 183f, 185
Acker, J. D., 102
Ackerman, A. M., 136f, 137
Ackerman, P. L., 222
Adan, A., 151, 152
Aguirre, G., 95
Ahlsén, 37
Akiyama, H., 141, 144
Alba, J. W., 123, 164
Albert, M., 119
Albert, M. L., 203
Albert, M. S., 97, 103
Alexander, A. H., 79–80, 179, 181, 185
Alexander, R. A., 222
Allard, L., 203
Alloy, L. B., 259
Allport, A., 154
Almirall, H., 152
Alpert, N. M., 103
Anagnopoulos, C., 184, 197, 203, 206
Anderson, E. S., 203
Anderson, J. R., 121, 133
Anderson, M., 151, 152
Anderson, N. D., 103, 104
Andres, D., 199
Anes, M. D., 191
Anschutz, L., 118
Arai, Y., 140
Arbuckle, T., 199
Arenberg, D., 134
Armbruster, T., 242
Armon, C., 30
Arthur, W., Jr., 222
Arvey, R. D., 227
Asburn, G., 205
Atkinson, J. W., 269
Atkinson, R. C., 76
Attig, M. S., 202, 259
Avery, D. H., 152
Avolio, B. J., 225

B

Babcock, R. L., 81, 226
Back, K. W., 238

Bäckman, L., 33, 35, 36, 37, 75, 104
Baddeley, A. D., 10, 76, 81, 132, 182, 186, 224, 241
Bagdanovitch, N., 101
Bahrick, H. P., 143, 144
Bahrick, P. O., 143
Baldi, R. A., 119, 120
Baldwin, C. L., 24
Ball, K. K., 70, 71, 223
Balota, D. A., 100
Baltes, M. M., 25
Baltes, P. B., 16–17, 18, 18f, 24, 25, 26, 27, 28, 29, 30, 31, 32, 43, 79, 182, 226, 233, 254
Bandura, A., 119, 120
Banich, M. T., 109
Bargh, J. A., 121, 122, 124
Baron, A., 64
Barrett, A., 100
Barrett, G. V., 222, 223, 224
Barsalou, L. W., 121
Bartlett, F. C., 87
Bartolucci, G., 204, 207
Bates, P. B., 3
Bayles, K., 203
Beard, B. L., 71, 223
Beasley, D. S., 186, 190
Beauvois, M. F., 81
Beckwith, B. E., 151, 152
Belli, R. F., 141, 144, 238, 242
Ben-Ishai, R., 223
Ben-Zur, H., 84
Bennett, J., 221
Benson, K. A., 140
Berg, C. A., 28, 31, 99
Berry, J. M., 116, 117, 119, 120
Bertus, E. L., 63, 64
Bess, F. H., 186, 190
Bettman, J. R., 261, 262
Betz, A., 132
Bhatt, A., 161
Bielby, D. D., 199
Billington, C., 198, 206, 207
Birchmore, D., 221
Birren, J. E., 9
Bischoping, K., 141, 144
Bishop, G., 238

Blair, E., 241
Blankenship, S. E., 156
Blanton, R., 108
Boden, D., 199
Bodenhausen, G. V., 151, 156, 164, 245
Bogner, M. S., 219
Boich, L. H., 187, 198, 205
Bonnet, M. H., 152
Bookstein, F., 106
Boone, D. R., 203
Borkowski, J. G., 118
Bosman, E. A, 34, 37
Botwinick, J., 97, 238, 268, 269
Bourhis, R. Y., 204, 207
Boyes, C., 198
Bradburn, N., 233, 235, 240, 241, 245, 247, 249
Brady, C. B., 61
Brandstädter, J., 33, 34
Bransford, J. D., 82, 178
Brant, L. J., 181
Brass, C., 151, 152
Braune, R., 64
Brehmer, B., 257
Brennan, P. L., 85
Breton, M. E., 222
Brewer, M. B., 124
Brewer, W. F., 131, 132
Brock, T. L., 166
Brouwer, W. H., 64, 224
Brown, G. M., 102
Brown, N. R., 132
Brownell, H., 185, 200, 201
Brownlee, S., 177
Bruni, J. R., 223
Brunswik, E., 255
Buckner, R. L., 35, 36
Buela-Casal, G., 152
Bunge, S. A., 101, 102
Burke, D. M., 15, 77, 84, 85
Burt, C. D. B., 132
Burton, S., 241
Butler, R. N., 137
Butters, N, 137
Byrd, M., 4, 10–11, 82, 83
Byrnes, A. M., 222
Byrnes, J. P., 259

C
Caballo, V. E., 152
Cabeza, R., 103, 104
Cacioppo, J. T., 165
Calev, A., 98
Calhoun, R. E., 268
Camp, C. J., 118

Caplan, D., 185, 186, 201
Caporael, L. R., 198, 204
Cappeliez, P., 137
Capps, J. L., 184, 202
Carpenter, P. A., 81, 82, 182, 184, 185
Cassileth, B. R., 220
Castellan, N. J., 257
Cattell, R. B., 43
Cavanaugh, J. C., 13, 115, 116, 117, 119, 120, 121, 122, 123, 124, 125, 184
Cave, C. B., 100
Cavigelli, S., 79–80, 179, 181, 185
Cerella, J., 27, 254
Cermak, L. A., 85
Cermak, L. S., 137
Ceurvorst, R. W., 269
Chace, P. M., 137
Chalfonte, B. L., 84
Chantraine, Y., 198
Chao, L. L., 106, 107, 108
Chapman, J. P., 259
Chapman, L. J., 259
Chapman, S. B., 203
Charness, N., 32, 34, 227
Chasseigne, G., 258, 259
Chassein, B., 236
Cherry, B. J., 109
Cherry, K. E., 11–12, 12f, 18, 58, 85, 99, 100
Cheung, H., 184, 198, 202, 205, 206, 207, 208
Cissell, G. M., 223
Clancy, P., 203
Clancy, S. M., 60
Clark, F., 236
Clark, H. H., 235
Clemons, T., 227
Cohen, B. M., 95
Cohen, G., 85, 140, 187, 202
Cohen, J., 102
Cohen, N. J., 137
Coleman, R. E., 103
Collins, L. M., 242
Colonia-Willner, R., 227
Colsher, P. L., 238
Commons, M. L., 30
Connor, L. T., 15
Conrad, H. S., 24, 43
Convit, A., 102
Conway, M. A., 131
Cooksey, R. W., 255
Coquhoun, W. P., 151
Corbetta, M., 35, 36
Corkin, S., 75
Costa, P., 137
Coupland, J., 199

Coupland, N., 199
Cowan, N., 155
Craik, F. I. M., 4, 8, 10–11, 13, 14, 27, 63, 64,
    75, 76, 78, 79, 81, 82, 83, 84, 86, 87, 101,
    102, 103, 104, 106, 186, 254
Crook, T. H., 225
Crossley, M., 64
Crovitz, H. F., 132, 135
Cueto, E., 152
Culbertson, G. H., 204
Cupchik, G. C., 134
Curley, S. P., 267
Czaja, S. J., 227

D
D'Alonzo, G., 151
Damasio, H., 95f, 263
Daneman, M., 80, 80f, 81, 82, 181, 182, 184, 185
Davidson, N., 11, 237, 238
Davidson, R. J., 109
Davies, D. R., 58
Davis, B., 177
Davis, W., 268
Dawes, R. M., 259, 264, 265
de Leon, M. J., 102
De Santi, S., 102
Degl'Innocenti, A., 104
Delbecq-Derouesne, J., 81
Delis, D., 97
Dell, G. S., 77
Dell, T. C., 226
DeMaio, T. J., 240
Dennehey, D. M., 119
Dennehy-Basile, D., 119
Denny, L. L., 103
D'Esposito, M., 95
Deutsch, B., 243, 243t
Diener, E., 261
DiVesta, F. J., 269
Dixon, R. A., 23, 24, 25, 26, 27, 28, 30, 31,
    33, 35, 36, 37, 38, 75, 116, 117, 119, 123, 188
Dobbs, A. R., 81
Donnell, A., 203
Doren, B., 202
Doussard-Roosevelt, J. A., 59–60
Dreisen, N. R., 108
Dror, I. E., 267
Ducharme, J. L., 189
Dudley, W. N., 11–12
Dulaney, C. L., 67
Dumais, S. T., 65
Dupuis, J. H., 102
Dweck, C. S., 120
Dywan, J., 78, 88

E
Earles, J., 6, 7f, 13, 14f, 15, 224, 264
Eaton, T. A., 219
Ebbesen, 133
Echt, K. V., 227
Edwards, H., 207
Eggers, 94
Elias, C. S., 269
Elias, J. W., 61
Elias, M. F., 227
Elias, P. K., 227
Eraker, S. A., 267
Ericsson, K. A., 32
Ershler, W. B., 109
Evans, G. W., 85
Eysenck, H. J., 268
Eysenck, S. B. G., 268

F
Fabiani 97, 104
Farber, E. I., 222
Faulkner, D., 85, 140, 187
Faust, M. E., 100
Fazio, R. H., 123
Fein, D., 97
Feldman, J. M., 117, 118, 119, 120, 121, 122,
    123
Ferreira, F., 191
Ferrs, S. H., 102
Fiedler, K., 242
Filion, D. L., 107
Fischer, S. A., 240
Fischhoff, B., 268
Fischoff, B., 122
Fisk, A. D., 66, 67
Fiske, S. T., 122
Fitzgerald, J. M., 137, 140
Fitzgibbons, P. J., 181, 186, 190
Fivush, R., 131
Flavell, J. H., 116, 118
Folkard, S., 151
Fossum, J. A., 227
Foster, J. C., 43
Fox, C. R., 266
Fozard, J. L., 181
Franklin, H. C., 137
Franks, J. J., 82, 178
Frieske, D. A., 6, 7f, 11–12, 12f, 13, 14f, 15,
    221, 224, 264
Fritz, S., 152
Fromholt, P., 139, 140
Fry, A. F., 267
Frye, K. J., 140
Fuster, J. M., 102

Hilton, D. J., 235
Hippler, H. J., 235, 236, 237, 238, 239, 243, 243t, 247
Hiscock, M., 64
Hitch, G. J., 81, 241
Hof, P. R., 101–102
Holding, D. H., 137
Holland, C. A., 223
Holliday, S. G., 269
Hoptman, M. J., 109
Horne, J., 151, 152
Horwitz, B., 102, 103, 106
Houle, S., 102, 103, 104
Howard, D. V., 78
Howes, J. L., 138
Hoyer, W. J., 60, 100
Hrushesky, W., 151
Hulicka, I. M., 134
Hultsch, D. F., 26, 119, 123, 125, 188
Hummert, M. L., 3, 28, 187, 197, 198, 199, 205
Humphrey, D. G., 69
Hunter, J. E., 225
Hunter, R. F., 225
Hunter, S., 16
Hupet, F. A., 198
Huppert, F. A., 203
Hutchinson, J. M., 203
Hutchinson, J. W., 123
Hutchison, S. L, Jr., 268
Huttenlocher, J., 132
Hyland, D. T., 136f, 137

I

Inhelder, B., 259
Inman, V. W., 81, 254
Intons-Peterson, M. J., 152
Ishihara, K., 152
Ivry, R. B., 98, 99f

J

Jackson, B., 141
Jackson, K., 268
Jacoby, L. L., 6, 77–78, 88, 218
James, W., 57, 61, 62, 64–65, 68, 70
Janowsky, J. S., 104
Jansari, A., 136f, 138
Jarvi, S. D., 140
Jeeves, M. A., 108, 109
Jennings, J. M., 8, 13, 14, 27, 75, 76, 78, 79, 81, 86, 101, 103, 106, 186, 218
Jensen, M., 203
Jerdee, T. H., 227
Joanette, Y., 203
Jobe, J. B., 131
Johnson, C. A., 242

Johnson, E. J., 261, 262
Johnson, M. B., 45
Johnson, M. K., 84
Johnson, M. M. S., 263, 264
Jones, H. E., 24, 43
Jones, T. R., 221
Jonides, J., 105, 106, 107, 109
Just, M. A., 182, 184, 185

K

Kahneman, D., 223, 261, 266
Kane, M. J., 69, 161
Kaplan, E., 97
Kapur, S., 102, 103
Kardes, F. R., 123
Kastenbaum, R., 137
Kaszniak, A. W., 104, 203
Katona, M., 267
Katz, A. N., 138
Kausler, D. H., 260
Kelley, C. L., 227
Kelly, G. A., 121
Kemp, S., 132
Kemper, S., 184, 197, 198, 201, 203, 204, 205, 206, 207, 208
Kempler, D., 185, 203
Kemtes, K., 197, 201
Kerkhof, G. A., 152
Kidder, D., 221
Kihlstrom, J. F., 104, 122
Kiku Annon, T. A., 202
Kincaid, D., 221
Kintsch, W., 180
Kirchner, W. K., 254
Kjelgaard, M. M., 187
Klayman, J., 257
Klein, S. G., 122
Klitz, T., 79
Kluger, A., 102
Knäuper, B., 11, 123, 141, 144, 233, 236, 237, 238, 239, 240, 244, 244t, 246, 247
Knauth, P., 151
Knight, R. T., 102, 106, 107, 108
Knops, U., 204, 207
Knowlton, B. J., 260
Koenig, O., 100
Koeppe, R., 106, 107, 109
Kogan, N., 268
Koh, K., 190f, 191
Konkle, D. F., 186, 190
Koriat, A., 84, 120–121
Korving, H. J., 152
Kosslyn, S. M., 100
Kostovic, I., 101
Koustaal, W. E., 78

McKoon, G., 77
McLachlan, D., 84
McLellan, K., 152
Mecacci, L, 152
Medina, J. J., 24
Mednick, S. A., 156
Meier, R. P., 175
Meinz, E. J., 48
Mello, N. K., 95
Mendelson, J. H., 95
Menon, G., 243
Mentis, M. J., 102, 103
Meredith, S. D., 208
Merikle, P. M., 185
Merrill, S., 119
Metcalfe, J., 115
Meyer, B. J. F., 220, 268
Midkiff, K., 152
Mihal, W. L., 223, 224
Miller, A., 96, 106, 109
Miller, R., 71
Miller, R. L., 223
Milner, B., 75, 100, 104
Mischel, W., 267
Mitchell, D. R., 81, 226
Mitchell, W. W., 152
Mittelman, M. S., 102
Miyake, S., 152
Miyaki, A., 184, 185
Miyasita, A., 152
Miyata, Y., 152
Moes, P., 108, 109
Monk, T. H., 151
Moon, S. J., 177
Moore, R. L., 223
Moore-Ede, M., 151
Morrell, C. H., 181
Morrell, R. W., 11–12, 219, 221, 227
Morris, C. D., 82
Morris, L. W., 81, 83–84, 104
Morris, R. C., 82
Morris, R. G., 81, 104, 254
Morris, R., 97
Morrison, J. H., 101–102
Morrison, M. L., 223
Morrow, D. G., 154
Morton, K. R., 118, 121, 123, 124, 125
Moscovitch, M., 101, 102–103, 103, 105
Müller, G., 236
Mullet, E., 258, 259
Mungur, K., 267
Murdock, B. B., 76
Murphy, D. R., 79
Murphy, K. R., 226
Mushaney, T. J., 202

Mutter, S. A., 258, 259
Myers, S. D., 200
Myerson, J., 97, 267

N
Nair, S., 227
Narens, L., 120–121
Narr, K., 108
Navon, D., 154
Nebes, R. D., 61, 86, 99, 134
Nef, F., 198
Neilsen-Bohlman, L., 102
Neisser, U., 117, 131, 143, 241
Nelson, T. O., 120–121
Nesselroade, J. R., 233
Nestor, P. G., 71
Nicholas, M., 203
Nisbett, R. E., 115, 124
Noelle-Neumann, E., 236, 247
Noller, P., 207
Norman, D. A., 81
Norman, K. A., 78
Norman, S., 184, 198
Norris, M., 119
Nussbaum, J. F., 199
Nyberg, L., 103, 104

O
Obler, L. K., 203
O'Brien, B., 205
Oden, G. C., 267
Okun, M. A., 268, 269
Olson, P. L., 224
Onken, J., 263
Orange, J. B., 203, 207, 208
Ostberg, O., 151, 152
Ostrom, T. M., 239
Othick, M., 198, 205, 206, 207, 208
Outerbridge, A. N., 225
Overman, R. A., 189
Owsley, C., 70, 223

P
Pahl, B., 268
Palmer, H. T., 219
Palmon, R., 226
Paradise, C. A., 227
Parasuraman, R., 58, 61, 62, 71
Parducci, A., 239
Park, D. C., 3, 4, 6, 7, 7f, 8f, 11–12, 12f, 13, 15,
    16, 18, 27, 85, 217, 218, 219, 220, 221, 224,
    225, 226, 227, 233, 237, 238, 244, 244t,
    246, 264
Parkin, A. J., 104, 107, 136f, 138
Parkinson, S. R., 81, 254

Pascualy, R. A., 152
Patalano, A. L., 221, 259
Pavelchak, M., 122
Payne, J. W., 261, 262
Pearson, J. D., 181
Perlmutter, M., 25, 26, 116, 117, 123
Perry, W. I., 30
Persanyi, M. W., 79
Petersen, S. E., 35, 36, 70
Peterson, M. A., 100
Petros, T. V., 151, 152
Pettitt, S., 151, 152
Petty, R. E., 165, 166
Piaget, J., 259
Piasecki, M., 269
Pichora-Fuller, M. K., 79, 80, 80f, 181, 182
Pickett, J. M., 179
Pietrini, P., 102, 103
Pliske, R. M., 258
Plude, D. J., 59
Pogash, R., 269
Pollack, I., 179
Ponds, R. W. H. M., 64, 224
Poon, L. W., 144, 186, 187, 190, 200, 219
Posner, M. I., 70
Post, G. M., 269
Powell, M. C., 123
Prather, P., 185, 200, 201
Pratt, M. W., 198
Presser, S., 233, 235, 245, 246, 247
Pressey, S. L., 24
Pressley, M., 118
Prill, K. A., 63, 64
Proctor, R. W., 71
Prohaska, V., 132
Provenzale, J. M., 103
Prull, M. W., 101, 102
Puckett, J. M., 260
Puglisi, J. T., 6, 7f, 11–12
Pulling, N. H., 224

Q
Quadrel, M. J., 268

R
Rabbitt, P. M. A., 138, 223
Rabinowitz, J. C., 81, 118
Rabinowitz, S., 226
Raghubir, P., 243
Rahhal, T. A., 144, 156, 166
Raichle, M. E., 35, 36
Ranney, T. A., 224
Rapcsak, S. Z., 100
Rapoport, S. I., 106

Rash, S. R., 198
Rasinski, K. A., 233, 245
Ratcliff, R., 77
Ratte, D. J., 223
Rau, M. T., 203
Rauch, S. L., 103
Raz, N., 85, 95, 102, 104, 108
Reese, H. W., 233
Reilly, C., 152
Renshaw, P. F., 95
Reuter-Lorenz, P. A., 93, 96, 106, 106f, 107, 108, 109
Revelle, W., 263
Rhodes, S. R., 225
Ribot, T., 137
Rice, K., 198, 205, 206, 207, 208
Richards, F. A., 30
Rieger, C., 141, 144
Rietveld, W. J., 152
Ripich, D. N., 203
Rips, L. J., 132, 241
Robbins, M. A., 227
Robbins, N. E., 227
Robertson, L. C., 98, 99f
Robins, S., 198
Robinson, J. A., 131, 137, 138
Rocchetti, G., 152
Rocchi, P., 152
Rodgers, W. L., 238
Rodin, J., 119
Rodriguez, M., 267
Roenker, D. L., 71, 223
Rogan, J. D., 63, 64
Rogers, W. A., 57, 63, 64, 66, 67
Rohde, P., 240
Romaniuk, M., 137
Rosen, B., 227
Rosen, M. J., 190f, 191
Ross, M., 125, 242
Ross, M. H., 95
Rubin, D. C., 86, 131, 132, 133, 133f, 134, 135, 136f, 137, 138, 139, 139f, 140, 141f, 143f, 144
Rubin Wetzler & Nebes 86, 134
Rule, B. G., 81
Rupert, M., 227
Rusinek, H., 102
Russo, C., 220, 268
Rutenfranz, J., 151
Ryan, E. B., 125, 187, 205, 207, 208
Rybash, J. M., 100
Rypma, B., 15, 69, 95

S
Sabey, B. E., 223

Swanson, J. M., 83
Swinney, D., 185, 200, 201

T
Tabachnik, N., 259
Talbot, A., 220, 268
Tang, J., 100
Tanke, E. D., 154
Taylor, G. A., 43
Taylor, R. N., 226
Terrell, B. Y., 203
Teuber, H. L., 75
Thielbar, P. R. S., 140
Thomas, C. W., 79
Thompson, C. P., 132
Thompson, K., 203
Thompson, P., 108
Tilse, C. S., 124
Titone, D., 187
Toga, A., 108
Tomoeda, C. K., 203
Tomsak, R., 79
Toppino, T., 87
Tourangeau, R., 131, 233, 234, 245
Trevithick, L., 37
Trott, 97, 104
Tubi, N., 98
Tulving, E., 76, 78, 84, 102, 103, 104, 132
Tun, P. A., 185, 186, 190f, 191, 202
Turkington, T. G., 103
Tversky, A., 266

U
Ulatowska, H. K., 203
Ungerleider, L. G., 102, 103
Upshaw, H. S., 239
Uttal, D. H., 25, 26
Uttl, B., 85

V
Valdiserri, M., 104
van der Geest, W., 152
van Dijk, T. A., 180
van Wolffelaar, P. C., 64, 224
Van Zandt, T., 71
Vandeputte, D., 198, 205, 206, 207, 208
Verhaeghen, P., 48
Vitiello, M V., 152
Vroom, V. H., 268

W
Wade, E., 85
Wagenaar, W. A., 131, 241
Waldfogel, S., 135

Waldman, D. A., 225
Wallace, R. B., 238
Wallach, M. A., 268
Walter, B. M., 107
Wäncke, M., 237
Warren, A., 205, 206
Warren, J., 198, 205, 206, 208
Warrington, E. K., 76, 86
Waters, G. S., 185, 186, 201
Watson, P. C., 36
Waugh, N. C., 81
Wayland, S. C., 187
Weaver, R., 151
Webb, W. B., 152
Weber, E. U., 266
Webster, J. D., 137
Wechsler, D., 97
Weingartner, H., 203
Weiss, R. L., 134
Welford, A. T., 43
Wells, G. L., 166
Wentura, D., 33, 34
Wenzel, A. E., 132, 134, 143f, 144
West, R. L., 105, 116, 119, 188f, 225
West, T., 152
Wetzler, S. E., 86, 134
White, M. F., 223
Wickelgren, W. A., 134
Wickens, C. D., 64, 83
Wildgruber, C., 151
Williams, A., 199
Wilson, A. A., 102
Wilson, B.A., 36
Wilson, G. D., 152
Wilson, J. A., 267
Wilson, T. D., 115, 124
Winbald, B., 101
Wingfield, A., 79–80, 81, 175, 179, 181, 183,
    183f, 184, 185, 186, 187, 189, 190, 190f,
    191, 200, 201, 202
Winkielman, 236
Winocur, G., 101, 102, 103, 105
Winograd, E., 131
Winthorpe, C., 138
Witherspoon, D., 77–78
Withey, S. B., 242
Wittlinger, R. P., 143
Wixted, 133
Wohlwill, J. F., 26
Woodcock, R. W., 45
Woodruff, D. S., 30
Woodruff-Pak, D. S., 94, 101
Worthley, J. S., 85
Wright, L. L., 61

Wu, G., 266
Wurf, E., 121
Wyer, R. S. 123, 245

Y

Yates, J. F., 221, 259, 267
Yoon, C., 151, 152, 153, 154, 156, 164, 165f, 166
Yurgelun-Todd, D. A., 95

Z

Zacks, R. T., 13, 14, 15, 16, 27, 68, 69, 75,
    76, 82, 154, 155, 157, 162, 197, 202, 254, 260

Zajonc, R. B., 87
Zandri, E., 227
Zani, A., 152
Zarahn, E., 95
Zelinski, E. M., 85, 117, 119, 185, 202
Zhang, W., 268
Zola-Morgen, S., 137
Zuckerman, M., 268
Zupiks, R. V., 220
Zurif, E. B., 185, 200, 201
Zwahr, M. D., 6, 7f, 13, 14f, 15, 219, 220, 221,
    224, 264

Subject Index

Elderspeak, 187, 204–207
Environmental support
  on cognitive aging, 34
  on working memory, 11–12
Episodic memory, 82–84
Estimation, and judgment, 255–260
Estimation strategies, for behavior questions,
  241–245
Estrogen replacement therapy, 220–221
Everyday life, cognitive aging on, 217–228. *See
  also* Cognitive aging, and everyday life
Executive function, 105–108
Experience, in workplace competence, 226

F
Factor analysis, single common, 47–48, 48f
Focused attention, 60–61
Formal operations, in life span development,
  30–31
Frequency scales, 236
Frontal lobes
  and content memory, 102–104
  and context memory, 104–105
  and working memory, 105–108, 106f

G
Gains, in cognitive aging, 23–39
  beliefs about, 27–29
  change and development in, 23–24
  conceptualization of, 24–25
  as a function of losses, 35–38
  gain and loss conceptualization in, 24–25
  gains qua gains in, 30–32
  and loss, as complementary perspectives,
    25
  as losses of a lessor magnitude, 32–35
  scholar's perspective in, 26
  textbook portrayals in, 26–27
  vs. cognitive decline, 25
Gains qua gains, 30–32
Garden path sentences, 180
General knowledge, memory of, 141–145
Goals, adjustment of, 33–34

H
Health, cognitive aging on, 219–222
Hemispheres, of brain
  right, laterality studies of, 98–100, 99f
  right, verbal *vs.* nonverbal ability decline in,
    96–98
  structure of, 95f
Heuristics
  in circadian arousal patterns, 164–165, 165t
  in inhibition, 164–165, 165t

I
Illusory correlations, 259
Impairment, organic, on behavioral gains, 36
Independent influences, in age-related
  cognition, 47–48, 47f
Inductive reasoning performance, composite,
  52f, 53f
Information, selection of, 59–60, 59f
Inhibition
  on attention, 68–69
  in cognitive function decline, 14–16
Inhibition, in circadian arousal patterns, 155–
  167
  access function of, 156–157, 157t
  deletion function of, 157–160, 159f
  heuristics in, 164–165, 165t
  persuasion on, 165–167, 166t, 167t
  stop signal of, 160–161, 160f
  susceptibility to, 163–164, 164f
  synchrony of, 161–162, 162t
Intellectual behavior, circadian patterns on,
  153–154
Intelligence, fluid *vs.* crystallized, 43. *See also*
  Cognitive aging, process and product in
Interference effects, on short-term memory,
  107
Interference susceptibility, in circadian arousal
  patterns, 163–164, 164f
Intergenerational communication, 199
Interhemispheric interactions, 108–109
Interviews, face-to-face, 240

J
Judgment, and decision making, 253–270
  choice in, 260–264
  judgment and estimation in, 255–260
  risky decisions in, 264–269
Judgment recall/computing, 239

K
Knowledge
  acquired, 48–49
  retention of, 217–218

L
Language comprehension, 184–186. *See also*
  Speech perception
Language processing, 179–180
Lateralized stimulus presentations, 98–100, 99f
Lens model, 257–258
Lexical access, 67
Life span development
  beliefs about, 27–29
  postformal operations in, 30–32

Life span development (*continued*)
  scholars' perspective on, 26
  textbook portrayals of, 26–28
Limited time mechanism, 9–10
Literal meaning, 235
Long-term memory, 100–105
Loss. *See also* Cognitive function decline,
    mechanisms of
  change factor in, 23–24
  conceptualization of, 24–25
  and gain, as complementary perspectives, 25
  and gain, in cognitive aging (*See* Cognitive
    aging, gains in)

M

Mattis Organic Mental Status Syndrome
    Examination, 223
Meaning, literal *vs.* pragmatic, 235
Mediation, and age-process relationship, 46–
    47, 47f
Medical care, and cognitive aging, 219–222
Memory, 75–88
  autobiographical, 131–145
  episodic, 82–84
  implicit *vs.* explicit processes in, 77–78
  metamemory as, social-cognitive perspective
    of, 115–126 (*See also* Metamemory)
  perceptual representation system in, 78–80,
    80f
  primary, 80–81
  procedural, 77–78
  remote, 86
  semantic, 84–85
  spatial, 85–86
  truth effect in, 87
  types of, 75–77
  word, 7–8, 7f, 8f
  working, 80–81
  working, processing speed in, 13–14, 14f
  working. research findings on, 6–8, 7f, 8f
Memory, autobiographical, 131–145
  early childhood, 134–136, 135f
  public events and general knowledge, 141–
    145, 142f–144f
  recent past, 132–134, 133f
  remainder of life span, 136–141, 136f, 139f,
    141f
Memory beliefs, 119–120
Memory search tasks, 66
Memory span tests, 163–164
Mental processing power, indexes of, 4
Messages, production and comprehension of,
    197–208
  auditory-based discourse on, 200–201

production changes in, Alzheimer's disease
    on, 202–204
production changes in, by older adults, 197–
    199
production changes in, to older adults, 204–
    207
text-based discourse on, 201–202
Metamemory, social-cognitive perspective of,
    115–126
  attributional processes in, 123–124
  automaticity in, 124
  awareness in, 124
  empirical research on, 118–120
  future directions in, 125–126
  interfaces in, 120–122
  personal attributes recall in, 125
  schematicity in, 122–123
  taxonomy of, 117
  theoretical frameworks in, 118
Morningness-eveningness questionnaire
    (MEQ), 152–153
Morningness-eveningness tendencies
  on behavior, 153–154
  measurement of, 152–153
Motor commands, 94
MouseLab, 261–263, 261f
Multiple regression model, for process times
    product cognition, 51

N

Native capacity, 43
Negative priming effect, 68–69
Neuropsychology, 70
Neuropsychology, cognitive, 93–110
  brain structure in, 93–96, 95f
  frontal lobes in, 105–108, 106f
  interhemispheric interactions in, 108–109
  long-term memory in, 100–105
  right hemisphere aging in, 96–100
Noncompensatory strategies, 263
Nonverbal ability, *vs.* verbal ability, 96–98
Numeric values, in rating scales, 237

O

Occipital lobes, 94
Off-peak time, 156–161
Open questions, *vs.* closed questions, 235–236
Organic impairment, on behavioral gains, 36

P

Palliative meanings, 33–34
Past, recent, memory of, 132–134, 133f
Perception, of speech, 175–192. *See also*
    Speech perception

Perceptual representation system, 78–80, 80f
Permastore, 143–144
Personal attributes recall, 125
Persuasion
    in circadian arousal patterns, 165–167, 166t, 167f
    on inhibition, 165–167, 166t, 167t
Phonological analysis, 177–178
Physical behavior, circadian patterns on, 153–154
Picture memory, 6–7, 7f
Postformal operations, 30–31
Pragmatic meaning, 235
Preceding questions, 237–238
Presbycusis, 80, 80f, 181–182
Primary memory, 80–81
Priming effect, negative, 68–69
Priming paradigm, 77–78
Procedural memory, 77–78
Process, 44–48, 44f–48f
    times product, 50–53, 52f, 53f
    vs. product, 43–44
Process disassociation, 218
Processing resources. See also Cognitive resources
    in working memory, 10–11
Processing speed
    on driving, 224
    on speech perception, 186–189, 188f
Processing speed theory, 9–10
Product, 48–50
Prosody, 187
Prosthetic environment, 34
Public events, memory of, 141–145

Q
Questionnaires. See also Self-reports
    "don't know" answers in, 238
    formal features of, 235–237
    preceding questions in, 237–238
Questions
    attitude, 245–246, 246f
    behavior, 241–245
    open vs. closed, 235–236
    order effects on, 245–247, 246f
    preceding, 237–238

R
Random restoration, 190–191
Range effect, 239–240
Rating scales, 236–237
    context on, 239
    numeric values in, 237
Raven's Advanced Progressive Matrices, 79, 227

Reading, 179
Reasoning performance, composite inductive, 52f, 53f
Recall, free vs. cued, 14, 14f
Recency effect, 247–248
Recent past, memory of, 132–134, 133f
Referential communication task, 198
    elderspeak in, 205–207
Regression analyses, of Woodcock-Johnson sample, 51–52
Reminiscence, 136–141
Remote Associates Test (RAT), 156–157, 157t
Remote memory, 86
Respondents' tasks, 233–238
Response alternatives, 243–245, 243t, 244t
Response editing, 240
Response order effects, 247–248, 248f
Retention interval, 144–145
Rheumatoid arthritis, 221–222
Right hemisphere aging hypothesis, 96–100
Risky decisions, 264–269

S
Schema-based processing, 164–165
Schematicity, in metamemory, 122–123
Search tasks, for memory, 66
Seattle Longitudinal Study, 33
    age-process relationship in, 45, 45f
Selective attention, 58–60, 59f
Self-reports, 233–249
    attitude questions in, 245–246, 246f
    behavior questions in, 241–245
    judgment recall/computing in, 239
    respondents' tasks in, 233–238
    response editing in, 240
    response formatting in, 239–240
    response order effects in, 247–248, 248f
Semantic memory, 84–85, 143
Sensory function, in cognitive function decline, 16–19, 18f
Short-term memory, interference effects in, 107
Single common factor analysis, 47–48, 48f
Skills, substitutable, 36–37
Slowing, 186
    of speech, 189–191
Slowing hypothesis, in processing speed theory, 10
Source amnesia, 83–84
Spatial memory, 85–86
Speech comprehension, 79–80
Speech perception, 175–192
    auditory acuity in, age on, 180–182, 182f
    comprehension and working memory in, 179–180

Speech perception (*continued*)
  language comprehension in, 184–186
  phonological analysis steps in, 177–178
  processing speed in, 186–189, 188f
  speech input slowing in, 189–191, 190f
  speech rate in, 176
  top-down *vs.* bottom-up processing in, 178–179
  waveform in, 176–177
  working memory in, age on, 182–184, 183f
Spoken language, comprehension of, 175–192.
    See also Speech perception
Stability theories, in estimation strategies, 242
Stimulus presentations, lateralized, 98–100, 99f
Stop signal, on inhibition, 160–161, 160f
Stroke, 36
Stroop color-word task, 67, 105
Stroop effect, 67
Subjective theories, of respondents, 242
Substitutable skills, 36–37
Success criterion, 33
Sulci, 94
Sustained attention, 61–62
Sustained frontal negativity, 106
Switching, of attention, 62–64, 63f
Synchrony, in circadian arousal patterns, 158–159, 161–162, 162t
Syntactic restoration, 190–191
Syntax, 177, 179, 184–185
  in message comprehension, 201–202

T
Tacit Knowledge Inventory for Managers, 227
Technology aptitude, 227–228

Television consumption, 243, 243t
Temporal lobe, 100–102
Text-based discourse, 201–202
Text processing, 200–201
Top-down processing, *vs.* bottom-up, 178–179
Truth effect, 87

U
Useful field of view (UFOV), 70–71

V
Verbal ability, *vs.* nonverbal ability, 96–98
Verbosity, 199
Vigilance tasks, 61–62
Visual acuity, 79
Visual fields, in laterality studies, 98–100
Visual search tasks, 59–60, 59f

W
Waveform, acoustic, 176–177
Wisdom, 31–32
Woodcock-Johnson Cognitive Abilities Test, 45, 49
  in process times product, 51, 52f
Word-cued memory, 141, 141f
Word memory, 7–8, 7f, 8f
Work, cognitive aging on, 225–228
Working memory, 80–81
  contents of, 155
  on driving, 224
  frontal lobes in, 105–108, 106f
  processing speed in, 13–14, 14f
  research findings on, 6–8, 7f, 8f
  in speech perception, 179–180
  on speech perception, 179–180, 182–184, 183f

#0144 - 250517 - C2 - 234/174/17 - PB - 9780863776922